THE
LIBERTY INCIDENT
REVEALED

A JAY CRISTOL

THE
LIBERTY INCIDENT
REVEALED

THE DEFINITIVE ACCOUNT
OF THE 1967 ISRAELI ATTACK ON THE U.S. NAVY SPY SHIP

Naval Institute Press
Annapolis, Maryland

Naval Institute Press
291 Wood Road
Annapolis, MD 21402

Library of Congress Cataloging-in-Publication Data

Cristol, A. Jay
  [Liberty incident.]
  The Liberty incident revealed : the definitive account of the 1967 Israeli attack on
the U.S. Navy spy ship / A. Jay Cristol.—[Revised and expanded edition]
      pages cm
  Previously published: The Liberty incident : the 1967 Israeli attack on the U.S.
Navy spy ship / A. Jay Cristol. Washington, D.C. : Brassey's, 2002.
  Includes bibliographical references and index.
  ISBN 978-1-61251-340-9 (hardcover : alk. paper)—ISBN 978-1-61251-387-4
(ebook) 1. Israel-Arab War, 1967—Naval operations. 2. Liberty (Ship) I. Cristol,
A. Jay, date II. Title.
  DS127.6.N3C74 2013
  956.04'6—dc23

                    2013016521

∞ Print editions meet the requirements of ANSI/NISO z39.48-1992
(Permanence of Paper).
Printed in the United States of America.

21 20 19 18 17 16 15 14 13   9 8 7 6 5 4 3 2 1
First printing

To the memory of Adm. Isaac C. Kidd Jr., U.S. Navy,
and Vice Adm. Donald D. Engen, U.S. Navy—giants
in the history of the U.S. Navy

CONTENTS

ILLUSTRATIONS

PREFACE TO THE SECOND EDITION

When I began this research project some twenty-seven years ago I thought, perhaps naively, that by collecting hard original evidence, analyzing it, and publishing it I would answer the question of whether or not the attack on the USS *Liberty* was a premeditated act by Israel against a U.S. warship or a tragic case of mistaken identity and "friendly fire." Sadly, I have learned over the years that there are many persons and entities who, pursuing their own agendas, are not even remotely interested in facts or truth and are concerned only with using this sad story as a means to attack and try to undermine the outstanding special relationship between the United States and Israel.

When the first edition of *The* Liberty *Incident* was published in 2002, there remained unanswered questions about audiotapes intercepted by the National Security Agency (NSA) that were alleged by some to contain absolute proof that the Israeli attack had been premeditated. My subsequent Freedom of Information Act lawsuit against the National Security Agency resulted in the release of those tapes. They are now available on the NSA website (www.nsa.gov), and one may listen to the tapes in the original Hebrew or review their preliminary and final translations. The NSA tapes and the Israel Air Force tapes may be compared in appendix 2 of this book.

Although the tapes clearly establish that the Israeli armed forces believed they were attacking a hostile ship, anti-Israel sources now insist that the NSA tapes are fraudulent and are part of a conspiracy between the National Security Agency and this author to deceive the American public!

In 2004, less than a year after I obtained the release of the above tapes, the U.S. Department of State held in Washington, D.C., a conference in connection with the release of *Foreign Relations, 1964–1968, Volume XIX, Arab-Israeli Crisis and War, 1967.* I was invited to deliver a lecture at that conference, which was moderated by Dr. Marc Susser, the historian of the Department of State. Dr. David Robarge, of the Central Intelligence Agency history staff; Dr. David Hatch, a historian for the National Security Agency; Dr. Michael Oren, then a scholar at Shalem Institute in Jerusalem and now Israel's ambassador to the United States; author James Bamford; and Dr. Charles Smith of the University of Arizona, as commentator, were on the panel with me.

As indicated below, in chapter 18, the U.S. State Department in its summary of the USS *Liberty* incident unequivocally concluded that the attack was a tragic mistake. Since then, it has been claimed that the State Department is a coconspirator with the National Security Agency and this author!

Thereafter, in October 2009, I was invited to appear on a panel at the National Security Agency and present a paper on the *Liberty* incident. My paper urged the National Security Agency to make an affirmative statement that the attack was a case of mistaken identity, but the National Security Agency, for reasons that remain known only to it, continues to decline to state publicly a position on the issue. This is rather strange, in view of the NSA's own conclusions in its 1981 document "Attack on a SIGINT Collector the U.S.S. *Liberty*" that "the knowledge that the tragedy resulted not only from Israeli miscalculation but also from faulty U.S. communications practices was even more difficult to accept" and "while these reports revealed some confusion on the part of the pilots concerning the nationality of the ship, they tended to rule out any thesis that the Israeli Navy and Air Force deliberately attacked a ship they knew to be American."

Furthermore, the historian for the National Security Agency, Dr. Thomas R. Johnson, in his history of the agency, clearly states that the attack was a tragic mistake. I have been unable to find or obtain any internal NSA document suggesting that the attack was a premeditated one against an American warship. The strongest negative statement on the issue within the NSA was made by Louis W. Tordello, who served as deputy director from 1956 to 1974. On July 5, 1967, in an interim decision, Judge Yeshayahu Yerushalmi, a judge on the Military Court of Appeals, in his capacity as examining judge under section 283 of the Israel Military Justice Law of 1955, ruled, "It appears to me, prima facie, that offenses of negligence may have been committed." The hearing was adjourned and reconvened, and it concluded on July 21, 1967, after testimony of thirty-four witnesses and receipt in evidence of fourteen documents. A final decision was rendered on July 21, 1967. Page 41 of the 1981 NSA report states, "When NSA's Deputy Director read the decision of the Israeli Defense Forces preliminary inquiry, he summed up *his personal feelings* [emphasis added] on the subject by calling it 'a nice whitewash.'" He was displeased with the Israel examining judge's ruling: "I hold that there is no sufficient amount of prima facie evidence justifying committing anyone for trial." However, Tordello never provided any evidence in contradiction of the tragic mistake theory.

In 2002, after the publication of the first edition of this book, the Israel Air Force conducted a study of the incident. It did not contain anything not previously released except an annotation that the Israeli air force and navy had coordinated meetings to establish procedures to prevent similar tragic mistakes from occurring again.

It seems quite clear to this author that the shadow of the *Liberty* incident continues to haunt the Israel Navy. On January 3, 2002, Israeli naval commandos in the Red Sea captured an old ship named the *Karine A* that was being operated by the Palestinian Authority and attempting to transport fifty tons of weapons manufactured in Iran and Russia to the Gaza Strip. It is significant that the go-ahead for the actual seizure of the ship was not approved until the Israel Defense Force chief of staff, Lt. Gen. Shaul Mofaz, personally flew over the ship, observed it, and confirmed that it was the target ship. Likewise, on March 15, 2011, when the Israeli navy captured the *Victoria,* another ship attempting to smuggle Iranian-supplied arms to Gaza, the actual seizure of the ship was not approved until its identity had been confirmed by the very highest authority in the Israeli military and the prime minister had approved the operation.

This second edition is based on all of the evidence that has now been declassified, including what the National Security Agency describes as its remaining papers on the *Liberty* incident, finally declassified on June 6, 2007. The NSA issued a press release on June 6, 2007 that stated, "NSA/CSS Releases Documents relating to the 8 June 1967 Attack on the USS *Liberty*—In recognition of the 40th anniversary of the attack on the U.S. Navy ship USS *Liberty,* the National Security Agency/Central Security Service (NSA/CSS) has finalized the review of *all remaining material* [emphasis added] relative to the attack and published this material on NSA website at www.nsa.gov. This additional release adds to the collection of documents, audio recordings, and transcripts previously posted to the site on 02 July 2005." All of the facts are now available for review. A quarter of a century of intensive research in Israel and the United States, including in all relevant archives (both classified and declassified documents) and interviews with all then-living individuals directly involved in the incident, has made the factual and documentary record clear.

Nevertheless the official records, facts, and truth are of no interest or concern to persons and organizations motivated by hidden agendas, who wish to keep alive conspiracy theories, or who are trying to feed sensations.

This author attests that the conclusions of this book are the truth, the whole truth, and nothing but the truth.

April 2013

A Jay Cristol

ACKNOWLEDGMENTS

What originally began as a short walk turned into a twenty-seven-year odyssey. Along the way I met many people in the United States, Israel, England, and Egypt who have been of invaluable help in the research and preparation of this manuscript. Not only did they contribute to my research, but most also became my friends. My sincere thanks go out to all of them.

In the United States
Curt Civin, MD, Regina Greenwell, Cdr. Richard Holzknecht, Adm. Jonathan T. Howe, Adm. Jerome L. Johnson, Cdr. Tom Krupp, Ivy Lapides, John Long, Robert S. McNamara, Ambassador Richard B. Parker, Ambassador Dwight Porter, Dean Rusk, Carl F. Salans, Capt. Frank Snyder, Rear Adm. Paul E. Tobin Jr., Wright Walden.

In Israel
Rear Adm. Ami Ayalon, Maj. Gen. Avihu Ben-Nun, Rear Adm. Abraham Ashur, Lt. Col. Michael Bloch, Moshe Fogel, Capt. Ari Gavish, Gila Gerson, Hirsh Goodman, Lt. Col. Matti Greenberg, Eitan Haber, Uri Meretz, Gen. Uzi Narkis, Pinchas Pinchasy, David Rubinger, Meir Shamgar, Commo. Chaim Shaked, Rear Adm. Paul Shulman, Ambassador Michael Shiloh, Col. Joel Singer, Rear Adm. Biny Telem, Judge Yeshayahu Yerulshalmi, Aharon Yifrach, Dan Pattir, Mark Regev.

In Egypt
Maj. Gen. A. Z. M. H. Abdin, Maj. Gen. Ahmed M. Halim, Ambassador Mahmoud Kassem.

In England
Rex Bloomstein, Mary Horworth, Adrian Pennick.

USS Liberty *Crew Members*
Capt. William L. McGonagle, Cdr. Maurice H. Bennett, Lt. George Golden, Communications Technician First Class Joe Lentini, Signalman Second Class Russell O. David, Seaman Stephen J. Richard.

Special Thanks
Adm. Isaac C. Kidd Jr., USN, Vice Adm. Donald D. Engen, USN, Capt. Ernest C. Castle, USN, John Hadden, Norman Polmar, Christina Davidson, Michael Weeks, Joann Rosoff, Rick Russell, Dr. Haim Shaked, Dr. Vendulka Kubalkova, Mitchil Debach, Maxine Schwartz, Yitzhak Rabin, Ambassador Ephraim Evron, Brig. Gen. Oded Erez, Rear Adm. Michael Ram, Rear Adm. David Ben-Bashat, Vice Adm. Eli Marom (Chiny), Rear Adm. Shlomo Erell, Rear Adm. Yechezkel Mashita Mor, Capt. Yaacov Nitzan, Col. Danny Shapira, Col. Raanan Gissin, Lt. Col. Danny Grossman, Juval Aviv, Maj. Gen. Iftach Spector, Royal Flight leader, Michael Shuldinger, Arthur Hertz, David Horan, Karen Horan, Cheryl Kaplan, Barbara Cargill, Jennifer Rolph, Lisa Walsh, Greg Koldys, William Cassidy, Glenn Lapides, Olga Cusell, Louise Bauer, Jill Bauer, Stephen M. Cristol, and David A. Cristol.

A Very Special Acknowledgment
To my beloved wife, Elly. Without her patience, understanding, and help, this book could not have been completed.

Chapter 1

ROLL IN ON TARGET

Kursa Flight leader glanced over his left shoulder to keep his eyes on the target as he rolled his Mirage IIICJ to a heading of 100°.[1] The plane rolled out of the turn with its nose pointing to the tiny gray ship on the surface of the Mediterranean Sea almost ten thousand feet below.

His right thumb pushed forward on the electric trim tab, easing the nose down into a dive and positioning the ship in the center of the ring of the gun sight projected on his windscreen. With only the smallest of smooth corrections, he flew the crosshairs on the sight to line up on the bridge of the ship. In the dive the plane accelerated to nearly six hundred miles per hour,[2] and he reduced the throttle ever so slightly to prevent the plane from buffeting against the edge of the sonic barrier. Under the circumstances, there was no need to go supersonic. He was descending toward the target, closing at the rate of a half mile every three seconds. Automatically his left hand let go of the throttle and flipped on the master armament switch. His hand then moved to the gun selector switch located next to it. His right hand continued to steady the stick while his feet lightly stabilized the rudder, continuing to hold the crosshairs on the target.

Without conscious thought, the index finger on his right hand slipped under the trigger safety guard, pushed it up, and found the trigger. As he approached to within one mile of the ship, which was about six seconds from the target, he slightly increased the pressure on the trigger to actuate the gun camera His eyes quickly searched for any sign of antiaircraft fire coming from the ship. He saw none. The structure of the attack was perfect. The target ship was steering westerly into the sun, which was at his back. His wingman was a short distance behind him in an identical pattern. The moment was now.

1

His two DEFA 5–52 30 mm guns began firing a steady burst of over nineteen rounds per second from each barrel.[3] He had never fired at a ship before, but something out of his past, the memory of his father being lost at sea on a ship, gave him an eerie sensation. He was transfixed in awe and horror as he thought he saw the incredible damage being caused by his gunfire. Attack doctrine dictates releasing or firing your weapon and pulling up at once to avoid being struck by your own exploding or ricocheting ordnance or fixating on the target and flying into it while counting your hits. The margin for error was only three seconds, during which the Mirage would travel almost half a mile.

He heard his wingman shout over the radio, "Look out for the masts!" He abruptly applied back pressure on the stick, pulling heavy g-forces as he hurtled skyward and began a steep left turn to reposition his aircraft for a second run. As he passed abeam of the ship, he noticed a huge fire and a great pall of black smoke spewing straight up from the ship. His target was the United States Ship *Liberty* (GTR 5).

Commencing at 1358 local time on June 8, 1967,[4] the *Liberty*, a U.S. intelligence-gathering ship, was attacked by Israeli air, and later by naval, forces while steaming the Mediterranean in international waters some twelve to fourteen miles off the coast of the Sinai Peninsula in the vicinity of the town of El Arish. Prior to the start of the third Arab-Israeli War in June 1967, known in the West as the Six Day War, the Sinai had been controlled by the United Arab Republic (Egypt). By the fourth day of the war, Israeli armor had swept through the Sinai, and Israeli tanks were on the banks of the Suez Canal. At the time of the attack, Israel controlled El Arish and the military airfield located just south of the town. The attack had concluded by 1440.

This event has been the subject of at least ten official investigations by the U.S. government and three official investigations by the Israeli government, and it has been the subject of five television productions. It is mentioned in more than a hundred books, several of which have been devoted entirely to the event, while others have dedicated chapters to it. Many more make mention of it. More than thirty years later, the incident still finds its way into numerous magazine stories, newspaper articles, and letters to the editor.

Dozens of theories speculate on what exactly happened that day. Both the United States and Israel classified much of the data concerning the incident for more than ten years, which only fueled the fires of the intrigue, conspiracy, and cover-up theories. However, significant portions of most of the official investigations have now been declassified or are readily obtainable.

To evaluate and understand what happened on that day in June 1967, it is necessary to understand the state of world affairs at that time. The USS *Liberty* operated during the height of the Cold War. The Soviet Union had been publicly humiliated five years earlier during the Cuban Missile Crisis of 1962, when it had backed down in the face of superior U.S. nuclear and naval power. This embarrassment prompted Soviet leader Nikita Khrushchev (in office 1953–64) to accelerate the construction of a "blue water" navy, a fleet of major warships that could project Soviet power on the high seas.

Soviet and U.S. warships began confronting each other on the high seas, particularly in the Mediterranean. Typically the Soviets would trail U.S. ships and intentionally interfere with their operations, in part to test American response. A Soviet ship, such as a destroyer, would steer a collision course with a U.S. destroyer; the two captains would wait as long as they dared to see who "chickened out" and changed course first to avoid collision. Incidents occurred where neither side gave way and ships "bumped," inflicting and suffering varying degrees of damage. Significantly, the Soviets were not always the initiators of these dangerous games. Eventually, the progressive escalation of such incidents led to the Incidents at Sea Agreement signed by the U.S. Navy and the Soviet Navy on May 25, 1972.[5]

In June 1967, however, the "incidents at sea" still occurred with regularity. For instance, the morning of June 7, 1967, one day prior to the *Liberty* attack, began with one such incident. Vice Adm. William I. Martin, the commander of the U.S. Sixth Fleet (COMSIXTHFLT) in the Mediterranean, operating about five hundred miles from the Sinai war zone, sent the following message to the Soviet guided missile frigate DLG 383,[6] which was shadowing the U.S. task group centered on the aircraft carrier *America:*

> Your actions for the past five days have interfered with our operations. By positioning your ship in the midst of our formation and shadowing our every move you are denying us the freedom of maneuver on the high seas that has been traditionally recognized by seafaring nations for centuries.
>
> In a few minutes the task force will commence maneuvering at high speeds and various courses. Your present position will be dangerous to your ship, as well as the ships of this force.
>
> I request you clear our formation without delay and discontinue your interference and unsafe practices.

Martin sent the message both by flashing light and voice radio in English and Russian. The Soviets did not acknowledge receipt of the message.[7]

One of the lessons of the Cuban Missile Crisis brought about the setting up by the United States and the Soviet Union of a teletype hotline between Washington and Moscow under a memorandum of understanding signed on June 20, 1963. Both parties realized that they had come closer than either had intended to a nuclear exchange. The hotline provided direct and nearly immediate, or "real time," communication, with the hope that a communication failure would not cause nuclear war. After its installation, however, the hotline was not used except for the formal exchange of New Year's greetings each year. This nonusage changed dramatically following the start of the 1967 Six Day War.

In June 1967, thousands of miles east of and away from the Sinai, a major armed conflict raged in Vietnam. By June 1967, some four hundred thousand American troops were already deployed in South Vietnam, and their number, as well as the number of casualties, increased almost daily. The situation in Vietnam, badly managed and poorly understood, was beginning to generate significant public discontent within the United States. In simplistic terms, the United States backed the "anticommunist" forces in South Vietnam, while the Soviets backed the "communists" in North Vietnam, all part of a more comprehensive Southeast Asian or, indeed, global competition. A serious potential existed that a specific confrontation would escalate from a "cold war" to a shooting war between U.S. and Soviet forces.

In fact, on June 2, 1967, U.S. Air Force fighter-bombers accidentally attacked the *Turkestan,* a Soviet merchant ship in Cam Pha harbor in North Vietnam. According to Phil G. Goulding, then Assistant Secretary of Defense for Public Affairs, the pilots of the attacking planes reported the whole story to their commander when they returned to their base in Thailand. They claimed that while strafing a battery of antiaircraft guns, another battery began firing at them. In an effort to save themselves and each other, they had opened fire with everything they had to suppress the antiaircraft fire long enough to get away. The tactic had worked, but the *Turkestan* was accidentally in the way. A Soviet crew member was killed and several others were wounded. The U.S. pilots' commander—a colonel who had been on many missions with his pilots and whose life had been saved twice by one of the pilots involved—"stuck by his men," destroyed the gun camera film, and covered up the incident.[8] With no verifiable report of the attack, the U.S. government formally denied the Soviet charge that American planes had strafed a Soviet ship. When the facts ultimately became known to the U.S. Department of Defense, the U.S. government, substantially embarrassed, retracted its denial of the attack but claimed that the attack had been an accident. *Pravda* quoted the master of the Soviet freighter *Turkestan*, Capt. Viktor Sokolov, as saying, "We were bearing all the markings of the Soviet government. A Soviet flag was flying from the stern mast. The stack was painted with a red stripe and a hammer and sickle. The *Turkestan* was about 400 meters from shore. The visibility was excellent. There is no possibility of talking about an accidental attack. The American pilots aimed their guns at the central superstructure where the crewmen live and work."[9]

In Leningrad, now St. Petersburg, a mob spat on American diplomat John Guthrie and his wife, and demonstrators marched outside an American exhibit there. Public meetings throughout the Soviet Union denounced the "pirate actions of the U.S. Military."[10] Tass, the official Soviet news agency, charged a U.S. cover-up of this "provocation against the Soviet Union."[11]

The *Turkestan* and the *Liberty* incidents occurred only days apart during a sequence of very sensitive international events, among them the outbreak of the Six Day War and the first detonation of a hydrogen bomb by China on June 17, 1967.[12] The *Turkestan* incident caused great concern at the U.S. State Department, because Soviet premier Alexei Kosygin was about to arrive in the United States as the head of a delegation to speak at the United Nations General Assembly session on the Middle East. The U.S. government feared that Kosygin would attack the United States before the United Nations, resulting in a further deterioration of relations at a time when the United States hoped for a summit between Kosygin and President Lyndon Johnson to discuss nuclear de-escalation.[13]

Focusing on the Cold War, the War on Poverty, and the Vietnam War, President Johnson anxiously hoped to avoid a conflagration in the highly sensitive Middle Eastern region, where U.S.-Soviet competition was at a high. Nevertheless, a rapidly deteriorating Middle Eastern situation became a shooting war on June 5, 1967.[14] Early that morning, Israel sent off its entire air force in a surprise strike. The Israel Air Force completely destroyed the Egyptian air force in less than eighty minutes. By day's end, Israel's two hundred or so first-line combat aircraft had effectively eliminated the Egyptian, Syrian, and Jordanian air forces. Flying their strikes, returning to base, rearming, and taking off to strike again with an on-ground turnaround time of six to eight minutes, Israeli aircraft achieved almost a thousand strikes on the first day. The Arab air forces, in many instances, could not turn an aircraft around on the same day.[15] For this reason, many Arab military leaders charged that the United States and Britain supplied attacking aircraft to the Israel Air Force. They were very vocal with their charges, even after they became aware that the United States and Britain had not been involved. In fact, the Israelis substantially embarrassed President Nasser and King Hussein by recording them fabricating a false press release on the subject.[16]

In addition to an understanding of the international political-military climate as it existed in 1967, some knowledge of the structure of the Israel Defense Forces (IDF), especially the relationship between its navy and the air force, is required in order to properly evaluate the *Liberty* incident. The IDF came into being officially with the establishment of the state of Israel on May 14, 1948.[17] The air force initially looked to Great Britain for inspiration, and one of its important commanders, Gen. Ezer Weizman, had started as a British Royal Air Force–trained pilot.[18] Israel's first prime minister, David Ben-Gurion, came to the United States and recruited an American U.S. Naval Academy graduate, Lt. Cdr. Paul Shulman, as the first chief of the Israel Navy.

From the Arab-Israeli War of 1948–49, known in Israel as the War of Independence, the Israel Air Force had taken control of the air and kept it. By 1967, Israel's military buildup emphasized the air force (and the armored units), on the basis of lessons from the 1956 war (the Suez campaign) in the Sinai. The Israel Navy did not have any impressive accomplishments in the 1948–49 war. The only reported naval air action during that war involved two Israeli pilots, in a Beechcraft Bonanza aircraft, who attacked an Egyptian ship. The attack failed, and the plane crashed during the attack, killing both fliers; the Egyptian ship remained unharmed.

During the 1956 Suez campaign, on October 31 the Egyptian destroyer *Ibrahim al-Awwal* shelled the port city of Haifa.[19] To the Egyptians' surprise, the French destroyer *Kersaint,* which happened to be in the Haifa harbor at the time, returned fire.[20] The *Ibrahim al-Awwal* withdrew. Shortly thereafter, two Israel Air Force Ouragan jet aircraft strafed the Egyptian destroyer. She was then confronted by an Israel destroyer flotilla consisting of two old British-built Z-class destroyers, the *Eilat* and the *Jaffa.* The Israel destroyers signaled by flashing light the code "A-A," which in international maritime code means "What ship?" or "Identify yourself!"[21] Lt. (jg) Moshe Oren, gunnery officer on the destroyer *Jaffa,* observed the Egyptian ship signal back "A-A."[22] Thereupon the Israeli destroyers opened fire on the Egyptian ship and disabled it. The damaged ship was then boarded and captured.[23] After extensive repair she became the third destroyer in the Israel Navy, renamed the *Haifa.*

Moshe Oren's personal and the Israelis' general experience with the Egyptian destroyer and its signaling "A-A" in 1956 would prove fatal eleven years later with the *Liberty*. For years, the Israel Air Force and the Israel Navy disagreed over the capture of the *Ibrahim al-Awwal*. The air force claimed that the Ouragan fighters' strafing attack had precipitated the surrender of the ship, while the navy claimed that naval gunfire had disabled the destroyer's rudder and made its capture possible.[24] By 1967, the Israel Air Force was known as an elite, highly sophisticated, and advanced force in the forefront of Israel's defense lines, while the Israel Navy was, in the words of its then commander, Rear Adm. Shlomo Erell, "at its lowest ebb."[25]

When the war broke out, the Israel Air Force had seventy-six state-of-the-art Mirage IIICJ aircraft, plus Super-Mystère B-2s and Mystère IVs, as well as a cadre of well-trained pilots. The Israel Navy, on the other hand, possessed only three obsolete destroyers, nine motor torpedo boats (three of which were deployed in the Red Sea), some obsolete submarines, and some miscellaneous small craft.[26] The navy was poised for a great leap forward into modern naval warfare, but that leap would be taken only in 1968, with the acquisition of modern missile boats.[27]

High-strung competition between various arms of the military is not a phenomenon peculiar to Israel. The tension between Israel's navy and air force in 1967 is evident from some of the conversation between Royal Flight leader and air control during the air attack on the *Liberty*. At 1409, about eleven minutes into the air attack and about three minutes before the chief air controller ordered Royal Flight to "leave her," Royal Flight leader says to air control, "if you had a two plane formation with bombs, in ten minutes before the navy arrives, it will be a *mitzvah* (good or worthwhile deed). Otherwise the navy is on its way here."[28] Evidently, Royal Flight leader wanted the attack completed by the air force, suggesting prompt assignment of properly armed aircraft to the mission to allow its effective completion *before* the navy's arrival. A few minutes later the navy's motor torpedo boats (MTBs) arrived. The same Moshe Oren who participated in the capture of the *Ibrahim al-Awwal* commanded MTB Division 914.

Aharon Yifrach, a twenty-year-old combat information center officer on the division commander's MTB, probably best expressed the feelings of the Israeli MTB sailors.

On the first night of the 1967 War, the Israel Navy inserted six naval commando teams [known in Israel as "frogmen"] into various Arab ports. The team sent into Latakia, Syria, was unable to complete its mission, as was the situation with all the other teams. The Navy became concerned about their safety and sent MTB Division 914 to help extract them. They were withdrawn but in the milling around, one MTB collided with another, making a hole in its bow about the size of a dinner plate. The boat was taken back to [the] Ashdod [port] where, in a short time, the hole was repaired as good as new. It was now the fourth day of the war. The Air Force had destroyed all the Arab air forces and controlled the skies. The armor had conquered the Sinai and were dipping their feet in the Suez Canal. The paratroopers had captured the entire West Bank, East Jerusalem and Israeli troops were praying at the Western Wall. And the Navy—we had made a hole in one of our own boats. We were anxious to get into the action.[29]

Abraham Rabinovich, author of *Boats of Cherbourg,* confirmed Yifrach's analysis: "Frustrated at the Navy's inactivity while the Army was overrunning Sinai and the West Bank and the Air Force was scoring its spectacular victories, the Navy command had been hoping to find an enemy ship that would enable it to get in on the war."[30]

Thus, the scene for a tragedy was set. The *Liberty,* following orders issued on June 1, 1967,[31] sailed toward an active war zone without knowledge that on June 7 the U.S. National Security Agency, through the Joint Chiefs of Staff, had ordered her withdrawn from harm's way.[32] What followed was the worst disaster in fifty years of U.S.-Israeli relations.

Chapter 2

THE TWO-MONTH CRISIS

The spring of 1967 was a period of escalating crisis in the Middle East. For months there had been unrest along the Syrian-Israeli border with at least fourteen terrorist incursions over that border from Syria into Israel. Retaliation and counterretaliation escalated from rifle fire to tank and artillery duels. Israel made some strong statements about further retaliations against Syria, which added to the concern.[1]

April 7: Attack on the Liberty *Minus Sixty-Two Days*
As had been done previously in the dispute between Israel and Syria over the right of Israel to farm in the demilitarized zones of the Syrian-Israeli border, an Israeli farmer drove a tractor into the zone. The Syrians responded with shell fire, which the IDF returned, first with ground fire and then by air force strikes against Syrian gun positions. Shortly thereafter Syrian MiGs were spotted heading toward the demilitarized zone. The Israel Air Force countered, and by the end of the afternoon, in two separate aerial battles, six MiG fighters were shot down. Several MiGs went down close to Damascus, to the humiliation of the Syrians. No Israeli aircraft were lost.[2]

May 2: Attack Minus Thirty-Six Days
The USS *Liberty* departed her home port of Norfolk, Virginia, for a scheduled four-month African deployment.[3]

May 13: Attack Minus Twenty-Six Days
The Soviets told the Syrian government that Israel was concentrating ten or eleven brigades along its border in preparation of an attack.[4] In fact, there were only about 125 Israeli troops in the area. The Soviets also gave this false

information to the Egyptians. The Israelis invited the Soviets, through their military attaché in Tel Aviv, to visit the Israeli-Syrian border area and check the situation for themselves. All such invitations were declined. Even today some scholars wonder if the Soviets really believed the story of the Israeli military buildup or if they knew it was false.

Why the Soviets passed this disinformation remains a mystery. The Egyptian chief of staff, Gen. Muhammad Fawzi, did not believe it. U.S. officials told the Egyptians that the report was untrue, and there were numerous means of independent verification, but the Egyptians seemed uninterested in verification. This might prove what some historians have suggested: that Egyptian leader Gamal Abdel Nasser himself did not believe the report and that he was playing a game of brinkmanship.[5] The unfortunate result for Egypt and the region of his misjudging the location of the brink was that he stumbled over it and into an unexpected and unwanted war.

In May 1967, President Nasser had a plateful of his own problems. In addition to major domestic troubles, his best troops were engaged in a protracted civil war in faraway Yemen. Egyptian tanks were stationed in Baghdad to control the local population while the Iraqi military was in the field fighting the Kurds.[6] As part of a war of words and subversion between "progressive" or revolutionary Arab countries, led by Egypt, and conservative or monarchical Arab countries, Jordan and Saudi Arabia attacked President Nasser every day in the Arab media, claiming that he was soft on fighting Israel and only contributed rhetoric to the struggle.[7]

Regardless of who knew what and who believed what, the government of Egypt took the official position that there was a concentration of Israeli troops on or near the Syrian border and that Egypt was going to demonstrate its leadership of the Arab world and come to the rescue of its Syrian sister country.

May 14: Attack Minus Twenty-Five Days
Egyptian Field Marshal Abd al-Hakim Amer (sometimes spelled "Amr") ordered Egyptian troops into the Sinai and put the Egyptian armed forces on full alert.[8]

Egyptian troops moved ostentatiously through Cairo on May 14, on their way toward the Sinai, and at least one armored division crossed the Suez Canal on the fifteenth. On May 14, Under Secretary of the United Nations Ralph Bunche met with Israel's UN representative, Gideon Raphael, who stated that he "wished to emphasize that there had been no concentration of Israeli troops on the Syrian border." He added that there was "no reason for anyone to be concerned about military action by Israel as long as the other side took none."[9]

May 16: Attack Minus Twenty-Three Days

Egyptian general Muhammad Fawzi sent a letter to Indian major general Rikhye, the Commander of the UN Emergency Force (UNEF), and asked for the removal of the UN force that had been deployed in the Gaza Strip following the Sinai campaign. The letter was passed to U Thant, secretary-general of the United Nations, who asked for clarification.

May 17: Attack Minus Twenty-Two Days

Egyptian forces reached El Sabha and El Amr, the UNEF posts near the Sinai-Israel border. U Thant informed the Egyptian representative to the United Nations, Muhammad Awad al-Kony, in writing, that there were no recent indications of Israeli troop movements or concentrations that should give Egypt cause for concern.[10]

May 18: Attack Minus Twenty-One Days

At noon, Egypt advised the secretary-general of the United Nations that it had decided to "terminate the presence of United Nations Emergency Force from the territory of the UAR and the Gaza Strip."[11]

May 19: Attack Minus Twenty Days

Israel's Foreign Minister, Abba Eban, informed the Soviet Ambassador that "there will be no war if the Egyptians do not attack and do not interfere with Israel's right of navigation" [through the Strait of Tiran].[12] U Thant cabled Cairo that UNEF would be withdrawn. Israel was advised of the withdrawal order and began a large-scale mobilization of its massive reserve forces.[13] On the same day, the UNEF contingent of Yugoslav troops withdrew from Sharm al-Shaykh, and Egyptian forces began to move in.[14]

May 20: Attack Minus Nineteen Days

The U.S. Joint Chiefs of Staff issued orders restricting the movements of the U.S. Sixth Fleet in the Mediterranean, positioning the fleet more than three hundred miles from the potential combat zone.[15] The Syrian defense minister, Hafez Assad, spoke of a disciplinary blow to Israel.

May 21: Attack Minus Eighteen Days

In the morning President Nasser addressed Egyptian air force officers at the Bir Gafgafa air base in the Sinai. He told them he was closing the Strait of Tiran in the Gulf of Aqaba. (*Al Arham* carried this story on page 1 of its May 22 edition.) A key element of the 1957 agreement for Israel's withdrawal from the Sinai, brokered by the U.S. government and the secretary-general of the United Nations, secured Israel's freedom of navigation to and from its only southern port, Eilat. Little was put in writing. There was a private written memorandum between UN secretary-general Dag Hammarskjold and President Nasser that memorialized some of the agreements and understandings, but it did not include all the agreements.[16] Sensitive to its ability to trade by sea with African and Southeast and Far East Asian countries without having to circumnavigate the whole African continent, Israel stood firm during the negotiations on the Strait of Tiran issue, and it was made clear to President Nasser that Israel considered a future closing of the Strait as a casus belli. Abba Eban had made public reference to that only two days before Nasser closed the strait.

On the same day, Richard Nolte, the U.S. ambassador-designate to Egypt, who had replaced Ambassador Lucius Battle but had not yet presented his credentials in Cairo, received a telegram drafted by Eugene Rostow, Under Secretary of State for Near East Affairs, relaying a message from President Lyndon Johnson to President Nasser. In view of Nasser's speech at Bir Gafgafa, Ambassador Nolte suggested delaying the delivery of the message. He was told to deliver it at once, and he delivered it that morning. Johnson's message was most conciliatory and suggested that Vice President Hubert Humphrey would be sent to the Middle East to talk to Arab and Israeli leaders after the tension subsided. President Johnson and Secretary of State Dean Rusk were still optimistic that the crisis could be resolved by diplomacy. U.S. intelligence analysis indicated that Egypt was not ready for a war, and Israel had offered assurances that there would be no war if its navigation rights were not disturbed. On this same day the Soviet government gave notice required under the Montreaux Convention that ten warships would transit from the Black Sea through the Bosporus and the Dardanelles into the Mediterranean.[17]

May 23: Attack Minus Sixteen Days

The U.S. National Security Agency (NSA) requested the Joint Chiefs of Staff to move the *Liberty* to a position off Port Said, Egypt.[18] It was standard operating procedure for NSA-controlled intelligence-gathering ships like the *Liberty* to sail off the coasts of various nations listening to and recording various types of signal emissions and charting the locations of their sources. They also listened for anything else that might be of political or military value in the Cold War, such as recording commercial radio broadcasts that would be passed to the Foreign Broadcast Information Service (FBIS).[19] Frank Raven, a civilian employee of NSA, protested sending the *Liberty* into an area where war might break out at any time. He was overruled, and the *Liberty* was given her fateful orders.[20]

May 24: Attack Minus Fifteen Days

At 0530Z the *Liberty* departed Abidjan[21] on the Ivory Coast on orders to traverse at her best speed the three thousand nautical miles to Rota, Spain, just outside the entrance to the Mediterranean through the Strait of Gibraltar. The Cairo newspapers reported that Egypt had mined the Strait of Tiran.

May 25: Attack Minus Fourteen Days

U.S. diplomatic dependents began leaving Israel and Egypt. Egyptian minister of war Shams Badran flew to Moscow and conferred with Premier Aleksei Kosygin, Foreign Minister Andrei Gromyko, and the newly appointed minister of defense, Marshal Andrei Grechko. There is no record that Party Secretary Leonid Brezhnev was consulted. The Soviets sent a mixed message of caution and support to Nasser.

May 26: Attack Minus Thirteen Days

Egypt assailed the United States as the number-one protector of Israel. Foreign Minister Abba Eban of Israel arrived in Washington after visiting President Charles de Gaulle in Paris and Prime Minister Harold Wilson in London. He was not publicly invited to the White House but was brought in through a side door in the evening and taken to President Johnson's living quarters. He met there with the president, Secretary of Defense Robert S. McNamara, and Under Secretary of State for Political Affairs Eugene V. Rostow, the third-ranking man in the State Department.[22] Johnson was seeking more time and looking for means to solve the crisis without Israel responding militarily. Eban was looking to impress upon the United States the seriousness of the crisis and to judge what diplomatic support there would be should Israel end up taking military action. When the meeting ended, Johnson, McNamara, and Rostow all walked Eban to the elevator. After Eban got in the elevator and the elevator door closed Rostow said to Johnson, "Do you think they'll go?" Johnson said, "They'll go."[23]

May 27: Attack Minus Twelve Days

While the Israeli cabinet was meeting, Abba Eban arrived at Lod Airport from Washington and rushed to Jerusalem to report on his meetings with De Gaulle, Wilson, and Johnson. There was much discussion about attacking at once.[24] The cabinet met past midnight and again the next day. It was decided to allow up to two or three more weeks for the United States to find a solution.

On the same day Vice Adm. William I. Martin, commander of the U.S. Sixth Fleet, was instructed by Adm. John S. McCain Jr., Commander in Chief, U.S. Naval Forces, Europe (CINCUSNAVEUR), not to operate aircraft within one hundred nautical miles of the coast of Egypt.[25]

May 28: Attack Minus Eleven Days

Syria and Iraq signed a military agreement for cooperation of their armies against Israel.[26]

May 29: Attack Minus Ten Days

President Nasser told the Egyptian National Assembly, "We are now ready to confront Israel," and, in a press conference that same day, he said he was ready to restore the situation to what it had been before 1948—before the creation of Israel.

May 30: Attack Minus Nine Days

In a move that Western governments did not expect, King Hussein Ibn Talal of Jordan flew to Cairo and signed a military pact with Egypt that placed the Jordanian armed forces under Egyptian command. Israeli officials felt the ring around them was closed: Egypt to the south, Syria and Iraq to the north, and now Jordan to the east.

June 1: Attack Minus Seven Days

The *Liberty* arrived at the U.S. naval base at Rota, Spain.[27] Additional linguists, trained in Arabic and Russian, reported on board.[28] There were no Hebrew linguists assigned to the ship.[29]

The Israeli cabinet met and formed a national unity government. Moshe Dayan was appointed minister of defense, a portfolio that previously had been held by Prime Minister Levy Eshkol. "Minister without portfolio" positions were given to Menachem Begin of the Herut Party and Joseph Sappir of the Liberal Party.

Retired U.S. ambassador Charles Yost arrived in Egypt. Ambassador Yost had been a colleague of Egyptian foreign minister Mahmoud Riad when the latter served as ambassador at both the United Nations and Damascus. The Yost mission was to obtain some access to President Nasser through Foreign Minister Riad. President Nasser had scheduled a June 5, 1967, date for Ambassador-designate Nolte to present his credentials. In the interim the United States did not have an accredited ambassador in Cairo.[30] Nasser also would not receive or speak to a deputy chief of mission, so the United States was out of direct contact with the person calling the shots in Egypt. There was an Egyptian ambassador in the United States, but he did not seem to enjoy access to President Nasser.

June 2: Attack Minus Six Days

Ambassador Yost urgently contacted Egyptian foreign minister Mahmoud Riad and told him that the U.S. government was ready to receive Vice President Zakaria Muhieddin of Egypt in Washington. Riad telephoned Nasser, and a June 7 meeting was set.

The *Liberty* departed Rota for the eastern Mediterranean, bound for Point Alpha, a designated point for the start of her patrol pattern located at 31-27.2 north and 34-00 east, about thirteen nautical miles off the coast of Egyptian-controlled Sinai and about thirty-eight nautical miles from the coast of Israel.[31] On that day, in North Vietnam, U.S. Air Force F-105D fighter-bombers accidentally attacked the Soviet merchant ship *Turkestan* in Cam Pha harbor.

June 3: Attack Minus Five Days

Prime Minister Eshkol and his advisers heard from Gen. Meir Amit (Ret.), the head of Mossad, the Israeli foreign intelligence agency. He had just returned to Israel from Washington and reported that U.S. efforts to open the Strait of Tiran were not making any progress and that the U.S. government apparently was resigned to Israeli military action against Egypt. Eshkol and his advisers decided to put the issue before the full cabinet on the following day.

June 4: Attack Minus Four Days

Iraq signed a pact in Cairo placing Iraqi troops under Egyptian command. The Israeli cabinet met and voted to go to war.

June 5: Attack Minus Three Days

In the early morning hours, the Israel Air Force launched nearly all of its combat aircraft.[32] At 0745, Israeli aircraft simultaneously struck all Egyptian air bases, catching almost the entire Egyptian air force on the ground. In particular, the Israelis were concerned about concentrations of Soviet-built

Tu-16 Badger bombers, which had the capability of bombing population centers in Israel. The bombers were totally wiped out.

Shortly after the start of the war, at 1240 local time (0640 Washington time, eastern daylight time [EDT]), the first hotline message was sent from Premier Kosygin to President Johnson asking that the United States cooperate with the Soviet Union in halting the conflict. The UN Security Council assembled in New York. The Israelis also sent a back-channel message to King Hussein of Jordan, requesting him to stay out of the war.[33] Hussein disregarded the message, the Jordanians attacked Israel on the central front, and the Israelis reacted accordingly.

An Israeli destroyer and several motor torpedo boats engaged Egyptian Osa missile boats off Port Said. The Osa missile boats retreated to Port Said. No missiles were launched. The commanding officer of one of the Israeli motor torpedo boats was quite distressed that the destroyer commander allowed them to disengage and withdraw.[34]

June 6: Attack Minus Two Days

The Israelis destroyed more than 150 Egyptian tanks in the Sinai and captured the West Bank of the Jordan River and East Jerusalem from Jordan. President Nasser of Egypt and King Hussein of Jordan announced that the United States and Great Britain had sent aircraft that had attacked Egypt.

President Nasser broke diplomatic relations with the United States and closed the Suez Canal. The UN Security Council in New York voted unanimously for a cease-fire. The only warring country to accept this resolution was Jordan.[35] Israel, Syria, Egypt, and Iraq ignored this call and persisted in the fighting.[36]

Six Israeli underwater demolition team swimmers were captured in the port of Alexandria.[37]

Syrian troops attacked and shelled a number of northern Israel border settlements. (The shelling continued throughout the war but the attacks were driven off.)

June 7: Attack Minus One Day

At one minute after midnight Greenwich mean time (GMT) (0201 Sinai time, 2001 on June 6, Washington time) the *Liberty* "chopped"—that is, the operational control of the ship was transferred from Admiral McCain, Commander in Chief, U.S. Naval Forces, Europe, to Vice Admiral Martin, commander of the Sixth Fleet.[38] This was accomplished by normal message procedure.[39]

Orders for ships in the Sixth Fleet normally came from the commander of the Sixth Fleet, not from the very top of the chain of command of the U.S. military. But the *Liberty* was not a normal warship, and though chopped to the Sixth Fleet, she was operating independently on orders from the Joint Chiefs of Staff. This transfer merely added one more layer to her chain-of-command structure.

The U.S. naval communications system is structured so that an order to a warship travels down through the chain of command. The purpose of this system is to keep everyone informed. When the initial message is sent, the ultimate recipient of the message is usually sent a copy of the message as an information addressee; thus the ship being ordered is usually expecting the message containing the order from the senior commander before it is actually received through the chain of command. From June 7 forward, orders for the *Liberty* from the Joint Chiefs of Staff in Washington had to be sent first to the headquarters of Gen. Lyman D. Lemnitzer in Stuttgart, Germany (USCINCEUR), whence they were transmitted to the headquarters of Admiral McCain in London (CINCUSNAVEUR). From there they were transmitted to Admiral Martin on board the cruiser *Little Rock* (CLG 4), flagship of COMSIXTHFLT, whence they were transmitted to the *Liberty*.

On this same day, as mentioned previously, Admiral Martin warned a Soviet warship shadowing his ships to stay out of the vicinity of Sixth Fleet operations.

During the midafternoon in New York, the UN Security Council again voted unanimously for a cease-fire, to take effect at 1600 Washington time (EDT), which was 2200 Sinai time. Egypt rejected this resolution.[40]

At 1830 Washington time, 2230 London time (GMT), and already 0030 on June 8 off the coast of the Sinai, the Joint Chiefs of Staff began sending a number of orders directing the *Liberty* to remain clear of the combat zone. The *Liberty* was still about 120 nautical miles away from the Sinai coast when the first "stand off" message was sent. A total of five stand-off messages were sent from or through various commands, but as a result of mistakes, faulty protocols, and other problems with the U.S. military worldwide communications system, the flurry of messages that directed the *Liberty* to stand off were not received by the *Liberty* prior to the attack.[41]

June 8, 0310 Sinai Time: Attack Minus Ten Hours, Forty Minutes
The second message directing the *Liberty* to stand off one hundred miles was generated by the Joint Chiefs of Staff and transmitted top secret/

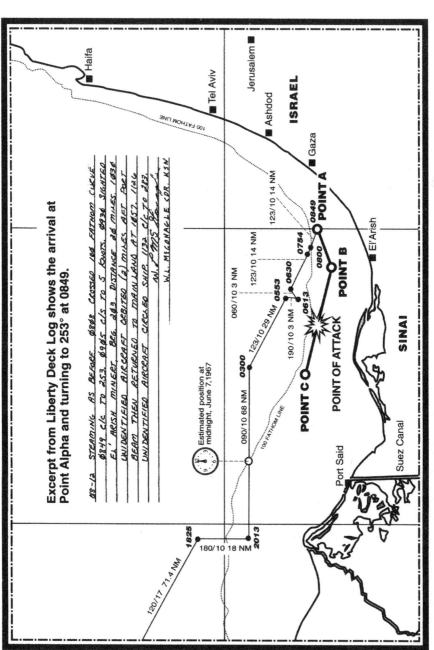

Plotting Map: The projected track of the *Liberty*

Note: This chart is not constructed with the precision of current navigation standards. The data used are from the *Liberty* deck logs. This map fairly demonstrates *Liberty*'s approach to Point Alpha.

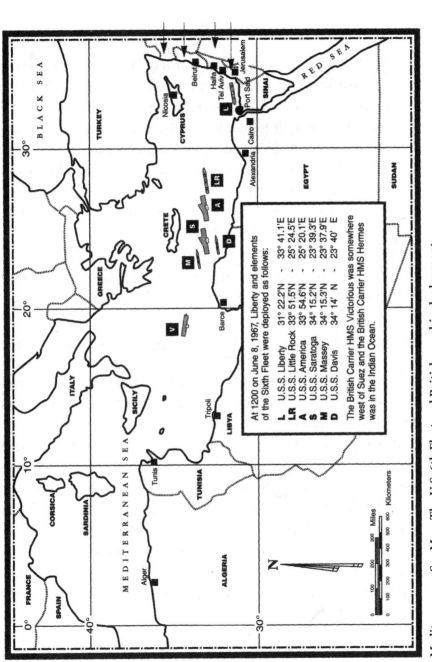

Mediterranean Sea Map: The U.S. 6th Fleet and British warship deployment

Note: There were numerous Russian and Egyptian ships in the area whose routes and positions were not known. Though the Syrians had some ships in the area, it is believed that they did not leave port. Deployment of the Israeli vessels is not shown.

At 1200 on June 8, 1967, Liberty and elements of the Sixth Fleet were deployed as follows:

L	U.S.S. Liberty	31° 22.2'N	33° 41.1'E
LR	U.S.S. Little Rock	33° 51.5N	25° 24.5'E
A	U.S.S. America	33° 54.6N	25° 20.1'E
S	U.S.S. Saratoga	34° 15.2N	23° 39.3'E
M	U.S.S. Massey	34° 15.3N	23° 37.9'E
D	U.S.S. Davis	34° 14' N	23° 40' E

The British Carrier HMS Victorious was somewhere west of Suez and the British Carrier HMS Hermes was in the Indian Ocean.

immediate. At this time, the *Liberty* was just slightly inside the hundred-mile limit.[42]

June 8, 0556: Attack Minus Eight Hours

At about 0558 Sinai time an Israeli air force reconnaissance aircraft with a naval observer on board spotted the *Liberty*, at a position about seventy miles west of Gaza. Ens. John D. Scott, USNR, testified about the aircraft:

A. Yes sir. On the morning of the 8th, I had the 4 to 8 officer of the deck watch on the bridge. It was a routine watch. The only thing out of the ordinary was we had one reconnaissance plane that flew by us and made a few circles off our port beam. He circled around about three or four times, then took off.

Q. About what time?

A. About 0515, I was not able to identify the aircraft. We looked at it with binoculars. Due to the distance we could not see any markings or insignia of any sort on it.

President: That was local time, Mr. Scott.

A. Yes sir. The plane circled around several times then took off in a true direction towards Tel Aviv. About 30 minutes later I got a call from coordination, sir, and Chief CT [Communications Technician] Smith was on the phone; wanted to know if I had an air contact that was fairly close in the last half hour. I told him I did and he wanted to know which direction it went after it left the vicinity of the ship. I told him, "Tel Aviv." He said, "Fine, that's all I want to know." I did manage to take four pictures of the aircraft with the camera on the bridge.[43]

Upon landing, the Israeli naval observer reported the ship sighting to Lt. Cdr. Uri Meretz, the Israel Naval Intelligence liaison officer assigned to debrief the returning aircrews at Lod Airport.[44]

From its beginning, the Israel Navy has not had any organic naval aviation and has always depended on the air force to provide it with aircraft. During the 1967 war, the Israel Air Force provided two naval reconnaissance flights a day, one at first light and one at sunset.[45] On June 8, the early morning flight, a Nord 2501 flew south to near Port Said and then flew an arc to the north to near the coast of Syria. The *Liberty* was observed and identified by her bow marks. The naval observer on board the flight apparently also saw a freighter hull and identified it as a U.S. Navy supply-type ship. How he concluded that the ship was a U.S. vessel at this early morning point in time is not known.[46] The flight engineer on the aircraft told Thames TV, "It was a grey colour and—uhm—no cannons on it and—uhm—not too big, not too small, like a cargo ship. There was no flag on that ship—that's something I'm sure about. . . . What we could see was the letters that was written on that ship. and we gave this letter—letters—to the ground control."[47]

The flight engineer said the plane got down to three thousand to five thousand feet in height and about a half mile "close to the ship [the *Liberty*]." This essentially corroborates the testimony of Ensign Scott.

In fact, when the Nord landed at about 0700 upon the completion of its patrol, the naval observer described the ship and its bow letters and number, GTR 5, to Lt. Cdr. Uri Meretz, who looked in *Jane's Fighting Ships* and specifically identified the ship as the USS *Liberty*.[48] He passed the information by telephone to the naval intelligence headquarters at Stella Maris in Haifa.[49] Uri Meretz commented that the *Liberty* was similar in appearance to the Egyptian ship *El-Quseir* and cautioned naval intelligence in Haifa not to mix up the two ships. Approximately an hour later, at about 0800, his twenty-four-hour watch over, Meretz went off duty and was relieved by Lt. Cdr. Moshe Tabak.

The naval liaison officer to air force headquarters in the Kirya—the Kirya ("city"), the equivalent of the Pentagon, is the Tel Aviv neighborhood where the Ministry of Defense and IDF general headquarters are located—Lt. Cdr. Pinchas Pinchasy, also reported the presence of the U.S. ship to the naval command center, and as a result of these reports the *Liberty* was marked by a "wedge" on the navy's plotting table and designated a "skunk," or unknown. Admiral Erell observed the wedge and inquired about it. He ordered it changed from "skunk" to "neutral."[50]

June 8, 0640: Attack Minus Seven Hours, Eighteen Minutes
The *Liberty*'s copy of the hundred-nautical-mile second stand-off message arrived at the U.S. naval communications station (NCS) in the Philippines as a result of misdirection and was rerouted.[51]

June 8, 0655: Attack Minus Seven Hours, Three Minutes
Commander in Chief, Naval Forces Europe, sent a wire note (the third stand-off message) to Commander Sixth Fleet directing the withdrawal of the *Liberty* to no closer than one hundred nautical miles from the combat zone.[52]

June 8, 0825: Attack Minus Five Hours, Thirty-Three Minutes
Commander in Chief, European Command, sent fourth stand-off message
to Commander in Chief, Naval Forces Europe.

June 8, 0849: Attack Minus Five Hours, Nine Minutes
The *Liberty* arrived at Point Alpha and began patrol.

June 8, 1100: Attack Minus Two Hours, Fifty-Eight Minutes
Just before 1100 Sinai time, the *Liberty* wedge was ordered removed from
the Israel Navy plotting table. In the words of the command duty officer,
Avraham Lunz:

> I got on—on—er—duty in the morning about 8 o'clock. The situation was
> very calm. I had some old information. One of them was about an AGI—in-
> telligence gathering ship, American Type, in the southern part of the arena.
> The information was quite old, it was dated six hour this morning. Around
> 11 o'clock, checking the situation and knowing that no ship would stay on
> its place, and five hours old information would be quite old, we took off
> without knowing where it went. . . .
>
>   COMMENTARY: It was standard procedure to remove out of date
> information from the battle control board.[53]

From that moment on, the existence of the *Liberty* was no longer marked
on the plotting table at the Israel Naval Command Center.

June 8, 1117: Attack Minus Two Hours, Forty-One Minutes
The Commander Sixth Fleet sent the fifth stand-off message to the *Liberty* or-
dering her to stand off one hundred nautical miles from the combat zone.[54]
The fifth stand-off message to the *Liberty* was transmitted from the Sixth
Fleet flagship, *Little Rock,* to Naval Communications Station, Morocco. NCS
Morocco sent it to the Army defense major relay communications station
(DCS) in San Pablo, Spain. DCS Spain sent it to Army Defense Communications Station, Asmara. DCS Asmara sent it to Naval Communications
Station, Greece. NCS Greece was apparently aware that the *Liberty* was not
monitoring NCS Greece and sent the message back to DCS Asmara, which
then passed the message to Naval Communications Station Asmara, where
it was placed on fleet broadcast at 081525Z, approximately two and one-half
hours after the attack.[55]

Chapter 3

WHY WAS THE *LIBERTY* IN HARM'S WAY?

On May 15, 1967, large numbers of Egyptian troops started crossing the Suez Canal and taking up positions in the Sinai Peninsula. Under the U.S.-brokered 1957 agreement concluding the British, French, and Israeli 1956 Suez campaign, the Sinai-Israel border was being monitored by the UN Emergency Force (UNEF), as a confidence-building force, on the Egyptian side of the Israel-Egypt border.[1] There was continuous consultation between Israel and the United States on the crisis.[2] The U.S. embassy in Tel Aviv was in daily communication with the Israel foreign ministry and was aware of the Israeli side of the situation.[3] In Cairo, Ambassador Richard Nolte had arrived at the U.S. embassy but had not yet presented his credentials; therefore the United States had no direct line of communication with President Nasser.[4]

It is useful to consider the intelligence situation in Washington in late May and early June 1967. There was wide-open exchange of information between Israel and the United States.[5] President Johnson was being advised daily about the situation by Israel, and corroboration was available through the U.S. embassy in Tel Aviv, as well as through the CIA. But President Johnson did not know the details of the situation on the ground in Syria and in Egypt. The Egyptians had publicly announced the imminent withdrawal of UNEF and the entry of Egyptian forces into the Sinai. The U.S. intelligence community had little or no real-time access to events in the Sinai. Some photography was available from the U.S. Corona satellite, but it was imagery only and not real-time. Therefore the United States had no way of verifying Egyptian activity in the Sinai.[6] Consequently President Johnson did not know, in real time, what, or how many, Arab forces were being introduced into the Sinai in the area from which the UN forces had been withdrawn.

The *Liberty* had the U.S. Navy hull designation AGTR 5: *AG* indicated a miscellaneous auxiliary, and *TR* stood for "technical research," the ship's "cover." The *5* indicated that she was the fifth AGTR. (As was done on many auxiliary-ship types, the *A* was not included in the hull marks; the Navy considered it obvious and simply painted "GTR 5" on her hull.) The most visible technical features of the ship were her forty-five antennas. She was armed with four .50-caliber machine guns, located in two forward gun tubs and two amidships tubs. Several rifles and pistols were also on board.

The *Liberty* was fitted with a Technical Research Ship Special Communications System (TRSSCOMM). TRSSCOMM could bounce a ten-thousand-watt microwave signal off the moon to an antenna at Cheltenham, Maryland, from where it was sent to National Security Agency headquarters at Fort Meade, Maryland. The system could work only in the very limited periods when the moon was visible to both the ship and the receiving antenna at NSA.[7] This limitation on its usage made it unreliable for real-time capability. It rarely worked at all, and the system was ultimately junked when more capable satellites became operational shortly after the *Liberty* incident.

The *Liberty* sailors liked to call themselves "spooks" and to refer to the *Liberty* as a "spook ship."[8] In fact, the *Liberty* was a warship and met the standard of a warship under international law as well as the criteria established by the U.S. Navy.[9] She was painted gray, the same shade (haze gray) as all U.S. Navy warships. She was armed, albeit inadequately. She was commanded by a naval officer and registered as a warship of the United States. As long as she plied the high seas and did not enter the territorial waters of a neutral or belligerent nation, she had every right under international law to innocent passage or, as the French translate it, "inoffensive passage," including the right to listen to every communication she could intercept. While the high seas are open to all, however, entry into a combat zone is not without risk, and any vessel that sails into a combat zone places herself in harm's way.[10] Under U.S. naval doctrine, a neutral ship may be destroyed if she is aiding the enemy. This would include passing radio intercepts to the enemy.[11]

The primary job of the *Liberty* was gathering signals intelligence from the electromagnetic spectrum, an activity unequivocally permitted under international law. Nevertheless, there was a policy of shrouding the *Liberty* and her sister ships in secrecy, because the United States had made a technological breakthrough that permitted electronic eavesdropping to an extent never before imagined possible. Since the *Liberty*'s specific capabilities were not known outside the U.S. intelligence community, little was done by countries whose coasts she traversed to interfere with her passage or to prevent her from listening to and intercepting communications and radar transmissions.[12] The *Liberty* also listened to and recorded routine commercial and government radio broadcasts. Most of the *Liberty*'s mass of electronic gear permitted eavesdropping on a varied spectrum of electronic transmissions—such as low-, medium-, high-, very-high, and ultra-high-frequency radio transmissions—and also gave her the ability to intercept telephone-line and microwave transmissions. This technology was the state of the art in 1967, and this capability was unknown to most of the world. Despite the U.S. technological eavesdropping advances, however, the *Liberty*'s radio capability in the very-high-frequency/ultra-high-frequency spectrum did not permit her to monitor Israeli VHF/UHF message traffic.

VHF and UHF radio waves travel in straight lines.[13] High-, medium-, and low-frequency radio waves bend with the curvature of the earth. In contrast, very-high and ultra-high-frequency waves can be heard only out to the horizon, a distance of nineteen statute miles, or 16.5 nautical miles, under normal conditions;[14] at that point they continue straight out into space. Such communications can be heard and intercepted only by a listener within the line of sight of the transmitter. As soon as the listener goes over the horizon, the VHF and UHF radio waves can no longer be heard or intercepted. *Liberty*'s operational area was adjacent to the withdrawal route of the UN emergency force, along the Sinai coastal road, through El Arish to Port Said. The coast of Israel, as well as the nearest point of Israel within *Liberty*'s listening range, across the Gaza Strip (which prior to the 1967 war was controlled by Egypt), was over the horizon from the deck of the *Liberty*. Therefore, *Liberty*'s mission could not have been to intercept Israeli VHF/UHF message traffic.

According to James Ennes, who served as an officer on the *Liberty*, Lt. Cdr. David Lewis, the head of the NSA cryptologic detachment, advised the *Liberty*'s commanding officer, Cdr. William McGonagle, on the eve of *Liberty*'s arrival at its assigned operating area, that withdrawal over the horizon would degrade the ship's mission by 80 percent.[15] The *Liberty* had been given her orders for patrol along the coastal road only a few days after UNEF had been ordered to pullout and Egyptian forces began to move into the desert. It may be logically concluded that the original mission of the *Liberty* was to monitor Egyptian communications in the Sinai. The *Liberty* could have listened to and recorded lower-frequency broadcasts from Israel, but because she did not have any Hebrew linguists on board, she could not provide real-time information on those intercepts, and very few if any military transmissions were on other than VHF/UHF.

Note: FM comdesron one two to Ruqkrq / Cincusnaveur
SECRET

For Admiral McMan from Kidd, deliver at breakfast.

1. Ref telecon, your 141740 Z not rcved as of 1423552; however requested 8 june chronology follows:

A. Approaching land from the west during the early morning hours of 8 June, projected operations of Liberty for the morning and afternoon of the day was to proceed to a Point 13 nautical miles from the coast of UAR at 31-27.2 N 34-00E (Point Alpha) thence to 31-22.3N 33-42E (Point Bravo) thence to 31-31N 33-00E, (Point Charlie) retracing this track until new orders received. Ship would operate north of this track line at all times. If fixes could not be accurately obtained as Point Charlie was approached it was intended to head due north until the 100 fathom curve was crossed and the track moved to the north to more or less move back and forth on the general average of the 100 fathom curve. (*Excerpt U.S. Navy Court of Inquiry Ex 27*)

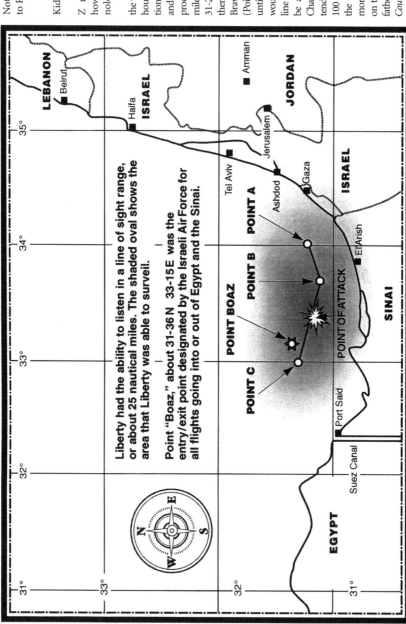

Situation Map: The projected track of the *Liberty* on the day of the attack and her VHF/UHF listening range

Cdr. Birchard Fosset, at the National Security Agency, was in charge of scheduling technical research ships. In late May 1967, he was instructed by his superiors in the Joint Reconnaissance Center of the Joint Chiefs of Staff to move a ship to the eastern Mediterranean Sea. Francis A. Raven, a civilian at NSA,[16] argued that it was unwise to send the *Liberty* to the eastern Mediterranean. He is reported to have said: "If war breaks out, she'll be alone and vulnerable. Either side might start shooting at her."[17] Such concerns were ignored by Raven's military superiors at NSA.

A message was sent to the *Liberty* at Abidjan, Ivory Coast, on May 24, 1967. "Make immediate preparations to get underway. When ready for sea ASAP [as soon as possible] depart Port Abidjan and proceed best possible speed to Rota, Spain to load technical support material/personnel. When ready for sea proceed to operating area off Port Said. Specific areas will follow."[18] The operating area designated in this first message as "off Port Said" should be noted, for later the operating area of the *Liberty* was moved about a hundred miles farther east, to coordinates (known as Point Alpha) off the Sinai near Rafah. At this easternmost point, the *Liberty* was about thirty-six nautical miles from the coast of Israel.

Admiral Martin's concern about the "unpredictability of UAR actions" following the outbreak of hostilities resulted in a message from the Sixth Fleet to the *Liberty* on June 6, 1967. The safety of the *Liberty* was an obvious concern. "In view of Arab/Israeli situation and unpredictability of UAR actions maintain a high state of vigilance against attack or threat of attack. Report by flash precedence any threatening or suspicious actions directed against you or any diversion from schedule necessitated by external threat."[19] For reasons that remain unknown, the *Liberty* did not receive this message.[20]

Owing to multiple human errors not only at the U.S. Joint Chiefs of Staff level but also at headquarters of the Commander in Chief, U.S. Naval Forces Europe, and Commander Sixth Fleet, and various communications stations in the Mediterranean—the messages meant to direct the *Liberty* to remain at least one hundred nautical miles off the coasts of Egypt and Israel—either never reached her or were broadcast and received well after the attack.

At the time a serious flaw existed in U.S. military communications with regard to passing messages from the highest level of command, like the JCS, to an operating unit, like the *Liberty*. Such as message was always sent via the chain of command—JCS to USCINCEUR to CINCUSNAVEUR to COMSIXTHFLT to the *Liberty*. The higher-level commands were equipped to receive and decode top-secret messages automatically. Lower-level, seagoing units like the *Liberty* were not so equipped. The normal procedure was to list commands and units with an interest as "information addressees" on messages to alert the ultimate recipient that a message was on its way. Thus a JCS confidential message with the *Liberty* as an information addressee would have been expected to be received by the ship at almost the same time it reached the initial "action" addressee, in this case USCINCEUR. However, the JCS message 080110Z June 67, which directed *Liberty* to remain at least one hundred miles from the coast, was classified at too high a level for the *Liberty* to receive it via the on-line encryption method. Thus before the attack, when possibly there was still time for her to turn away and sail farther out to sea, when the *Liberty* received a USCINCEUR message to "take for action" a forthcoming JCS message, she had not received her information copy, either because it was misdirected or, even if there was no misrouting, because of its elevated security classification. The stand-off order itself arrived through the chain of command well after the incident.

The exact time that Admiral McCain's headquarters in London could have received the USCINCEUR message intended to keep the *Liberty* away from the combat area and directing the admiral to "take for action" the orders that would have sent the *Liberty* out of harm's way is not precisely known, but it was after 1117 Sinai time. Cdr. Maurice Bennett had the following comment on this issue:

> The bungling of communications by the U.S. was a major contributing factor. Immediately prior to the attack the XO [executive officer], LCDR Lewis—the Research Officer and I were in research communications spaces puzzling over a FLASH precedence message from 6th Fleet (I think) telling us to take [a] JCS msg for action—we commented that we all presumed that we would get the JCS msg (telling *Liberty* to pull away from the coast) momentarily—when the first wave hit—we finally got the JCS message a day or two *after* the attack.[21]

Confirming Commander Bennett's conclusion, the House Armed Services Investigating Subcommittee stated in its report:

> A garbled version of this message [USCINCEUR 080625Z June 67] was placed on Fleet Broadcast at 1059Z [1259 Sinai time], June 8th, and there was some question whether it had been received by U.S.S. *Liberty*. But as Rear Adm. Fitzpatrick testified "It is a moot point whether the ship

received it or not for two reasons: If it did receive it, it was probably use-less to them and number two, even if they had received it, it wouldn't have made any sense to them because all it said was to take some other JCS message for action, some higher commander, and they wouldn't have known what the other message was because, as we know, that other message from the Joint Chiefs of Staff, which they had the information copy on, didn't get to them.[22]

Another contributing factor was that the communications system in the Mediterranean was simply overwhelmed by the volume of messages gener-ated in direct response to the Arab-Israeli War.[23] The question has often been asked, Was there a direct back-channel circuit by which NSA could communi-cate directly with the crypto compartment on board the ship? This author has not discovered any such back channel and does not believe it existed, with the possible exception of the TRSSCOMM system, which, as noted, rarely worked and was dependent on the position of the moon.[24] If sending a message from NSA over regular channels addressed only to the *Liberty* is considered back-channel communication, then, if it existed and was used, one would wonder why the crypto compartment receiving a stand-off message would not have passed it to the commanding officer of the ship. No *Liberty* crew member has ever claimed such a back-channel link existed. It should be remembered that U.S. intelligence ships like the *Liberty* were not first-line naval combatants but rather platforms for gathering routine FBIS material and tediously collecting huge amounts of data on radar and voice transmissions for further analysis later. There was no perceived need for real-time or back-channel communica-tion. If such a back channel existed, there is no evidence that it was used in any way related to the *Liberty* incident.

The U.S. government has never released a formal statement accurately describing the overall mission and assigned tasks of the *Liberty* in the eastern Mediterranean on June 8, 1967. Phil G. Goulding, the Assistant Secretary of Defense for Public Affairs, wanted to "take the public affairs initiative, leveling with our people from the beginning."[25] Goulding proposed saying, "This ship collects intelligence."[26] Numerous arguments were made in opposition. There was concern that if it was disclosed that the *Liberty* was gathering intelligence, other intelligence-gathering ships would not be welcome in ports where U.S. "research ships" had been quite welcome. Another argument was that Middle East countries might be offended by the United States sending a ship to eaves-drop on them. Secretary of Defense McNamara listened to all the arguments, and though he personally favored Goulding's suggestion, he ultimately yielded to the security and diplomatic arguments and authorized reference to the *Liberty* only as "a U.S. Navy technical research ship."[27] The official statement on technical research ships was, "The mission of this ship is to conduct technical research operations in support of U.S. Navy electronic research projects which include electromagnetic propagation studies and advanced communications systems."[28] The press release further stated that the *Liberty* "arrived at her position this morning to assure communications between the U.S. government posts in the Middle East and to assist in relaying information concerning the evacuation of American dependents and other American citizens from the countries of the Middle East."[29] Egypt had broken diplomatic relations with the United States following the Israeli air attacks of June 5, 1967. Evacuation of U.S. diplomats from Cairo and Tel Aviv started on May 25, 1967, and was completed long before the *Liberty* arrived at Point Alpha. It may be argued that because there were still American citizens in the region, the cover story was valid, but other than the press release, there is no evidence of any sort to support the claim that the *Liberty* was there to "relay information concerning evacuation of American dependents and other American citizens."

There are apparently two valid primary reasons, and possibly a third, self-serving reason, that may explain the failure of the United States to candidly disclose, even after the incident, all of the facts regarding the decision to send the *Liberty* to the coast of the Sinai in late May and early June 1967 and regarding her mission there. The primary reasons reflect both security and political concerns. The self-serving reason is the normal reflex tendency of any bureaucracy to prevent the full exposure of its internal failures.

The security reason is quite valid. The United States had moved far ahead of the rest of the world in the development of listening and message-interception capabilities, a fact virtually unknown to almost everyone else. The United States thus had a tremendous intelligence edge, and it wanted to keep it as long as possible. For this reason, no doubt, the National Security Agency document "United States [deleted], Attack on a SIGINT Collector the U.S.S. *Liberty* (S)-CCO," written by William D. Gerhard and Henry W. Millington and published in 1981, was originally classified top secret, with a declassification review date of April 2011.[30] Although a great deal of information about the *Liberty* has been disclosed since June 1967, some of the intercept technology of 1967 probably still requires security classification. There was, then, a certain legitimate amount of holding back for security reasons, which still may cover some technical data relating to the capabilities of the equipment on board the *Liberty*. If some technical data of this nature remains hidden behind the veil of secrecy, it is doubtful that it goes to the issues explored in this book.

The political reason for lack of candor is more complex. Since the beginning of the twentieth century, the United States has had a many-faceted foreign policy in the Near East, often complicated by contradictory forces and needs. The United States has substantial business interests in the Middle East related to oil. During the Cold War, it also desired to be "evenhanded" in the region while maintaining and continually expanding its influence, wishing to contain Soviet influence in the Arab world and to prevent the establishment of Soviet hegemony in the Middle East. At the same time, the United States wished to maintain a "special relationship" with the state of Israel. The many hats worn (then as now) by the United States made it difficult to chart a course of action. Not unlike Great Britain, the United States has many times found itself on both sides of the Arab/Israeli conflict.

The third, self-serving reason not to be candid was that it was an attempt to prevent disclosure of one's own errors. Such action is not uncommon. The foreword to the NSA document on the history of the *Liberty* incident states, "The knowledge that the tragedy resulted not only from Israeli miscalculation but also from faulty U.S. communications practice was even more difficult to accept."[31] The presence of the eavesdropping *Liberty* off the coast of Sinai in the middle of the 1967 war was potentially a source of embarrassment to the United States. Moreover, it was by an innocent series of errors that *Liberty* entered the war area, without the intent or real-time knowledge of upper-level U.S. policy makers. She was there as a result of communication failure that misdirected her orders to remain well clear of the war zone. Thus the less-than-candid press releases by the U.S. Department of Defense were an effort to explain away an unwelcome but undeniable fact. Like most efforts of this kind, it was not successful, as to this day the false press report is widely recognized as just that.

But was there a cover-up of any aspect at all of the event? The dictionary meaning of the word "cover-up" is "an effort or strategy intended to conceal something as a crime or scandal."[32] Deputy Secretary of Defense Cyrus Vance, the number-two person in the Department of Defense at the time, says in a letter to this author dated March 24, 1994, "As to the allegation there was a cover-up and I was in charge of the cover-up, it is simply untrue." Goulding, however, says there was a cover-up.[33] In view of the false public statement of the United States about *Liberty*'s mission, it is difficult to disagree with Goulding's assessment. The United States never truthfully stated the precise mission of the *Liberty*. It made up a false press release and let the false press release stand as "our cover story"[34] for the event. Obviously, Secretary McNamara and Deputy Secretary Vance saw this as an appropriate effort to protect security and diplomatic relations, while Goulding, a newspaperman by profession, saw it as violating the public's right to know. Whether one prefers the Goulding description of "cover-up" or the Vance conclusion of "no cover-up" is related not to the issue of whether there was a cover-up about the attack but rather to the reason the NSA initially sent the *Liberty* on a mission to the eastern Mediterranean.

There was no effort to cover up mistakes made by either the United States or Israel. The Navy, the Department of Defense, and Congress had an intense interest in discovering all the facts, and U.S. failures in particular, to prevent such a tragedy from occurring again. Even if there had been an effort to cover up the errors that were made, it would not have succeeded, in view of the multiple investigations and the very large number of personnel involved.

It is important to understand that the false statement, or cover-up, regarding the mission of the *Liberty* was made not to conceal the failure or wrongdoing of any individual or to hide any errors and mistakes relating to the attack but rather to protect a perceived national interest of the United States in the area of security and diplomatic relations. Secretary of State Dean Rusk agreed with Vance in his interview with Thames TV.

> Interviewer: They say Mr. Rusk, that there's been a coverup for 20 years on behalf of successive American administrations to examine and explore the affair.
> Rusk: Oh, I don't think so, I think it's simply that the feeling that once something like this has happened you have to continue to work toward constructive ends, you don't allow an incident of this sort to poison the entire relationship.[35]

While there is obviously substantial dispute about a cover-up, it is clear that the dispute rages over the reason the *Liberty* was sent on her mission and not about the mistakes by the United States that put her in harm's way and the mistakes by Israel that resulted in the attack.

Chapter 4

THE *LIBERTY* TARGETED

The *Liberty* reached Point Alpha at 0849 on June 8, 1967, and began her patrol, steaming to the west with her bow pointed in the general direction of Port Said, Egypt.[1] The *Liberty*'s commanding officer, Cdr. William L. McGonagle, knew she was in a potentially dangerous position. It has been written that he contemplated sailing away from the coast, but because he was "not in the loop"—that is, he did not know the reason for the *Liberty*'s mission, he apparently was persuaded by the advice of Lt. Cdr. David E. Lewis, the head of the cryptologic detachment, to remain in harm's way.

There was the *Liberty*, in eye view of the war, painted haze gray, armed with .50-caliber machine guns, in an area where, unbeknownst to her, the previous day the U.S. defense attaché at the U.S. embassy in Tel Aviv had advised Washington by message that Israeli forces had reported being shelled from the sea.[2]

On that same morning of June 8, the Israelis held the ground at El Arish and also controlled the air above. Explosions were occurring at El Arish.[3] Ennes reports, "At 1130 the ship arrived at Point Bravo. . . . Coastal plotting remained difficult. . . . Suddenly a large explosion rocked the town of El Arish. . . . I located Captain McGonagle in the wardroom to tell him of the fire and smoke ashore." At noon, thick black smoke extended for miles along the beach.[4]

Commander McGonagle testified at the U.S. Navy court of inquiry,

At the commencement of the drill [1300] it was possible to see a large billowing cloud of black smoke rising from approximately 15 to 20 miles to the west of El Arish on the beach. The exact identity of the cause and location of this explosion is not positively known, although it was believed to be near the beach area. This was noted about 1300. At about 1330 a smaller cloud of

black smoke was noted to the west of El Arish estimated five to six miles and
also along the coastline. . . .

So that they would be impressed I pointed out to the crew at the
time that the column of black smoke on the beach should be sufficient
evidence that the ship was in a potentially dangerous location.

When these explosions occurred, the Israeli troops at El Arish wrongly
concluded that, as reported the day before, they were being shelled from
the sea. In fact, either Egyptian sappers, caught behind Israeli lines, were
detonating Egyptian ammunition dumps or the explosions were part of IDF
cleaning-up operations. With hindsight it is clear that there was no shelling
from the sea and that one or both of the above activities caused the explosions and the resulting columns of smoke along the coast near El Arish, but
the Israeli forces on the scene at El Arish did not know that at the time.

Perhaps, if the *Liberty* had not been in sight, about fourteen miles off the
coast, the Israeli army units might not have come to the conclusion that they
were being shelled from the sea.[5] Of course, the *Liberty* did not have guns
that could reach the beach from fourteen miles, but a ship's details were not
discernible at that distance, especially to soldiers. Consequently the troops
stationed at El Arish advised the high-command headquarters at the Kirya
in Tel Aviv that they were being shelled from the sea. The people at the Kirya,
following normal IDF procedures, determined this to be a naval matter. A
call was placed to navy headquarters in Haifa at Stella Maris, and the navy
was told to investigate.

Following the 1956 Suez campaign, the Israel Air Force recognized the need
to move its headquarters from Ramla, about twelve miles southeast of Tel Aviv,
to the Kirya in the center of Tel Aviv, where it was installed next to the headquarters of the IDF chief of staff. The Israel Navy headquarters remained in Haifa,
more than sixty miles away, linked to the Kirya by closed telephone.[6]

The war log at the navy headquarters in Stella Maris indicates a call from
the Kirya was received and that the navy first ordered two destroyers to head
toward El Arish. That order was canceled and a new order directed Motor
Torpedo Boat (MTB) Division 914,[7] which had departed the port of Ashdod
at 1120 and was still in the vicinity of Ashdod, to proceed toward El Arish.
At this point, the MTB division was not told of the reason for the order; it
was only told "turn to El Arish for patrol."[8]

MTB Division 914 consisted of three diesel-powered motor torpedo
boats named after birds of prey—203, named the *Aya;* 204, named the *Daya;*

and 206, named the *Thames*—all under the command of Lt. Cdr. Moshe Oren. The boats were built in France and were powered by two Napier Deltic diesel engines and capable of forty-two knots, according to *Jane's Fighting Ships*. They carried a normal crew of fifteen and were armed with one 40 mm cannon facing aft, one 20 mm cannon on the bow, and two .50-caliber machine guns, one on each side. They carried two German aerial nineteen-inch torpedoes mounted on launchers or throwers, which were often referred to as "torpedo tubes." They were not torpedo tubes in the classic sense but rather throwing devices that pushed torpedoes over the side and away from the boat. The boats were equipped with old U.S. World War II–surplus Kelvin-Hughes radar, but only one boat had true motion radar. They also had UHF radios that had been installed about a week earlier. Only boat 206's UHF radio was operable.

Division 914 steered toward El Arish, a distance of about fifty miles, at top speed of about thirty-six to thirty-eight knots.[9] At 1330, division commander Oren was advised that "El Arish is being shelled from the sea."[10] At 1341, a target was detected at the extreme radar limit of motor torpedo boat 204, which the Israeli radarman called about twenty-two nautical miles.[11] Using the map from the 1982 *IDF History Report* on the *Liberty* incident and the times indicated in that report on page 18, it can be calculated that took the MTBs about forty-four minutes to close the distance of about twenty-two miles from their position to a position about two miles from the *Liberty*. With the MTBs moving at thirty-six to thirty-eight knots toward the *Liberty*, and with the ship moving away from the MTBs at her patrol speed of about five knots, the relative motion between the two was thirty-one to thirty-three knots. It would therefore take about forty-one to forty-four minutes to traverse twenty or twenty-one nautical miles. The figures are not precise and suggest that the speeds may have been a knot or two different than reported by the MTBs or by the *Liberty*, or that the times may have been off a minute or two, or a combination of all of the above.

The Israeli radarman on the MTB division commander's boat, 204, a young enlisted man called Gulli,[12] accurately reported to his combat information center (CIC) officer that the target was steering west (the actual heading was 283 degrees). This information, together with a range, was used by the CIC officer to calculate the speed of the target as thirty knots. This was inaccurate. How could such a mistake have been made? The radar operator watched a round radar screen shaped much like a large dinner plate. The center of the screen represents the position of the boat. A line from the center of the screen to the top indicates the direction the MTB was traveling. The radar beams emitted by the radar and returned or reflected by the target causes a bliplike image to appear on the radar screen.

A sweep swings 360 degrees, indicating the rotation of the radar antenna. Each time the sweep finds the target, it is illuminated on the screen. The screen momentarily retains the illuminated image. The image, or target, thus appears to move on the screen. If the radar is stationary and the target is moving, the calculation is easier. If both radar and target are moving, the calculation is more complex. When the target is moving away from the radar and the radar is moving toward the target, as was the case of the *Liberty* and the MTBs, the speeds of both are factors in the equation.

The round radar screen is about eighteen inches in diameter. Thus, from the screen's center, which represents the MTB, where the radar is located, looking forward, the screen is about nine inches from center to top. If the center to the extreme range is twenty-four miles, then a mile is represented by three-eighths of an inch.[13] The *Liberty*'s speed of five knots is a mile and a half per minute or a deflection of 1/32 of an inch per minute on the screen. During a one-minute period, on the radar scope the MTB moved a little less than 9/32 of an inch toward the target. At the same time, if the target was moving at thirty knots, the target moved away from the MTB on the radar scope 6/32 of an inch. If the target was moving at five knots, it would move away 1/32 of an inch. Dealing with such tiny measurements in a small dim room with only minutes to make calculations and while en route to a twenty-year-old naval officer's first combat engagement is a recipe for error.

Modern radars have cursors that can be placed on a target, and the distance course and speed of the target instantly appear in digital format.[14] This was not the case in 1967. There was a cursor that could be projected from the center of the screen to the target to provide range information. The operator on MTB 204 viewed the scope and, upon measuring the distance to the target, orally passed that data to the CIC officer, Ens. Aharon Yifrach.

The CIC officer had a dead-reckoning tracer (DRT), which was an illuminated map board or plot of the area. Beneath the plot was an illuminated dot surrounded by the 360 degrees of the compass, which is called in Hebrew *shoshanat haruchot,* which translates as "rose of winds." In English it is usually referred to as a compass rose. The position of the illuminated dot at the center of the rose of winds beneath the map of the area was stabilized by a gyroscope. It was run by an electric motor, and the position was calibrated and set before leaving harbor. The accumulated error in the position usually did not vary more than one nautical mile per hour. It was customary to reset the rose of winds when a fix was obtained.

The speed calculations were made not on the radar scope by the radar operator but by the CIC officer on the plotting table, or DRT. The plotting table was described to this author by Aharon Yifrach, the CIC officer on boat 204. He said the plotting table was about three feet by three feet and was located in the CIC compartment, which was about two meters (a little over six feet) by three meters (a little over nine feet). The compartment was big enough for either the CIC officer or the radar operator to sleep on the deck while the other stood watch. The CIC compartment was below the main deck, and the ladder to the main deck came out just behind the bridge, which was a few additional steps higher. Yifrach communicated with the bridge via an intercommunications system that consisted of a large rubber microphone with a speaker on the bridge. The intercom was a single system, not a duplexer. The user could either talk or listen but not both.

Communication between the MTB and Stella Maris was possible from the bridge or from the CIC compartment by VHF radio if the MTB was north of Tel Aviv. In the El Arish area, well south of Tel Aviv, communication with Stella Maris was only possible by single-sideband (SSB), but there was no SSB unit on the bridge. Yifrach believes the SSB radio was made by Collins and was called a T-618 or 618-T. Communication between the MTBs was by a designated VHF radio frequency; the radio was on the bridge and not in the CIC. Ensign Yifrach confirmed that new UHF radios for communication with aircraft had been installed on the MTBs just before, or at the very beginning of, the 1967 war. These radios were on the bridge. They were new and very complicated to use. On the command boat, only Yifrach knew how to operate the air-link radio, and he was not near it. For that reason, the one other MTB that was able to use the UHF air-link radio talked to the *Kursa* flight and relayed the messages to Division Cdr. Moshe Oren via surface-communication VHF radio. The communications systems left a great deal to be desired.

The initial position of the target was marked on MTB 204's plotting table. The calculations are not simple. The initial calculation of the distance from the MTB to the target was made by a nineteen-year-old enlisted radar operator in a dimly lighted radar compartment, in an MTB skipping across the water at thirty-six to thirty-eight knots, rushing to his first combat. The twenty-year-old CIC officer made a mark on the plotting table with a pencil to indicate the position of the target. Then, in a minute or two, he got a second target position and marked it on the plot. Next, he measured the distance of the movement with a straight-edge ruler. If he used a one-minute measurement, he multiplied the distance the target moved by sixty to calculate the speed in distance per hour. If he used a two-minute measurement, he multiplied by thirty, and if he used a three-minute minute measurement, he multiplied by twenty. Yifrach, the CIC officer, believes the initial radar position was in error. He initially calculated the target speed as thirty knots. Upon request for verification, he recalculated twenty-eight knots.

In the first UHF radio communication from *Kursa* flight received by MTB 206 and relayed to MTB 204, the lead MTB with Commander Oren on board, the pilot stated that the ship had a single funnel with a mast forward and a mast aft. This information was passed from the bridge of the MTB, where it was received, to Yifrach in CIC with the comment that the target was a Zed-class destroyer (i.e., a former British Z class). In retrospect, accepting this report was another error, because, although the Egyptian Z-class destroyers had a single funnel (or stack) and masts fore and aft, the two Egyptian Z-class destroyers were in the Red Sea and could not have come back into the Mediterranean because the Suez Canal was now closed as a result of the war. However, the report seemed logical to Yifrach in view of the report that El Arish was being shelled from the sea. The only Egyptian warships capable of the shelling from a distance of fourteen miles would have been destroyers or Soviet-built Osa or Komar missile boats.[15] But this target was reported as a destroyer, and its computed speed was thirty knots. For the target to have been shelling from the sea as reported, it must have been a destroyer, and a destroyer can steam at thirty knots.

Some authors reject the explanation that the radar "painted," or showed a reflected target, at twenty-two miles and that the Israel Navy miscalculated the actual speed of the *Liberty*. The error in calculating the speed is explained above. There are a number of possible explanations of the reported radar distance. A review of the electronics literature discloses a phenomenon called "channeling," or "refraction."[16] On dry, clear summer days, radar beams sometimes bounce or curve and are able to reach targets even beyond the normal line-of-sight range. June 8, 1967, was a dry, clear summer day. Thus the channeling or refraction theory is most likely and is supported by the fact that as the *Davis* approached the *Liberty*, the latter appeared on the *Davis'* radar over the horizon at eighty-five nautical miles. A message from CTG 60.5 to COMSIXTHFLT and CTF 60 090004Z June 1967 reads, "1. Tentative identification Liberty lat 32-35 N long 31-05 E 85 miles ahead of me ETA 0430Z." It is interesting to note that *Davis* personnel were able to accurately estimate their rendezvous time with the *Liberty* approximately four and one-half hours in advance.

If channeling were not involved, the distance beyond the horizon is not significant and can be accounted for by the projection of both the radar antenna of the MTB above the surface of the sea, about eighteen feet, and the projection of the superstructure of the *Liberty* above the sea surface. It is also possible that the MTBs and the *Liberty* were two or three miles closer together than the reported radar range calculation.

The reported speed of the *Liberty* as thirty knots had two important implications. First, under Israeli naval doctrine, a radar target moving faster than twenty knots was presumed to be a warship. U.S. naval doctrine at that time made essentially the same assumption. The U.S. doctrine in 1967 was that speed of a vessel of twenty-five knots or more observed on radar identified the vessel as a warship.

Since the *Ibrahim al-Awwal* incident in 1956, there had been an ongoing dispute, still very much alive, between the Israel Air Force and the Israel Navy over which service was entitled to credit for the capture of the Egyptian destroyer. As a result of air force–navy rivalry, air force controllers at ground radar control sites would not let naval liaison officers serving with them talk on the air defense net.[17]

Many persons intimately familiar with the navy–air force rivalry believe that if the Israel Navy had believed it could reach and overtake the target, it is inconceivable that it would have called for help from the air force. Other experts point out that the information available to the motor torpedo boat crews—that is, that the target was running at twenty-eight or thirty knots and therefore must be a destroyer—indicates that a call for air support would have been both appropriate and prudent. It is the opinion of this author that the navy would not have called for air force assistance if the navy believed it had the remotest chance of overtaking the target, even if it was certain that the target was a destroyer.

In any event, the navy did call for air support. The MTB division commander determined that the target had its bow pointed toward Port Said, which lay about sixty nautical miles from the *Liberty*'s 1300 (local time) position.[18] *Liberty*'s undisputed heading was 283°. If the *Liberty* continued at twenty-eight knots, as the Israeli naval force thought, and the MTBs chased at thirty-six, they could not close the twenty-two-mile gap before the target entered the safe haven of Port Said. The MTB message to naval headquarters at Stella Maris was recorded as: "Division 914 is reporting that targets are sailing west at 30 knots. An order was made to double check speed [of the target]. He [referring to MTB Division 914] can not chase them. Suggests dispatch aircraft."[19]

At Stella Maris, Rear Adm. Shlomo Erell, the chief of the navy of Israel, had been in direct operational command of Israeli naval forces from the early morning hours of June 8. After the 0600 reconnaissance flight had sighted the *Liberty* at her early-morning position, Erell had a "neutral" wedge placed on the plotting table.

At 1100, the second in command of the navy, Capt. Issy Rehav, assumed tactical command when Erell left Stella Maris on Mount Carmel to go down to the port of Haifa. Shortly before Rehav took tactical command, the command duty officer, Cdr. Avraham "Ramy" Lunz, directed removal from the plotting board of the wedge marking the ship.[20] Not only did Lunz order removal of the wedge, but also he did not inform Captain Rehav of his action when Rehav took command.

Why did Commander Lunz fail to advise Rehav? His explanation was that ships do not stand still. He was of the opinion that the ship had moved at least seventy-five miles from the point where it was previously sighted steering south at fifteen knots. The *Liberty* deck log shows her speed at 0600 that morning as fifteen knots. It also reflects that the *Liberty* changed course at 0555, made a right turn toward the coast of Egypt, and steered 190° for about ten minutes before turning left to 060° and correcting back on her track of 130°, which was her original course to Point Alpha. The *Liberty* maneuvers began at the time that the Israeli morning naval reconnaissance plane was near the ship. The maneuvers may have been undertaken to deceive the aircraft into thinking that the ship under observation was heading for Port Said.

Five hours on 190° at fifteen knots would have put the *Liberty* in the vicinity of Port Said at about 1100. It is not known if Commander Lunz considered that possibility when he ordered the wedge removed. As a result of removing the wedge and failing to tell Captain Rehav about it, Lunz was named a party in the judicial inquiry by the Israeli examining judge who later investigated the incident.[21]

The MTBs had requested an air attack on what they initially believed from their radar to be an Egyptian destroyer running from them toward Port Said. The call went by telephone from navy headquarters in Stella Maris to Lieutenant Commander Pinchasy, the naval liaison officer at air force headquarters in the Kirya in Tel Aviv. Though Pinchasy had also been aware of the *Liberty*'s 0600 position, he did not associate this information with the MTBs' report of an Egyptian destroyer shelling El Arish from the sea

Pinchasy's location was in a small room on the first floor of the command-and-control center in the "pit," or high-command post, of the IDF command-and-control center, in the Kirya. The pit was somewhat akin to the U.S. National Military Command Center in the Pentagon. In the pit, or war room, area is a series of underground bunkers. In 1967, the minister of defense had a very small room off the army spaces. The army command post had separate rooms for each army command or theater and for various functions. One very important room was the incoming communications room. All incoming messages were received there and distributed to the room or rooms to which they were related. The army bunker was not like the navy or the air force command posts in Stella Maris or the pit, as it had no real-time plot of the entire ground situation. The air force command center was near, but not directly accessible to, the high command or army bunker.

The Israel Air Force command center was two stories in height from floor to ceiling. A large tabletop map displayed the entire country of Israel and portions of surrounding countries. Facing the map on the second-floor level was a raised platform where the air force commander in chief, Maj. Gen. Mordechai "Motti" Hod, sat. To his left, behind a glass partition, sat the chief of air force intelligence, Lt. Col. Yeshayahu "Shaike" Bareket. To the right of Hod sat Col. Rafael "Rafi" Har-Lev, the deputy air force commander, and to Har-Lev's right sat the chief air controller. The second-floor platform had some depth, and behind the four front-row seats sat or stood various members of staff, such as the deputy chief air controller, who sat behind his chief. On the opposite wall, data was posted for quick reference.

Airmen worked on the first floor around the table, placing and moving wedges in a manner similar to the scenes of Royal Air Force war rooms in World War II movies. Below this second-floor platform was a series of additional rooms on the first floor housing other staff, such as the air defense controller (who had very little work during the 1967 war) and the naval liaison officer to the air force. The staff members in the rooms on the first floor were linked by telephone to the level above them, and the naval liaison officer communicated with the navy command post by closed telephone line. It was necessary to initiate a call and wait for the telephone to be answered. This was much less efficient than an open-line system, where the telephone was never hung up and a person constantly listened at each end. A stairway went from the first floor to the second floor, where General Hod was seated. Lieutenant Commander Pinchasy made his request for an air attack by telephone to General Hod on the second floor above him. The request was denied.

To understand the situation in the Kirya and the attitude of General Hod, it is necessary to be aware of an event that had taken place on the night of June 7, 1967. Israel Defense Force coastal radar had reported three large ship targets steaming north along the coast. The air force and the navy were alerted, the latter dispatching its three destroyers—the *Eilat*, the *Jaffa*, and the *Haifa*—to meet the ships, which were presumed to be Egyptian destroyers. The air force launched several flights of Mirage fighter-bombers. Broken clouds moved across the night sky.

The air force pilots reported to General Hod that through the breaks in the clouds they could see three wakes of ships moving at high speed. They asked for permission from General Hod to attack. Hod was on the telephone with Rear Admiral Erell, who was at the navy command center at Stella Maris in Haifa, and told Erell that his pilots had the enemy ships in sight and he wished to authorize the pilots to attack. Because this was a naval matter, protocol gave the navy the last word, and Erell said no. Hod argued that his planes had limited fuel, and that if they could not attack at once he would pull them off. Erell insisted on illumination. Reluctantly, Hod ordered a plane to dive below the clouds and drop a flare. A moment later the flare illuminated the *Eilat*, the *Jaffa*, and the *Haifa*. There were no Egyptian ships. The radar blips had been false images, or "ghosts."[22]

The climate remained cool between the navy and the air force as an aftermath of what Hod believed to be the wasting of his limited air assets the night before. Lieutenant Commander Pinchasy reported his lack of success in securing air support to Stella Maris and was told to be more forceful. He got up from his desk and went upstairs to the second floor platform to confront General Hod directly, much to Hod's annoyance. Hod did not wish to commit his limited air assets to another wild-goose chase for the navy. "Do you have a target?" Hod asked. Pinchasy answered, "Yes."[23]

General Hod passed the order for air support to Col. Shmuel Kislev, his chief air controller, seated two chairs to Hod's right. Kislev's deputy, noting that *Menorah* flight,[24] consisting of four Mirage IIICJs armed with conventional bombs, was outbound to the south, asked Kislev if he should divert *Menorah* flight to this target. Kislev replied, "No."

Menorah was en route to strike surface-to-air missile (SAM) sites along the Suez Canal, and Colonel Kislev deemed that mission more important than running an errand for the navy. Ironically, Kislev's decision not to divert *Menorah* flight proved to be to the *Liberty*'s benefit, because *Menorah* flight was armed with conventional iron bombs; had they attacked the *Liberty*, it is very likely that they would have sunk her in minutes. Kislev next looked over his airborne assets and noticed *Kursa* Flight, two Mirage IIICJ aircraft armed with 30 mm guns and air-to-air missiles, on combat air patrol over the Suez Canal and near the end of its time on station. *Kursa*'s return route would take it over Point Boaz,[25] just a few miles from El Arish and the *Liberty*. Kislev thus directed *Kursa* Flight to proceed toward El Arish and ordered the flight leader "to bang," or attack, the target "if it is a warship," warning the flight leader, "but be careful, we have MTBs in the area." He also gave Kursa a UHF frequency on which to communicate with the torpedo boats and the code name of MTB Division 914, which was "Pagoda."[26]

Kursa Flight departed the Suez Canal and flew toward El Arish. Upon arrival near El Arish the *Kursa* Flight pilots saw a ship steering west and then observed other boats to the north. At first they thought there were only two other smaller boats, but then they observed three. Although *Kursa* had authority to attack "a warship" in the vicinity of El Arish, *Kursa* attempted to establish direct radio communication with the Israeli naval boats.[27] Air-to-ship communication, however, was not easy. The Israel Navy had installed UHF radios with aviation frequencies in all three MTBs shortly before the war began, but only MTB 206 was able to operate the equipment properly and communicate with *Kursa*. MTB 206 then passed the communications to Lieutenant Commander Oren, the division commander, in MTB 204.

The *Kursa* leader orbited the *Liberty* looking for the "Blue Max,"[28] which was the identifying mark the Israelis placed on their hardware to help identify them as friendly. He did not see a flag on the ship.[29] *Kursa* Flight leader had carefully sorted out the non-Israeli warship from the Israeli torpedo boats. Now he contacted air control for specific permission to attack. It was granted at 1355, subject to verification that "it is a warship."

At 1357 the *Kursa* Flight leader, as well as his wingman, rolled into shallow dives from west to east with the sun at their backs.[30] His right index finger found the trigger of his 30 mm guns, and the air attack began. Traveling at six hundred knots (perhaps a little slower, see chapter 1, note 2), the attacking plane closed on a slow-moving surface target at the rate of ten miles per minute, or a mile each six seconds. Less than three seconds were available for firing (he may have had four seconds rather than three), followed by a pull-up and turn back for another firing run. It is extremely dangerous to remain in the attack run too long, because of the rapid closure rate with the target. The phenomenon is called target fixation. It is a fascination with the run that compels the pilot to continue the run rather than pull up a safe distance from the target. Because very little time remains after firing ceases until the aircraft will fly into or strike a surface target, fighter and attack pilots are told repeatedly to fire and pull up. Most pilots, including this author, will confess that they have in fact delayed pull-up to observe their hits. The *Kursa* Flight leader and his wingman did so that day.

As the stream of 30 mm rounds struck the *Liberty,* they tore into the unarmored superstructure and deck, slaying men and destroying equipment with equal ferocity. They also struck the *Liberty*'s motor whaleboat stored amidships on the starboard side just aft of the bridge, puncturing and setting on fire two fifty-five-gallon drums of gasoline stored on the port side on the 01 level (one level above the main deck).[31]

Chaos and horror reigned on the bridge. Shattered glass, mutilated bodies, and blood were everywhere. Amid it all, Commander McGonagle remained calm and continued to command his ship. He even got the ship's camera out of the safe and took pictures of the second wave of attacking aircraft.[32] The initial attack so disrupted the *Liberty*'s radio transmission capability that she was unable to transmit on her standard encrypted transmitters. The ship's radio shack began transmitting on the CINCUSNAVEUR high-command (HiCOM) unsecure high-frequency voice circuit, initially without success. Someone had accidentally moved the frequency dial one kilocycle. This was quickly discovered and corrected by Radioman Chief Wayne L. Smith, and the transmitters worked at once. This transmission problem, along with other problems, such as destroyed connections, is the source of the myth that the *Liberty*'s radio transmitters were "jammed." Compare the testimony of Radioman Chief Smith, in the U.S. Navy court of inquiry transcript (p. 94):

> Word was passed on the 1MC to pass over hicom that we were being attacked, to any station. I immediately picked up the hicom transmitter which was on UIC 32, auxiliary radio. We started to transmit with it. No station heard us, and five minutes or so later the transmitter was reported to have blown out. I immediately switched to a work two transmitter in the transmitter room, and we couldn't get out on that either, so, in between attacks by this time I went down to the transmitter room and I found or discovered that somebody had accidentally knocked the

frequency dial one KC [kilocycle] off. I corrected this and ran back to the radio shack and we got hold of stations schematic on which we passed the attack message.[33]

The initial report of the attack to reach the Sixth Fleet was received and understood by the aircraft carrier *Saratoga* (CVA 60), call sign "Schematic," at 1210Z (1410 Sinai).[34] Immediately after the air attack began, the *Liberty* began transmitting: "Any station from Rock Star, over, any station from Rock Star we are under attack we are under attack over."[35]

The logs reflect a response two minutes later from the aircraft carrier *Saratoga:* "Rock Star from Schematic u are garbled, say again, over." The log entry notes four minutes later: "Switching xmitrs but no luck." The log entry reporting the transmission of the message about the torpedo strike was entered as 1218Z/1418 Sinai, which makes clear that time entries in the radio logs are a number of minutes earlier than the actual events occurred. The log entry reads: "Schematic from Rock Star be advised we have been hit by torpedo listing about 9 deg request immed assist over."

Pinchas Pinchasy provided much of the data for this chapter during an interview by this author on January 12, 1990, in his office at Technion University in Haifa, where Pinchasy was on the development staff. Pinchasy was most gracious with his time and allowed the interview to be taped. After several hours the interview ended. The tape recorder was turned off, and this author was putting his pad and pencils in his briefcase when Pinchasy leaned forward and said words that made this author's hair on the back of his neck stand up and sent a chill down his spine. Pinchasy said: "Now I am going to tell you something as one naval officer to another which I have never told to anyone else before. I am going to tell you what really happened out there that day, and you may do with it what you wish." At that stage of the research this author was still looking for a possible smoking gun—that is, for evidence that the attacks were not caused by mistakes but rather that they were intentional attacks on a U.S. warship. And here it was. A confession about to be made by a senior Israeli naval officer who was at the Kirya at the time of the attacks. The tension was enormous.

Pinchasy continued: "What caused this terrible tragedy was the intense competition between the navy and the air force." The tension disappeared. This author thanked Pinchasy for the information but explained to him that this was not a new theory and told him that, in addition to other sources, the theory could be found in the Rabinovich book *The Boats of Cherbourg.*

Chapter 5

THE AIR AND SEA ATTACKS

The first rounds fired by *Kursa* Flight leader struck the *Liberty* at about 1358. There is some debate on whether rockets or missiles were fired by the aircraft. It was the recollection of the *Kursa* Flight leader on June 10, 1992, twenty-five years and two days after the event, that his Mirage carried a couple of air-to-air missiles.[1] The *Kursa* Flight leader and *Kursa* wingman each made three strafing runs and exhausted their ammunition by about 1404. *Kursa* Flight then left the target area for home.

As *Kursa* Flight leader steered slightly east of north to return to Hatzor Air Base, he was haunted by the attack he had just made. It was the first time he had attacked a ship. It stirred memories of his boyhood. His father had been a poet and a sailor. In 1941, during World War II, he had left on a boat with twenty-two other members of the PALYAM, a British-led Jewish naval commando group, on a mission to Vichy-controlled Tripoli, Lebanon. None of the commandos was heard from again. It had been a difficult experience for the small boy to grow up on a kibbutz with his widowed mother. But grow he did. He became a poet, like his father, and a fighter pilot in the Israel Air Force.[2]

Col. Shmuel Kislev, the chief air controller, sitting in the pit at the Israel Air Force command center in Tel Aviv, two chairs to the right of General Mordechai Hod, had located another flight, on its way to interdict Egyptian troops and armor in the Sinai. This flight, call sign "Royal," consisted of two Super-Mystère B2 jets, armed with the same 30 mm guns fitted in the Mirages. Each of these planes also carried two canisters of napalm, in addition to two 216-gallon (U.S.) drop tanks. Kislev vectored Royal Flight toward El Arish and, following a momentary delay, authorized Royal Flight to attack. The Royal aircraft made their initial runs from stem to bow, dropping their napalm as they passed over the hapless ship. At least three canisters missed.[3]

Capt. R. L. Arthur, fleet material officer, Service Force, COMSIXTHFLT, later sent a message from COMSIXTHFLT to COMSERVFORSIXTHFLT stating in part: "1E. Flash fire stbd wing of bridge. No major damage."[4]

The two Royal Flight Super-Mystères pulled up in left turns to the west and then made 270° turns to come back across the ship broadside, from west to east, with the sun at their backs.[5] The *Liberty* had turned from west to north, putting the sun to her port side and the ship's own shadow on the starboard side. As Royal Flight leader crossed the ship, firing at her in an effort to hit the boilers, he observed on her bow what appeared to be a letter and some numbers on the up-sun (port) side of the hull.[6]

Back at air force headquarters in the Kirya, Chief Air Controller Kislev, ever the professional, kept asking Royal Flight leader, "Is there any *Nun Mem?*" *Nun Mem* is a Hebrew acronym comprising the letters *nun,* which translates as *N,* and *mem,* or *M.* It stands for *neged matossim,* which translates as "anti or against aircraft" and is used by the Israel Defense Forces the same way the U.S. forces use "AA" to denote "antiaircraft" or "triple A" for "antiaircraft artillery."

Although the official U.S. Department of Defense press release stated that the *Liberty* fired her machine guns against the aircraft,[7] there is no such report in the *Liberty*'s log. There is some testimony in the U.S. Navy court of inquiry record that the ship's guns were fired at the aircraft. Whether or not this took place, neither *Kursa* Flight nor Royal Flight reported any antiaircraft fire. Thus eight or nine minutes into the air attack both Kislev and Royal Flight leader became concerned. As Royal Flight leader passed over the ship observing the bow marks, he radioed to air control, "This ship is marked P 30, I am going down for another look." At 1411 Royal Flight leader reported, "Pay attention, this ship's marking is Charlie Tango Romeo 5 [CTR 5]." While the flight leader repeated this "CTR 5" identification twice, he was in error, because actually the first letter on the *Liberty*'s bow was *G,* not *C.* At almost six hundred miles per hour, this is an understandable mistake. It was also grave news. First, both Royal Flight leader and Kislev knew that Arab ships were marked in Arabic script, not with Roman letters, and that therefore the ship was not Arab.

Twenty years later on Thames TV, Kislev said that when he heard the identification, he threw down his headset and swore; it was then that he believed the ship was American. Shmuel Kislev does not explain why at that point he thought the ship was American. In the Thames TV production, Kislev first justifies the attack:

One has to try to put yourself in—in the shoes of the pilot. What is he told now? He's told now—he's not told to look for an American ship—he's not told to look for a French ship. He's told that there is an enemy warship that is running to the west, that the navy is chasing it, that it has shelled our positions, and now all he is told to do, please find it. And on top of that, he is told just to make sure that it's that ship were talking about. It's not something else. That's all you have to do. More than that, I would say, we are telling him that there are no other military ships in the vicinity—so if you will be sure that it is a military ship, you can hit it.

He added, "At that time, I was sure it was an American ship and I was sure that we did—that we had that mistake."[8] Persons who were present have told me that Kislev's words were, "Damn it! The navy has f——ed us again." A minute after Royal Flight leader's transmission, at 1412, Kislev gave Royal Flight the terse order "Leave her!" and Royal Flight turned toward home to the Hatzor Air Base.

Different IDF personnel in Israel had learned or concluded at different times that the vessel that been targeted was a U.S. ship. Lt. Cdr. Uri Meretz, the naval intelligence officer at Tel Aviv, decided the *Liberty* was a U.S. ship shortly after sunrise on the morning of June 8. But Meretz went off duty at 0800. He had passed the information to navy intelligence, and the information was in a room down the hall from the navy command-and-control room at Stella Maris on Haifa's Mount Carmel. Rear Adm. Shlomo Erell knew from a report from Lieutenant Commander Pinchasy, the naval liaison officer at the air force control center, that a U.S. Navy supply-type ship was north of Port Said near dawn, but Erell had left the command center and gone down Mount Carmel to the port of Haifa. The navy command duty officer, Cdr. Avraham "Ramy" Lunz, was aware that a U.S. ship had been near Port Said about dawn, but he did not associate that ship with the warship reported shelling Israeli troops near El Arish. Since the Israelis considered the United States a friendly country and it was not reasonable for Lunz to have concluded that the ship reported to be shelling the troops was American, obviously it could only be Egyptian.

As indicated previously, Kislev remembers that at 1412 he concluded that the target of *Kursa* and Royal Flights was American. It is clear, however, from the recordings that during the remainder of that afternoon, as the tragedy was unfolding and he was listening to the radio traffic on his headset, he changed his mind several times, still thinking that the ship might be Egyptian.

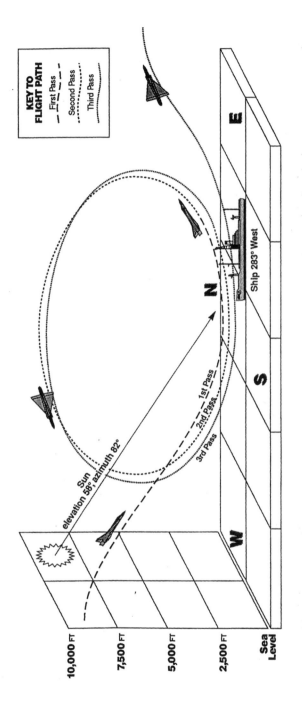

Air Attack *Kursa:* Two Mirage IIIC aircraft attack from bow to stern

At about 1358 hours, the *Liberty* was steering 283° degrees, or west. The sun's position was at an elevation of 58° 50'; azimuth of 82° 20'. Two Mirage IIIC aircraft made three passes each.

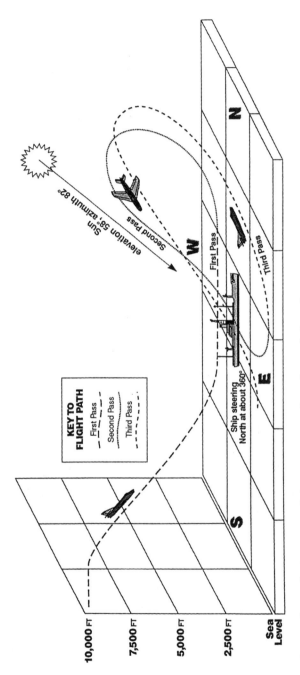

Air Attack Royal: Two Dessault Super Mystère aircraft attack from bow to stern

At about 1406 the Royal Flight approached from the stern to the bow and then made a left turn then attacked broadside west to east. Aircraft came from out of the sun on the second and third passes.

Within the figure:

KEY TO
FLIGHT PATH

First Pass
Second Pass
Third Pass

Sun
elevation 58°, azimuth 82°

Second pass
First Pass
Third Pass

Ship steering
North at about 360°

N
W
E
S

10,000 FT
7,500 FT
5,000 FT
2,500 FT
Sea Level

Others in the Kirya who heard the report "marked CTR 5" and who were aware that there were half a dozen Soviet intelligence gathering ships in the area, all of whose identification marks began with the letter *C*, were shocked and horrified that the target might be a Soviet ship! Some Soviet intelligence-collection ships were designated *sudno svyazyy*, or "communications vessel." On their bow they had pennant numbers preceded by the letters *SSV*. In the Cyrillic alphabet used in Russian, they resemble the Roman letters *CCV*. Hence the confusion over the *C*, the mistaken *G* in the *Liberty*'s "GTR 5" bow markings.

The *Liberty*'s commanding officer testified at the U.S. Navy court of inquiry that her flag was shot away in the first strafing run. The *Liberty* had a motor whaleboat stored amidships on the starboard side, just aft of the bridge. On the port side two fifty-five-gallon drums of gasoline were stored on the 01 level. The initial strafing ignited the gasoline drums, causing a large fire, as well as igniting the fuel contained in the motor whaleboat, and it is most likely that the resulting flames burned through the halyard holding the five-by-eight-foot national ensign. The main halyard was a line attached to a pulley on the main mast below the yardarm and below the radar dish, in the vicinity of the *Liberty*'s bridge. It is the customary location for hoisting a ship's colors. In any event, there is no disagreement that the flag was gone early in the air attack. However there is substantial disagreement on whether or not the five-by-eight-foot American flag was extended, and therefore visible to the attacking airplanes, at the very start of the attack.

The Israelis involved were mistaken regarding the perception that she flew no flag. Before the air attack began, the ensign was there. Whether it was sufficiently extended to be observable or whether the Israeli pilots were close enough to see a flag of this size is the question. (See chapter 7 for a detailed discussion of this issue.)

At 1412 the air attack was over. At Tel Nof Air Base, a flight of two Mystère IV aircraft, Nixon Flight,[9] armed with conventional bombs, was on takeoff roll. The flight's target was that ship off El Arish. Time to the target at subsonic speed would have been twelve to fourteen minutes.[10] Thus Nixon Flight probably would have beaten the navy MTBs to the scene. However, shortly after ordering Royal Flight to "Leave her!" Colonel Kislev diverted Nixon Flight to a target in the north. Consequently this second flight, which could well have quickly and efficiently sunk the *Liberty* with its iron bombs, did not attack the ship.

Motor Torpedo Boat Division 914 continued to approach the *Liberty* from the northeast, on a southwesterly heading. Its personnel observed the

USS *Liberty* under way. View from starboard bow. At six hundred miles per hour and almost a half-mile farther away, clearly "GTR" could be mistaken for "CTR." *Photography Laboratory U.S. Naval Air Station, Norfolk, VA , 11-1-66*

air attack and watched the aircraft depart. Before them was a ship spewing a huge cloud of black smoke and steaming west; this, they thought, meant that it was running toward Port Said. The MTBs were somewhat down-sun, approaching the starboard side of the ship. According to the testimony of Commander McGonagle, *Liberty*'s bow was pointed 283°. In June the sun is at about twenty-four degrees north, so it would have been slightly off the port bow of *Liberty*, and her starboard side would have been in shadow, facing the approaching MTBs. Following the loss of the steaming flag, a larger flag had been hoisted on the port halyard, which was on the other side of the ship from the approaching Israeli MTBs.[11] The MTBs stopped at a distance of about a mile from the *Liberty*. They began signaling with a flashing Aldis lamp. While there has been no dispute that the MTBs stopped and began signaling, there were clearly misperceptions on both sides about what was signaled. The MTBs were sending "A-A," which in international maritime code means "Identify yourself," or "What ship?"

Perhaps because of the huge pall of smoke, the crew on the *Liberty* was not able to understand the message from the MTBs. At the U.S. Navy court of inquiry held in June, there was no testimony about anyone signaling back from the *Liberty*. On June 13, 1967, CINCUSNAVEUR requested the commander of Destroyer Squadron 12 (COMDESRON TWELVE), "Please ask *Liberty* . . . did *Liberty* at any time use any signals such as blinker light, flag hoist, etc. to identify herself to Israeli attackers?"[12] The *Liberty* responded, "Did not attempt to signal planes with flashing light or any other method at any time."[13] While the question asks the *Liberty* if she signaled the Israeli "attackers," the answer limits itself only to the attacking planes and fails to refer explicitly to the MTBs. In a secret message dated June 19, 1967, SECNAV asked CINCUSNAVEUR specifically, "Did *Liberty* attempt to answer signals from patrol boats prior to attack?" The *Liberty* responded, "Yes, [Israeli] Patrol boat signals were partially obliterated by flames and smoke from burning whaleboat abaft starboard wing of bridge. Patrol boat signals could not be understood by Liberty who attempted establish communications by Aldis lamp. Other signal lights had been shot away."[14]

The message the *Liberty* transmitted on July 6 to the Chief of Naval Operations (CNO) stated that "Aldis lamp not utilized until after the torpedo attack."[15] This was apparently a handheld Aldis lamp, because the starboard twenty-four-inch Aldis lamp had been destroyed in the air attack. Commander McGonagle testified at the court of inquiry that "the center boat of the [Israeli] formation was signalling to us. . . . It was not possible to read the signals because of the intermittent blocking of view by smoke and flames."[16] While the *Liberty* testimonies indicate no signaling in response to the MTB signals, the MTBs thought they saw a response of "A-A." A U.S. embassy officer in Tel Aviv spoke with an Israeli MTB officer and reported: "The source officer said he was comm[unications] officer on his MTB and worked the signal light himself. He sent the international request for identification to *Liberty*, A-A and *Liberty* responded with A-A."[17]

Whether the Israeli officer (who was probably Aharon Yifrach) saw flashes of light or just imagined he saw a return signal of "A-A" will never be known. Perception at that moment was more important than reality, whatever that reality was.

As the MTBs were signaling with their lights and trying to communicate with the smoking ship, the *Liberty* opened machine-gun fire on the MTBs.

This fact is beyond dispute and was clearly reported in the testimony of Commander McGonagle before the court of inquiry on June 13, 1967, and in a videotaped press conference given by McGonagle on board the *Liberty* on July 29, 1967,[18] the day *Liberty* arrived at her home port in the United States. McGonagle said, "I had previously directed a man from the bridge to proceed to the forward starboard gun mount and take the torpedo boats under fire in an attempt to defend ourselves. When I saw what appeared to be the Israeli flag, I yelled to the fo'c'sle because I had no phone communications with the men and I yelled to him to tell him to hold fire. But before he was able to understand what I was trying to tell him, he opened fire on the boats as I had [previously] directed."[19]

There is some disagreement about the number of *Liberty*'s guns that fired and whether one gun fired as a result of flames detonating its ammunition or was fired by a gunner.[20] At least one MTB commander has told this author that he was not certain that the MTBs knew they had been fired upon. However, as early as the IDF report by Col. Ram Ron, dated June 16, 1967, the Israelis mention gunfire emanating from the *Liberty* and directed at the MTBs, and Commander McGonagle was of the impression that the boats knew they were being shot at. The Ram Ron report quotes the Division 914 war log, "At 1435 the torpedo boats reported seeing gun flashes from the ship's direction."[21] The 1982 *IDF History* report states that "the latter [the division commander] discerned flashes of gunshot fire emanating from the ship, and the commander of T-203 saw the fire and reported hits in the vicinity of T-206."[22]

A very important factor that added to the MTBs' misperception was that the *Liberty* opened machine-gun fire on them. When the *Liberty* began shooting at the MTBs as they signaled, a new reality set in, rendering any light signal response or lack of response from the *Liberty* unimportant. Commander McGonagle testified on June 13, 1967, "As far as the torpedo boats are concerned, I am sure that they felt that they were under fire from USS *Liberty*."[23]

It gets worse. The MTB division commander, Cdr. Moshe Oren, is the one who ordered the signal "A-A" sent to the smoking ship in front of him. The formal definition of signaling repeatedly "A-A" as a flashing-light transmission is stated as "Call for unknown station or general call." The formal answering signal would be a continuous sequence of "TTTT" (four *T*s). A sequence of signal exchanges would then follow and would finally result in the vessels transmitting their respective identification codes to each other. In everyday use on the high seas, the formal sequence is shortened to flashing repeatedly a series of "A-As." The receiving vessel is expected to signal its international identification code, which for the USS *Liberty* was "NIYR." The originating ship would then respond with its identification code. This of course assumes that the receiving ship understands what is being signaled.[24]

Looking for an enemy ship, Oren was not without prior experience in this type of situation. Eleven years before, he had been the gunnery officer on the destroyer *Jaffa* when she engaged the Egyptian destroyer *Ibrahim al Awwal*. On that occasion, the *Jaffa* had signaled "A-A." *Ibrahim al Awwal* had signaled back "A-A." Now, on June 8, 1967, Oren said to himself, "Déjà vu. You ask an Egyptian ship to identify itself and it returns the same signal back."

Each MTB carried an IDF-produced ship-identification guide called the "Red Book." The formal title of the guide was *Identification of Arabian Navies*.[25] As Oren observed the smoking ship and thought he saw a signal of "A-A," the MTB commanders on the other two boats each looked at their Red Books. They saw in the water before them an "old tub" of a ship covered with smoke. The ship had a superstructure and one funnel in its center, as well as one mast forward and one aft. The Egyptian Z-class destroyers also had one funnel, with two masts, but they had substantial gun mounts, which this ship did not have. The only other ship in the Red Book with that configuration was the old Egyptian transport *El Quseir*. At about the same time, the boat commanders of MTBs 203 and 206 independently identified the target as the *El Quseir*. Moshe Oren was certain the target was Egyptian. When he heard that the other boat commanders identified her as the *El Quseir*, he said, "If [name not released],[26] the commanding officer of boat 203, says it is the *El Quseir*, it is the *El Quseir*." Uri "Chera" Tsur, a junior officer in training, stood next to the commanding officer of boat 206 as he compared the burning target with the picture of *El Quseir* in the Red Book and was not satisfied with the identification, but what is a junior officer in training to do when his opinion differs from that of his superiors?[27]

Shortly after 1417, about five minutes after Colonel Kislev stopped the air attack, air force headquarters in Tel Aviv contacted navy headquarters in Haifa by telephone to advise that the air force had some question about the identification of the target ship. At about the same time, Commander Oren, the MTB division commander, was transmitting by radio to Capt. Issy Rehav, the officer then in tactical command of the navy, at the navy command center in Stella Maris, Haifa, requesting, "*Tesha vuv*." *Tesha vuv* is Hebrew for "nine V," which was the coded authorization to launch torpedoes.

Rehav was getting some information by telephone from the air force in the Kirya concerning the identification of the ship. He responded, suggesting the MTBs hold up because there was some doubt about the identification of the ship.[28] Now Oren, with his boats under fire, informed Rehav that he had no doubt about the identification of the ship as an enemy vessel, simply because it was shooting at him![29] It would have been difficult to deny a request for permission to attack to a commander on the scene who was taking enemy fire. Indeed, if the MTBs were engaging an Egyptian destroyer, they were in mortal danger. Four Soviet-built Egyptian destroyers were armed with four 5.1-inch guns each, and two British-built Egyptian destroyers were armed with four 4.5-inch guns each. Whether anyone remembered that the British-built Z-class destroyers were in the Red Sea is not known, but the four Soviet-built Skory-class destroyers were in the Mediterranean. A direct hit from any of those guns could easily penetrate the wooden hull of an MTB and blow the craft to smithereens. Captain Rehav had a few seconds to make his decision.

If Rehav was not aware of the identification of the target as *El Quseir* and believed the target was an Egyptian destroyer, as earlier suspected and reported, then his authorization of the torpedo attack was appropriate. Yet the naval headquarters war log and the report of Col. Ram Ron make it clear that by 1424, Rehav had received a report that the target "may be a commercial vessel or a supply ship," and by 1436 the MTB division had reported that the identification as *El Quseir* was definite. Nevertheless, Rehav responded, "*Tesha vuv* approved." The time was about 1430.

Commander Oren, in the lead torpedo boat, boat 204, immediately began racing toward the *Liberty* for a torpedo attack. Doctrine and training demanding simultaneous runs from different angles from both sides of the target vessel were ignored. The other two boats followed as best they could, ultimately launching five torpedoes. The *Liberty,* on her part, did not execute any evasive maneuvers. Commander McGonagle testified, "I elected to maintain a course of 283 at maximum speed."[30] Only one of the five torpedoes struck the *Liberty*. The torpedo that hit came from MTB 203. The other torpedo from boat 203 passed ahead of the ship and was seen by some of *Liberty*'s crew. The other three torpedoes, two from MTB 206 and one from MTB 204, passed astern the *Liberty*. When the captain of MTB 204, Gil Keren, was asked by the other boat captains why he had launched only one torpedo, he replied, "Moshe Oren said 'launch torpedo,' not 'launch torpedoes.'"[31] A graphic of the torpedo attack was prepared based on an interview of the commanding officer of MTB 203,

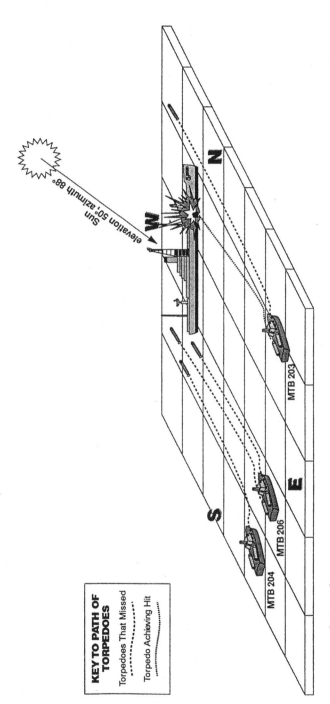

MTB Torpedo Attack

Torpedo attack all MTBs on the starboard side of *Liberty*. Attack was toward the sun at an elevation of 50° and azimuth 88°.

who told this author that the *Liberty* had turned to the north and the MTBs attacked on a westerly heading. Commander McGonagle testified that the *Liberty* maintained a heading of 283°, which is thirteen degrees north of west. In either situation the MTBs would have had the sun somewhat in their eyes during the torpedo run. It is possible that the *Liberty* was still steering a little more north of west than her skipper remembered following the air attack, and it is also possible that the MTB commander was incorrect in his recollection. The difference in headings is not significant. Notwithstanding the precise headings of the *Liberty* and the MTBs, the attack was carried out essentially in the manner depicted in the graphic.

According to Rear Adm. Benjamin "Biny" Telem, the commander in chief of the Israel Navy during its most successful period of operations, the 1973 war,[32] the torpedoes on MTB 203 and MTB 204 were German-made nineteen-inch torpedoes, acquired as part of the Israel Navy's worldwide shopping efforts. The torpedoes on MTB 206 were eighteen-inch torpedoes purchased from Italy. All of the torpedoes were originally aircraft torpedoes that had been converted for use by Israel Navy surface ships. The only one of these torpedoes that ever actually hit a target was the one that hit the *Liberty*. According to Telem, over a period of several years prior to the attack on the *Liberty*, and including the five torpedoes launched against the *Liberty*, the Israel Navy had launched about fifty torpedoes, mostly in training exercises. Forty-eight of these torpedoes missed their targets. Of the remaining two, a few years before 1967, one torpedo ran hot and circled back to hit the Israeli ship that had launched it.[33] The other one hit the *Liberty*.

Throughout the torpedo attack, the MTBs fired their .50-caliber machine guns as well as their 20 mm and 40 mm cannon in a response to the fire from the *Liberty*. They continued firing, as standard procedure would warrant. As they passed the *Liberty*, they reported a flag hanging limp and partially obscured by the smoke. Following the air attack but prior to the torpedo boat attack, the *Liberty* hoisted her larger, seven-by-thirteen-foot holiday ensign. According to an interview with Aharon Yifrach, the MTBs distinguished the red color in the flag and immediately reported to their command center that they thought the target might be Soviet. Within minutes they passed the curved stern, which bore the name *Liberty*, and observed non-Arabic letters on the ship. This is different from entries in both the Israel Navy headquarters war log and the MTB Division 914 war log. The MTB Division 914 log reads: "1451—Report to SEA/3: 'vessel may be Russian.' SEA/3 asked on what basis? DIV Commander replied: Based on writing on back [stern] of vessel." The IDF Navy headquarters war log reads: "1451—May be Russian nationality, based on writing on aft. An order was made to dispatch a tug boat from Ashdod."

MTB 203 then recovered one of the damaged life rafts that had been put over the side by the *Liberty* crewmen in anticipation of abandoning ship.[34] The raft had "U.S. Navy" painted on it. At this point the crew of MTB 203 concluded the ship was American. Commander McGonagle testified that "immediately after the ship was struck by the torpedo the torpedo boats milled around astern of the ship at a range of 500 to 800 yards. One of the boats signaled by flashing light in English 'Do you require assistance?'" The *Liberty* log reports indicate (and McGonagle later testified before the U.S. Navy court of inquiry) that the first offer of help from the Israeli MTBs occurred at 1503, a little less than thirty minutes after the torpedo hit the ship. According to Ensign Yifrach, the CIC officer on MTB 204, at about 1630 Sinai time the MTBs again approached the *Liberty* to a distance where they could speak by megaphone and again offered help. Official U.S. reports state that the offer of help was declined.[35] Yifrach said, "They told us to go to hell."

Admiral Erell arrived back at the navy headquarters in Stella Maris after the authorization for the torpedo attack had been given but before the report of the torpedo strike was received at the navy command center. Upon being briefed on the situation, he immediately countermanded the order, and his order was transmitted by radio to the MTB division commander on board MTB 204. Commander Oren stated he did not receive the order. There is evidence that the order was received by the CIC officer on MTB 204. It is not possible to know for certain if the order was given or received before the torpedoes were launched or after the torpedoes were in the water.

The MTBs were communicating by radio with the navy command center at Stella Maris. The air force planes communicated by radio with the Kirya and with the MTBs by UHF radio. The air force communicated with the navy by land line or conventional telephone. If the incident were not so tragic, some of the air force controller's transmissions would be humorous. As is clear from the air control recordings, the Israel Air Force had just been through a roller-coaster ride: it is an Egyptian ship; it is an American ship; it is a Soviet ship; it is an American ship! The air force air controllers were confused as to whether they were initiating rescue operations of friends or capturing Egyptian enemy prisoners.

The first Israeli search-and-rescue Super Frelon helicopter pilot to reach the *Liberty* after the air attack and the torpedo strike saw no one on deck and did not see a flag.[36] He remembers that occasionally a door or hatch would open and a crewman would scurry in or out, and some waved him away. About thirty minutes after the conclusion of the attacks, at about 1512, the second Israeli helicopter pilot reported to the air force command center that he saw an American flag on the ship.[37] James Ennes, George Golden, and many others have claimed that there exists a recording of an Israeli pilot stating he saw an American flag on the *Liberty* before or during the air attack. Thus far no one has produced such a tape. The only publicly released recorded statement of an Israeli pilot reporting an American flag on the ship is the report of the second helicopter pilot made at least forty-four minutes after the air and sea attacks had been terminated.

The translations of the transcripts of the tapes of the Israeli air traffic controllers recorded in Hebrew at Israel Air Force command headquarters reveal a great deal. It is clear from the conversations between the air controllers that they were still trying to sort out the identity of the *Liberty* thirty to forty-five minutes after the last shot was fired. (See excerpts of the translations of the transcriptions of the Israel Air Force tapes in appendix 2.) Although the air attack lasted twelve to fourteen minutes and the sea attack was over by approximately 1440, many of the *Liberty* crew members remained terrified, fearful of further attacks, until after the sun went down, approximately four hours after the attacks were over.

Meanwhile, over five hundred miles to the west, the Sixth Fleet was responding to the information that a U.S. ship was under attack near geographic coordinates 31-23 N, 33-25 E. Admiral Martin, the Sixth Fleet commander, ordered F-4B Phantom jet fighters and A-1 Skyraiders launched to defend the *Liberty*. The naval messages transmitted, including the situation reports sent by Admiral Martin to Admiral McCain, Commander in Chief, Naval Forces Europe, indicate that the aircraft were launched at about 1600 Sinai time from the carriers *America* and *Saratoga* and were recalled by Martin following receipt of the message from Commander Castle, the U.S. naval attaché in Tel Aviv, advising that the Israelis had attacked the ship by mistake. The records of the messages establish that Martin recalled the aircraft before or at about the time the first word of the attack reached President Johnson in Washington. When the Israeli high command in the Kirya became aware with certainty that the target was a U.S. Navy ship, Lt. Col. Michael "Mike" Bloch, an IDF army intelligence officer serving as liaison with foreign military attachés, was ordered to advise the U.S. naval attaché in Tel Aviv of the situation. Bloch contacted Cdr. Ernest Castle at the U.S.

embassy by telephone and advised him of the attacks and offered to send a car to take him from the U.S. embassy on Hayarkon Street in Tel Aviv to the high command headquarters at the Kirya.

Bloch later told this author that he has had better duty than telling his friend at the American embassy that Israel had just attacked a U.S. ship. Castle told this author that he had never seen his usually self-confident Israeli counterparts so totally shattered, nor had he ever been offered a car before, or was he thereafter. A brief meeting took place between Bloch, Lt. Col. Arye Shalev, and one other Israeli officer. When Commander Castle arrived, they were studying a volume of *Jane's Fighting Ships*. Castle was told that they believed they had attacked a U.S. Navy ship. Castle, who had not been aware of the incident until informed about it by Bloch, was angry and later recalled that it was difficult for him to remain restrained. He was then driven back to the U.S. embassy, arriving at about 1600 Sinai time. He reported the incident to Ambassador Walworth Barbour, who had just received a similar report from the Israel Foreign Ministry.

Castle prepared a flash message from the office of the U.S. defense attaché to COMSIXTHFLT, CINCUSNAVEUR, CNO, the White House, and others. The date-time group on the message was 081414Z June 67, which was 1614 Sinai time and 1014 Washington time. The message was released about the time of its date-time group and was transmitted and received in Washington about thirty minutes later. The Castle message reached the Sixth Fleet before it was received in Washington. The message stated that the Israelis reported mistakenly attacking a U.S. ship at 1400 [Sinai time], that rescue efforts were under way, and that they apologized. Ambassador Barbour requested a helicopter from the Israel Foreign Ministry to fly Commander Castle to the site of the incident to attempt to identify the ship.[38] The request was honored, and on his way out of the embassy door Castle invited Lt. Lynn Blasch, an assistant naval attaché, to accompany him. They were driven to Sde Dov Airport on the north side of Tel Aviv,[39] where they were met by an Israel Air Force Sud-Aviation SA-321K Super-Frelon helicopter. They took off at about 1800 Sinai time and flew toward the last reported position of the ship. They arrived over the *Liberty* about 1840. It was twilight. There was no radio voice communication between the helicopter and the *Liberty*, as aircraft radios and ships' radios do not normally use the same frequencies.

Commander McGonagle refused to halt the ship or to allow the helicopter to lower anyone onto the *Liberty*. After efforts to land or lower someone on board were rebuffed, the helicopter flew back to Sde Dov, arriving at about 1910.[40] Castle returned to the U.S. embassy to find Ambassador Barbour waiting in the atrium, just inside the front entrance. This was unusual, as it was usually an attaché who was waiting at the door for the ambassador.[41] Barbour told Castle that General Getty at National Military Command Center (NMCC) in Washington, D.C., wanted to talk to him. Castle called Getty at about 2300 Israel time and briefed the general on his helicopter flight to the *Liberty*.[42]

Chapter 6

IN THE AFTERMATH

While the air and sea attacks were taking place in the afternoon in the eastern Mediterranean, it was still the morning of June 8, 1967, in Washington, D.C. At the White House at 0949 eastern daylight time, 1549 Sinai time,[1] President Johnson was in his bedroom with his press secretary, George Christian. He received a telephone call from Walt Whitman Rostow, his National Security Advisor. Rostow had been advised of a flash (highest-priority) voice message that had been received by telephone at the National Military Command Center at 0911 (1511 Sinai time) from the Commander in Chief, U.S. Forces Europe (CINCEUR). Rostow was now informing the president of the message.

The message was, "Mr. President: We have a flash report from the Joint Reconnaissance Center [in the Pentagon] indicating that a U.S. ELINT (electronics intelligence) ship, the *Liberty*, has been torpedoed in the Mediterranean. The ship is located 60 to 100 miles north of Egypt. Reconnaissance aircraft are out from the Sixth Fleet. We have no knowledge of the submarine or surface vessel which committed this act. We shall keep you informed."[2] President Johnson hung up the telephone, turned to George Christian, and repeated Rostow's words. He then looked Christian squarely in the eyes, became very grave, and said, "George, if this attack is by the Russians, this means war."[3]

The *Liberty* had been attacked by aircraft at about 1400 (0800 EDT) and torpedoed at about 1435 (0835 EDT). At the time of the attack, the aircraft carriers of the Sixth Fleet were over 530 miles from the *Liberty*.

It was a busy day for the president, who had been working since 0745, when his breakfast tray was brought to his bedroom. He had already made or received eleven telephone calls, received a hotline message,[4] and met with White House staff member Marvin Watson. Upon receiving the message

about the attack on the *Liberty,* the president immediately ordered a meeting of his top Middle East advisers in the Situation Room in the basement
of the West Wing of the White House. While the advisers were gathering, a
launch of aircraft was dispatched by the Sixth Fleet to protect the *Liberty*.
It is not clear if the message that stated, "Reconnaissance aircraft are out
from the Sixth Fleet," relayed by Rostow to the president, referred to aircraft
already in the air or to the aircraft that were about to be launched. It is most
likely that the reference was to the aircraft that were about to be launched or
were already in the process of being launched when the message was sent.
U.S. aircraft flying from the Sixth Fleet off Crete toward the Arab-Israeli war
zone were a matter of urgent concern to Johnson.

He and Kosygin had previously assured each other that neither the United
States nor the Soviet Union intended to intervene in the Middle East war.
There were many Soviet warships in the Mediterranean, including at least
half a dozen intelligence-gathering vessels, and the United States knew that
information about U.S. warplanes flying toward the Middle East war zone
would arrive in the Kremlin in a very short time after takeoff. At 1100 Johnson approved a hotline message to Premier Kosygin, transmitted at 1117
Washington time, advising him that the planes were being sent to the scene
where the *Liberty* had been torpedoed "to investigate." The message stated,
"We have just learned that U.S.S. *Liberty,* an auxiliary[,] has apparently been
torpedoed by Israel Forces in error off Port Said. . . . We wish you to know
that investigation is the sole purpose of this flight of aircraft, and hope that
you will take appropriate steps to see that proper parties are informed."[5]
Johnson was most anxious not to provide any provocation to the Soviets.

Johnson left his bedroom and arrived at the Oval Office at 1104 with
George Christian and deputy press secretary Tom Johnson.[6] They were met
at the door by special presidential assistant Marvin Watson and immediately
left the Oval Office for the Situation Room on the floor below.[7] Johnson ar-
rived at 1106 to find all the president's men gathered together: Secretary of
State Dean Rusk, Secretary of Defense Robert McNamara, National Security
Advisor Rostow, special adviser McGeorge Bundy, ambassador to the So-
viet Union Lewellen Thompson, chair of the Foreign Intelligence Advisory
Board Clark Clifford, and the number-two man at the State Department,
Nicholas Katzenbach.[8]

Until minutes before the president arrived in the Situation Room, little
additional information had been received. The individuals gathered in the
Situation Room were not aware of what President Johnson already knew. The

atmosphere in the room was therefore extremely tense. Who was attacking a U.S. warship? Was it the Egyptians? A strong case could be made that it very well might have been the Egyptians, since they had broken diplomatic relations with the United States and accused the United States of helping Israel. Although it had lost nearly its entire force on the first day of the war, the Egyptian air force still had some MiGs flying, and the Egyptian navy had naval vessels. Was the *Liberty* being attacked by the Soviet Union? This was McNamara's first conclusion,[9] albeit not the conclusion of senior U.S. naval officers in the Sixth Fleet. Were the Soviets entering the conflict on the side of the Arabs? Was this the beginning of World War III? How should the United States respond? Could the situation in the Mediterranean escalate into a nuclear exchange?

In the Israel Air Force command center at the Kirya at about 1400 Sinai time (0800 in Washington, D.C.), the word was spreading that Israel Air Force jets were attacking an Egyptian ship off El Arish. As reports of fire and smoke billowing from the ship were heard over the air-control radio speakers, a state of euphoria broke out, and some of the staff in the command center began cheering. Abruptly, however, at about 1410 Sinai time, the euphoria turned to horror when the leader of Royal Flight reported markings on the bow of the ship to be in lettering other than Arabic and, especially, that the initial letter was a *C*. No one knew that he had made an error in his sighting, but everyone in the command center knew that Arab ships were marked in Arabic script and that therefore the ship could not be Egyptian. In addition, many were aware that the Soviets were operating at least half a dozen intelligence-gathering vessels off the coasts of Israel, Egypt, and Syria and that the call letters of some if not all of the Soviet ships began with the Cyrillic letter *C*.[10] The gloom was deepened when the MTBs passed close to the *Liberty* following the torpedo attack and Ensign Yifrach observed a large flag hanging in the smoke that appeared to him to be red. Another MTB crewman misread the writing on *Liberty*'s stem as being in Russian. This information was reported to the navy command center in Stella Maris and passed on to the air force command center by telephone. The "dream war" was turning into a nightmare.

The immediate reaction of the officers assembled in the air force command center was that by attacking a Soviet ship, Israel had given the Soviet Union an excuse to intervene in the war on the losing Arab side. All the gains of the IDF would now be annulled by the intervention of Soviet military forces. Only a short while later, at 1520, the MTBs confirmed the identity of the ship as American rather than Soviet.[11] By about 1530, after much confusion, the Israelis concluded that their navy had just torpedoed a U.S. Navy ship. According to Lt. Col. Michael Bloch, a foreign military liaison officer to attachés, "A huge wave of relief swept over the Kirya."[12] Ironically, it was much better news. It remained to order Bloch to inform the U.S. embassy in Tel Aviv of the mistaken attack.

Commander Castle's flash message date-time group 081414Z (1614 Sinai/ 1014 EDT) was received by the White House shortly before 1100 EDT/1700 Sinai.[13] The message from Castle was rushed to the Situation Room. Before the message reached the White House and made its way to the Situation Room, a tense debate was taking place. Both Secretary of State Rusk and Secretary of Defense McNamara told this author of the extreme concern of all the men in that room. Then the president told them of the Castle message. In an instant the mood changed. It was Israel that had been the attacker. The United States was not at war. The Soviets were not involved. The issue of a nuclear exchange was not on the table. According to Rusk, "A wave of relief swept through the situation room."[14] With relief, McNamara called the Joint Chiefs of Staff at the Pentagon and ordered a message sent that canceled the previous JCS "use of force" authorization.[15] The aircraft had already been recalled by the Sixth Fleet commander, Vice Admiral Martin, who had received the Castle message at 1028 Washington time, almost half an hour before it was received at the White House.[16] President Johnson left the meeting at 1145 and at 1246 joined President Hastings Kamuzu Banda of the Republic of Malawi in the Oval Office as a prelude to a state luncheon.

When Vice Admiral Martin, Commander, Sixth Fleet, first received word of the attack on the *Liberty* on June 8, he was on the cruiser *Little Rock,* at sea in the eastern Mediterranean near Crete. The *Little Rock* was steaming in formation with two U.S. aircraft carriers, the *America* and the *Saratoga,* within the defense screens provided by their destroyer squadrons. Alongside the U.S. formation was the Soviet warship to which Vice Admiral Martin had sent his demand to stop harassing the Sixth Fleet twenty-four hours before. Not only the Americans but also the Soviets were now able to hear *Liberty*'s voice transmissions and were aware of the attack on a U.S. ship taking place about 530 nautical miles away. Neither had any additional information about the attack. Each force eyed the other, and the Americans wondered if it was time to open fire.

Stewart M. Harris, a twenty-five-year-old lieutenant (junior grade) serving at the time as the Destroyer Squadron 12 communications officer on board the destroyer *Davis* (DD 937), remembers two heavily armed U.S. Navy A-1 aircraft flying in a racetrack pattern over the Soviet destroyer that was steaming along with the carrier *Saratoga*.[17] The Americans and the Soviets were facing each other eyeball to eyeball, with guns loaded, although there is no documentation that either force went to battle stations.[18] Harry J. Stathos, an embarked United Press International reporter, had the following message, date-time group 082041Z June 67, transmitted as news copy by the USS *America* on his behalf: "Shortly after the attack occurred at about 3 p.m. (1500 GMT), Task Force Sixty of the Sixth Fleet, which has been operating in the eastern Mediterranean during the Middle East crisis, was ordered into condition two, a high state of combat readiness." Suddenly a copy of the message from Commander Castle to the White House was received at the communications center on the *Little Rock*. Cdr. Francis M. "Frank" Snyder, the Sixth Fleet communications officer, told this author, "A wave of relief rolled over the Sixth Fleet headquarters upon learning that the attackers of the *Liberty* were Israeli and not Soviet or Egyptian.[19]

At the American embassy in Cairo, the atmosphere on that day was also very tense. Following the accusations by President Nasser that U.S. military planes had assisted Israel in the attack on Egypt, the U.S. embassy was under siege by street mobs, and newly arrived Ambassador Richard Nolte did not know whether the government of Egypt would continue to use the Egyptian army or police to protect the U.S. embassy. Richard B. Parker was then a political counselor at the embassy and worked closely with Ambassador Nolte and the deputy chief of mission, David Nes. The initial word of the attack on the *Liberty* off the coast of Sinai sent chills through the Cairo embassy staff, who were certain the attackers were not Egyptian and therefore initially presumed they were Soviet. When the word was received that the attackers were Israeli, according to Parker, "A wave of relief swept through the U.S. Embassy in Cairo."[20]

The United States publicly disclosed that the attackers of the *Liberty* were Israeli on June 8, 1967, through a press release by the Public Affairs Office of the Department of Defense.[21] The disclosure willy-nilly admitted that a U.S. warship described as "a U.S. Navy Technical Research Ship" was within eyeball distance from the war rather than over a hundred miles away, as the United States had told the world from the United Nations two days before.

Arthur Goldberg, the U.S. ambassador to the United Nations, had told the Security Council on June 6 that the U.S. ships were hundreds of miles from the combat area. In addition, the U.S. Department of Defense had issued a news release on June 5 and another on June 6 that concluded with the statement, "The Sixth Fleet carriers and their aircraft have been several hundred miles from the scene of the fighting."[22] The United States, anxious to avoid possible Soviet intervention in the hostilities, was urging a hands-off policy for both the United States and the Soviet Union. Most likely Arthur Goldberg had no idea that the *Liberty* was en route to the Sinai coast when he made the statement.

As a result of the *Liberty* incident, the United States now had the proverbial egg on its face. Its previous statements were demonstrated not to be true, and the United States now had a lot of explaining to do to both the Arabs and the Soviets. Word that the *Liberty* had sailed from Rota, Spain, to the combat area—information that was included in the June 8 U.S. Department of Defense press release—generated an inquiry from the highest levels of the Spanish government, which was very much concerned that Spain might be seen as supporting U.S. efforts on behalf of Israel and against the Arabs. An article with the byline Ross Nark appeared in the June 9, 1967, edition of the Madrid newspaper *El Alcazar* and claimed the *Liberty* was based at Rota. The Spanish government was advised by the U.S. embassy in Madrid that the *Liberty* had called at Rota only for refueling. The Spanish government was "gratified" by the reply. Nevertheless the U.S. embassy in Madrid advised the U.S. Secretary of State in a telegram with "immediate" precedence, "Request Dept caution official USG [U.S. government] spoxesmen [*sic*] observe greatest care in any references to Spain during current M.E. crises. Walker."[23]

The first political casualty of the incident in the United States was the longtime warm relationship between Eugene V. Rostow, the assistant secretary of state for Near Eastern affairs, and Clark Clifford, the chair of the president's Foreign Intelligence Advisory Board. On June 9 very few of the details of the incident were known. Investigations had just begun, and the feelings of the members of the National Security Council already were not in accord. At a National Security Council meeting on June 9, 1967, Clifford urged that the United States treat Israel the same way it would have treated the Soviet Union or Arabs if either of the latter had attacked the *Liberty*.[24] Eugene Rostow was outraged at Clifford's suggestion that the United States should treat a country that it supported in the same manner that it would treat a country with which relations had been severed or a country with which it had a merely formal relationship.[25]

President Johnson immediately assigned Clifford the task of investigating the incident and reporting back to him. Clifford conducted his investigation without staff and relied primarily on the Department of Defense for his fact finding. Over a month later, after reviewing materials provided by the Defense Department, he concluded that the attack was not an intentional attack on a ship known by the Israelis to be a U.S. ship. Clifford's report was couched in very strong language and was extremely critical of the Israeli military. The report remained secret until October 25, 1995, when both the report and the cover letter transmitting it from Clifford to W. W. Rostow were declassified.[26] The transmittal letter from W. W. Rostow to the president remained classified until June 25, 1998.

In the transmittal letter, which was declassified at the request of this author under the Freedom of Information Act, W. W. Rostow advised the president that "it [the report] is based on the study of literally thousands of pages of evidence." It is difficult to understand why this letter remained classified thirty-one years after the event. It is also difficult to understand why Clifford took such a strong position on how to treat Israel in view of the fact that he was always considered a friend of Israel. While serving as executive assistant to President Harry Truman in 1948, Clifford had bumped heads with both Secretary of State General George Marshall and Dean Rusk (who worked for the Department of State but did not yet have a title), who advised Truman not to recognize the state of Israel on the declaration of its independence by David Ben-Gurion. In fact, when this author interviewed Dean Rusk in 1989 and discussed the Clifford report and the fact that Clifford had concluded that the attack on the *Liberty* was not an intentional attack on a U.S. ship, Rusk commented, "I would have expected him to side with the Zionists."[27] In spite of Clifford's ultimate conclusion in his report in favor of Israel, the relationship between Eugene Rostow and Clifford remained chilly.

Ironically, Secretary of State Dean Rusk's position on how to treat Israel was softer than Clifford's. Rusk was bitterly disappointed that Israel had struck preemptively on June 5 and had not waited until Egyptian vice president Zachary Mohieddin arrived in Washington on June 7, 1967, for a meeting Rusk had scheduled.[28] Rusk was certain he could have resolved the crisis diplomatically. On June 8, 1967, Israel's ambassador to the United States, Avraham Harman, and his deputy chief of mission, Ephraim Evron, were at the U.S. Department of State to discuss matters relating to the war. They were taken by Lucius Battle, former U.S. ambassador to Egypt, to Secretary Rusk's office. At that point the two men had been away from Israel's embassy since morning and had not yet received the report of the *Liberty* incident. They were completely mystified when a very angry Rusk demanded information from them about the *Liberty*. Rusk's demeanor was shocking to both Harman and Evron, as Rusk had always been polite and cordial in the past. Ultimately Rusk refused to accept the Israeli explanation and branded the attack as irresponsible.

If there was extreme tension in the White House Situation Room, the Sixth Fleet flagship, and IDF headquarters in Tel Aviv, the situation in Cairo was chaotic. Anti-U.S. sentiment was running strong as a result of Nasser's announcement that the United States had fought for the Israelis against Egypt. The security of the U.S. embassy in Cairo was in doubt. Ambassador Richard Nolte cabled the State Department in Washington, "We had better get our story on torpedoing of USS *Liberty* out fast and it had better be good. Nolte."[29]

The State Department was receiving other inquiries from Muslim countries and from nations sympathetic to the Arab side of the Arab-Israeli conflict. In general, the issue revolved around what the *Liberty* was doing in the combat zone. The war caused the Arab countries to begin breaking diplomatic relations with the United States at an alarming rate. On June 6, 1967, Egypt (UAR), Syria, and Algeria broke diplomatic relations with the United States. On June 7, 1967, Sudan, Iraq, Mauritania, and Yemen followed suit.

The fact that a U.S. ship had been attacked in the war zone during the Arab-Israeli War was quite extraordinary. Dozens of reporters were, in fact, embarked on board the carrier *America* and were about to begin a press conference on the issue of whether the United States was actually involved in the conflict when first word of the attack on the *Liberty* was received by the Sixth Fleet. When the *Liberty* arrived in Malta, numerous reporters and correspondents sought the *Liberty* crew. However, a little more than three hours after the attack, Cyrus Vance, the Under Secretary of Defense, had issued an order by telephone that all news releases on the *Liberty* incident would be made at the Washington level and not from ships in the fleet.[30] After the Associated Press reported, on the day of *Liberty*'s arrival in Valletta, that an unidentified officer on the aircraft carrier *America* had said, "To put it bluntly she [*Liberty*] was there to spy for us. Russia does the same thing,"[31] a message was sent to *America* "to pipe down." Secretary McNamara issued a press release that stated in part: "Many rumors and reports about the attack have been circulating. The Department of Defense has no evidence to support some of these rumors and reports. Others appear to be based on partial evidence. Some appear to be accurate on the basis of present information here, which is incomplete. Until the Court has had an opportunity to obtain the full facts, the Department of Defense will have no further comment."[32]

Many vastly different stories and tales have been told by numerous crew members and others about a gag order. Former ambassador James E. Akins wrote:

While in Malta most of the surviving officers and men were interviewed in several groups by Rear Admiral Isaac Kidd, who ostentatiously took off the stars on his uniform in each case and said, "Now, tell me, man to man, everything that happened." They all did. Then he equally ostentatiously put the stars back on and said, "Now I'm talking officially; you are never, repeat never to discuss this with anyone, not even your wives. If you do you will be court-martialled and will end your lives in prison or worse."[33]

Some of the tales have reached the extreme. For instance, Egyptian ambassador Mahmoud Kassem reported that the families of crewmen who were lost on the *Liberty* were prohibited by the U.S. government from holding memorial services for them.[34] However, this author has not been able to locate a documented case of anyone ever being prosecuted, court-martialed, or disciplined as a result of talking about the *Liberty* incident.

As the news about the outcome of the Israeli-Egyptian-Syrian-Jordanian war was spreading, most of the press was euphoric in its reporting of the David-versus-Goliath story of Israel's defeat of the Arabs in a "six-day war." The June 19, 1967, issue of *Newsweek* magazine included in its "Periscope" column a comment regarding the *Liberty*. This was the first-ever suggestion in the world media that the attack on the *Liberty* had been an intentional Israeli attack on a ship that Israel knew to be American. A week later (June 26, 1967) the same "Periscope" column ran a story, "U.S.S. *Liberty:* Caught in Political Currents?," presenting a fascinating theory.[35] It first confirmed that sources in the State Department and the Pentagon backed Israel's story that the attack was an unfortunate accident. It then went on to say, "Some members of the Administration decided to talk about the possibility of a calculated attack for what they considered important political reasons. The supposed fears: that U.S. diplomats' maneuvering ability in the Mideast would be severely hampered unless some way was found to deflate pro-Israeli sentiment in the U.S."[36]

The next week *Newsweek* (July 3, 1967) wrote that "the Navy turned up no evidence to indicate the attack was anything but a tragic blunder. . . . In fact, no one seemed to doubt that judgment—not even Cairo.[37] . . . The Israelis were for once exact when they said that the bombardment of that ship . . . was a mistake."[38]

About seven weeks later (August 28, 1967) the following appeared in *Newsweek* under the headline, "The U.S.S. *Liberty:* Tragedy of Errors":

Defense Secretary McNamara is satisfied that the strafing of the U.S. ship *Liberty* by pilots during the Mideast war was unintentional. He recently told a closed session of a Congressional committee that "there is no evidence that the individuals attacking the *Liberty* knew they were attacking a U.S. ship." McNamara blamed the attack on "inadequate communications and an inexcusable error of professional tactics." The Israelis are yet to report on their own investigation into the attack in which 34 U.S. seamen died.[39]

The September 4, 1967, *Newsweek* reported that Israel was not going to take court-martial action against any of the pilots or seamen who fired on the USS *Liberty*.[40] An Israeli court of inquiry headed by Examining Judge Yeshayahu Yerulshalmi concluded that the *Liberty* had been attacked because she greatly resembled an Egyptian supply ship and, when asked to identify herself, she had replied, "Identify yourself first."

The *Liberty* issue quickly faded from the print media as a result of continuing unsettling news from Vietnam and the unfortunate race riots that broke out in the United States at the time. Within the U.S. administration, there was a major debate on how much the United States should disclose to the public about the event. Assistant Secretary of Defense for Public Affairs Phil G. Goulding suggested going public with the simple truth. The State Department objected to truthful disclosure, because it feared the impact on future Arab-U.S. relations. A stronger argument against Goulding's position came from the intelligence community. The *Liberty* and her sister ships were described—indeed disguised—as auxiliary general technical research ships and were believed by the National Security Agency to be safe and generally welcome around the world. The NSA's argument was, "These ships had access to many ports as research ships where they would not be welcome if they were branded intelligence gatherers."[41] Although Secretary of Defense McNamara allegedly leaned toward the Goulding approach, he was ultimately persuaded to go with what Goulding later described as a "cover-up."[42]

On June 8, the Department of Defense issued a press release, penned by Goulding himself, which said, "A U.S. Navy technical research ship, the U.S.S. *Liberty* (AGTR-5) was attacked about 9:00 a.m. (EDT) today approximately 15 miles north of the Sinai Peninsula in international waters of the Mediterranean Sea. The *Liberty* departed Rota, Spain, June 2nd and arrived at her position this morning to assure communications between U.S. Government posts in the Middle East and to assist in relaying information concerning the evacuation of American dependents and other American citizens from the countries of the Middle East."[43] When asked in 1991 about this press release, Dr. Harold Saunders, who in June 1967 was on the Near East desk at the National Security Council, replied, "For every covert operation, there has to be a cover story, that is our story."[44] The cover story about the *Liberty*'s purpose did not exactly work. It is still called a cover-up by many.

In addition to this inaccurate and misleading press release, the Department of Defense issued a press release on June 28, 1967, no. 594–67. It consisted of a cover sheet, "a summary of the proceedings of the U.S. Navy Court of Inquiry" and an edited transcript of the testimony of the commanding officer of the *Liberty* before the court. The summary is inaccurate. It states "facts" and conclusions that do not appear anywhere in the court of inquiry proceedings, and it omits substantial significant facts and conclusions that put an entirely different spin on the release. The author of this June 28, 1967, press release remains unknown. When read against the findings and conclusions of the court of inquiry, it is at once apparent that its contents are more the imagination of the author than an accurate report of the court's findings and conclusions.

The notion that intelligence-gathering ships of the *Liberty* class were generally safe and welcome anywhere was shattered less than a year later, on January 23, 1968, when the USS *Pueblo*, an auxiliary environmental research ship, or AGER, similar to the *Liberty* was captured by the North Koreans off the coast of North Korea, to the further great embarrassment of the United States.[45] Certainly the use of ships like the *Liberty* and the *Pueblo* was a calculated risk. Only the NSA has the data necessary to establish whether the intelligence collected by these ships was worth the price of the *Liberty* and *Pueblo* disasters.

On Friday morning, June 9, 1967, the *Davis* (DD 937) and the *Massey* (DD 778), two U.S. Sixth fleet destroyers, rendezvoused with the *Liberty*. The *Davis* and the *Massey* had been with the carriers of Task Force 60 near Crete, about five hundred miles northwest of the location of the *Liberty* when she was attacked. After continuous steaming through the night at thirty knots, as dawn broke the destroyers came upon the *Liberty* lying dead in the water.[46] A nineteen-inch-diameter German torpedo had blasted a hole in the hull of the *Liberty* large enough for a Greyhound bus to drive through. The original estimate was that the hole was twenty feet by thirty feet, but when the torpedo hole was measured it was found to be in excess of forty feet by forty feet. The torpedo had struck the ship on the starboard side, just forward of amidships. It was a square hit on the NSA, or "spook," compartment and caused the death of twenty-five persons in the compartment. Some *Liberty* crewmen insist that the Israeli torpedo was aimed precisely at the NSA compartment to put it out of action. However, this assumption of precision does not explain why the other four Israeli torpedoes missed completely.[47]

Blast damage and bullet holes covered much of the *Liberty*'s topside area, and she was listing nine or ten degrees to starboard. Her radio facilities were very limited. The first order of business was the evacuation of casualties. It was accomplished that day by helicopters from the Sixth Fleet's aircraft carrier *America*. Most of the surviving crew and personnel were suffering from shock and exhaustion. The uninjured men (and some with minor injuries) remained on the ship and assisted with the salvage operation.

Lt. Paul E. Tobin, the engineering officer of the *Davis*, came on board and supervised the damage control and engineering repairs on the *Liberty*.[48] When Tobin came on board, he was assigned a stateroom. Sadly, it had belonged to Lt. Stephen Toth, a former classmate of Tobin's at the U.S. Naval Academy who had died on the bridge during the air attack.

After seven hours of damage control and repair under Tobin's direction, his men from the *Davis* and the remaining *Liberty* crew, working together as a salvage team, determined that the tanks and voids nearest the keel had not been damaged. They calculated that there was a sufficient margin of transverse stability to ensure adequate "righting moment" if heavy weather was encountered. Some of the 250,000 gallons of fuel oil remaining on board was transferred from starboard to port, and the ship was righted and stabilized. The *Davis* engineers, together with the engineering staff of the *Liberty*, then went to work on the ship's steam plant to see if the ship could sail on her own power. When this was accomplished, Admiral Martin ordered the *Davis* to escort the *Liberty* to Souda Bay, Crete, for temporary repairs. After they got under way, the destination was changed to Valletta, Malta, where a dry dock was available.

En route, the electricians worked at repairing the ship's electrical system. This was accomplished with amazing speed, and within hours lighting and ventilation were restored. The Navy fleet tug *Papago* (ATF 160) arrived but did not have to tow the *Liberty*, because Tobin had been able to restore the propulsion plant. During the slow transit to Malta, most of the ship's vital systems, including the main gyro, sound-powered phone circuits, and a main fire and flushing pump, were restored to service.

Once the ship was under way to Malta, a suction effect drew large amounts of debris out the ship's torpedo hole. There was intense concern about secret documents that might float out through the gaping hole in the hull, the major worry being the code keys and other cryptologic documents. All the way to Malta precautions were taken to prevent any ship, in particular Soviet warships, from retrieving documents from the wake of the *Liberty*.[49] The *Papago* sailed immediately astern of the *Liberty* and collected and sifted through whatever material could be recovered as it washed out of the flooded space. One hundred and fifty miles east of Malta the wind and sea conditions deteriorated to the point that unusual noises were heard from the damaged portion of the ship. Tobin would later recall: "The bulkhead on the forward side of the flooded hold was visibly panting as hogging and sagging stresses distorted the ship's structure. The unusual noises were determined to be the sound of breaking surf and the impact of desks, chairs, and equipment being violently tossed around in the hold."[50]

The ship was slowed to allow bracing and shoring; these heroic efforts were successful. Finally, after a day, the rough weather subsided, and the *Liberty* entered Valletta. Lieutenant Tobin was awarded the Bronze Star for meritorious achievement in bringing the *Liberty* safely to port.

Chapter 7

FRIENDLY FIRE KILLS

H istory is replete with cases in which military forces have made mistakes that resulted in the killing or wounding of their own people or allied personnel, friends, or neutrals. The lessons to be learned from the tragedy of the *Liberty* are many and varied. Col. Charles R. Shrader, in his outstanding research survey *Amicicide: The Problem of Friendly Fire in Modern War,* documents the sad fact that modern warfare carries with it the burden of losses to "friendly fire."[1] Shrader coined the word "amicicide"; the U.S. Navy has long referred to it as "blue on blue," and the Israelis use the Hebrew words *esh* (fire) *yedidutit* (friendly).

According to Shrader, all modern military forces, including those of the United States, suffer amicicide casualties at the rate of about 2 percent. Moreover the percentage of friendly fire casualties has changed very little in modern times. The percentage was perhaps a little higher for the French in World War I, and it was terribly high for the United States in the Gulf War, where almost as many British troops were killed by the United States as by the Iraqis. In each case the tragedy occurs because of a mistake in identification.

The display of a flag as a means of identification or protection against air attack is not effective in practice. The *Liberty* had a five-by-eight-foot U.S. flag hoisted on her main halyard at the time of the air attack. It was shot away in an early strafing run by the attacking Israeli aircraft and replaced before the MTB attack with a seven-by-thirteen-foot holiday ensign on the port halyard—opposite the side from which the MTBs approached the *Liberty.*[2] In his book *Assault on the "Liberty,"* James Ennes tells how on the morning of the day of the attack he stressed to the *Liberty* signalman the importance of flying the ship's only remaining new flag, because the *Liberty* was operating in a dangerous area.[3] Since the incident much has been made of whether the flag was drooped or extended at the time of the air attack. Many crew members believe it was extended and should have been seen and identified as an American flag by the attacking aircraft. However, according to Marvin Nowicki:

> In reconstruction of the attack, the *Liberty* crew makes much of flying the American flag, as if it would somehow protect them in harm's way (see Ennes p. 152). Little does the crew appreciate the difficulty of identifying a ship from an aircraft merely on the basis of a flag or even a hull number (GTR-5 displayed by the *Liberty*). Based on my experience of flying many "low and slow" reconnaissance flights over ships in the Med and Atlantic with VQ-2, unless the flights are almost overhead, target identification is virtually impossible. High powered binoculars are not much good in a bouncing low-level aircraft. Even post facto photos do not always reveal identification. See for example, Ennes' photo of the ship on page 146. The crisp overhead photo does not clearly show the identity of the American ship. So how could the attacking Israeli forces conclude this was a friendly ship?[4]

To get a better idea of the size of *Liberty*'s flag, it is useful to compare it to the "star-spangled banner" that was "seen through the night" on September 12, 1814, during the War of 1812. That flag, flown by Maj. George Armistad over Fort McHenry, in Maryland, was thirty feet by forty-two feet, and each stripe was two feet wide. The *Liberty*'s flag was forty square feet, while the banner over Fort McHenry was 1,260 square feet, or more than thirty-one times larger than *Liberty*'s flag, which was much more akin to the flags flown on private homes on national holidays than to the huge flags frequently flown by American automobile dealerships. The ship also had her abbreviated hull designation, "GTR 5," painted on both sides of her bow and stem in white letters and numbers with a black shadowing. The number 5 was about ten feet tall, while the letters were about half that size. Many crew members believe that these features should have been sufficient for identification by the approaching aircraft. Also, many crew members believe that the ship, with her various arrays of antennae, was so unique that her configuration should have been identified by the attacking aircraft as well as by the motor torpedo boats.

Many people have held these beliefs for more than thirty years, and in most cases they are not likely to reconsider them. The primary argument, frequently referred to as the "*Liberty* was clearly marked" argument, is that

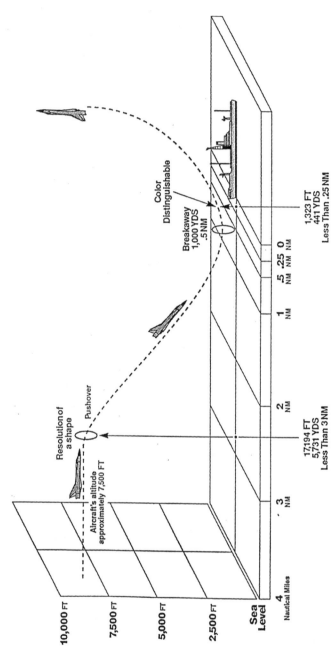

Attack profile of a Mirage IIIC: Aircraft flying against ship displaying 5 x 8 foot flag

The pilot could discern a 5 x 8 foot shape at about three nautical miles out. However the pilot could not discern color, or distinguish the stripes, outside of one quarter of a nautical mile.

SHIP'S FLAG AS SEEN WITH 10 KT WEST WIND.

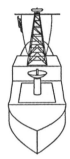

Wind 15 KTS from the bow. The flag is flying and is seen streaming aft. The pilot has no view of the flag.

SHIP'S FLAG AS SEEN WITH 5 KT EAST WIND.

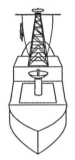

Zero wind across the deck. If the ship is steaming west at 5 KTS, and the wind is from the east at 5 KTS, then the flag would be seen as drooped.

SHIP'S FLAG AS SEEN WITH 15 KT CROSS WIND.

(North or south illustration shows south wind.)

If the ship steamed west at 5 KTS, it would require a wind in excess of 15 KTS to extend the flag perpendicular.

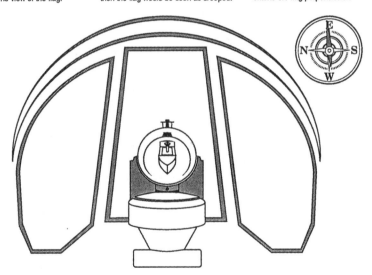

What does a pilot see during a head on run at a ship?

The ship is steering west at 5 nautical mph. The plane is flying east at about 600 mph.

June 8, 1967, was a clear day, a fact not disputed by anyone; that the *Liberty* was in international waters, which is also undisputed but also not really significant, since she was in eye view of hostilities; and that she was clearly marked by flying on the main halyard, a five-by-eight-foot U.S. flag that was fully extended at the time of the attack. The flag was visible to crewmen on the deck of the *Liberty;* therefore, the argument goes, it had to have been seen and identified by the attacking aircraft.

The first question one must ask is, from how far away could a pilot of an attacking military aircraft see a flag? If the flag was perpendicular to the approaching aircraft and in good light, according to the mathematical formula for visual acuity, the red and white stripes on a five-by-eight-foot U.S. flag might be identifiable at 1,323 feet.[5] A military aircraft pilot approaching at almost a thousand feet per second (almost six hundred miles per hour) would have a little less than two seconds to see and identify the flag. A jet airplane attacking at high subsonic speed would complete firing its guns in two to three seconds during its attack run and would have pulled off the target before getting closer than 2,500 feet, which is not close enough to see or identify a five-by-eight-foot flag.

But suppose the flag could have been seen from a distance longer than the calculated 1,323 feet. What, then, does a pilot see during a head-on run at a ship? If the flag was extended and flying in a normal manner—that is, corresponding to and parallel with the length of the ship—a pilot attacking from the bow would see the edge of the flag, which would be of no assistance in identification. It is this author's conclusion that under the wind conditions at the time of the attack, the flag was not extended but rather drooped on the halyard and did not help in identification. A number of the *Liberty* crew have recollections of looking up at the flag and seeing it fully or partially extended. Appendix H of the Ennes book, *Assault on the "Liberty,"* "Ship Weather Observation Sheet" for June 8, 1967, shows wind observations up to 1100 GMT, 1300 Sinai time, about an hour before the air attack. The document shows light winds and calm seas. It is possible to argue with the Ennes calculations, but it is not necessary, because the report ends an hour before the attack and therefore contributes nothing other than a history of the morning weather conditions. The U.S. Navy court of inquiry in June 1967 concluded that "the calm conditions and slow ship speed may well have made the American flag difficult to identify." In a separate message Admiral McCain advised the Secretary of the Navy on June 14: "Following received from *Liberty*. Quote: . . . c. Flat calm condition and slow (5) knot

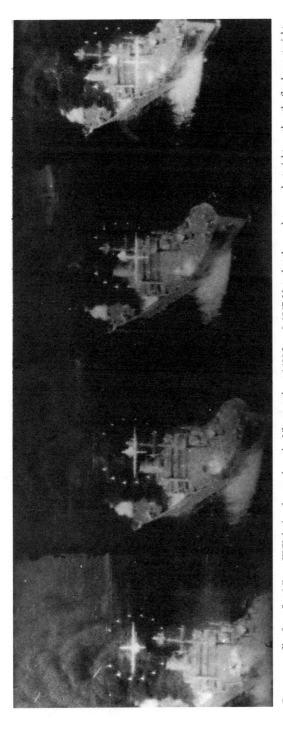

Gun-camera film from first Mirage IIICJ during the attack on the *Liberty* at about 1400 June 8, 1967. Note that the smoke ascends straight up; thus the flag hung straight down as the air attack took place. Kursa *Flight Leader Photos*

speed of *Liberty* in forenoon when she was being looked over initially may well have produced insufficient relative wind for steaming colors to be seen by pilots."[6]

Royal Flight leader, the attacking Israeli pilot of the second flight to hit the *Liberty*, reported to air force control that there was no flag (actually, that they saw no flag) on the ship, as is evident from the recording at 1412. This was stated again in *Kursa* Flight leader's pilot debriefing report filed at 1500 Sinai time on June 8: "We had an identifying run around her and saw it did not have an Israeli Navy sign as published. There also was no flag on the mast."[7]

The best evidence of the status of the flag at 1400 comes from *Kursa* Flight leader's gun-camera film. When *Kursa* Flight leader made his attack runs on the *Liberty*, his gun camera recorded the conditions. An examination of the films, a frame of which is shown on the cover of the first edition of this book, and of other frames shown here, shows that the huge pall of smoke from the fire on board the *Liberty*, which was in the vicinity of the main halyard where the flag was hoisted, is ascending straight up. If the smoke rose straight up, then the flag drooped straight down, as, indeed, the U.S. Navy court of inquiry concluded.

The Israeli gun-camera film was not available for examination by the court of inquiry, but pictures were taken on the *Liberty* itself during the attacks. These pictures were available to the court and are contained in exhibits in its official record. The pictures include both the attacking aircraft and the attacking motor torpedo boats.[8] These pictures independently establish what the Israeli gun-camera film shows: a straight-up ascent of smoke rising from the ship, confirming that there was hardly any relative wind.[9]

Assuming for the sake of argument that the wind and the light were right and the Israeli pilots got close enough to see the flag for a second or two, would that have been enough to make an identification? Americans are familiar with the U.S. flag, consisting of red and white horizontal stripes and a field of blue studded with stars. The Liberian flag also has horizontal red and white stripes and a field of blue (as does the flag of Malaysia). At any given time in the last half-century, there were probably more ships on the high seas flying Liberian flags than U.S. flags, because of the ever-increasing practice of flagging ships in Liberia. No U.S. warship had made a port call in Israel since November 1963. Israel Air Force pilots did not often see the U.S. flag flying on a naval ship so near the coast in the eastern Mediterranean, although most Israelis would probably recognize an American flag quite easily if they had a clear view of it. But many more ships flying the Liberian flag than the American flag had made port calls in Israel in the years between 1948 and 1967.

Further, the International Committee of the Red Cross has pointed out in its *Law of War Handbook* that a flag is not a reliable means of identifying the nationality of a warship.[10] This is because the law of naval warfare permits warships to fly a false flag as a "ruse of war."[11]

In one of the most famous naval battles ever fought by the American navy, on September 23, 1779, Capt. John Paul Jones sailed the *Bonhomme Richard*, flying a British flag, alongside the British ship *Serapis:* "[British captain] Pearson hailed, 'What ship is that?' Paul Jones, in order to get into close action, was flying British colors. . . . [The *Serapis*] hailed again, 'Answer immediately, or I shall be under the necessity of firing into you.' Jones struck his British colors, caused a big red white and blue striped American ensign to be raised, and gave the word to fire his starboard broadside."[12]

During World War II, German captain Hans Langsdorff flew a French flag from the German pocket battleship *Graf Spee* while approaching his targets before attacking.

> Now Langsdorff used a new technique. He steamed straight at his victims, believing rightly that they would not recognize him head-on as a German and would probably think he was French. Sometimes he flew the French flag, and changed it at the last moment for the German swastika.[13]
>
> The *Graf Spee*'s crew ran to action stations with the prospect of the first bit of excitement for more than three weeks. Again the French Tricolor was hoisted, and the 5.9-inch guns were loaded.[14]

It is thus recognized in professional military circles that the identification of a warship by means of its flag is neither practical nor conclusive.

The size of a ship on the surface is of little help in identifying it from the cockpit of a plane. In May 1941 the British were chasing the German battleship *Bismarck*. The British cruiser *Sheffield* was a few miles behind the *Bismarck*. The British carrier *Ark Royal* launched its Swordfish torpedo bombers. They promptly dove through the clouds and launched their torpedoes against the *Sheffield*, a vessel just under a fifth the displacement of the *Bismarck*.[15] Fortunately for the *Sheffield*, the Fleet Air Arm pilots' aim was no better than their ship identification. All the torpedoes missed. It made no difference to the Royal Navy pilots that the *Bismarck* was about eight hundred feet long and displaced about 42,000 tons, while the *Sheffield* was only 591 feet long and displaced only nine thousand tons.[16] The *Sheffield* was less than 73 percent of the length of the *Bismarck* and almost one-fifth of its displacement. The *El Quseir* was 275 feet long, or about 60 percent of the *Liberty*'s 455-foot length, and displaced 2,640 tons, less than a quarter of the *Liberty*'s 10,680-ton displacement.[17]

Over the water, with no points of reference, it is very difficult to judge height or distance, or the length or displacement of a ship. An observer cannot be certain whether a ship is smaller and closer to the observer, or larger and farther away. It is interesting, however, to compare the silhouettes of the *Liberty* and the *El Quseir;* each had a mast forward, a mast to the rear, a superstructure in the middle, and a single smokestack. The CIA report concluded they could easily be mistaken by an overzealous pilot. It is even more interesting to compare the silhouettes of the *Bismarck* and the *Sheffield*. The *Bismarck* has two single-pole masts, while the *Sheffield* has two tripod masts; the *Bismarck* has one smokestack as compared to two on the *Sheffield*.

The Israeli pilots and motor-torpedo-boat sailors had never before seen either the *Liberty* or the *El Quseir,* while the British pilots from the *Ark Royal* had been fully briefed on their target, the *Bismarck,* and had also been steaming in company with the *Sheffield* for weeks.

In the U.S. Navy, naval aviators were trained to report ship traffic by the configuration of the bow, number of masts, number of smokestacks, placement of the stacks, and placement and description of the superstructure. They were seldom expected to identify ships by name or even type. An Israel Air Force officer told this author that the Israel Navy had "two types of ships, big Dabours and little Dabours." In fact, the Israel Navy had six types of large missile boats of the Saar class (*saar* means "tempest") and two types of smaller patrol boats of the Dabour class (*dabour* means "wasp"). The typical Israel Air Force pilot was not well trained in the identification of ships at sea.

On June 4, 1967, the commander of the United Nations Emergency Force, Maj. Gen. Indar Jit Rikhye of the Indian army, was flying in his personal plane from Cairo to El Arish. Passing Port Said, the general remembers that

> the captain of the aircraft, who looked extremely excited, came up to me, and pointing at some ships at sea below, said "Sixth Fleet! They're just a few miles off Port Said." He was referring to the United States Sixth Fleet stationed in the Mediterranean area.
>
> We made several circuits, gradually losing altitude. Through a pair of binoculars all I could see were a number of oil tankers, whereas the captain

insisted he had seen an aircraft carrier. I was taken up to the cockpit to get a better view, where a very excited first pilot . . . shouted "Sixth Fleet! Sixth Fleet!" . . . All I could see, however, were oil tankers steaming towards the north end of the Suez Canal . . . I was amazed at the inability of the air crew, probably all of whom at one time or another had served in the UAR air force, to differentiate between an aircraft carrier of nearly fifty thousand tons and oil tankers, none of which was over ten thousand tons.[18]

General Rikhye's comparison of the ten-thousand-ton tankers to the "fifty thousand ton" carriers is similar to the disparity between the *Bismarck* and the *Sheffield;* the *Bismarck* was about five times the displacement of the *Sheffield*. In fact, the carriers *America,* at 61,174 tons, and *Saratoga,* at 59,098 tons, were each approximately six times the displacement of the ten-thousand-ton tankers. The tankers were being observed by persons on an aircraft who had the luxury of making "several circuits, gradually losing altitude" without the stress of a war in progress within view.

It has been said that under wartime tensions and pressures one will find whatever one wants to find. If one wants to find enemy infiltrators, one will find them; if one wants to find an enemy submarine, one will find it; if one wants to find an enemy ship, one will find it. During the American Civil War, on May 2, 1863, Confederate soldiers wanted to find infiltrating Yankees. They found them, and as a result, the Confederate army lost one of its most famous and able generals. "Stonewall" Jackson died after his own troops mistook him for the enemy and mortally wounded him as he was returning from a scouting mission. In a parallel event during the 1948 War for Independence, an Israeli sentry, looking for an Arab infiltrator, shot and killed Brig. Gen. Mickey Marcus, mistaking the American volunteer for an enemy infiltrator. Marcus, a West Point graduate, had joined the Israel Army in 1948 and was in command of the Israeli forces fighting for Jerusalem.

According to Geoffrey Regan in his book *Blue on Blue: A History of Friendly Fire,* "The most remarkable example of amicicide in naval history occurred in 1905 during the Russo-Japanese War," when Russian admiral Zinovi Rozhestvensky identified a British trawler fleet of hundred-ton vessels fishing off the Dogger Bank in the North Sea as a fleet of Japanese torpedo boats and attacked them.[19] Only the terrible aim of the Russian fleet kept the tragedy from being worse.

On October 15, 1918, the British Q-ship *Cymric* was looking for a German submarine. Instead, she sank the British submarine *J-6*. "*Cymric* noted a limp ensign flying from the submarine's flagpole, but took no notice of that—they had been fooled by false colors in the past." According to Regan in *Blue on Blue,* "In World War I, three times, British submarines mistook British ships for German and tried to torpedo them."[20] Regan notes, "Conversely, three British cruisers tried to ram British submarines, mistaking them for German U-boats."[21]

Mistaken identification of a ship by an aircraft is not a new phenomenon. On February 22, 1940, a lone German bomber sank two German destroyers at a cost of 578 lives.[22] The *Lebrecht Masse* was struck with two bombs, broke in two, and sank. In 1974 off Cyprus, Turkish F-4s sank their own former U.S. *Fletcher* (DD 445)–class destroyer with the flotilla commander on board.

During the 1956 Suez campaign a flight of four Israeli Mystère aircraft, led by Danny Shapira,[23] were finishing bombing runs when they observed an Egyptian Z-class destroyer in the Gulf of Aqaba.[24] They immediately attacked the ship, inflicting slight damage. Soon they learned that the "Egyptian" destroyer had been in fact HMS *Crane,* a British destroyer that had proceeded to a point in advance of where the Royal Navy had advised Israel that it would be operating.[25] The largest tank battle of the 1956 Suez campaign occurred at Abu Ageila, where two Israeli tank units fought each other with devastating results.[26] The United States and the Israelis have each suffered from amicicide in every war in which they have fought.

The myth of the invincible and faultless Israel Defense Forces has been replaced with the analysis that the IDF is a superior fighting force but neither invincible nor faultless. Israelis do make mistakes. On June 5, 1967, the Israel Air Force bombed a column of Israeli Sherman tanks during the battle for Jerusalem. On June 8, 1967, the IAF bombed and strafed the Israel Army just a few hours before the attacks on the *Liberty* began. In the preceding days, Israeli forces had mistakenly killed a number of Indian and Brazilian UN troops in the Sinai.

Adm. John S. McCain Jr., the Commander in Chief, U.S. Naval Forces Europe, who endorsed Admiral Kidd's U.S. Navy court of inquiry report with the comment, "The attack [on the *Liberty*] was in fact a mistake" (see chapter 12), was aware from personal experience that a flag flown on a surface vessel offered little in the way of identification and protection against friendly air attack. During World War II, McCain commanded the U.S. submarine *Gunnel* (SS 253) on a secret mission to guide the U.S. invading armada to the beaches of Morocco. When the *Gunnel*'s mission was complete,

McCain was ordered to sail away from the invasion site on the surface flying an American flag illuminated by a spotlight. While proceeding as ordered, the *Gunnel* was attacked and strafed by an American P-40.[27]

Unfortunately, another more recent example underscores the difficulty of positively identifying the enemy under stressful conditions. On April 14, 1995, in northern Iraq, on a clear day, in broad daylight with visibility unrestricted, U.S. Air Force F-15s shot down two U.S. Black Hawk helicopters, each with six large U.S. flags prominently painted on all sides. No shooting war was taking place at the time. There was no adrenaline flowing. The helicopters had little or no offensive capability as far as the F-15s were concerned, nor were they a threat to U.S. or coalition forces in the area. This tragedy was compounded by the fact that the F-15s had state-of-the-art Identification Friend or Foe transponder equipment on board and were being controlled by a U.S. Airborne Warning and Control System aircraft with state-of-the-art radar and electronic surveillance equipment.

- In 1991, during the Gulf War, almost as many British soldiers were killed by United States forces as by Iraqis.
- In Afghanistan in 2002, the U.S. Air Force dropped a laser-guided five-hundred-pound bomb that killed four Canadians and wounded eight.
- Later in Afghanistan, National Football League star Pat Tillman was killed by members of his own Army unit.
- On the first day of the Iraq war, the United States shot down a British jet and incredibly the next week shot down a U.S. Navy jet.
- On May 7, 1999, the United States, by mistake, bombed the Chinese embassy in Belgrade, Yugoslavia; to this day the Chinese refuse to accept the explanation that the bombing was a mistake.

In military operations, attention to detail is important. The smallest detail or oversight can result in inefficiency, ineffectiveness, failure, and even disaster. With the *Liberty,* there were many little mistakes on both sides, each of which, if it had not occurred, might have broken the chain of events that led to the tragedy. Military operations require precision, attention, and knowledge in order to succeed. It is prudent to keep friendly forces advised of force movements and deployments.

It is useful to remember that the United States had announced in the Security Council of the United Nations that no U.S. ship was within hundreds of miles of the war zone. This announcement did not contribute to the safety of the *Liberty*. In 1943, an American transport was sunk by an American torpedo boat whose officer had relied on assurances that there were no friendly vessels in the area.[28] During the Allied invasion of Sicily in July 1943, when transports laden with paratroopers overflew a U.S. amphibious force that was undergoing a German bombing attack at night, the amphibious force opened fire and shot down twenty-three U.S. planes, killing sixty air crewmen and about forty paratroopers. Cdr. Thomas Krupp, the naval attaché at the U.S. embassy in Tel Aviv during 1989 and 1990, was asked if he had an opinion on whether the attack on the *Liberty* was a mistake.[29] He replied: "The only time I was wounded during my naval career was on April 16, 1972, while serving on the destroyer *Worden* (DLG 18) off Vietnam. The *Worden* was attacked by U.S. Air Force F-4 aircraft."[30]

The *Liberty* incident is a classic illustration of the terrible results that can occur when friendly forces fail to keep their friends informed of their movements. Intelligence operators are typically paranoid about the security of their missions. The general rule is that security is based on the need to know. It is well established that the National Security Agency did not inform either the U.S. embassy in Tel Aviv or any entity in Israel of the intended operations of the *Liberty* close to the war zone. On the contrary, as noted, the U.S. government had officially stated that there were no U.S. ships in the area. If the NSA had advised the Israel Defense Forces of the voyage of the *Liberty* along the coast of Sinai, very likely the *Liberty* incident would not have occurred.

Lt. Col. Danny Grossman (Ret.) of the Israel Air Force sent the following e-mail to this author on August 21, 2001:

> I know only too well from dealing with bereaved families of soldiers killed in combat by friendly fire that this is a situation where no explanation can ever be satisfactory. It is one thing to lose a loved one who falls in combat while defending his country and protecting his buddies. Families and survivors learn to deal with this. It is much harder to accept the idea that a loved one is gone due to thoroughly avoidable circumstances. Our [Israel's] own experience in Lebanon and the U.S. experience in the Gulf War has shown that many parents and survivors [of friendly fire] can never rest until they feel that someone has been made to account for their loss. The facts may never be sufficient for many survivors, but they should be presented in order to help those who are able to finally make peace with the reality that caused so much pain.[31]

Chapter 8

SURVIVORS' PERCEPTIONS

By the time the Israeli attacks on the *Liberty* were over, 34 Americans, most of them working directly for the National Security Agency, were dead and 171 were wounded, many severely.[1] On June 8, 1967, William L. McGonagle was the commanding officer of the USS *Liberty*.[2] Although wounded in the air attack, he refused to leave his duty station on the bridge of his ship and continued to command her, directing damage control and the departure from the area following the air and sea attacks. That night he lay on his back on the deck, steering the ship by reference to the stars, to a dawn rendezvous with the U.S. destroyers *Davis* and *Massey*. For his "conspicuous gallantry and intrepidity at the risk of his life above and beyond the call of duty," President Johnson awarded McGonagle the Medal of Honor.

On June 13, 1967, five days after the attack, McGonagle testified under oath before the U.S. Navy court of inquiry that, following the air attack and as the MTBs were approaching, "I realized that there was a possibility of the aircraft having been Israeli and the attack had been conducted in error."[3] This author first met Captain McGonagle in Washington, D.C., on June 7, 1991. He had refused to comment publicly on the *Liberty* incident since his press conference in June 1967, other than to praise the professionalism and valor of his crew in saving the ship. This author learned that he and Captain McGonagle had a common interest in flying and that following his retirement from the navy, McGonagle had obtained a commercial pilot's license in preparation for a career in civil aviation. (He was not able to pursue that career, because he could not maintain his aviation medical certificate as a result of deteriorating vision.)[4] Thereafter a warm, friendly relationship developed by correspondence and telephone.

Captain McGonagle was under the impression that he had been intentionally slighted by President Johnson because he received his Medal of

Honor at the Navy Yard, while the president awarded twelve other Medals of Honor at the White House on the same day. This author provided him with information that resulted in his writing a letter on August 20, 1998, stating:

> Thank you so much for sending a copy of President Johnson's Daily Diary for June 11, 1968.
>
> I stand corrected on my long held erroneous belief that the President had presented 12 Medals of Honor at the White House on the same day that I received my medal at the Navy Yard. . . .
>
> Your thoughts about " . . . if President Johnson wished to diminish the honor (of the award) he could have declined to sign the Citation . . ." seems to me to be sound reasoning.[5]

The President of the United States of America takes pleasure in presenting the
MEDAL OF HONOR to

CAPTAIN WILLIAM L. McGONAGLE
UNITED STATES NAVY

for service as set forth in the following

Citation: Captain (then Commander) William McGonagle U.S. Navy, U.S.S. *Liberty* (AGTR-5), for conspicuous gallantry and intrepidity at the risk of his life above and beyond the call of duty. Sailing in international waters, Eastern Mediterranean, on 8-9 June 1967, the *Liberty* was attacked without warning by jet fighter aircraft and motor torpedo boats which inflicted many casualties among the crew and caused extreme damage to the ship. Although severely wounded during the first air attack, Captain McGonagle remained at his battle station on the badly damaged bridge and, with full knowledge of the seriousness of his wounds, subordinated his own welfare to the safety and survival of his command. Steadfastly refusing any treatment which could take him away from his post, he calmly continued to exercise firm command of his ship. Despite continuous exposure to fire, he maneuvered his ship, directed its defense, supervised the control of flooding and fire, and saw to the care of the casualties. Captain McGonagle's extraordinary valor under these conditions inspired the surviving members of the *Liberty's* crew, many of them seriously wounded, to heroic efforts to overcome the battle damage and keep the ship afloat. Subsequent to the attack, although in great pain and weak from the loss of blood, Captain McGonagle remained at his battle station and continued to command his ship for more than 17 hours. It was only after rendezvous with a U.S. destroyer that he relinquished personal control of the *Liberty* and permitted himself to be removed from the bridge. Even then, he refused much needed medical attention until convinced that the seriously wounded among his crew had been treated. Captain McGonagle's superb professionalism, courageous fighting spirit, and valiant leadership saved his ship and many lives. His actions sustain and enhance the finest traditions of the United States Naval Service.

Captain McGonagle's Medal of Honor citation

Capt. William L. McGonagle, commanding officer of USS *Liberty*, wearing his Medal of Honor. *U.S. Navy photo*

When this author's doctoral dissertation was published by the Graduate School of International Studies of the University of Miami in 1997, two copies were provided to Captain McGonagle at his request. He wanted one for himself and another that he said he planned to forward to the Hoover Institution at Stanford University.

A trip together to Israel to meet with Israeli participants in the attacks was discussed, but it was not to be. McGonagle died of lung cancer on March 3, 1999. He was buried with full military honors at Arlington National Cemetery on April 9, 1999. The *New York Times* obituary quoted him as declaring, at a gathering of *Liberty* survivors in Washington, D.C., in 1997:

> I think it is about time that the state of Israel and the United States Government provide the crew members of the Liberty and the rest of the American people the facts of what happened and why the *Liberty* was attacked 30 years ago today.
>
> For many years I have wanted to believe that the attack on the *Liberty* was pure error. It appears to me that it was not a pure case of mistaken identity. It was, on the other hand, gross incompetence and aggravated dereliction of duty on the part of many officers and men of the state of Israel.[6]

This author agrees with Captain McGonagle that it is time to declassify the few remaining classified documents relating to the *Liberty* incident. In September 2001 this author obtained from the Israel Air Force the transcripts of audiotapes of communications between Israeli air controllers and transmissions of the pilots in the attacking aircraft recorded at IAF command headquarters on June 8, 1967. The tapes show the confusion of the attacking forces regarding the identification of the target. It is time for the U.S. National Security Agency to grant this author's Freedom of Information Act appeal and release the transcripts and translations of the tapes recorded by the NSA team on board the U.S. Navy EC-121 aircraft under the supervision of Dr. Nowicki, at the same time the Israel Air Force tapes were recorded, in order to corroborate the Israeli tapes and bring closure to this matter.

The *Liberty* crewman and personnel assigned to the NSA detachment are a fine group of men who risked their lives in the service of their country. Some of the *Liberty*'s survivors are bitter and hold various grievances as a result of their traumatic, tragic experience. It is bad enough when shipmates are hit by an enemy. It is probably worse when they are the victims of friendly fire.

Following the incident of June 8, the crew of the USS *Liberty* were assigned to other ships and stations throughout the fleet. Some left the Navy. Most were disappointed with the treatment they received when they returned to the United States. Like many servicemen during the Vietnam conflict, they did not receive the triumphant welcome home and the warm, affectionate attention that had been showered on their predecessors upon their returns home from World War II. By June 1967 the general public mood of America had turned against the military because of the fierce debate surrounding the Vietnam conflict, and the *Liberty* veterans were treated just like their comrades in arms who were coming from that theater. While this mistreatment was neither appropriate nor fair, it had nothing to do with their involvement in the *Liberty* incident. However, some of the *Liberty* veterans, including some who were suffering from post-traumatic stress disorder, perceived their treatment as being connected to the tragic event itself.

In 1981, the *Liberty* Veterans Association was formed.[7] Its first reunion was scheduled for Washington, D.C., on June 5 and 6, 1982. While the real motives of some of the founding members who had not served on the *Liberty* and certain actions of the association itself might be questionable, it has become an excellent support group for the surviving crew members in general, especially those still suffering from post-traumatic stress disorder. The association attempts to hold annual reunions each June and publishes a newsletter several times a year.

The *Liberty* Veterans Association is composed of individuals who differ in their views about many issues, including the question of whether the Israeli attack was a case of mistaken identity or an intentional attack on a U.S. Navy ship. A short while after the association was formed, a letter from one *Liberty* officer, who wished to remain anonymous, complained: "I hope you will tone down the radical and extremist nature of the newsletter and that you will avoid outrageous claims. For instance, can you substantiate your claim that *Liberty* men were held against their will in San Juan and questioned while under the influence of sodium pentothal? I don't recall press curb or coverup except before the court report was published or with regard to classified material. Can you substantiate these claims?" The letter was signed, "A *Liberty* officer who requests anonymity."[8]

When people are shot at and their shipmates are killed or wounded, it is difficult for them to accept the idea that such an attack was a mistake, let alone to be objective. The *Liberty* Veterans Association continues to request a congressional investigation of the incident even though *five* congressional investigations have been conducted since 1967. Certainly, the U.S. government has not been completely forthcoming about the incident. In fact, the U.S. government did release a false statement, but only about the *Liberty*'s mission off the coast of Sinai on the day she was hit. The Clifford Report of July 1967 was not declassified until October 1995, and the record of proceedings of the U.S. Navy court of inquiry of June 1967 was kept classified for more than nine years, until 1976. As a result, some members of the association have been crying "cover-up."

On the day of the incident, even before the aerial attack, *Liberty* crew members observed a good many aircraft around their ship that they presumed were Israeli. As has been mentioned earlier, the ship was observed and positively identified as the *Liberty* by the Israeli air force routine morning reconnaissance flight. On the other hand, since a major war was being fought in this vicinity, it could be argued that not all the Israeli or other aircraft observed were concerned with the *Liberty*. In addition, the presence of "a ship" off El Arish was observed and even reported to the Israel Air Force headquarters by other Israeli high-altitude aircraft the *Liberty* crew never sighted.[9]

About twenty years after the *Liberty* incident, word of the theory that the Israelis intentionally attacked a U.S. ship reached a British Thames TV producer, who subsequently came to the United States and listened to the story as told by a number of crew members. He spent a great deal of time with them in 1985 and 1986. The producer believed that some of the survivors were still suffering from post-traumatic stress disorder.[10] The *Liberty* veterans themselves confirmed this as recently as 1996 in their newsletter, *Liberty News*,[11] in an article entitled "Post-Traumatic Stress Disorder."[12] The severe trauma experienced and the lingering after effects are, undoubtedly, deserving of sympathy, but they do not enhance the ability of the victims to impartially analyze the incident.

The argument made by some *Liberty* veterans that the Israeli attacks were conducted in the knowledge that the *Liberty* was a U.S. ship and were not a result of mistaken identification is not supported by the evidence. These veterans adopt and repeat a number of allegations about the attacks and believe that they are true. All of the surviving *Liberty* crew members suffered a horrible experience on June 8, 1967. Many continue to suffer from that experience to this day. Like many other victims of "friendly fire," they have become obsessed with the cause of their pain as they perceive it, all the more so since they have attracted willing but unholy allies who, if anything, have fanned the flame in order to promote their own agendas. With all the respect that is certainly due the survivors of the *Liberty* incident, their objectivity is lost or tainted.

Lt. Cdr. George Golden was a lieutenant and the engineering officer on the *Liberty* on June 8, 1967. He was third in command, and upon the death of Lt. Cdr. Phillip Armstrong, *Liberty*'s executive officer, Golden became second in command. He testified at the court of inquiry and was the signatory on the *Liberty*'s engine bell book, which was admitted in evidence as Court of Inquiry Exhibit 15. He and his chief machinist mate, Richard J. Brooks, heroically manned the engine room of the *Liberty* and kept her engines operating.

Lieutenant Commander Golden, former president of the *Liberty* Veterans Association, has an excellent memory of many details of events that he personally observed inside the engine room on June 8, 1967, and also many memories of his participation in the production of the Thames TV documentary *The Attack on the "Liberty"* (see chapter 14). However, Lieutenant Commander Golden confirms that all he knew about the Israeli side of the attack was what he had heard from others.[13]

Chief Machinist Mate Richard J. Brooks was the senior chief petty officer on the *Liberty*.[14] His general quarters station, or battle station, was in the engine room. When the general quarters alarm sounded at the commencement of the air attack, he went immediately to the engine room, where he remained with Lieutenant Golden until both the air and sea attacks were over. He has a vivid recollection of what took place when the torpedo struck: "Within an instant the *Liberty* assumed a 9° list and the lubrication alarms sounded as a result of the oil shifting in the oil tanks." Chief Brooks immediately began pumping oil into the tanks from the reserve tanks. Chief Brooks recalls frantically running the oil from the reserve tanks, because without sufficient oil, the power trains would overheat and self-destruct in seconds. Chief Brooks was emphatic that the ship's movement from a normal upright position to the nine-degree-list position occurred in an instant.[15] This prompt action kept the engines running and was a major factor in keeping the ship under power and ultimately saving her. Chief Brook's prompt professional action was recognized by the award of the Silver Star. He also was awarded a Purple Heart.

Seaman Steven Richards was in the aft deck division locker room with Seaman Thomas Anthony Quintero when the air attack began. Seaman Richards heard a loud noise and thought the TRSSCOMM dish antenna had tipped over. Then the general alarm sounded, and he ran to his battle station, which was forward on the flying bridge on the 04 level. He heard the aircraft but did not see them. He recalls a slight upheaval of the ship when the torpedo struck, followed by a resettling in the water and then a slow roll to the nine-degree-list position.[16]

The two different recollections of the same event, the ship rolling to a nine-degree list, give a classic example of how perception may differ from reality. Chief Brooks's perception was influenced by an urgent situation that needed resolution with all possible haste, while Seaman Richards's perception was not subject to the impending disaster like the one that Chief Brooks was urgently trying to prevent. Thus when recollections of the same event differ, the reason for the difference in most instances is the observer's perspective rather than lack of candor.

In 1979, James M. Ennes Jr., a *Liberty* crew member, published a book entitled *Assault on the "Liberty": The True Story of the Israeli Attack on an American Intelligence Ship.*[17] By his own testimony, Ennes was seriously wounded in the leg during the first few minutes of the Israeli air attack and was taken below deck for medical treatment.[18] His knowledge of the remainder of the air attack and the subsequent naval attack was based on what he heard or was told rather than on what he observed at first hand.

In June 1967, as Lieutenant Ennes and his wounded shipmates lay in their hospital beds in the sick bay of the carrier *America* and ashore, they began to contemplate the events of the previous few days. Some soon concluded that the Israeli attacks had been part of a planned and carefully executed plot. Twelve years later Ennes, in his *Assault on the "Liberty,"* traced back his views to those hospital days: "The hospital executive officer brought me a message from the Department of State. Israel's ambassador to Italy wanted to talk to me. Would I consent to see him? . . . *Anyway, I was convinced that the attack was deliberate, premeditated murder. . . .* No, I said."[19] Thus, within a week after the attack, without recourse to research or access to additional firsthand information, Ennes had already reached his own conclusion. He then did some research and wrote *Assault on the "Liberty,"* but as the following examples demonstrate, statements he presents as facts are not always accurate.

In the hardcover edition, Ennes alleges in a parenthetical comment that President Johnson knew the Israeli attack on the *Liberty* had been made with knowledge that it was a U.S. ship: "(According to *Liberty*'s Lieut. Bennett [a cryptology officer in the NSA detachment], he [President Johnson] did know. After years of silence on this subject, Bennett told me that in 1967 Senator William Fulbright informed Captain McGonagle and Chief of Naval Operations Adm. David L. McDonald in Bennett's presence that the President knew the attack was deliberate and had ordered the information covered up for political reasons.)"[20]

Ennes elaborates in the footnotes:

On January 21, 1974, while buying coffee from a machine in a Navy building in Washington, D.C., Bennett ended almost seven years of silence on this subject to tell me: "The government knows the truth. Knew it all the time. Senator Fulbright told us that Johnson ordered a cover-up to protect Israel and to avoid causing a ruckus." Bennett remained fairly close-mouthed about the Pentagon meeting, however, and when witnesses were near he sometimes denied there was a cover-up at all (he was still on active duty and could have been hurt by excessive candor). During the following four years, however, he repeatedly confirmed with gist of the Pentagon discussion: The President knew the attack was deliberate and ordered it covered up for political reasons.[21]

This is triple hearsay. Ennes states that Bennett said that Fulbright said that President Johnson said. None of President Johnson's writings or papers support Ennes's claim. Admiral McDonald told this author that he had no recollection of Senator Fulbright making such a statement.[22] Senator Fulbright denied to this author that he made such a statement. Furthermore, he explained that the claim was not plausible. Senator Fulbright had been chair of the Senate Foreign Relations Committee since 1958. When Lyndon Johnson became president in 1964, Fulbright, who yearned to be secretary of state, expected his former U.S. Senate "buddy" Lyndon Johnson to appoint him to that office. Johnson did not. Consequently, their friendship cooled, and so, as Fulbright pointed out, in 1967 they were not even speaking to each other, much less sharing secrets.[23]

Interestingly, the paperback edition of the Ennes book published in 1986, a few years after publication of the hardcover edition, omits, on page 250, both the above-quoted text and footnote 5. This author interviewed Cdr. Maurice Bennett, USN (Ret.), in an effort to learn more about the disappearing quote from the Ennes book. Commander Bennett said that Senator Fulbright was a friend of one of Bennett's mother's brothers from Fayetteville, Arkansas. Bennett's parents had made an unannounced impromptu stop at Senator Fulbright's office during a visit to Washington to request tickets for a White House tour. While they were in the office, Senator Fulbright happened to come out of his office to the reception area, and the senator and Bennett's parents had a brief, informal conversation. In the course of that conversation, Bennett's mother told the senator that her son had been on the *Liberty*. According to Bennett's recollection of his mother's account of the visit, "at no time did Fulbright make a definitive official statement that he knew or had information about the attack." Bennett further states, "I do not recall a conversation with Ennes at a coffee machine. I also do not recall participation in a meeting with Admiral McDonald."[24] Most important, Bennett confirms that he was never in the presence of Senator Fulbright.

Other statements Ennes asserts as facts are also not accurate. For instance, Ennes reports that the USNS *Private Jose F. Valdez* (T-AG 69), proceeding from the eastern Mediterranean toward Norfolk, Virginia, passed the *Liberty* during the night of June 4 and morning of June 5, the day the war began.[25] An examination of the deck log of the *Liberty* reflects her position at 0800 on June 5, 1967, as 36-32.7 N, 13-58.2 E—that is, in the Mediterranean approaching Sicily. The *Jose F. Valdez* deck log reflects her position at exactly the same time on that same day as 36-34 N, 52-15 W—that is, in the mid-Atlantic on course toward New York, almost three thousand miles to the west of where Ennes reports her.

Another illustrative example is an Ennes report of seeing three (not two) Mirage aircraft approach the *Liberty* from the northeast. "The airplanes were fully loaded with eighteen large rockets visible under each wing."[26] According to Bill Gunston's *Illustrated Guide to the Israeli Air Force*, the Israeli Mirage IIICJs were wired for two or three air-to-air missiles but they never carried rockets.[27] They usually carried fuel tanks on the inboard hard points and air-to-air ordinance on the outboard hard points.[28] All Mirage IIICJ aircraft had only five hard points; therefore, even if the Mirage Israeli IIICJs were wired for rockets, they could not carry more than five each. Other Israeli jet aircraft were wired for rockets in 1967, but they carried them in pods that looked somewhat like fuel tanks. Since the rockets were stored internally, they could not be seen from the outside.

In the same volume, the winter 1985–86 issue of *American-Arab Affairs,*[29] in which the Ennes article was published, included under the heading "Documentation" an item listed in the table of contents as *The USS "Liberty": Discrepancies between Israeli Inquiry and U.S. Navy Court of Inquiry, September 21, 1967*. The preparer of the document, Carl F. Salans, was incorrectly described as "the legal adviser of the State Department." The legal adviser of the State Department at that time was Leonard Meeker; Salans was one of about fifty young attorneys who worked for Meeker. Ennes claimed in the article mentioned above that the document was prepared for Under Secretary of State Eugene V. Rostow.[30] In an interview by this author, Rostow stated that he never saw the document and pointed out that the address on the document was to code "U," which was the code for the number-two person in the State Department, Under Secretary of State Nicholas Katzenbach, not Rostow.[31]

Ennes described the document as "devastating" to the Israeli position but concedes that "The Salans report does not contain an overall conclusion as to whether the attack was deliberate."[32] This author corresponded with and interviewed Carl F. Salans in 1993. At that time Salans was practicing law in Paris with Salans, Herzfeld & Heilbronn, an international law firm with offices in London, Paris, Moscow, and New York. In a letter to this author dated March 17, 1993, Salans confirmed that he had "very little memory of my memorandum or its preparation." He did recall that he had not spoken to Clark Clifford but believed that he had seen the "Clifford Report."

The Salans document does nothing more than compare the reports of Clark Clifford, the U.S. Navy court of inquiry, and the Israeli examining judge for consistency, without comment. All three concluded that the attack was a case of mistaken identity. To the question put by this author to Salans during an interview on March 29, 1993, "Some people argue that your memo proves the attack was deliberate. Is that your interpretation?" Salans replied: "The Under Secretary asked me for an analysis, not an effort to draw any conclusion or place any blame." Furthermore, Ennes comments that "a report prepared for President Johnson by presidential advisor Clark Clifford has since vanished from government files."[33] This author located the Clifford Report, classified secret, and prevailed on an appeal of classification. The report was declassified on October 27, 1995.

The linchpin of the motive argument in the Ennes book is that Israel was trying to keep the United States from learning of its plan to attack Syria on June 9, 1967. This theory has a number of weaknesses, many the same as those of the arguments of Richard K. Smith. First, when the *Liberty* set sail for its patrol area off the Sinai, prior to the commencement of hostilities on June 5, 1967, the Gaza Strip was controlled by Egypt. The *Liberty*'s basic capability for listening extended only to the horizon (about twenty to twenty-five miles). A projection of the listening range from the *Liberty*'s patrol area out to a maximum twenty-five miles does not place the *Liberty*'s "ears" over any Israeli territory. Rather, it overlays the coastal road from Port Said, Egypt, to the Gaza Strip (see page 26). Any Israeli radio communications about Syria would have come from IDF headquarters in Tel Aviv, approximately sixty miles from the northernmost listening point of *Liberty*'s twenty-five-mile "collection zone." If by some chance the *Liberty* could have listened all the way to Tel Aviv, sixty miles to the north, or north of Tel Aviv, the question remains: Who would have done the real-time eavesdropping? The *Liberty*'s linguists were primarily Russian speakers. At Rota, Spain, the *Liberty* took on board Arabic and Russian linguists, including Marine staff sergeant Bryce F. Lockwood, but *there were no Hebrew linguists on board the ship.*[34]

But assuming that somehow the *Liberty* could or even did overhear Israeli plans to attack Syria, how big a secret was it on June 8? Israeli tanks were being withdrawn from the Sinai and transported north toward Syria on roads through Tel Aviv, within a few blocks of the American embassy. This movement had already been observed by the CIA station chief and reported to Washington.[35] Secretary of State Dean Rusk confirmed the receipt of this information to this author.[36] In his television series *Israel: A Nation Is Born,* former foreign minister Abba Eban comments on a call he received from McGeorge Bundy: "I received a call from a high U.S. official. He hinted that it would be illogical if the war were to end with the Syrians suffering no penalty for having provoked it."[37]

Another puncture to the "hide plans for the attack on Syria" theory seems to be provided by the *Times* of London of June 8, 1967. On its front page is the headline "Blow at Syria Now." The article, written by Charles Douglas-Home, told of the forthcoming attack on Syria, with a dateline of Tel Aviv, June 7, 1967, the day *before* the *Liberty* was attacked by Israel. Of course it might not have been convenient for the president of the United States to read about the "Syrian blow" secret in the London *Times.* It is perhaps for that reason the chief of intelligence of the Israel Defense Forces, Gen. Aharon Yariv, briefed Harry McPherson, President Johnson's special representative, in the presence of U.S. ambassador Walworth "Wally" Barbour hours before the attack on the *Liberty* and told them, "There still remained the Syrian problem and perhaps it would be necessary to give Syria a blow." Yariv went on to say, *"There were no ground operations in Syria yet, unfortunately"* (emphasis added).[38] It is difficult to understand why, hours before their attack on the *Liberty,* the Israelis would tell the representative of the president of the United States and the U.S. ambassador to Israel about the impending attack on Syria the following morning and then attack the USS *Liberty* just a short time later in the afternoon to prevent the United States from learning about the same impending attack.

The U.S. naval attaché in the embassy in Tel Aviv in June 1967, (then) Cdr. Ernest Castle, commented on this theory in the Thames TV documentary: "Let us presume the Israeli high command was so fearful that the United States would learn of what was an evident Israeli plan to take the Golan [Heights from Syria], or any other plan on the part of the Israelis, when they say, that will irritate the United States—our great friend—we'd better not do that, or let that happen, so let's sink their ship instead? That's how I address anyone who thinks the Israelis purposely sank [*sic*] that ship to keep us from knowing something."[39]

On the same video he said further:

Let us presume it was a premeditated plan—for whatever reason—to get rid of a United States ship that was a threat to Israel. Then the nation that had just, in 22 minutes, destroyed an entire Egyptian air force—had captured all of the Egyptian armor in the Sinai—if they had decided they had to sink a United States ship, I believe they would have done so. And I think it would have been done with *ruse de guerre,* and done during the night, so that there was never any real evidence of who had done it—if the Israelis had really wanted to sink a United States ship.

In his book Ennes concedes, in regard to the official investigations of the *Liberty* incident, "Each of the reports either concluded that the attack was probably conducted in error, or avoided making conclusions by lamely reporting that it could find no evidence that the attack was deliberate."[40] Lack of evidence is not considered a lame excuse but rather a valid reason for not finding guilt.

Furthermore, Ennes's lack of knowledge regarding naval matters and weapons makes his allegations highly questionable. In *Attack on the "Liberty,"* while discussing the reaction by the U.S. Sixth Fleet to news of the attack, he writes: "Two *nuclear armed* [emphasis added] F-4 Phantom jets left *America*'s catapults and headed almost straight up, afterburners roaring. Then two more became airborne to rendezvous with the first two, and together the four powerful jets turned towards *Liberty,* making a noise like thunder."[41]

Unfortunately for the credibility of his story, no F-4 Phantoms operated by the U.S. Navy or Marine Corps (the latter also flying from aircraft carriers) in 1967 were fitted with or wired to carry nuclear weapons. Further, a carrier commander could not launch nuclear-armed aircraft without explicit direction from the highest authority, the president, and in some special instances a theater commander, and there is no evidence that such direction was given or that any other American planes were loaded with nuclear weapons that day. The Ennes book is flawed by so many other errors of simple fact, major and minor, that it is more a product of imagination than documented research. Even statements that rely on his own firsthand experience and recollection cannot be accepted as "nothing but the truth."

Causing further harm to his credibility, in the years since the *Liberty* attack, Ennes has taken an irrationally harsh line against Israel. He has made statements such as, "The fact is Israel would have no enemies if they did not constantly raid their neighbors, steal their land, take their water and kill their children."[42] He also stated in a letter, "It is Israel that daily maims and murders an unarmed population in Palestine. It is Israel that daily bulldozes homes of suspected adolescent rock-throwers"[43]

The following is another example of how multiple contradictory stories can be created with only a slight basis in the same reality. In 1988 a U.S. naval officer assigned to the National Security Agency detachment on board the *Liberty*, Lt. Cdr. David E. Lewis, told an incredible story in a private interview with an American reporter, Dale Crowley Jr.[44] According to Lewis, Rear Adm. Lawrence Geis, the commander of the U.S. carrier task force in the Mediterranean, had told him that as soon as the *Liberty*'s calls for help were received (approximately 1410 Sinai time, 0810 Washington time EDT), Geis launched fighter-bombers to defend the *Liberty* and radioed the Pentagon of the action. Apparently, Geis chose to bypass his immediate superior, COMSIXTHLFLT, as well as CINCUSNAVEUR and USCINCEUR in the chain of command and call the Pentagon directly. Lewis then quotes Geis as saying, "A few minutes later I received a call from Secretary of Defense Robert McNamara ordering me to recall the planes because they were carrying nuclear arms." It remains unexplained why the Secretary of Defense, like Rear Admiral Geis, bypassed the chain of command and gave direct orders to a two-star rear admiral at sea.

Lewis goes on to say that Geis told him that after the recall of the first aircraft launched, he "immediately rearmed another squadron with conventional weapons, deployed it and reported to the Pentagon." Again, Admiral Geis is reported to have bypassed his chain of command and dealt directly with the Pentagon. Lewis quotes Rear Admiral Geis further as saying: "A few minutes later I got another call from McNamara ordering me to recall these planes too. I was angry and mystified and exercised my prerogative to go the next higher level of authority to have McNamara's order reversed. Seconds later President Lyndon Johnson was on the radio telephone, and I made my case to him."

Again it is hard to imagine a two-star rear admiral going over the head of Commander Sixth Fleet, Commander in Chief U.S. Naval Forces, Europe, Commander in Chief European Command, and the Joint Chiefs of Staff to deal directly with the secretary of defense on this issue, and then even going over the head of the secretary of defense, demanding to speak to the U.S. president and actually speaking to him on radio telephone. If Admiral Geis had been willing to tell his story to Commander Lewis, a subordinate and a total stranger, one might infer that he would also at least have told his wife about such an important conversation with the president. On the contrary, his widow has no recollection of ever being told by her husband of such a conversation.[45]

What also remains unexplained is the nature of these radio telephone calls between Admiral Geis in the Mediterranean and Secretary McNamara and President Johnson in Washington. In 1967, the United States did not have the ability to make a secure telephone link between Washington and a ship in the Mediterranean.

Capt. Joseph M. Tully Jr., USN (Ret.), who was commanding officer of the *Saratoga* on June 8, 1967, told this author that he was on the bridge of the *Saratoga* that day when he received word of the attack on the *Liberty*, at 1432 Sinai time. He said he tried to reach the commander of Task Force 60—that is, Rear Adm. Lawrence Geis—on board the *America*. Unable to do that, he said, he announced over voice radio that he was turning into the wind and launching his "ready group"; then between 1440 and 1450 he launched four F-4Bs, four A-4s, four A-1s, and four A-4 tankers (sixteen aircraft in ten minutes on eight minutes' notice). Captain Tully then went on to tell this author how the aircraft were immediately recalled by Admiral Geis.[46]

The records created that day, including Captain Tully's own messages released by him and sent on June 8, 1967, tell a different story. The only support for a launch from the *Saratoga* at 1440 is a log entry that states that at 1440 the *Saratoga* changed course to 315° and increased speed to twenty-five knots. The log does not reflect two launches. According to the *Saratoga* deck log, the first aircraft launched to defend the *Liberty* were launched at 1602 Sinai time, which was 1002 Washington time. The *America*'s log does not have a message indicating the exact time. However, the *America* probably launched its four F-4s slightly before the *Saratoga*.

Lewis and Tully claim the planes were launched from the *Saratoga*. Ennes claims they were launched from the *America*. Lewis and Tully claim that Admiral Geis said the aircraft were recalled by voice command of Secretary of Defense McNamara and confirmed by voice command of President Johnson, both speaking to Admiral Geis. Ennes claims the aircraft were recalled by Secretary McNamara and the Chief of Naval Operations, Adm. David McDonald, giving voice orders from the Pentagon to Commander Sixth Fleet (Admiral Martin) rather than to Admiral Geis.[47] However, McNamara was not in the Pentagon that morning during the time frame when Ennes claims McNamara called Admiral Martin.

Secretary McNamara later confirmed that he never spoke on the telephone or radio to anyone in the Sixth Fleet that day.[48] The president had called a meeting in the White House Situation Room and arrived there at 1106 Washington time, 1706 Sinai time. McNamara was already in the Situation Room. Pictures taken by the White House photographer show McNamara at the White House at times when the Ennes story places him at the Pentagon.[49]

Secretary McNamara told this author that the only order he gave to recall aircraft was issued in the Situation Room at the White House after the message from Commander Castle in Tel Aviv was received by the White House, advising that the attack on the *Liberty* had been made by Israel.[50] That was about 1125 Washington time, which was about 1725 Sinai time. At that time all aircraft had already been recalled by Vice Admiral Martin, the Sixth Fleet commander, who canceled all strikes at 1040 Washington time.

Messages sent by Admiral Martin in June 1967 flatly contradict the stories told by Lewis, Ennes, and Tully. Admiral Martin told a press conference that he did not get any instructions from Washington at any time and that he, not Tully and not Geis, ordered the *Liberty*-defense aircraft launched and recovered. He also stated that he had provided copies of every message he sent during the *Liberty* incident to his superiors, CINCUSNAVEUR and CINCEUR.[51]

The *Liberty* Veterans Association concedes that in spite of the conflicting tales of two launches of aircraft told by Ennes, Lewis, and Tully, the official position of the U.S. Navy is that there was only one launch. They also, however, imply that this official denial indicates something more insidious than a simple assessment based on established fact.[52] But all records, message traffic, and statements made at the time or immediately after the attack indicate that only one launch was made to protect the *Liberty.*

Although these stories have really nothing to do with the question of whether the Israelis attacked with knowledge that the target was a U.S. ship, they are told with great passion by conspiracy theorists, some of whom claim they prove a conspiracy to betray the United States and the *Liberty* between the president, the secretary of defense, and all the top admirals involved.[53]

At periodic intervals the commander of the Sixth Fleet was required to compile a command history and file it with the Chief of Naval Operations. Excerpts from the command history of the U.S. Sixth Fleet, declassified on September 30, 1981, confirm the launch and recall times of the aircraft launched to defend the *Liberty:*

> June 8, 1967—Communications ship *Liberty* erroneously attacked in international waters by Israeli aircraft and torpedo boats. Israel offers immediate apologies for incident. . . .
>   Pertinent message traffic can be found in Annex A. . . .

Z 081250Z JUN 67 [1450 Sinai time, 0850 Washington time]
     FM COMSIXTHFLT
TO USS SARATOGA
     USS AMERICA
INFO CTF SIX ZERO
     CTG SIX ZERO PT TWO
CONFIDENTIAL

1. America launch four armed A4's to proceed to 31-23N 33-25E to defend USS Liberty who is under attack by gun boats. Provide fighter cover and tankers. Relieve on station. Saratoga launch four armed A-1's ASAP same mission.

Z 081339Z JUN 67 [1539 Sinai time, 0939 Washington time]
     FM COMSIXTHFLT
TO USS AMERICA
     USS SARATOGA
USS LIBERTY INCIDENT

1. IAW CINCUSNAVEUR Inst PO3120.5b forces attacking Liberty are declared hostile.

2. You are authorized to use force including destruction as necessary to control the situation. Do not use more force than required. Do not pursue any unit towards land for reprisal purposes. Purpose of counterattack is to protect Liberty only.

3. Brief all pilots contents of this message. In addition brief pilots that Egyptian territorial limit only 12 miles and Liberty right on edge. Do not fly between Liberty and shoreline except as required to carry out provisions para 2 above. Brief fighter cover that any attacks on attack aircraft, Liberty, or themselves is hostile act and para two above applies. GP-4

081414Z JUN 67 [1614 Sinai time, 1014 Washington time]
     FM USADO TEL AVIV ISRAEL
TO WHITE HOUSE/OSD/CNO/DEPT STATE/COMSIXTHFLT/
CINCUSNAVEUR/JCS/DIA/USUN/CINCEUR-USEUSOM/CTG SIX
ZERO PT TWO/USAFE/CINCUSAREUR/CTG SIX
ZERO/CINCSTRIKE
     CONFIDENTIAL 0825 JUN 67
ALUSNA called to FLO to receive report. Israeli aircraft and MTB's erroneously attacked U.S. ship at 08/1200Z, position 31-25N 33-33E. Maybe Navy

ship. IDF helicopters in rescue operations. No other info. Israelis send abject apologies and request info of other US ships near war zone coasts. GP-3.

Z 081440Z JUN 67 [1640 Sinai time, 1040 Washington time]
    FM COMSIXTHFLT
TO USS AMERICA
    USS SARATOGA
CTF 60
    CTG 60.2
CONFIDENTIAL
1. Recall all strikes Repeat recall all strikes GP-3

Another problem with the Lewis story is its lack of consistency. Lewis went public with this story in 1988, many years after the event. John Borne, in his book published in 1995 (see chapter 9), quoted Lewis as the source of a different version of this story.[54] The story was also told differently by Lewis himself in a videotape produced in 1991 by Sligo Productions;[55] it was told differently once again by Lewis in the NBC video production of 1992, *The Story behind the Story.*[56]

Lewis was badly burned in the torpedo attack on the *Liberty*. His perception of events that day and during his period of recuperation has perhaps allowed imagination to fill in some of the gaps in his memory of the event and the immediate aftermath. Ennes tells his story without citation to any source, and the Tully story told twenty years later is in conflict with Tully's written records created at the time.

Lt. (now Cdr.) Maurice H. Bennett, USN (Ret.), who was a cryptographic officer attached to the NSA detachment on board the *Liberty* on the day of the attack and who was awarded the Silver Star, shared this perception:

I think that a number of us who were coming up from the torpedoed research spaces thought at first the attack was by Egypt. We at that time had no idea who to blame. I remember when the helos flew over the first time many of the people from the research spaces were cheering them on to "get" the Egyptians. It wasn't until later that we realized it was Israeli attack. Of course those on the bridge had made the identification as Israeli and knew who was attacking.[57]

The U.S. Navy recognized the heroism of the crew by awarding many individual citations as well as the highest unit award, the Presidential Unit Citation, issued for "exceptionally meritorious and heroic achievement." Communications Technician First Class Joseph Lentini was wounded in the torpedo attack. By chance he was outside the NSA compartment when the torpedo hit, killing twenty-five of his shipmates. He has said, "The best way to remember those men is the way I try to remember them every day. And every time I get a chance to voice their memory—they were serving their country and every one of them was a hero."[58]

Chapter 9

CONSPIRACY THEORIES

The conspiracy theories about the attack on the *Liberty* range from a simple rejection of the conclusion that it was a case of mistaken identity to some rather incredible theories. Some of these theories may have their genesis in the perception, wishes, or agendas of their propagators. Notwithstanding the fourteen official U.S. and Israeli investigations of the case, all of which concluded that the incident was caused by a tragic series of mistakes or that there is no evidence that the Israeli attack was not a tragic case of mistaken identity, the following assertions to the contrary have become a part of the growing *Liberty*-related literature. Is this a conscious effort to deceive the American public and U.S. decision makers? Probably not in the case of those whose own perceptions have led them to their conclusions—but probably yes in the cases of special interest groups or individuals promoting their own agendas.

Why have these stories persisted? McGeorge Bundy, President Kennedy's National Security Advisor and later chairman of a special committee in charge of the Middle East crisis appointed in June 1967 by President Johnson, provided a simple explanation: "The American people love conspiracy."[1] This is evident, for example, in some of bizarre stories still circulating over fifty years later about the 1963 assassination President John F. Kennedy and numerous other conspiracy tales that are told and retold in magazines, books, films, and elsewhere.

For patriotic Egyptians and other Arabs, it is emotionally more desirable to accept a defeat at the hands of the United States than a defeat by Israel. National pride is assuaged, even if national interests are not served by refusing to accept reality. From the point of view of the leaders of Egypt, who knew or should have known the reality, there was a political motive to maintain public support by focusing blame on an insurmountable outside entity.

On July 27, 1967, Yevgeny A. Primakov, who has a long history of favoring the Arab side of the Arab-Israeli conflict, was serving as an editor of the Communist Party newspaper *Pravda*. He published an article about the *Liberty* incident that states:

> Now it is known that among the *Liberty* crew members were superlative Arab language experts. While moving along the Sinai towards the Israeli border, they were intercepting operative communications between commanders on the Egyptian side. It was also leaked out that the *Liberty* maintained two-way communications with Israeli radio stations. It is possible that when it was necessary to cover up any evidence of U.S. espionage activity there was a scenario which was played out in the Israeli motor torpedo boat attack upon the *Liberty*, which turned out to be a tragedy for the crew of the ship. A similar version agrees that the Israeli head of government decided to mask the fact of its cooperation with the CIA by an attack on the *Liberty*; in any case, this has already been circulated in the world press.[2]

Thereafter Primakov and others wrote a book about the 1967 war entitled *The "Dove" Has Been Released*, which was printed in the Soviet Union in Russian in 1968.[3] This book claims that the United States and Israel used the *Liberty* to send false or "cooked" messages to the Egyptian forces in the Sinai, directing them to withdraw. In electronic warfare, "cooking" refers to intercepting and altering enemy messages. It can be as simple as rendering the message unintelligible so that it is of no use to the enemy or as sophisticated as altering the content of the message to affect the enemy's action in response to the message. Many of the theories of those who doubt, or do not accept, the mistaken-identity theory attribute various cooking capabilities to the Israelis. Primakov and his coauthors further allege that "in order to erase the participation of this ship in the Sinai campaign, it was necessary to stage an attack."[4]

Thus, in the Primakov story the United States was on Israel's side, actively fighting against the Arabs, and the attack on the *Liberty* was made in collusion with the United States to cover up the U.S. participation on behalf of Israel. Many Arabs interviewed by this author have heard this story and accept it as true. The Arab affection for this Soviet version of the events is further reinforced by Primakov's insistence that the Israeli victory over the Arabs was due only to assistance from the United States, Britain, and West Germany: "Newspaper reports that the U.S. and British planes participated in the raids on Arab airfields were not confirmed. But that in no way disproves the extensive indirect participation of the U.S., British and West German imperialist hordes in the Israeli venture."[5]

In an article coauthored by Primakov and published in 1968, the authors go on to claim that Israeli officers received "extensive" military training in special camps in the United States and the Federal Republic of Germany and were also trained by their participation in the fighting in Vietnam.[6] The Primakov story served the national and political interests of the Soviet Union in its quest to establish influence in the Arab world at the expense of the United States. The Primakov story is not supported by any evidence.

Another interesting cooking story has been related by Egyptian ambassador Mahmoud Kassem.[7] In this case the cooking goes one step farther, according to Ambassador Kassem, as it was not a conversation between two other parties but rather a conversation between one party, King Hussein, and the "cookers," who instantly created the responses of the purported second party, President Nasser, who was not in fact a party to the conversation at all.

Ambassador Kassem, who worked in the office of President Nasser during the 1967 war, believes that the attack on the *Liberty* was an intentional attack by Israel against a U.S. ship, because, as he claims, the *Liberty* had intercepted a telephone conversation between Jordan's King Hussein that purported to be from Egypt's President Nasser but which in reality was from the Israelis and had been cooked to mislead King Hussein into believing he was talking to President Nasser. The ambassador believes that Israel tricked King Hussein into entering the war and that Israel did not want this successful trick to be disclosed and therefore attacked the *Liberty* to prevent the disclosure.

His theory is that Israel had recorded conversations of Nasser's speeches and spliced individual words together. These words were used by the Israelis to create responses to Hussein in Nasser's voice and thus lead Hussein to believe that he was talking with Nasser, when in fact Nasser was not a part of the conversation at all.[8] Israel had developed superior electronic intelligence (ELINT) capabilities, and its abilities in 1967 far superior to the Arab ELINT capabilities. However, even with today's highly advanced, fully computerized technologies, it would be absolutely impossible to hear a statement from Hussein, decide on the response, locate and retrieve on stored audiotapes the individual words needed for the cooked response, splice them into a sentence or phrase, and then transmit them in time. Even if one could accept the notion that the Israelis were able to accomplish such a remarkable feat in 1967, how could the Israelis possibly have known that the cooked message had been intercepted by the *Liberty*?

There is another major problem with Ambassador Kassem's theory: on the relevant date, June 6, the *Liberty* had not arrived in the area. She was still two days away from the coast of the Sinai. Moreover, even if one assumes that the *Liberty* had somehow intercepted the Israeli cooked telephone conversation, why has this intercept never been leaked or disclosed in any fashion?

Ambassador Kassem told this author that he had "heard that Moshe Dayan ordered the sinking of the *Liberty*. He also said that he heard that the U.S. government had forbidden the families of the crewmen lost on the *Liberty* to conduct memorial services for them.[9] No evidence indicates any support for either of these claims.

In 1977 Anthony Pearson published a book entitled *Conspiracy of Silence*.[10] Pearson's conspiracy theory is that the Israelis deliberately attacked the *Liberty*, because Israel had demanded the withdrawal of the ship from the area and the United States had refused to move it out. Pearson first told this story in the May 1976 and June 1976 issues of *Penthouse* magazine.[11] According to Pearson, the *Liberty* arrived "off" its designated station at midday on June 5, 1967,[12] and was operating off the Sinai and passing information to the United States for several days prior to June 8, 1967. Pearson ignores the documented fact that the *Liberty* arrived on station at Point Alpha at 0849 on the morning of June 8, 1967. Also, Pearson never states specifically to whom or how the information gathered by the *Liberty* was passed, but he does state that the *Liberty* was "well out of the striking range of the Egyptian coastline" and was ordered to move closer to the Sinai coast on the morning of June 8 by a "communication."[13] He does not say from whom or how the communication was sent.

In fact, on the morning of June 8, the National Security Agency and the Joint Chiefs of Staff were trying to transmit orders to the *Liberty* directing her to stay one hundred miles clear of the combat zone. The failure of these orders to reach the *Liberty* was the subject of the House Armed Services Committee investigation of military worldwide communications in 1971.[14] Pearson makes no mention of that investigation in his book. He explains the situation in this way:

What no one knew—except those at the highest levels of the Israeli and American governments—was that Israel was violating a predetermined plan formulated by the CIA, top officials of the Johnson administration, the Israeli General Staff and leading Israeli politicians. According to the plan, Israel should have fought a contained war with the Arabs which would not have affected territorial lines between Israel and Syria and Jordan. But the *Liberty* had discovered Israel's violation or the scheme, and on the evening of June 7, the Israeli ambassador in Washington was told that the attacks had to stop. Eight hours later orders were given in Tel Aviv to destroy the ship.[15]

The core of the Pearson story is that it was the *Liberty* that "had discovered Israel's violation of the scheme" (a day before she arrived in the area) and that therefore she was ordered destroyed by the Israelis on the morning of June 7. This is curious, because on Wednesday, June 7, Israel's chief of staff, Gen. Yitzhak Rabin, publicly announced that Israel was in possession of the Sinai, Sharm el-Sheikh, Jerusalem, and the West Bank of the Jordan River.[16] In fact, hundreds, if not thousands, of newspapers around the world carried major front-page stories of the capture of the West Bank, East Jerusalem, and the Western Wall before the *Liberty* was in a position to hear anything. The validity of the Pearson story wilts on the time line, since the *Liberty* arrived off the Sinai coast about 0849 on the morning of June 8.[17] Pearson places the *Liberty* in times and places where she simply was not. For example, he places the *Liberty* at a point twenty-eight miles due northwest of Tel Aviv at 0850 on the morning of June 8, 1967. According to the *Liberty* deck log, at 0849 on that morning she turned to a westerly heading of 253° after arriving at Point Alpha, 31-27 N, 34-00 E. Her position was in fact about fifty-eight miles southwest of Tel Aviv, the closest she ever got to that city.[18] Furthermore, neither the U.S. government nor the Israelis have any record of any exchange of Pearson's alleged messages from the *Liberty* to Washington or from Washington to the *Liberty*.

By Pearson's own admission, he took on the *Liberty* story as a writing assignment for *Penthouse* "during the summer of 1975," when "he was broke" and needed money.[19] He explained: "The circumstances of the *Liberty* incident were related to me in Doha Qatar by an American film producer, Tito de Nagy Howard. I had met him early in April in the lobby of the Intercontinental Hotel in Dubai. When he discovered that I was an investigative journalist and that I was considered by the PLO [Palestine Liberation

Organization] to be pro-Palestinian, he eagerly gave me an idea to resurrect the *Liberty* incident as a whole new story."

Pearson describes Howard as "a man at war with the Israelis" who claimed to have won a court battle with the government of Israel over distribution of a documentary film and, according to Pearson, was "riding high through the Arab world on the euphoria of his legal victory." Howard is further described by Pearson as blaming "Zionist agents" for burning a nightclub he owned in an effort to bankrupt him and because he took a "radical pro-Arab stance."[20]

Pearson's book confirms his primary interest. He needed to write a story that would sell. An article or book confirming that the U.S. and Israeli official investigations were properly conducted and their conclusions were sound and that the incident had been a tragic mistake very likely would not have sold to *Penthouse* or to a book publisher looking for sensation. The Pearson story is entertaining, but it should be classified as fiction. Actually, it belongs in the "man bites dog" category of reporting.

In 1978, Richard K. Smith, a freelance aviation historian, wrote an article entitled "The Violation of the *Liberty*," which was published by the U.S. Naval Institute *Proceedings* in June of that year.[21] Smith's article provoked numerous letters to the editor of the *Proceedings* on all sides of the issue. Eighteen letters were published in the *Proceedings,* ranging from rational to highly emotional. Smith rejects the Israeli explanation that the incident was a mistake and argues that Israel attacked because

> a vital part of Israel's war plan was preventing the rest of the world from knowing about its military victories until they could be presented as a political *fait accompli.*
>
> After two or three days, this news blackout created great anxieties among the civilian population of Israel, but it was more important to keep foreign powers in the dark. The Israeli leaders feared superpower pressures for a cease-fire before they could seize the territory which they considered necessary for Israel's future security. Any instrument which sought to penetrate this smoke screen so carefully thrown around the normal "fog of war" would have to be frustrated.[22]

Smith concludes with an assessment that the Japanese were more regretful about sinking the U.S. river gunboat *Panay* (PR 5) on the Yangtze River in China in 1937 than the Israelis were about the *Liberty* incident.[23] He sums up his thesis: "If there is a timeless lesson to be relearned from the savage violation of the Liberty it is that nations do not have 'friends.' They have only interests. . . . In any given set of circumstances nations are guided to action by what they perceive to best serve their own interests."[24]

Smith does not provide evidence to support his assessment about Israeli regrets, nor does he address ample evidence to the contrary. Apparently he did not look at the message traffic generated by the incident, or he would have seen the cable from Ambassador Walworth "Wally" Barbour, stationed in Tel Aviv, to Secretary of State Rusk, that said, "Israelis obviously shocked by error and tender sincere apologies."[25] The records also contain:

- A letter of condolence from Israel's ambassador to the United States, Avraham Harman, to Secretary Rusk dated June 8, 1967
- A cable conveying condolences from Israel's minister of foreign affairs, Abba Eban, dated June 8, 1967, to Secretary Rusk
- A letter from Eban to President Johnson
- A message from Secretary Rusk dated June 8, 1967 (081815Z June 67), to the American embassy, Tel Aviv, which states, "[Harman] had learned of it [the attack] within the hour during call on Assistant Secretary [Lucius] Battle to whom he had expressed his great sorrow"
- A cable from the American embassy in Tel Aviv (number 008296, 090810Z June 67) to the U.S. secretary of state requesting that condolences of Israel's Prime Minister Levy Eshkol be transmitted to the president of the United States
- The letters of condolence sent by the ambassador of Israel to the United States to the families of those killed in the attack.[26]

At least the U.S. diplomats who met with the Israeli diplomats at the time seemed convinced of the sincerity of the latter's regrets, in clear contradistinction to Smith's assessment formed years later.

The Smith article offers no supporting evidence to establish that the attacking Israelis knew the ship was American. He reaches his conclusion by drawing an inference from his claim that the Israelis attacked to prevent the United States from learning the extent of the Israeli military success as of the afternoon of June 8, 1967. Smith ignores facts such as that, for example, there were no Hebrew-speaking personnel on board the Liberty and that thus the ship could not have provided real-time intelligence concerning Israeli military actions. Furthermore, Israel's high command headquarters was located in Tel Aviv, while its Naval Command Headquarters was located in Haifa, far north of Tel Aviv. A point farther north from where the *Liberty* actually sailed would have been a much better position for Smith's conjectured role.

However, worldwide public news on *and before* June 8 revealed the full extent of Israel's military victories, as is borne out by the front pages and headlines of U.S. and foreign newspapers, including the *Times,* London; *Le Figaro,* Paris; *Il Messaggero,* Rome; the *New York Times;* the *Wall Street Journal;* the *Washington Post;* the *Chicago Tribune;* and the *Miami Herald.* The Smith theory was best evaluated by Alfred Friendly, foreign correspondent for the *Washington Post,* who won the Pulitzer Prize for foreign reporting for his coverage of the 1967 war in Israel. In his response to the Smith article published in the U.S. Naval Institute *Proceedings,* Friendly says: "That the attack on the *Liberty* was ordered by the Israel High Command to prevent American and world knowledge of the capture of El Arish announced with fanfare in Tel Aviv more than two days before, or of further progress of the Israeli Forces to or near the Canal, also announced day by day, almost hour by hour, is a thesis that simply does not hold water."[27]

In 1980, Wilbur Eveland, a former CIA officer, published a book entitled *Ropes of Sand: America's Failure in the Middle East* that contradicts the official position of the Central Intelligence Agency set forth in its intelligence memorandum of June 13, 1967, and reconfirmed publicly many times thereafter. Eveland states that President Johnson authorized James Jesus Angleton to inform Ephraim Evron, the Israel deputy chief of mission at the Israeli embassy in Washington, that the United States would prefer that Israel lessen the tension but would not intervene to stop an attack on Egypt.[28] Eveland explains that he obtained this bit of information after he left the CIA. He states:

> Under orders from the Joint Chiefs of Staff, the USS *Liberty* was rushed to the waters off Israel's shore to permit this sophisticated communications-monitoring vessel to follow the fighting should the Israelis attack Egypt. The *Liberty* wasn't sent alone, for an even more important reason. Stationed below her was the Polaris nuclear submarine *Andrew Jackson,* for the Pentagon knew that the CIA had aided Israel in acquiring a nuclear capability. Moreover the U.S. had provided the Israelis with missiles, to which atomic warheads could be attached.[29] Thus, in case a bogged-down Israeli army decided to use ballistic missiles to win a war against the Soviet-equipped Egyptian army, the U.S. was in a position

to warn both Israel and Russia that the introduction of nuclear warfare would produce instantaneous retaliation.

. . . Message intercepts by the *Liberty* made it clear that Israel had never intended to limit its attack to Egypt. . . . *To destroy this incriminating evidence,* Moshe Dayan ordered his jets and torpedo boats to destroy the *Liberty* immediately. . . .

Then the U.S. Government shrouded the entire *Liberty* matter in secrecy under a cloak of national security considerations. . . . Why? Defense Minister Dayan had stated his government's position bluntly: unless the United States wished the Russians and Arabs to learn of joint CIA-Mossad covert operations in the Middle East and of Angleton's discussions before the 1967 fighting started, the questions of the lost American ship and how the war originated should be dropped. That ended the U.S. protestations![30]

Professional reviews of the Eveland book are critical and express doubt that he had plausible access to information to back up his "revelations." CIA director Richard Helms, referring to the Eveland book at a conference organized by Ambassador Richard B. Parker and held on the twenty-fifth anniversary of the 1967 war at the Center for the Study of Foreign Affairs of the Department of State's Foreign Service Institute in Rosslyn, Virginia, said: "Books like . . . Eveland's *Ropes of Sand,* and others: The Central Intelligence Agency has had the misfortune to have certain former employees who have written mischievous books, not necessarily based on fact, a lot of it just plain fiction."[31]

The Evans and Novak column in the *Washington Post* of November 6, 1991, included two conspiracy stories about the *Liberty* incident.[32] One involves U.S. ambassador Dwight Porter; the other relates to Seth Mintz and is discussed in chapter 10. Evans and Novak interviewed Dwight Porter, who was the ambassador to Lebanon in June 1967. That interview was by telephone and was brief. The column vividly dramatizes:

"It's an American ship!" the pilot of an Israeli Mirage fighter-bomber radioed Tel Aviv as he sighted the USS *Liberty* 15 miles off the Israeli-Egyptian coast on June 8, 1967.

The U.S. embassy in Beirut intercepted that frantic message and the reply from the Israeli Defense Forces headquarters. The decoded transmissions handed to U.S. Ambassador Dwight Porter shocked him and his staff. The reply from Tel Aviv disregarded the pilot's warning and ordered him to carry out his mission.

The column went on to say, "The remarkable intercepted radio traffic was chilling for Ambassador Porter, but he was preoccupied with official duties in Beirut. He was organizing a crisis evacuation of hundreds of U.S. citizens, including most of his own embassy personnel, as Arab militants called for throwing America out of the Mideast. He kept silent on the facts until we approached him."

Several issues emerge about the statements Evans and Novak attribute to the ambassador. First, the radio transmissions between the Israel Air Force Mirage and the Israel Air Force headquarters in Tel Aviv were by UHF radio and could only be heard in line of sight. They could not be heard over the horizon.[33]

The U.S. embassy in Beirut in 1967 was at sea level. The Mirage was off El Arish in excess of 180 miles away. If the Mirage was at an altitude of ten thousand feet, its UHF transmission could be heard at a distance of 123 miles, according to calculations based on the standard formula from the U.S. Department of Transportation publication *Instrument Flying Handbook*, which is published to advise pilots how far their transmissions on VHF/UHF radio can be heard.[34] But even if the Mirage were flying in space, like the space shuttle, at an altitude high enough for its UHF radio transmissions to be heard at sea level in Beirut, how could the embassy in Beirut have heard the response ordering the pilot to attack, which was allegedly transmitted from Israel Air Force headquarters at sea level in Tel Aviv?

A second, more important question is: Why would a distinguished professional diplomat, Ambassador Porter, disregard such important information and not disclose it to anyone in the State Department? Why would he disclose it to Evans and Novak in a brief telephone interview twenty-four years later? Finally, and strangely, the Evans and Novak column that was printed on November 6, 1991, differs substantially from the story Ambassador Porter told this author in an interview on November 21, 1991.

Ambassador Porter has a fine reputation and a distinguished career as a diplomat representing the United States. At the time of the interview with this author, he was alert and competent and authorized this authorized this author to record the interview.[35] On that tape Ambassador Porter said he had seen some transcripts of material in June 1967. He did not recall who presented the transcripts to him. He was under the impression that this event occurred on June 8, 1967, the day of the attack on the *Liberty*. He remembers reading some transcripts and then having them burned because the U.S. embassy was under siege by a street mob and the ambassador feared the mob might break into it. Contrary to the Evans and Novak column describing the data the ambassador saw as "intercepted radio traffic," Ambassador Porter confirmed to this author in a handwritten letter dated December 14, 1991, that "I certainly did not state that the interception was made by or in the Embassy."[36]

A Freedom of Information Act inquiry to the U.S. Department of State established that the day of the mob attack on the U.S. embassy in Beirut was June 6, 1967, not June 8, 1967. All this proves is that the memory of the ambassador about a very stressful event twenty-four years earlier was not perfect. This author was not privy to the telephone interview of Ambassador Porter by Evans and Novak. The information in this author's recorded interview of the ambassador and correspondence in the ambassador's own handwriting tells a quite different story from the story Evans and Novak allege he told them. This documentation, together with the physical facts relating to ability to hear UHF radio transmissions, suggests that the Evans and Novak column did not report accurately what Ambassador Porter said.[37]

In 1984, Stephen Green published *Taking Sides: Americas Secret Relations with a Militant Israel*.[38] His support for the Arab side of the Arab-Israeli conflict is well established. Green claims that the U.S. Air Force supported the Israeli war effort in 1967 with four RF-4C Phantom photo-reconnaissance aircraft.[39] The attack on the *Liberty* is described by him as an attempt to prevent the world from learning about this U.S. support through the *Liberty*'s radio intercepts.

Richard B. Parker, who in 1967 served as a political counselor at the U.S. embassy in Cairo and later as U.S. ambassador to several Arab countries,[40] examined this story in a detailed article published in 1997. This article put to rest the tale of the participation of the U.S. Air Force on Israel's side in the 1967 war.[41] One wonders: If the U.S. government was able to keep USAF participation in the 1967 war on Israel's side a secret for thirty years by telling the U.S. Air Force participants—and there had to have been quite a number of them—to keep silent, why could the U.S. government not have followed the same practice with the *Liberty* personnel? Those on board the *Liberty* who would have been privy to this knowledge were limited to NSA personnel, whose business was secrecy. Surely, they could have kept this story a secret if quite a few Air Force pilots, ground crews, and photo interpreters could do that.

If the NSA detachment on the *Liberty* or any other of the ship's crewmen had in fact learned of, let alone taken an active part in, USAF activity in the 1967 war on Israel's side and had become aware that they were attacked by Israel with the intention to suppress such information, it is very odd indeed that none of the *Liberty* survivors have come forward, in more than four decades, to tell this story. As noted, the *Liberty* survivors have been quite vocal about their own theories, but this is not one of them. If this theory is accurate, why does it have no support from the surviving victims?

According to Parker's article, former CIA director Richard Helms "categorically denied that there had been any U.S.-Israeli plot in 1967. . . . He also commented that there was no substance to the accusation contained in Stephen Green's book, *Taking Sides,* that a U.S. Reconnaissance Squadron had flown missions for Israel during the war. Neither Helms nor Robert Mc-Namara had ever heard of such missions, which would have been impossible without knowledge of either of the two."[42]

Still another approach to the *Liberty* incident was taken by Dr. John E. Borne in 1993. He became acquainted with the *Liberty* incident through the James Ennes book *Assault on the "Liberty."* He wrote a dissertation and then a book, *The USS "Liberty": Dissenting History vs. Official History.* Borne generally supports his argument that Israel attacked knowing that the target was a U.S. ship by reciting a number of unrelated anecdotes. His perception was established primarily through his study of Ennes's writings, and his dissertation relies heavily on Ennes. Borne's own research reflects little use of primary sources, and he is not especially careful with the rather limited amount of research he did perform.

For example, he states that the June 8 "Daily Diary shows a telephone call from McNamara to the president at 0838."[43] The diary does indeed report that call, except that it was not a call from McNamara to the president but from the president to McNamara.[44] The error would not seem significant except for the incredible claims that Borne then makes on the basis of the 0838 telephone call.

Borne claims that McNamara, by "personal voice order," recalled aircraft launched from the *Saratoga* at 0826 Washington time, 1426 Sinai time. First, all available evidence establishes that the earliest any aircraft could have been launched from carriers was 0850 Washington time, 1450 Sinai time. Second, there was no secure telephone link from Washington to ships in the Sixth

Fleet. The David Lewis story (see chapter 8) on which Borne relies claims that McNamara gave the recall from the White House and that it was immediately confirmed by President Johnson, while Borne places McNamara at the Pentagon at the time of the alleged "personal voice order" recall. Finally, Secretary of Defense Robert McNamara personally told this author that he never had any voice communication with anyone in the Sixth Fleet and that the only order to recall aircraft that he ever gave was from the Situation Room of the White House, after word had been received that Israel had advised the United States of its attack. The records of the message traffic and the Sixth Fleet command history confirm that all Sixth Fleet aircraft launched to protect the *Liberty* had already been recalled by Admiral Martin by the time McNamara issued his recall order at about 1125 Washington time, 1725 Sinai time. A review of the sanitized Naval Security Group file on the USS *Liberty* available from the Naval Historical Center (declassified on April 11, 1985) shows: "(C) 081415Z. LGEN [Lt. Gen.] Carter, DIRNSA, [Director of National Security Agency] telephoned Capt Cook to request that he pass by telephone to SECDEF McNamara info about the *Liberty*. . . . First attempts to reach Secretary McNamara personally by phone were unsuccessful. Capt Thomas held on the line until Secretary McNamara came to the phone at 081430Z [this is 1030 Washington time]." Borne's claim that Secretary McNamara knew about the attack on the *Liberty* at 0826 Washington time is clearly a figment of his imagination or the result of inadequate research.

In 1985, former U.S. congressman Paul Findley (R-Ill.) published *They Dare to Speak Out: People and Institutions Confront Israel's Lobby,* which in chapter 6 repeats several conspiracy theories amidst many factual inaccuracies.[45] For example, Findley states that a U.S. carrier "was only 30 minutes away . . . prepared to respond almost instantly."[46] Findley ignores the official records, which establish that the carriers were over five hundred miles away and that the first U.S. aircraft were not launched until 1602 Sinai time, more than an hour after the attack was over.

Findley was one of the first U.S. legislators to embrace the PLO and the Arab side of the Arab-Israeli conflict. His sentiments are clearly set forth in his books. Congressman Findley relied mainly on Ennes and thus generally follows the Ennes story, including the notion that the motive for the attack was to keep the secret of the impending Israeli attack on Syria. The rebuttal of the "Syrian attack secret" motive has been sufficiently discussed previously.

Without offering any source or authority for the claim, Findley asserts that CIA had learned a day before the attack that the Israelis planned to sink the ship.[47] Captain McGonagle heard this tale and was troubled by it. This author arranged a three-way telephone conversation between Captain McGonagle, this author, and the 1967 CIA chief of station at the U.S. embassy at Tel Aviv. The CIA chief of station (John Hadden) confirmed to Captain McGonagle that there was no record supporting that story and that he, who had been closely involved, knew nothing about it.

Furthermore, Congressman Findley quotes Vice Adm. Donald D. "Don" Engen, who was the captain of the carrier *America* that day: "President Johnson had very strict control. Even though we knew the *Liberty* was under attack, I couldn't just go and order a rescue."[48] Admiral Engen denied ever making that statement.[49] (Engen later confirmed his confidence in this author's research of the *Liberty* incident by a comment in his book, *Wings and Warriors*.)[50] Findley quotes Admiral Kidd as giving explicit orders: "Answer no questions. If somehow you are backed into a corner, then you may say that it was an accident and that Israel has apologized. You may say nothing else."[51] Admiral Kidd denied to this author that he ever made the quote attributed to him by Findley. Obviously, these problems call into question the entirety of Findley's work.

In 1984, Donald Neff wrote the second of his two books on the Middle East. His earlier book, *Warriors at Suez: Eisenhower Takes America into the Middle East,* had been published in 1981.[52] The second book, *Warriors for Jerusalem, The Six Days That Changed the Middle East,* deals with the *Liberty* incident.[53] Neff argues that the Israeli attack was a deliberate attack on a ship known to be American. He begins his story with some misinformation regarding a request by the *Liberty* to the Sixth Fleet for an armed escort and a reply to the request on Tuesday, June 6, 1967, "To the ship's [*Liberty*'s] request for an armed escort, Sixth Fleet commander Admiral Martin had replied: '*Liberty* is a clearly marked United States ship in international waters, not a participant in the conflict and not a reasonable subject for attack by any nation.' In the unlikely event of an attack, Admiral Martin promised, jet aircraft could be over the ship within ten minutes. The request was denied."[54]

In fact, this author has not been able to locate such a request or denial anywhere. The Russ report, which focused primarily on the message traffic involved, does not include any such messages. Neff does not provide a source other than Ennes for the denial of the *Liberty*'s request by Vice Admiral Martin. Ennes remembers such a message and in his book states that he can remember the message verbatim, but he does not provide a citation or reference. According to Ennes, the evidence is just missing.[55] If such messages had actually been exchanged, they would have been kept in the records of the Sixth Fleet commander on the cruiser *Little Rock* and very likely on other ships or shore stations, as it is customary to send copies of messages to other sites for their information, in addition to the action addressees. To arrange for such message records to vanish into thin air would have required a major conspiracy involving numerous naval personnel.

The Neff allegation suffers from yet another flaw that results from Neff's reliance on Ennes. In Neff's notes at the end of his book,[56] he confirms that he relies on a letter from Ennes that told him that "[Lt. Cdr.] Dave Lewis, who headed the SIGINT effort [on the *Liberty*], had authority to release messages without showing them to the Captain. The message was prepared by Dave and may not have been seen by McGonagle. In any case . . . the request was official, and it was scornfully declined by Admiral Martin." That Lewis had authority to release messages without showing them to the captain is probably accurate, in that Lewis could communicate with the National Security Agency about his SIGINT operations without including the ship's commanding officer in that loop. However, anyone who is familiar with U.S. naval procedures would find it very hard to believe that Lewis had "authority" to communicate with Commander McGonagle's own immediate superiors about an issue concerned with the operation and security of the ship without involving the latter.

If what Ennes wrote to Neff is true and Lewis did have such authority on June 6 to communicate directly with McGonagle's superiors, the story still falls apart, because on that date the *Liberty* was still under the command and control of Admiral McCain, Commander in Chief, U.S. Naval Forces Europe. *Liberty* did not "chop" to, or go under the command and control of, Vice Admiral Martin, the commander of the Sixth Fleet, until June 7, 1967. The idea that a subordinate cryptology officer (not a line naval officer) in the U.S. Navy would bypass the commanding officer on the ship to which his detachment was assigned, as well as Commander in Chief, U.S. Naval Forces Europe, to request assistance from a nearby fleet commander on a matter of ship's security is simply beyond belief.

For the sake of further discussion, it could be assumed that the message was sent and Vice Admiral Martin did promise jet aircraft over the ship in ten minutes. How could that have been possible? The nearest U.S. carriers would have been over five hundred miles away from *Liberty*'s assigned patrol area. The fastest U.S. jet fighter on board the carriers, the F-4B Phantom, at maximum subsonic cruise speed, would have required a minimum of sixty minutes to reach the *Liberty*. In "afterburner" mode at supersonic speed,[57] the time to target would have been twenty to thirty minutes, if they could remain supersonic that long. But in fact the aircraft could not have arrived over *Liberty*, because in afterburner they would have run out of fuel well before reaching the ship. Was Vice Admiral Martin so lacking in knowledge of the performance of his fighter planes that he promised more than he could deliver to his comrades in arms? Or is it more plausible that Ennes's memory of that message, which cannot be found anywhere, is simply not accurate?

Neff notes that when President Johnson learned of the attack on the *Liberty* he immediately advised Soviet premier Kosygin about it via the hotline. He goes on to say:

> While the Kremlin now knew about the Israeli attack on the *Liberty*, the American people did not. From the very beginning, the Johnson Administration gave every evidence of a determination to play down the attack. . . . Although there was reported skepticism that the attack was totally accidental, the inclination of the officials was to accept Israel's version since none of them could see why the Israelis would risk losing U.S. support by such a dangerous action. It may have been the result of a local trigger-happy commander, they agreed, though there was no evidence of that either. But even if that were the case, that did not amount to a hostile act ordered by the top echelons of the government.
>
> Beyond the lack of evidence, the President and his advisers were aware that they needed all the influence they could bring to bear on Israel to get it to stop fighting. A direct emotional confrontation at this time would only lessen Washington's ability to achieve a cease-fire. In the end, Clark Clifford was detailed to investigate the attack and everyone else was ordered to keep mum until his report was completed.[58]

Neff also tells a story about Israel's defense minister, Moshe Dayan, ordering the attack and repeats the theory that "Israelis do not make mistakes."[59]

While it is clearly established that President Johnson and both Secretary of State Dean Rusk and Secretary of Defense Robert McNamara were aware of Israel's impending "blow at Syria" from several sources, including having specifically advised of the plan by the chief of Israeli intelligence, Gen. Aharon Yariv, Neff turns the facts around and suggests that this "secret" was learned by the *Liberty* and provided to the United States. He does not explain how the information was passed to the United States at a time when the

Liberty was not in communication. In regard to the advance U.S. knowledge of the attack on Syria, he says: "Apparently the attack did not come as a surprise to the United States. In his memoirs, Lyndon Johnson asserted that 'we did know Israel's military intentions toward Syria' . . . could the *Liberty* have accomplished at least part of its task? Did its sensitive antennas pick up the orders for the Thursday June 9 attack on Syria and relay them to Washington?"[60]

The answer to Neff's question is no. From the various positions of the *Liberty* from the time of her arrival at Point Alpha until the time of the Israeli attack, she was far over the horizon from both Tel Aviv and Israel's Northern Command, which was responsible for the Syrian front. If somehow she could have heard transmission of orders to attack Syria, how would she have understood those orders in real time, since *Liberty* did not have any Hebrew linguists on board? It could be argued that perhaps she relayed raw data directly to NSA. But if *Liberty* had a direct communication link with NSA, why then did she not receive her stand-off orders over that same link?

Again, the United States did know of the impending attack on Syria, from several sources. For example, the CIA's June 8, 1967, intelligence memorandum, Arab-Israeli Situation Report (as of 9:00 a.m. EDT), indicates in paragraph 4 that the U.S. consul in Jerusalem on the morning of June 8, 1967, had a report of "intensive air and artillery bombardment of Syrian positions opposite the Central Demilitarized Zone . . . an apparent prelude to a large-scale attack in order to seize the heights overlooking the Israeli border."[61]

The most difficult story to believe was published in 1994 by John Loftus.[62] He had served as a U.S. Army officer and then worked in the Office of Special Investigations of the Department of Justice, whose function is to prosecute Nazi war criminals who had entered the United States illegally after World War II. His book *The Secret War against the Jews,* written with Mark Aarons, includes a chapter entitled "The *Liberty* Incident." Loftus claims that the CIA sent the *Liberty* to a position off the Sinai to spy on the Israeli forces and that the information obtained was then passed to the Egyptians via a British intelligence center in Cyprus. Loftus writes:

> Aramco and the other big players in the oil business were extremely concerned that American aid to Israel would alienate the Arab oil producers. It was not enough to withhold [U.S.] military assistance in the coming war. Everyone in the Moslem world knew that the United States was

still neutral in favor of Israel. The oil men wanted some under-the-table help for the Arabs. [This assertion is supported by his footnote 26, which reads: "Confidential interviews, former liaison to the NSA; former analyst, Naval Intelligence."]

President Lyndon Johnson had been in the "erl bidness" himself down in Texas and knew how the game was played. The oil producers got to LBJ or someone very close to him in the White House. Our sources were never able to find out who. The oil men asked if the President could throw the Arabs a bone, some sort of secret assistance that the public would never find out about but would make the Arab leadership grateful. The point was to keep the oil flowing no matter what happened in the 1967 war.

The White House approved a contingency plan to send the Arabs a little intelligence about the Israel Defense Forces.[63]

The "little intelligence" to which Loftus refers would be provided by the *Liberty*. Loftus describes the ship as having such sophisticated eavesdropping equipment that she was capable of hearing and recording every Israeli electronic transmission in the Sinai, including "intercom" transmissions inside individual tanks. This electronic bonanza was sorted out by the British in Cyprus, using massive computers, and passed to the Egyptians. Loftus claims, therefore, that in the 1967 war, on the southern-front battlefield, the United States and Great Britain were actually helping the Arabs against Israel.[64]

The allegations by Loftus that the CIA sent the *Liberty* to spy for the Egyptians, with the data being collected and passed to Cairo via a British intelligence computer base on Cyprus, began by placing the *Liberty* off the Sinai several days before she actually got there. He ascribed to the *Liberty* capabilities of listening equipment far beyond anything that the United States, or any other nation, had in the 1960s or probably would for the next decade or two. Anyone familiar with the literature on electronic intelligence (ELINT) could establish that Loftus's claims about the listening capability of the *Liberty* in 1967 are fantasy. But let us assume that the *Liberty* could have gathered electronic data from the Sinai nearly, or even completely, to the extent claimed by Loftus. How did Israel know the capabilities of the *Liberty* in June 1967? If this capability existed and Israel knew about it, what was to be gained by the Israelis attacking her as late as June 8? The battle for the Sinai was virtually over by June 7. Israeli forces had defeated the Egyptians and were mopping up in the Sinai and were in the process of securing the western bank of the Suez Canal.

Ironically, Loftus argument that the *Liberty* was involved in the 1967 war on the side of Egypt—that is, that it was fighting against Israel—would have provided a legitimate reason for Israel to attack the ship. Under the law of naval warfare, a belligerent may be attacked anywhere except in the territorial waters of a neutral nation, and a neutral aiding a belligerent is subject to the same rule.

The general thesis of the Loftus book is that intelligence organizations all over the world, throughout modem history, have conducted covert operations *against* the Jews in general and against Israel, the Jewish state, in particular. While there may be a grain of truth in some of his claims for certain organizations at specific times, and while invidious anti-Semitism is a historical fact, this author suggests that the book is far off the mark regarding the relationship in 1967 of the CIA and the Mossad, a relationship that has historically been symbiotic. Also, the *Liberty* was assigned to the National Security Agency, part of the Department of Defense. Therefore, neither the CIA nor the Navy was in control of her intelligence operations.[65] Loftus, like other writers, often confuses intelligence agencies and fails to understand their relationships, jurisdictions, and control, including their dealings with other governmental departments and agencies.

Loftus spends much of his time traveling around the United States lecturing to Jewish audiences, who are generally receptive emotionally to his thesis. Loftus tells Jewish audiences what they want to hear. While a great deal of what he says may be historically accurate, his chapter on the *Liberty* incident is neither documented nor accurate. Loftus mainly relies on the information of unidentified "old spies" and "old" or "former" intelligence officers. The only names disclosed by Loftus are of persons who are dead, and therefore it is not possible to corroborate what Loftus attributes to them. His theory on the attack on the *Liberty* is far from persuasive.

In 1980 James "Jim" Taylor privately published *Pearl Harbor II*. Taylor makes it immediately and abundantly clear that he is opposed to Zionism. The first seventy pages of his book are a tirade against Zionism. The *Liberty* is rarely mentioned. No research or new evidence is presented on the *Liberty* incident. He cites portions of the record of the U.S. Navy court of inquiry, which *do not* support his thesis. Material from the court of inquiry record that flatly contradicts his thesis is omitted.[66]

The highest-ranking U.S. military officer to reject the Israeli explanation of the *Liberty* attack was Adm. Thomas H. Moorer, a hero of World War II, who served as chairman of the Joint Chiefs of Staff from 1970 to 1974. When the

Liberty incident occurred, he was not directly in the loop. He became Chief of Naval Operations (CNO) on August 1, 1967. He had no personal knowledge of the incident, but he has a strong emotional attachment to the victims of the attack. Admiral Moorer knew Lt. Steven Toth personally as the son of Capt. Joseph Toth, who had been at the U.S. Naval Academy while Moorer was there.

Admiral Moorer has maintained the notion that the first aircraft launched from the carrier *Saratoga* were armed with nuclear weapons, as claimed by James Ennes and some other sources.[67] All available evidence points to the contrary.[68] Moorer says that he refuses "to swallow" the Israeli story. His main argument is that the *Liberty* was the ugliest ship in the U.S. Navy and that an attacking pilot had to recognize it as the U.S. Navy's *Liberty* and could not confuse it with an Egyptian ship.

This author respectfully acknowledges that Admiral Moorer, with his special knowledge of U.S. ships and his naval flying experience, probably would have recognized the *Liberty* from the air.[69] However, the CIA report differs from the admiral's assessment and specifically states that the *Liberty* could have been mistaken for the Egyptian ship *El Quseir*.[70] Admiral Moorer does not explain why Israel Air Force pilots, whose experience in naval matters was virtually nonexistent, should have been expert in U.S. ship identification. The history of Israeli naval aviation combat prior to the 1967 war was quite limited. For example, during the 1956 Sinai campaign, two Israel Ouragon jets strafed the Egyptian destroyer *Ibrahim Al-Awwal* near Haifa, and Israel Air Force colonel Danny Shapira led an attack by a flight of four Mystère aircraft against the British destroyer HMS *Crane* in the Red Sea, upon the mistaken assumption that the *Crane* was an Egyptian warship.

What little knowledge of warships they had was focused on the ships of navies of Arab countries with which Israel was at war. In fact, if they had been able to distinguish the antennae array, they would have been far more likely to have identified the *Liberty* as a Soviet intelligence collector, since there were several Soviet intelligence collectors operating in the eastern Mediterranean and no U.S. warship had visited an Israeli port in several years.[71]

The Israeli pilots of Royal Flight and the chief air controller recognized a problem after only ten to twelve minutes and terminated the air attack. Ultimately, the recognition had nothing to do with the beauty or ugliness of the ship but rather with its conduct during the attack—that is, she was not shooting back. Royal Flight leader identified *Liberty* as not being an Arab warship by her hull markings "GTR 5," not by her multiple antennas, her lack of beauty, or U.S. flag.

Admiral Moorer told this author that when he was Chief of Naval Operations, he did not talk one-on-one with the president or the secretaries of state or defense and never discussed the *Liberty* incident with them. (As CNO he did attend meetings, along with other senior officers and service chiefs, with the president and the secretary of defense once or twice a year.)[72] He was quoted by Jim Anderson in a United Press International article dated December 12, 1985: "Moorer, who was not in a position of command during the *Liberty* attack, told the news conference he did not investigate it when he became head of the Joint Chiefs because it was during the Vietnam war 'and I was concerned with what was about to happen, not what had happened.'" His position of "not swallowing" the Israeli story developed years later. Notwithstanding Admiral Moorer's eventual position of refusing to accept the explanation that the attack was a mistake, he apparently swallowed it when he was Chief of Naval Operations. The final endorsement on the U.S. Navy court of inquiry proceedings concluding that the attack was a tragic mistake was approved by his office on March 25, 1968.

It should always be understood that while in many instances perception is more important than reality, in most instances perception is not synonymous with reality. Thus different conspiracy theories, for the most part, focus on the notion that the Israeli attack was intended to keep the *Liberty* from discovering the military intentions or activities of Israel. The common threads in all these accounts tend to be: (1) a total and absolute disregard for all fourteen official U.S. and Israeli inquiries, and (2) disregard for facts when the facts disagree with the conspiracy theory. As Professor Dan Schueftan points out:

> Beyond the detailed and well substantiated macrodata, the *Liberty* conspiracy theory is fundamentally flawed in the macro perspective, since it disregards the political strategy of the Israeli decision makers at that time.
>
> In the summer of 1967 the Israel leadership considered American goodwill towards Israel to be its supreme political interest, second only to Israel's existence. The bitter lesson of the Sinai Campaign of 1956 and its aftermath in 1957, when Israel was forced to withdraw by American and Soviet pressure was only too vivid. In 1967 Israel could not risk another political defeat to follow her military victory. To preserve this goodwill, Israel waited for three weeks for an American approval before launching the war, even though Israel believed that her very existence was at stake. The Israeli leaders knew that only American support could

give their political strategy a chance to work to trade the territorial and strategic assets of the war for a lasting political settlement that would secure Israel's future in the region.

By June 8, the Israeli success in defeating the Egyptian threat had already manifested itself. To suggest that Israel would risk the fruits of her military victory by purposely attacking an American surveillance ship and killing US personnel indicates a total failure to understand the overall picture of the "Six Day War." None of the dubious theories presented to date offer a motivation for the attack on the *Liberty* that could be vital enough to override these considerations.

To suggest that Israel attacked the *Liberty* to keep the US in the dark about the offensive in the Golan is to assume that Israel was prepared to revert to the 1956 pattern, after it endangered its very existence for three weeks before the war to avoid just that. To suggest that it was done to cover up a major atrocity that did not even happen, hardly deserves a serious response. To suggest that such a major decision could be taken on a level lower than the Prime Minister or Minister of Defense is to ignore the way the Israeli Defense Force worked at the time (and still works today). Finally, an experienced student of Israeli media and political practices would know that if there were a grain of truth in these conspiracy theories, that truth would have surfaced in Israel long ago.[73]

Chapter 10

TALL TALES VS. REALITY

In 1984 Seth Mintz told a story to a *Liberty* crew member that caught the attention of the *Liberty* Veterans Association. According to his story, Mintz had been an intelligence officer in the Israel Defense Forces during June 1967, sitting quietly in the "Israeli War Room," where he saw and heard unidentified Israeli officers examine aerial photographs of the USS *Liberty* and then, with full knowledge that the *Liberty* was flying the U.S. flag, order the attack on the *Liberty*. The *Liberty* Veterans Association newsletter carried an item with the headline "An Israeli Major Speaks Up":

> In January, one of our shipmates was approached by a man claiming to be a former Israeli major who had observed the attack from the Israeli war room. "The business about no flag flying is a lie," the man said. "We could hear the pilots reporting during the attack that the ship flew an American flag." . . . The man does claim that Embassy officials were asked to move the ship away from the Israeli coast, and he claims that U.S. Embassy officials insisted that there were no American ships in the area.[1]

A more detailed variation on this story had been printed several weeks before by United Press International, dated March 18, 1984. The article does not mention Mintz by name but indicates that his name is known to UPI and to author Stephen Green. Green wrote about the *Liberty* incident in his 1984 book *Taking Sides*. Green does not mention Mintz or this story in his book, although he interviewed Mintz by telephone in two calls. Green passed his notes of this interview to Rich Bonin, an associate producer of the CBS News program *60 Minutes*. *60 Minutes* sent a crew to Maine to tape an interview with Mintz. It was never aired on *60 Minutes*. Bonin passed the notes to the research editor of the Thames TV production *Attack on the "Liberty,"* Adrian Pennink, who interviewed Mintz but did not use the Mintz story in the Thames TV production.

Pennink's notes of the Mintz interview contain a number of assertions made by Mintz that certainly raise questions about his credibility. Mintz told Pennink that "there were three attempts to contact the U.S. Embassy about the ship. He also remembers a phone call that Beni Moti made to the Military Attache at 9:00 a.m. in the morning." While there is some dispute about whether the IDF ever contacted the U.S. embassy to inquire about U.S. ships in the area, the call at 9:00 a.m. was just a few minutes after the *Liberty* arrived at Point Alpha. The air attack began just before 2:00 p.m. Did Mintz sit in the war room unnoticed for five hours? Mintz "remembers seeing the *Liberty* marker on their operation board stay throughout the day. It was not removed." All available evidence establishes that the wedge representing the *Liberty* was on the sea plot at naval headquarters at Stella Maris, Haifa. There was no ship plot at air force or army headquarters in Tel Aviv. Mintz said he heard "reports coming through the loud speakers from the pilots attacking the ship." The Israel Air Force has transcribed and translated the pilot and controller communications available. The tapes do not support the Mintz claims. Finally, Mintz "cannot remember exactly where Southern Command is but said he could easily find it were he in Tel Aviv." In 1967 the high commands of the air force and army were in Tel Aviv. (The Israel Air Force Command Center was not at all like Mintz's description of it.) Southern Command was with Maj. Gen. Yeshayahu "Sheike" Gavish on an armored personnel carrier moving through the Sinai toward the Suez Canal. It is suggested that these were sufficient reasons for Thames TV to reject Mintz's tale.[2]

Mintz was back in public view in 1991 when he was interviewed over the telephone for about fifteen minutes in connection with a column by Roland Evans and Robert Novak. The column, which appeared in the *Washington Post* on November 6, 1991, states:

American-born Israeli Maj. Seth Mintz, who was present in IDF headquarters for several hours before the Mirage fighter-bomber radioed that the ship he had been sent to attack was American. Mintz had been allowed to accompany his friend and mentor Gen. Benni Matti,[3] into the "war room"—a [highly classified] secure headquarters in Tel Aviv. As the minutes went by, he told us, the mood took a definitive turn from doubt to certainty as to the ship's identity. "They were discussing photographs of a ship that they thought was American," Mintz told us by telephone from his home in Houlton, Maine. "No one wanted to take responsibility."

He said the photos were sent to the U.S. embassy in Tel Aviv for identification. The embassy said it knew of no American ship in that part of the Eastern Mediterranean—a lie following the precepts of the intelligence game. IDF officers studied *Jane's Fighting Ships,* Mintz told us, and "everyone felt it was an American ship and that it was the *Liberty.* . . . There were comments about the markings, about the flag. Everybody in that room was convinced it was an American ship."

Mintz said the order to sink the ship came not from the war room but from superior officers. Immediately thereafter, Mintz said many Israeli officers "had doubts whether they had done the right thing." As for himself, Mintz told us: "The Israelis were guilty of an outrage, but the American refusal to admit the *Liberty* was there helped precipitate the outrage."[4]

The Evans and Novak column did not go unchallenged. Two days later, on November 8, 1991, senior *New York Times* editorial writer A. M. Rosenthal published an op-ed piece in the *New York Times* entitled "Anatomy of a Scoop." Regarding the portion of the Evans and Novak column relating to Mintz, Rosenthal had this to say:

> Evans-Novak reported that an American who was then an Israeli major was in the Israeli Defense Forces headquarters in Tel Aviv that day and corroborates "evidence that the Israelis were well aware that they were attacking an American ship."
>
> Like hell he does.
>
> Evans-Novak said their "eyewitness" was Seth Mintz, now a salesman of chemicals in Houlton, ME. When I called him, expecting a confirmation of hard reporting, I got a furious denial that he had ever "corroborated" that the Israelis knew. He said he told the reverse to Mr. Evans.[5]

The next day the *Washington Post* carried a letter to the editor signed by Seth Mintz of Houlton, Maine, and captioned "Attack on the *Liberty:* A Tragic Mistake." Mintz claims that Evans and Novak misquoted him. He says they changed the order of events and took his answers out of context. His letter concludes:

Finally, the columnists quote me as saying that the Israelis "had doubts whether they had done the right thing" as if I was referring to a deliberate attack on an American ship when, in fact, I was talking about uncertainty regarding the ship's identity that lingered among some of the officers, even after the embassy's second denial.

The *Liberty* incident was a terrible human tragedy. There is no excuse for using it to fan hatred through distortions and misrepresentations.[6]

Evans and Novak defended their original column in an article in the *Washington Post* on November 11, 1991, explaining that Mintz was now denying what he had told them because he was afraid "that he might be in danger." The column states, "Mintz told an Israeli newspaper that he doesn't need the Mossad and Shin Bet knocking at his door."[7] The column further confirms that the telephone call to Mintz from Evans occurred on October 22 and that Mintz "spoke to us for more than 15 minutes."[8]

The last word in this war of columnists was written by Hirsh Goodman, editor of the *Jerusalem Report,* whose column "The Last Word" was published on November 21, 1991. Titled "Messrs. Errors and No Facts," Goodman's column takes the Evans and Novak article apart, line by line, and chides the columnists for omitting much significant data and for relying on the Mintz story, because the story does not make sense and "was less than convincing."[9]

Seth Mintz has told a number of conflicting stories about what he knows of the *Liberty* incident. He first claimed in his story carried by the *Liberty* veterans newsletter to have been a major in the Israel Army, assigned to intelligence, and to have been in the Israeli military command center in Tel Aviv on June 8, 1967. Mintz's story was that he went to Israel as an American Jew at the age of fifteen and a half and spent some time on a kibbutz, which he identified as Kibbutz Magen. He told Adrian Pennink, the research editor for the Thames TV production on the *Liberty,* that the kibbutz was "located in the Negev on the Gaza Strip." There is indeed a Kibbutz Magen (which is the Hebrew word for shield) located in the Negev near a more famous kibbutz, Yad Mordechai. On June 20, 2001, at the request of this author, a representative of Israel TV Channel 1 contacted Kibbutz Magen and was advised by telephone that in November 1963 an adult male named Seth Mintz came to the kibbutz. He was not fifteen and a half years old, as Mintz told Adrian Pennink, but old enough to marry, and in fact he married a woman named Karen. They left the kibbutz together in September 1964 and were not heard from again. The kibbutz representative also stated that there was no important or well-known IDF general from the kibbutz during the 1963–67 time frame.

This is significant because Mintz claims to have been befriended by a senior Israeli general whom he identified as his "kibbutz father" and whose name he could not exactly recall in his earlier stories and to whom he did not refer at all in his interview with author Stephen Green.[10] He did, however, identify the general to Adrian Pennink as Benni Moti, and later as Gen. Benni Matti in the Evans and Novak article. Concerning Gen. Benni Matti, Goodman writes in his article, "There has never been such a person in the Israeli Army."[11] There is a well-known Israeli general named Daniel "Danny" Matt, but when he was asked by this author whether he was the kibbutz father or a friend of Mintz or Dagan, the alias Mintz claimed he used when he joined the IDF, the general replied that he was not and that he had never heard of Mintz or Dagan.[12]

Mintz claims he enlisted in the Israel Army under the pseudonym "Giora Dagan," in order to prevent loss of his U.S. citizenship. He claims his IDF serial number was 968409. He has not been able or willing to identify to Adrian Pennink anyone in Israel who can corroborate his story or who knew him during his five-year sojourn there prior to 1967. Pennink's notes reflect that Mintz did not have a stamped passport to establish that he ever traveled to Israel and did not have any other documentation to support his other claims. Col. Raanan Gissin, deputy spokesman of the Israel Defense Forces, researched the IDF personnel records looking for a Giora Dagan, IDF serial number 968409, and for Seth Mintz. Gissin found no record of Seth Mintz. He did, however, find there was a Giora Dagan with that serial number in the Israel Army in 1967, but Dagan was neither a major nor an intelligence officer. Dagan was a driver in a motor pool. The possibility that a motor pool driver had access to the air force command post during the 1967 war is very remote, to say the least. It is even less plausible that while just "sitting around" the command post Mintz saw Israel Air Force officers receive aerial reconnaissance photographs of the *Liberty* with the U.S. flag clearly visible, as he claims. Although Mintz claims to have heard them discuss the flag and to have heard them call the U.S. embassy and ask if the ship was American, the U.S. embassy has no record of such a call. According to Mintz, after a person at the U.S. embassy, whom he does not identify, advised the Israel Air Force officers that the ship was not American, Mintz heard them order the attack.

After "An Israeli Major Speaks Up" was published in the *Liberty* veterans newsletter of May 1984,[13] Richard Bonin, an associate producer of the CBS Television program *60 Minutes,* sent a television crew to Maine to interview Mintz on videotape for a *60 Minutes* segment. The producer told this author that he was not satisfied with Mintz's credibility and dropped the story.

When a Thames TV team arrived in Washington, D.C., to begin shooting the documentary *Attack on the "Liberty,"* Bonin passed the story to his friend Adrian Pennink, the research editor for the Thames production. According to Bonin, the Thames TV production team hired David Walsh, a "pro-conspiracy" public relations person in Washington, to assist them, and he put them in touch with both Seth Mintz and Stephen Green. Pennink brought Mintz and his wife, Barbara, to Washington and interviewed him but, like Bonin, did not find his story credible and did not include it in the Thames documentary.[14] Mintz also gave author Stephen Green a couple of telephone interviews, in which he told a similar story except that he placed the *Liberty* off the Sinai on the evening before the *Liberty* arrived there. Perhaps Mintz had read the Pearson stories.[15] In any event, Green apparently was not impressed with Mintz's story, because when Green published *Taking Sides,*[16] the Mintz story was not included. Of course the story Mintz told Green is quite different from the story Green told in his book as to the reason for the attack, which Green claims was to cover up U.S. Air Force assistance immediately prior to the war.

Mintz declined to be interviewed by this author.[17] But Mintz appeared live on camera in 1992 on the television NBC program *The Story behind the Story*. On this occasion his story, as broadcast, was again different from his prior tales. There was no mention of his earlier claim that he had been an Israeli intelligence officer. He was described by Richard Kiley, the narrator, as a twenty-year-old soldier in the Israeli army, visiting a family friend at the air force control center in Tel Aviv. He said there was no doubt among the Israelis that the ship was American and that sets of pictures of the *Liberty* were sent to the U.S. embassy, where the U.S. denied the ship was an American ship. (In prior stories he had said the embassy was contacted by telephone. Because he did not go to the embassy, it is not clear how he knew the embassy's reply.) He concluded his TV appearance with a somewhat convoluted statement of why the Israelis decided to attack. In his own words: "The Israelis were convinced that if the Americans weren't willing to acknowledge the existence of their own ship . . . the possibility, no matter how remote it was, existed that it was in fact not an American ship."[18]

Mintz is an enigma regarding the *Liberty* incident. In view of the many different versions of his story, it is clear that he is not reflecting a consistent, single perception; yet it is difficult to identify a special interest as the basis of, or motive for, his stories. Whether Dagan was Mintz is not certain. The fact that neither Mintz nor Dagan was an intelligence officer is clear. Also, Mintz's description of the "War Room" and its location is not accurate. His motives and objectives remain unknown. For a short time, "Major Mintz" was the darling of some of the conspiracy theorists. His letter in the *Washington Post* probably chilled that relationship. Rich Bonin, the CBS *60 Minutes* producer who rejected the Mintz story as not credible, commented to this author, "Mintz is a troubled soul."[19]

Adrian Pennink's research for the Thames TV production *Attack on the "Liberty"* unearthed an additional story. Pennink interviewed former congressman Paul N. "Pete" McCloskey, who told Pennink that he had visited an Israeli in a federal prison in Springfield, Missouri. McCloskey claimed that the prisoner, a certain Amnon Tavni, told him that he was an Israeli pilot who flew against the *Liberty* and that he had a clear identification of the *Liberty* as a U.S. ship when he made the attack.

Pennink called Tavni in prison, but Tavni told Pennink that he had never made such a statement to Congressman McCloskey. Pennink learned the name of Tavni's former girlfriend in New York and interviewed her. She stated to Pennink that Tavni had told her he served in the IDF but never mentioned being a pilot. The IDF spokesman could not find a record of Tavni as a pilot in the Israel Air Force nor as a member of any branch of the IDF.[20]

The Medical Center for Federal Prisoners at Springfield, Missouri,[21] confirmed to this author that Amnon Tavni, prisoner number 05818–054, was convicted in federal court for the Southern District of New York of robbery and conspiracy to rob a bank. He was sentenced to ten years in prison by U.S. District Judge Thomas P. Griesa.[22] Records indicate that Tavni entered prison on April 26, 1984, and served thirty months and twenty-five days. He was paroled on November 19, 1986, and returned to New York, where parole office records indicate he was deported to Israel in December 1986. Recent efforts by this author to locate Tavni in Israel have not been successful. This author has learned that after Tavni was deported to Israel in 1986, he changed his name and so cannot be located.[23]

Four Israel Air Force pilots were involved in the air attacks on the *Liberty*. Yaacov Hamermish, the pilot who flew as wingman in Royal Flight, died in a plane crash prior to 1979 while practicing for an air show.[24] Royal Flight leader, whose name is not to be disclosed, died in 2009. The two surviving pilots, who live in Israel, flew as *Kursa* wingman[25] and *Kursa* Flight leader.[26] *Kursa* Flight leader has since come out and has been identified as Brig. Gen. Iftach Spector, one of the Israel Air Force's top aces. No Israel Air Force record identifies a pilot who participated in the air attack named Amnon Tavni. Either Tavni or Pennink or McCloskey told a tall tale. It is also possible, of course, that Tavni told two different stories, one to McCloskey and another to Pennink. All things considered, the Pennink story is more believable, because Pennink "had no dog in this fight, while McCloskey has had a well-known aversion/opposition to Israel."

An even more fascinating story surfaced in July 1997, when the *Orlando Sentinel* printed a "My Word" column by Ronald M. Wade of Rockwell, Texas, entitled "Israel Should Own Up to the Truth about the *Liberty*." Wade wrote that he had worked in the engineering department of E-Systems Inc., a company that designed the data-collection systems installed in both the *Liberty* and the *Pueblo*. The most interesting part of the column stated:

> Among the Israelis assigned to our facility to oversee that contract [for the installation of surveillance systems in Israeli aircraft in Texas during the 1970s] was the airman who had been radar officer on the aircraft that had led the machine gun, rocket, and napalm attack on the *Liberty*.[27]
>
> In private conversations, he acknowledged that the attack had been well planned in advance and was broken off only when Israeli listening posts picked up radio transmissions from American carrier-based fighter aircraft coming to the *Liberty*'s aid.

It is interesting to note that Wade does not make clear whether he was a party to the "private conversations" and his information is firsthand or whether the "private conversations" were repeated to him and his information is hearsay. While the *Orlando Sentinel* did not provide the name of the Israel radar officer, Wade subsequently did. Ronald Wade amplified his earlier story in the *Intelligencer: The Journal of U.S. Intelligence Studies* (December 1999, p. 26) by including the name of the Israeli radar officer. The letter then appeared on the Internet on Saturday, January 8, 2000. "One of the Israeli officers assigned to monitor the program was Yohanan Levanon. One day when the subject of the *Liberty* came up, Levanon told a small group that he himself had been radar officer on the lead attack aircraft that strafed and napalmed the *Liberty*. He confided that the attack was well planned and coordinated with naval forces in advance."[28] Again Wade did not make it clear whether he was one of the "small group" or whether he was told second hand what Levanon allegedly told the small group.

Yohanan Levanon was an officer in the Israel Air Force with a specialty in electronics.[29] In a telephone interview with this author he stated that he did not fly at all during the 1967 war. He did fly as a nonpilot flight officer in Vautour aircraft after the Six Day War. He retired as a lieutenant colonel and, as a civilian electronics expert, was posted to E-Systems in Greenville, Texas. He spent considerable time in the United States, including a long stay in the burn center of a hospital in Albuquerque, New Mexico, as a result of serious injury in the crash of a civil aircraft. He currently resides in Israel. When furnished with both the *Orlando Sentinel* article and Ron Wade's Internet item, Levanon responded by sending an e-mail directly to Wade that read:

> Mr. Wade, I recently read your fax to a Mr. Anderson (date unknown) in which my name and my comments about the attack on the *Liberty* ship were mentioned.
>
> Yes, I was shown photographs of the damage done on the *Liberty* ship by one of the E-Systems engineers and in the conversation that followed I stated that I have a first hand information that the Israeli AF attack on the *Liberty* was by mistake. On the late afternoon of the attack while I was talking with Gen. Hod, the Israeli AF commander, two Israeli AF intelligence officers approached him and told him that the assumed Egyptian ship that was attacked was an American one, his reaction and sorrow were unmistakable.
>
> These were my words at that time and later on when I was approached about this subject. You misquoted me, actually inverted my words and that is as close as I can come to being politically correct. Were you really Director of Ethics for seventeen years?
>
> I did not fly during the 1967 war. While at E-Systems, I was employed by the company as a Senior Project Engineer and already retired from the Israeli AF therefore not a monitoring officer as you wrote.
>
> Yohanan Levanon[30]

Ron Wade responded by e-mail to Levanon's message with an admission that he never heard Levanon speak about the *Liberty* and that his source was hearsay from another person at E-Systems. He apologized to Levanon on March 18, 2000, by e-mail:

Dear Mr. Levanon:

The story I passed on concerning the subject of your 3/17 e-mail was related to me by a close friend whose veracity I had no reason to doubt. I did not claim I was present at the conversation but that the information was given to a small group by you. If this information is incorrect or if I was misinformed, please accept my sincerest apology. If you are innocent of association with the *Liberty* attack, we both have been victimized.

Ronald Wade[31]

In 1982, author James Bamford, in his book about the National Security Agency, *The Puzzle Palace,* described the attack on the *Liberty* as an attack on a ship known to be U.S., carried out because the Israelis did not want the United States to know that they were going to attack Syria. When interviewed by this author, Bamford made it quite clear that he was very sympathetic to the *Liberty* crewmen and that he had an intense dislike of Israel.[32] When the "Syrian attack secret" was effectively discredited by this author, by disclosure of the U.S. State Department cable from the U.S. ambassador in Tel Aviv to the secretary of state, another conspiracy theorist, John Borne, was quoted in the *Rutland (Vt.) Herald:*

> John Borne, a New York University adjunct professor of history who also wrote a dissertation on the *Liberty* and believes the attack on the U.S. ship was intentional, nonetheless agrees with Cristol that a clear motive is tough to pin down. "I mean if the ambassador is sending this message, there's no point in attacking the ship to prevent the ship from sending the message," Borne says. He says the crew will need to find "another motive, if they are ever able to prove their case."[33]

James Bamford produced such a motive in his book *Body of Secrets.*[34] Bamford reports that the motive for the attack was an effort by the Israelis to keep the *Liberty* from learning of war crimes and atrocities being committed at El Arish. There is no independent confirmation that Israel perpetrated the war crimes at El Arish. Yet, Bamford claims that, "[the NSA via the *Liberty*] recorded evidence of the numerous atrocities committed that morning only a few miles away [at El Arish]."[35] Bamford does not explain how electronic surveillance equipment could record evidence of war crimes being committed. Bamford also fails to explain why the evidence of these war crimes was not recorded by the Navy EC-121 aircraft or, if such evidence was recorded, why none of the Hebrew linguists who heard the transmissions on board that aircraft or later listened to the tapes at NSA headquarters ever mentioned it to anyone. The material provided to Bamford by one such Hebrew linguist is totally devoid of any mention of such evidence of war crimes.

In chapter 7 of his book, Bamford discloses the existence of tape recordings of the entire attack made by a Navy EC-121 electronic surveillance airplane that was flying high above the Mediterranean within line-of-sight reception of the Israeli airplanes attacking the *Liberty*. Bamford claims the information on these tapes proves that the attack was an attack on a ship the Israelis knew to be American. He claims that these tapes are among the "deepest darkest secrets" of the NSA. His source for this information is a retired U.S. Navy officer, Marvin Nowicki,[36] a Russian-Hebrew linguist who was on the EC-121 as it flew overhead near the site of the attack and who supervised the surveillance and recording of the attack. Following his retirement from the Navy, Nowicki earned a doctorate and became a professor and a Fulbright scholar.

Bamford claims that Nowicki told him that the Israeli radio transmissions that Nowicki had heard and that the EC-121 NSA crew recorded prove the attack was an Israeli attack on a ship known to be American. The NSA has never admitted publicly that such tapes ever existed. Whatever the EC-121 tapes ultimately prove, if they are ever released, the data provided to Bamford by Nowicki in an e-mail dated March 3, 2000, effectively destroys Bamford's credibility. Nowicki tells a not only interesting but very credible story about the event being recorded by the EC-121 for the NSA. Nowicki told Bamford exactly the opposite of what Bamford speculates in his book. The classic reason that courts do not allow hearsay evidence is that all too often the relator of hearsay, as in this case, tells a story that is quite different from the story told by the source.

The National Security Agency adds its comment on Bamford's credibility in their press release stating, "*Mr. Bamford's claim that the NSA leadership was 'virtually unanimous in their belief that the attack was deliberate' is simply not true.*"[37]

Bamford quotes Nowicki on four different pages of *Body of Secrets* in support of his argument that Israel attacked a ship it knew to be a U.S. ship.[38] The quotes of Nowicki are presented out of context in an ambiguous and broken narrative. Bamford presents no new evidence, although he leads his readers to believe that on the basis of what Nowicki told him, he has new evidence that the attack was made by the Israelis on a ship they knew to be American. A comparison of what Bamford attributed to Nowicki and what Nowicki actually told Bamford should give readers a better yardstick by which to evaluate the *Body of Secrets* claim. The Nowicki letter of March 3, 2000, to James Bamford states:

Dear Jim,

As a followup to our e-mail and telephone exchanges, I am enclosing sensitive information about U.S. intelligence collection techniques that I engaged in during a career in the U.S. Navy spanning over 20 years. Like you, l am interested in preserving certain historical events surrounding SIGINT collection. I believe it is important that future generations understand and appreciate the efforts of the Cold War warriors.

In this correspondence, I am concentrating on a single event that involved the USS *Liberty* in June 1967. As you know, Jim Ennes and members of the *Liberty* crew are on record stating the ship was deliberately attacked by the Israelis. I think otherwise. I have first hand information, which I am sharing with you. I was present on that day, along with members of an aircrew in a COMFAIRAIRRECONRON [Commander Fleet Air Force Air Reconnaissance Squadron] TWO (VQ-2) EC-121M aircraft flying some 15,000 feet above the incident. As I recall, we recorded most, if not all, of the attack. Further, our intercepts, never before made public, showed the attack to be *an accident on the part of the Israelis* [emphasis added].

To support my claim, I am forwarding four enclosures of information. My story is over 30 years old but there are certain events that are embedded in my memory, including a scary night flight into the battle zone and the attack on the *Liberty*. Enclosure (I) begins with a narrative entitled, "Assault on the *Liberty*: The untold story from SIGINT." Enclosure (2) provides a postscript to the attack in the years that followed. Enclosure (3) gives my views of additional evidence of a *mistaken attack by the Israelis* [emphasis added], contradicting Jim Ennes in his book. Enclosure (4) discusses Ennes' cover-up conundrum, asks who was ultimately responsible, and why the presence of our VQ mission was never revealed.

In addition, I am enclosing personal information about my 24-year career in the Naval Security Group. I am doing this for the purpose of helping you see how I might assist you with other aspects of your historical account of SIGINT. You may, for example, be interested in stories how we hunted Soviet TU-95 Bears [Soviet turbo prop reconnaissance aircraft] in the Atlantic and searched for SA-2 [missile] sites in southern Algeria during flights into the Sahara. A chronology of my duty stations and professional experience is found in Enclosure (5).

Finally, on a cautionary note I would appreciate it if you would cull any information that crosses the bar of national security, in addition to the names of colleagues cited herein. I do not have permission to use their names. If you have any questions or need clarification, please do not hesitate to contact me. Thank you and good luck with your book.

Sincerely,
Marvin E. Nowicki, Ph.D.[39]

The five enclosures to the Nowicki letter may be viewed on the Internet at www.thelibertyincident.com. Nowicki's letter to the *Wall Street Journal* confirming his rejection of Bamford's story was published on May 16, 2001 (p. A23).

How Bamford, a professional writer and researcher, could read Nowicki's letter and its enclosures and conclude Nowicki was telling him that the NSA tapes proved the attack was intentional staggers the imagination. James Bamford has never heard the tapes. Since his knowledge of their existence came exclusively from what Nowicki wrote him, the question is, did Bamford accurately report what Nowicki told him? Thus the issue is the integrity of James Bamford. The contents of Nowicki's letter make it clear that Bamford's book does not fairly and accurately report the information Bamford received. The Bamford tale is by far the apogee of this chapter about tall tales. Furthermore, Bamford continues to make completely false claims about the *Liberty* incident at public appearances and in letters to the editor, including a claim that there has never been an official investigation of the *Liberty* incident.

Additionally, this author learned from Nowicki that the other Hebrew linguist in the EC-121 aircraft, who was with him at the time and who also heard the original transmissions and listened to them again with Nowicki on the ground at Athens Airport shortly after the EC-121 landed, agreed with him that the transmissions established an attack in error.

The name of this U.S. Navy Hebrew (Special Arabic) linguist was known to Nowicki, this author, James Bamford, and the NSA. He had requested that his name not be made public but on June 26, 2008, he agreed to come out. He is Michael Prostinak. He did advise Nowicki that Bamford contacted him after Nowicki's letter was published in the *Wall Street Journal* and urged him to support Bamford's assertion that the NSA tapes show that the attack was intentional. He refused and advised Nowicki that he agreed with Nowicki's assessment that the transmissions and the tapes showed the attack to be a mistake.

In a conversation with Nowicki on Friday, July 27, 2001, this author inquired about opening communication with a third NSA Hebrew linguist, whose name had been withheld upon request but who has come out. He is Richard Hickman. Hickman spent a great deal of time listening to the EC-121 tapes at NSA headquarters at Fort Meade, Maryland, and he briefed the then director of NSA, Marshal Carter, on the contents of the tapes. Nowicki previously told this author that this third Hebrew linguist agreed with Nowicki that the tapes showed the attack was a mistake on the part of the Israelis. On that Friday afternoon Nowicki commented that Hickman mentioned to him something about the tapes that Nowicki had forgotten and that Hickman found quite persuasive. It was the clear confusion of the Israelis during conversations about whether the personnel on the ship for which rescue operations were being initiated were Egyptian or American and where to take the persons rescued, depending on which nationality they were. A very important aspect of this bit of information is that it corroborates that the NSA tapes coincide or at least agree with the Israel Air Force tape transcripts and translations that were released to Thames TV in 1987 and released by the Israel Air Force to this author in September 2001. An annotated translation of relevant excerpts of the Israel Air Force tapes and the NSA tapes is provided in appendix 2.

This author received an e-mail from Richard Hickman dated October 11, 2001, that stated in part:

Al Blue [the NSA Arabic linguist] was a friend of mine. We were both on the [U.S. Navy destroyer escort] *Valdez* during February–April of '67, having picked up the ship in Massaua, Ethiopia and rode it up the canal into the Mediterranean and out to Barcelona. When we re-turned "they" told us that we had to go right back out to get on the *Liberty*. I told them that I was due to be discharged from the Navy in June of '67 and it was unlikely the Navy would let me go, with so little time left. So, they agreed that I couldn't go, which resulted in "no" Hebrew linguist aboard the *Liberty*. But, they said that Al (Blue) had to go.

So, because of the fact that I lost a good friend in Al and of course NAVSECGRU shipmates and other wounded civilians—I was ready to blame the Israelis, along with everyone else who was angry. But, based on what I heard, both from eyewitnesses and the tapes, my conclusion has always been that it was a case of mistaken identity.

Clark Clifford, former chairman of President Johnson's Foreign Intel-ligence Advisory Board, told this author that he had considered "certain electronically gathered evidence" that convinced him that the attack was a mistake.[40] At that time this author was not aware of recordings made by an EC-121 aircraft in the possession of NSA and assumed that Clifford was referring to the Israel Air Force tapes. Now it appears more likely that he was referring to the NSA tapes.

Allegations abound in the conspiracy camp that a tape existed that proved that the attack was intentional. This author interviewed George Golden,[41] the engineering officer on the *Liberty*, who said, "Some of that could have counted also for the fact that Lieutenant Bennett brought some information and gave it to me. He said they had taped it, concerning the planning of the attack and I gave that to a member of Admiral Martin's staff the next morning and nothing came of that. I wish I was in a position to make a copy of it myself."[42]

The House of Representatives Armed Services Subcommittee on Inves-tigations conducted an investigation at the request of the *Liberty* Veterans Association from about July 1991 through about April 1992. Roy Kirk of the General Accounting Office was the chief investigator. Kirk told this author that he was told by various *Liberty* crew members about a tape (sometimes an audiotape, sometimes a videotape) and that he spoke to the person who was supposed to have had the tape and was told, "There are no such tapes. Those guys who claim the tapes exist are crazy."[43] In a March 2001 interview, Cdr. Maurice H. Bennett elaborated:

This story arose—and spread—from a remark I made shortly after the attack. I do not remember to whom I spoke or who was present.

The gist of my remark was that surely/probably somewhere in the morass of tapes made before and during the attack there should be/probably was/might be some intercept relating to the attack. I have/had no knowledge of such information in a definitive sense, it was speculative not definitive. As stories get retold, they get embellished/distorted and that is obviously what happened in this case.

The tapes which were on board *Liberty* were I think shipped back to NSA and it was always my understanding that no information relating to the attack, before or during, was found on them. NSA will have to provide a definitive answer.[44]

There is no tape in the exhibits to the record of the U.S. Navy court of inquiry. Admiral Kidd told this author that he did not receive such a tape.

Another report of a tape surfaced in 1998 when a *Liberty* Veterans Association member put the following message on the Internet:

Subj: [LIB] Taped interviews from Israel—voice
Date: 98–02–13 16:23:59 EST
From: tonktime@CO.TDS.NET (Phillip F. Tourney)
Flash! Flash! Flash!
It has come to my attention that valuable taped information from the players, our attackers, is in the hands of a very reliable and competent source. The tape reveals the debriefing of the Israeli torpedo crew as to their statements to anyone concerning the attack on the *Liberty*. They were told, as they have stood by in the public's eye, mistaken identity. This tape proves not so from their very own lips. Their mission was to destroy our ship and pay no attention to its nationality. The orders were to destroy the ship and crew. The tape also reveals the bewilderment of our attackers that the ship did not sink after all the air attack and torpedo attacks. These players have names that we are all familiar with and they are: Moshe Oren, former Lead Commander, Torpedo boats; Pinchas Pinchasy, former Naval Liaison Officer with the Israeli Air Force; Avraham Lunz, Former Duty Officer [*sic*; Command Duty Officer] in War Room to name a few. The unnamed source at this point will send the tapes to the proper authorities. After this is completed, copies will be made available, I am told.

At this point, I don't know when the tape was recorded or who recorded it, but it does exist. With this type of evidence maybe once and for all our nay-sayers and non-believers will join us in bringing this cover-up out into the open.

Phil Tourney

Until now Tourney's unnamed source has not made these alleged tapes available, as Tourney stated he was told would happen.

Why did NSA not disclose the existence of the EC-121 flight and its tapes? It should be remembered that in the 1960s NSA was publicly known facetiously as "No Such Agency" and as a matter of policy disclosed literally nothing about its activities. Assuming the tapes were made available to Clark Clifford and all the U.S. and Israeli governmental investigations officially concluded that the attack was a mistake, that there was no pressing need to make such disclosures. In addition, there was a valid political reason not to disclose the fact that a U.S. military aircraft was at a place at a time in which the United States had told the world in general and the Soviets and Arabs in particular that there were no U.S. military aircraft. Such a disclosure in 1967 would have reinforced the Egyptian and Jordanian claims about U.S. aircraft in the combat zone supporting Israel against the Arabs, a claim that the United States was actively denying at the time. As the NSA and its operations became better known and the agency became more relaxed, no doubt the NSA felt there was no need to know on the part of the public and there remained a continued valid operational reason not to disclose the capability of the technology on the EC-121. Who would have imagined the United States had such fabulous surveillance capability in 1967, or for that matter in 2002?

This author filed a Freedom of Information Act request with NSA on April 27, 2001, requesting the release of the EC-121 tapes, transcripts of tapes, and translations thereof. On June 14, 2001, in FOIA Case: 40039, NSA denied this author's FOIA request for any *Liberty* recordings and the EC-121 tapes. The NSA responded that "NSA can neither confirm nor deny the existence of any specific collection that may have occurred on that date by the *Liberty*. In addition, we have determined that the fact of the existence or non-existence of the other materials [the EC-121 tapes] you request is a currently and properly classified matter." This author appealed that denial on July 6, 2001, and requested declassification. The appeal was denied. When this book was originally published in 2002, this author concluded this chapter with the comment,

"Now is the time for the NSA to grant this author's Freedom of Information Act appeal and release the tapes, their transcripts and translations. The data on those tapes would provide valuable evidence relating to many of the conspiracy claims." Thereafter this author sued the NSA for release of the tapes under the Freedom of Information Act; NSA capitulated and released not only the tapes but other significant material as well on July 2, 2003. The tapes and translation thereof may be heard and seen on the NSA website, www.nsa.gov, as well as this author's website, www.thelibertyincident.com. Translation of the tapes is provided in appendix 2. A detailed analysis of the intercepts is included in chapter 16.

Chapter 11

DID DAYAN ORDER IT?

Some conspiracy theorists claim that the attacks on the *Liberty* were made on the direct order of Israel's minister of defense, Moshe Dayan. The most prominent claimant that Dayan did it was Norman F. Dacey, national chairman of the American Palestine Committee.

In September 1977 Dayan, who was then foreign minister, traveled to the United States on an official visit for talks with President Jimmy Carter and Secretary of State Cyrus Vance. On September 19, 1977, the *New York Times* carried on page 26 an advertisement paid for by Dacey. The ad began with a large-type headline, "Are We Welcoming the Murderer of Our Sons?"

Beneath the headline was a picture of Moshe Dayan. The ad told of the June 8, 1967, attack on the *Liberty* and claimed that "this Committee" had obtained three (unevaluated) intelligence documents from the Central Intelligence Agency under the Freedom of Information Act. Excerpts from three documents were presented in the ad. The release of these documents was highly unusual. This author has never been able to obtain the release of a CIA unevaluated intelligence document or any further information on the facts and circumstances surrounding this particular release for the *New York Times* ad. Each of the documents has certain portions blacked out or redacted; not all the original information is readable. The first document referred to the opinion of the Turkish General Staff (TGS) and stated: "2. The TGS is convinced that the attack on the U.S.S. *Liberty* on June 8, 1967 was deliberate. It was done because the *Liberty*'s CCNMO actively was having the effect of jamming Israeli Military communications."

Neither the name of the informant nor the exact place from which the information was obtained is readable. The second unevaluated intelligence document stated that "Israeli forces did not make mistakes." Like the first document, both the name of the informant and the source of the information were redacted. The third unevaluated intelligence document was dated November 9, 1967, and was entitled "Attack on USS *Liberty* Ordered by Dayan." The advertisement included paragraph 2 of the redacted document. "[Deleted] commented on the sinking [*sic*] of the U.S. communications ship *Liberty*. They said that Dayan personally ordered the attack on the ship and that one of his generals adamantly opposed the action, saying, 'This is pure murder!' One of the admirals who was present also disapproved the action and it was he who ordered it stopped. [Deletion] believe that the attack against the U.S. vessel is [deletion] detrimental to any political ambitions Dayan may have."

The advertisement then asks a series of questions, concluding with, "If for ten years you have had information disclosing the identity of the individual who deliberately ordered the attack which killed or maimed so many of our sons, why have you never demanded that he be brought to justice? While you have been deporting persons suspected of war crimes against Europeans 35 years ago, why have you done nothing about the perpetrator of this heinous war crime against American servicemen ten years ago?"

The advertisement ends with the statement, "It is time for the U.S. Government to end its silence on the *Liberty* tragedy. It is time the American people were given the truth!" A separate news article in the same issue of the *New York Times,* on page 7, described the American Palestine Committee as "a nationwide committee of Americans trying to help the Palestinians to get back into their homeland."[1] The story of this ad was picked up by the Associated Press and United Press International, and articles about it appeared in the *Washington Post* and other Washington, D.C., newspapers.[2]

On the day the advertisement appeared in the *New York Times,* the director of the Central Intelligence Agency, Adm. Stansfield Turner, appeared on the ABC television program *Good Morning America,* hosted by Steve Bell. It is rather sad that it was only on January 28, 1985, that the CIA approved for release a transcript of that portion of the *Good Morning America* show, more than seven years after it had been heard and seen by tens of millions of TV viewers! The transcript is enlightening (emphasis added below):[3]

Transcript—Good Morning America September 19, 1977
Steve Bell: There is a particular incident that has just come into the papers this morning; namely, that a group of Palestinian supporters in the U.S. has taken out an advertisement in *The New York Times* which uses raw CIA data

gained from the Freedom of Information Act. The accusation is made that Moshe Dayan specifically ordered the attack on the USS *Liberty* in the 1967 Middle East War. Can you give us any enlightenment on that?

Admiral Turner: I certainly can and I am glad Steve that you emphasized the word raw intelligence data. We are required under the Freedom of Information Act to produce to those who ask for it intelligence documents which can be unclassified. In those which we released there were several which indicated a possibility that the Israeli government knew about the USS *Liberty* before the attack. Also, we released an evaluated over-all document which said very clearly that it was our considered opinion that the Israeli government had *no such knowledge* at that time.

Approved For Release
Date 28 Jan 1985.

It is interesting to evaluate the unevaluated intelligence document that accuses Dayan. The informant and the place from which the paper originated are redacted or sanitized, so neither of these items is of any help.

- The document states: "—— commented on the sinking of the U.S. communications ship, *Liberty.*"
- This author's comment: The ship was not sunk.
- Document: "They said that Dayan personally ordered the attack on the ship."
- This author's comment: The issue is what weight should be given to the assertion that Dayan personally ordered the attack on the ship.
- Document: "One of the admirals who was present also disapproved of the action."
- This author's comment: The source suggests that the navy had more than one admiral; however, in 1967, the Israel Navy had only one admiral, Shlomo Erell. Erell was in Haifa on June 8, 1967, and Dayan was en route to Hebron. There was no admiral present with Dayan at the Kirya in Tel Aviv.
- Document: "It was he [the admiral] who ordered it [the attack] stopped and not Dayan."
- This author's comment: From what is known about Dayan's temper and style of command, it is most difficult to imagine a subordinate countermanding his order in his presence. (In fact there were two attacks: the first by aircraft, which was halted by order of the chief air controller at Air

Force Headquarters in the "pit" in Tel Aviv; the second was the attack by the motor torpedo boats, which was halted not from the navy headquarters in Haifa but by the motor torpedo boat division commander after the torpedo attack had been completed.)

- Document: "——— believe that the attack against the U.S. vessel is also detrimental to any political ambition Dayan may have."
- This author's comment: Wrong again. Dayan came out of the war a hero and remained the minister of defense and number-two person in the Israel government until after the 1973 war.

This author's conclusion: The unidentified informant was wrong, or inaccurate, about every other assertion made. This suggests that the assertion that Dayan personally ordered the attack suffers from lack of credibility. It appears that the unidentified informant was uninformed or spread misinformation about *every single* detail in the document, and his evaluation of Dayan's political future was far off the mark. How much weight, then, should be attached to the source's reported comment that "Dayan personally ordered the attack on the ship"? None.

Dayan's autobiography, *Story of My Life,* published in 1976, says that on June 8, he learned that Hebron had been captured and that he promptly set off for Hebron: "Shortly before noon on Thursday, Central Command reported to General Headquarters that its Jerusalem Brigade had linked up with Southern Command, having advanced South from Jerusalem and seized Bethlehem, Hebron, and Dahariah. I promptly set off for Hebron, meeting Uzi Narkiss [the general in charge of the Central Command] in Jerusalem and driving South with him."[4] Dayan's book makes no mention of the *Liberty* incident.

The Israel Defense Forces History Department reports that on the morning of June 8, 1967, Dayan went to Jerusalem, where he had Maj. Gen. Uzi Narkiss transport him to Hebron.[5] It is about a fifteen-minute drive from the Kirya to Sde Dov Airport, located on the north side of Tel Aviv, on the coast. It is a little over thirty miles from Sde Dov to Jerusalem as the crow, or helicopter, flies. A Super Frelon helicopter cruises at between 138 and 155 miles per hour; thus Dayan's flight time to Jerusalem was about twelve to fifteen minutes. His route then went south less than three miles from Jerusalem to Bethlehem, then another five miles to the Gush Etzion site, or Etzion Bloc,[6] where he and his entourage stopped for lunch, and finally on to Hebron, about ten more miles.

Is there any evidence that supports Dayan's alleged evil deed? Gen. Uzi Narkiss stated that on June 8 he was at his headquarters in Jerusalem when Dayan arrived by helicopter. Narkiss remembered that he was with former prime minister David Ben-Gurion and was about to take Ben-Gurion to the Western Wall, which had just been captured from Jordan.[7] Dayan said, "No, we are going to Hebron," so Narkiss got his command car, a few half-tracks, and some jeeps, and they started out for Hebron. Narkiss then told this author, "But don't take my word for it. . . . *Life* magazine published a special edition about the 1967 war that included a picture of Dayan having lunch that day on the road to Hebron."

A few days later, not knowing if the photo could be found, this author mentioned the *Life* magazine photo to Eitan Haber, a noted Israeli journalist.[8] Haber said, "Yes, I remember the picture, I am in it. I was with Dayan that day." In the photo Dayan was seated on the ground next to an Israeli brigadier. Further research identified the brigadier as Rehav'am Ze'evi.[9] This author interviewed Ze'evi, who remembered the trip and identified the site of the luncheon as being on the foundation of a building at the Etzion Bloc.[10]

Another officer standing in the rear of the *Life* photo was identified as Yitzhak Rager, who served as a battalion commander in 1967. This author interviewed Rager when he was the mayor of Beersheva, and Rager confirmed his identity in the picture.[11] Thus, there are corroborating witnesses to Dayan's location and inability to have given an order to attack the *Liberty* on June 8, 1967, between 1300 and 1400.

This author also learned from General Narkiss that on June 8, 1967, Narkiss had with him Pvt. Yaacov "Cobie" Sharett, whose duty was to keep a diary for the Central Command. Yaacov Sharett, son of Moshe Sharett, the second prime minister of Israel, confirmed making the trip with Dayan on June 8, 1967, and corroborated the story told by Uzi Narkiss.[12]

In an effort to learn more about Dayan, this author interviewed Dayan's longtime friend and confidant Shlomo Gazit.[13] Gazit stated that he and Dayan never discussed the *Liberty*. He went on to tell a story about an occasion when Dayan could not remember some details of an event. Gazit told him, "Dayan, you are cheating history, you should keep a journal." Dayan agreed and the next morning spent an hour writing about the previous day. Gazit said that Dayan never did it again. Instead, he appointed a man named Chaim Israeli to write the journal for him. This author found Chaim Israeli still working for the Defense Ministry and learned that he had nothing in his

Defense Minister Moshe Dayan eating lunch at Etzion Bloc on the road to Hebron at 1335 June 8, 1967. Photo from *Life* magazine special edition, June 1967. *David Rubinger*/Time-Life

journal about the *Liberty* on June 8, 1967. Israeli remembered that the military secretary assigned to Dayan on June 8, 1967, was Col. Itzhak Nissyahu.

Nissyahu lives in Ramat Gan, Israel. He recalled flying with Dayan on June 8 to Jerusalem and, in the early afternoon of that day, traveling with Dayan and Narkiss to Hebron in a convoy arranged by Narkiss.[14] Nissyahu rode in the lead jeep. On the way, they stopped for lunch at the Etzion Bloc and then drove on to Hebron, where Dayan visited the Cave of Machpelah. The convoy then drove to Beersheva, which is farther to the south. They returned from Beersheva to Tel Aviv in the early evening. Dayan first heard of the *Liberty* incident when he reached Beersheva in late afternoon. From there they flew by helicopter back to Tel Aviv. Upon arriving they went to the Kirya. Shortly thereafter, Dayan left headquarters at the Kirya to spend the night with his girlfriend in Tel Aviv. He returned early in the morning and began reading messages that had come in during the night. Suddenly, he came upon a cable from Nasser to Syrian president Nur el Din Attasi, intercepted at 3:30 a.m., stating, "I think that Israel is interested in concentrating its forces against Syria, in order to crush the Syrian Army. . . . I would like to advise you to agree to end the hostilities and let U Thant, the [UN] Secretary General, know in order to keep the Syrian Army intact. We have lost this battle. God will be with us in the future."[15]

Dayan flew into a rage at the night duty officer for not having called him when that message came in, for he interpreted this message as meaning that the war was over on the Egyptian and Jordanian fronts. He called Maj. Gen. David Eleazer, in charge of the Northern Command, who had been pressing for authorization to attack Syria for several days, and ordered him to launch an attack against Syria at once. He then called Prime Minister Levy Eshkol and advised him that he had ordered the attack on Syria, though he could still call it back. Eshkol was highly displeased that Dayan had acted without consulting him and immediately called a cabinet meeting, but the attack on Syria was not halted.

This author's research indicates that Dayan's total lack of involvement in the *Liberty* incident seems to be clear enough, based on the evidence discussed above. However, one additional material witness was discovered. In arranging for the use of the *Life* magazine photograph, this author learned that its photographer was David Rubinger, who twenty-five years later still worked for *Time-Life.* Rubinger's diary supports his memory that he met Dayan at Sde Dov Airport on June 8, 1967, flew with him to Jerusalem in the Super Frelon helicopter, then rode with Dayan and Narkiss in the command car, stopping for lunch at Gush Etzion. He recalled the command car as being an open vehicle with no

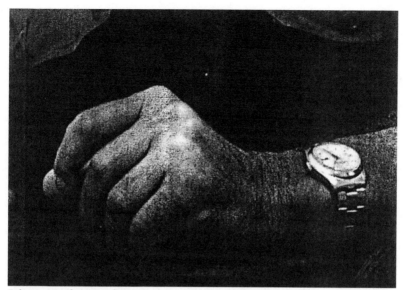

Enlargement of picture of Dayan's wristwatch made from another negative on the same roll as the preceding picture of Dayan. *David Rubinger/*Time-Life

radio. (Cellular telephones were not yet in existence.) He recalled that Dayan and his party were without the ability to communicate with the rest of the world from midmorning until they arrived in Beersheva.

A close examination of the picture shows at least three people wearing wristwatches. This author asked Rubinger if the photo could be enlarged to show the time on the watches when Dayan was eating lunch. In the *Life* magazine picture Dayan's watch was at an angle and could not be effectively enlarged, but Rubinger advised that he had taken multiple shots of that same scene, all within a minute or two. Those pictures could be enlarged along with the pictures of the other watches.[16] The time on the watches, including Dayan's own watch, was 1325, about seventeen minutes before the first order was given sending Mirage IIICJ aircraft in search of a warship off El Arish.

Dayan did not do it!

Chapter 12

AMERICA INVESTIGATES

Regulations of the U.S. Navy require an investigation of all incidents involving any death or injury or loss of, or damage to, Navy property.[1] The Commander in Chief, U.S. Naval Forces Europe, Adm. John S. McCain Jr., ordered a court of inquiry to be convened on the *Liberty* attack. Rear Adm. Isaac C. Kidd Jr., who was then serving as Assistant Chief of Staff, Logistics, for Commander in Chief, Allied Forces Southern Europe, was named president of the court.[2] Capt. Bert M. Atkinson Jr., USN, a Naval Academy graduate, and Capt. Bernard J. Lauff, USN, a highly respected veteran of Wake Island in World War II, were designated members. Kidd requested Capt. Ward Boston Jr., USN, as counsel for the court.[3] Boston brought two special assets in addition to his skill as a Navy lawyer. He had been a naval aviator in World War II and therefore had insight beyond that of one qualified only in the law. Also, Kidd knew him as a man of integrity. On an earlier matter Boston had been willing to bump heads with Kidd when Boston felt it more important to do the right thing than to curry favor with the senior who would write his fitness report.

The court convened in London at forty-six minutes before midnight on June 10, 1967, two days and a few hours after the attack. Testimony was taken in London from Capt. Leonard Robert Raish, the assistant chief of staff for Commander in Chief, U.S. Naval Forces Europe. The court remained in session until 0250 June 11. Rear Admiral Kidd then traveled with Captain Boston and a court reporter to Souda Bay, Crete, and boarded the *Liberty* at sea on June 12, while she was en route to Valletta, Malta. The other members of the court met the ship on June 14, 1967,[4] at the port of Valletta, Malta, and at 0730 the court went into session on board the *Liberty*.

The inquiry took testimony from nineteen witnesses;[5] transcribed testimony ran 158 pages; forty-nine exhibits, consisting of hundreds of documents and pictures, were received into evidence. The court completed taking evidence in Malta on June 15 and returned to London, where it took additional evidence. The court was closed at 1645 London time on June 16. The court concluded its deliberations two days later and presented its fifty-two findings, together with the record of its proceedings, to Admiral McCain.[6] The more important findings were:

1. Available evidence combines to indicate the attack on *Liberty* on 8 June was in fact a case of mistaken identity.
2. The calm conditions and slow ship speed may well have made the American flag difficult to identify. . . .
6. There are no available indications that the attack was intended against a U.S. ship.

Admiral McCain's lawyer, Capt. Merwin Staring,[7] was not happy with the form of the untidy, bulky document, which contained typographical errors, but Admiral McCain and his staff prepared a five-page "First Endorsement" and ordered "Ike" Kidd to deliver the findings and endorsement to the Chief of Naval Operations, Adm. David McDonald, in Washington.[8] The endorsement of Admiral McCain includes the following statement: "15. The foregoing comments by the convening authority lead to an overall conclusion that the attack was in fact a mistake."[9]

The record of proceedings and the first endorsement by Admiral McCain, plus two copies, were placed in a briefcase that was chained to the wrist of Rear Admiral Kidd. Also, he strapped a .45-caliber semiautomatic pistol in a shoulder holster to his chest. He was driven to Heathrow Airport and boarded a Pan American airliner bound for New York. He was booked first class. As soon as he got into his seat, he fell asleep. He remembers waking in the middle of the night to find a flight attendant trying to cover him with a blanket. He asked what she was doing, and the attendant explained that she was trying to cover the huge pistol on his chest, as the lady in the opposite seat was terrorized by it. He wondered ever after why he had been given the pistol, since he probably could not have used it effectively with the briefcase chained to his wrist.

He then fell back asleep until the plane arrived in New York. A Navy plane awaited him there and flew him to Washington. He was met upon

landing and driven to Bethesda Naval Hospital in the nearby Maryland sub-
urbs, where he arrived at dawn. Admiral McDonald was recovering from a
bout with pneumonia. Kidd felt it prudent not to awaken him and waited
outside his room.[10] As soon as McDonald awakened and heard that Kidd
was there, he sent for him. As Kidd walked into the room, McDonald said,
"Ike, was it intentional?" He replied, "No, Admiral." Then they went through
the record of the proceedings.[11]

In July 1967, almost a month after the U.S. Navy court of inquiry completed its report, Admiral Kidd added an amplification addendum to the
Liberty inquiry in a secret message, U.S. eyes only, 061222Z July 67, which
stated:

1. Req add following amplification as appropriate
   Addendum to *Liberty* inquiry pursuant your req for amplifying facts.
2. Following attested to by CO *Liberty* Cdr McGonagle; CTC Thompson; and Signalman David through Cdr McGonagle.
3. [deleted because not relevant]
4. Alleges AA from PTS was not repeat not read by *Liberty* prior to
   torpedo hit.
5. [deleted because not relevant]
6. [deleted because not relevant]
7. Thompson says first identifiable visual transmission from PTS read
   by anyone on *Liberty* was "Do you need help" followed by "Do you
   want us to stand by." . . .
8. Thompson states after Aldis lamp unlimbered, which was after he got
   to bridge which was after torpedo attacks, the only thing sent by light
   to PTS was "No thank you" in reply to offer of help.

The U.S. Navy court of inquiry did a remarkably competent and accurate job of collecting and analyzing evidence relating to the *Liberty* attack
and arriving at conclusions. While the investigation was thorough and the
court had the resources of the United States at its disposal, it did not hear
directly from Israeli witnesses. Nevertheless, the conclusions of the court
have stood the test of time and are supported and corroborated by later data
that became available from Israel.

In the United States, by tradition, human life is treasured. In normal
times any single life lost is a tragedy. But 1967 could not be considered normal times. The United States was engaged in armed conflict in Vietnam and

was in the process there of losing the lives of 55,000 of its military personnel. During the week of June 5, 1967, 187 more U.S. military personnel died
in Vietnam. The numbers of wounded were astronomical. Thus the loss
of lives and the woundings during the week of June 5, 1967, were neither
unusual nor unfamiliar to an American public that had been experiencing
these terrible human losses week by week for several years.

The Navy wanted to know what had happened. This concern was operational: How and why had it happened, and what could be done to prevent
similar events in the future? The relationship of the U.S. military and the
Israeli military in 1967, though cordial, was neither strong nor close, except perhaps at the most attenuated points of each military where personal
contact was made. For example, there was a friendly relationship between
Air Force colonel Anthony Perna, the U.S. defense attaché in Tel Aviv, and
his counterpart, Lt. Col. Y. S. "Shaike" Bareket, the Israel Air Force chief of
intelligence. Likewise, there was a friendly relationship between Navy commander Ernest Castle, the U.S. naval attaché, and his counterpart, Lt. Col.
Michael Bloch, the IDF foreign military liaison officer.

The court was not permitted, nor did Navy regulations require it, to take
evidence from the Israeli side.[12] The court took testimony only from U.S.
personnel and studied the ship and physical exhibits. If, as some critics suggest, the court's decision was controlled for political motives, it is difficult
to understand why that report was then classified for nearly ten years. It is
much more reasonable to assume that the report was classified for security
or operational reasons than that its conclusions were made under political
pressure. The United States was concerned about the fact that the ship was
an intelligence gatherer, a fact that neither the Department of State nor the
Department of Defense wanted disclosed. Also, the Department of State had
no desire to reinforce the Arab perception, from a political point of view,
that the United States had provided direct military support to Israel.

For reasons never explained, the findings of the court of inquiry and the
McCain endorsement were classified top secret and not declassified until
June 29, 1976, over nine years after the event. A news release was issued by
the Office of the Assistant Secretary of Defense (Public Affairs) on June 28,
1967. The "Summary of Proceedings" attached to the news release is strange.
It omits court of inquiry findings 1 and 6 as well as paragraph 15 of Admiral
McCain's endorsement. The summary appears to go out of its way to say
things not in the actual proceedings of the court. It also contains errors of
fact that are contradicted by the record of the proceedings. For example it

says, "*Liberty* fired her .50-caliber machine guns at the aircraft and torpedo boats, but only after she had been attacked and hit." She did fire her guns at the torpedo boats, but *before* they attacked. The transcript of Commander McGonagle's testimony confirms this.

One paragraph of the press release even seems to contradict the court's findings 1, 2, and 6: "Her configuration, as shown in the international standard naval identification book *Jane's Fighting Ships,* and her standard markings, were clearly sufficient for the aircraft to identify her properly as the non-combatant ship *Liberty*."[13] Two paragraphs later, the summary relates that this "non-combatant" ship was exercised at general quarters during most of the hour just prior to the air attack. When general quarters is sounded on a U.S. Navy ship, the boatswain's mate of the watch announces, "All hands man your battle stations." It is not possible to have it both ways. The *Liberty* may not have been adequately armed for combat, but she was a warship by international-law definition. One can only speculate as to why the press release called her a noncombatant and omitted, or distorted, a number of significant aspects of the actual findings of the court.

While the U.S. Navy conducted the court of inquiry, the Central Intelligence Agency conducted its own investigation of the *Liberty* attack, issuing a report on June 13, 1967, five days before the Navy court of inquiry completed its work.[14] The CIA report is accurate and is an excellent piece of work to have been assembled in only five days. However, in its rush to complete the report, the CIA overlooked the fact that while Washington was observing daylight savings time in June 1967, Israel was not. As a result, the times in the CIA report, although essentially accurate, are one hour off. That is, the attack began about 1400 Sinai time on June 8, 1967, but the CIA report reflects the time as 1500.[15] The CIA investigation was supervised by the chief of station in Tel Aviv and used U.S. sources in both Israel and the United States. The initial conclusion was that the attacks on the *Liberty* were a mistake.[16] The June 13, 1967, CIA intelligence memorandum has been declassified, but a subsequent memorandum dated June 23, 1967, remained classified until January 12, 2004. Although the reason for the continued classification is not known, the conclusion of the CIA that the attack was a mistake was reinforced in 1977 in an exchange of letters between the director and Senator James G. Abourezk of South Dakota. The agency was queried by the senator on behalf of Carl Marcy in a letter to the director dated November 18, 1977.

To the question "5. Finally, could I have your judgment and that of the Agency you head, based on information acquired by the Agency from all sources, that the Israeli attack on the USS *Liberty* was deliberate or an honest mistake?" Admiral Turner responded in a letter dated February 27, 1978, "Comment: 'It remains our best judgment that the Israeli attack on the USS *Liberty* was not made in malice toward the United States and was a mistake.'"

Throughout the many accounts of the *Liberty* incident, much ink has been expended on the issue of the similarities between the *Liberty* and the Egyptian warship *El Quseir*.[17] The June 13, 1967, CIA report states: "Although the *Liberty* is some 200 feet longer than the Egyptian transport El Quseir, it could easily be mistaken for the latter vessel by an overzealous pilot. Both have similar hulls and arrangements of masts and stack."[18]

While some naval experts may disagree with the conclusion of the CIA report that *Liberty* and *El Quseir* have similar hull shapes, the question is best answered by viewing the silhouettes of both ships. Page 40 of the NSA document shows unclassified pictures of USS *Liberty* and *El Quseir*. Each ship has a mast forward and a mast aft, a superstructure amidships, and a single smokestack. The simple silhouettes shown in the illustration reflect the similarities (*Liberty* above, *El Quseir* below). It is even more instructive to imagine a jet fighter pilot twenty one or twenty two years old who has never before attacked a ship approaching a target already identified as an enemy at almost six hundred miles per hour, or almost one-half mile each three seconds.

Liberty and *El Quseir* silhouettes

It was not only the Navy and the CIA that were immediately concerned with the cause of *Liberty* tragedy. The U.S. Joint Chiefs of Staff (JCS) were concerned as well that five messages directed to the *Liberty* had gone astray. Army major general Joseph R. Russ was directed by the JCS to commence a fact-finding study of the communications failure; he began the investigation on June 9, 1967.[19]

In part 2, section 1 of his report, Russ outlined thirty-six "Findings of Fact," most of which are followed by a "Discussion"; however, because of the charter of the fact-finding team, General Russ did not make any findings about the actual attacks.[20] The team collected, compiled, and analyzed all of the significant message traffic.

Russ was more concerned with errors and omissions by the U.S. military than with duplicating the work of the court of inquiry being conducted by Rear Admiral Kidd. The JCS was concerned with the inability of the U.S. military communications system to prevent the event. While this investigation gathered a very important compilation of U.S. messages, its focus was on failures and responsibilities of the U.S. military communications system. Therefore, the Russ Report is an invaluable resource in the study of the *Liberty* incident.

The most mysterious and elusive of all contemporary investigations was carried out by Clark Clifford, who chaired the President's Foreign Intelligence Advisory Board and was a close adviser to President Johnson.[21] He was asked two questions by the president through National Security Advisor, Walt Rostow. Question 1: Who fired the first shot in the 1967 War? Question 2: Was the attack on the *Liberty* intentional or a mistake? Clifford's answer to the first question remains classified, although it is generally believed that he concluded that Israel fired the "first shot."[22] The Clifford Report on the question of whether the attacks were intentional or a mistake remained classified top secret until this author obtained its declassification on October 25, 1995.[23]

The Clifford Report stated the following conclusions:

a. The information thus far available does not reflect that the Israeli high command made a premeditated attack on a ship known to be American. . . .

d. The best interpretation from available facts is that there were gross and inexcusable failures in the command and control of subordinate Israeli naval and air elements. . . .

f. The unprovoked attack on the *Liberty* constitutes a flagrant act of gross negligence for which the Israeli Government should be held completely responsible, and the Israeli military personnel involved should be punished.[24]

The bottom line was that Clifford found no premeditation but rather "inexcusable failures" constituting "gross negligence" on the part of Israeli subordinate military personnel. Clifford, looking through American eyes, concluded further: "e. There is no justification for the failure of the IDF—with the otherwise outstanding efficiency which it demonstrated in the course of the war—to ensure prompt alerting of all appropriate elements of the IDF of the fact that a U.S. ship was in the area."[25]

In an interview with this author, Clifford recalled that the *Liberty* attack was "a matter of enormous delicacy."[26] He obtained material from the Department of Defense, and after review he concluded that the attack was a mistake, in effect a case of "Murphy's Law."[27] He stated that his investigation had been conducted without staff and that he did not travel to the Pentagon. He recalls attending a couple of meetings in the Map Room of the White House,[28] and after "looking into it and listening to electronically recorded material it seemed to establish that it was an accident."[29]

In 1991 Clifford published a memoir entitled *Counsel to the President*. The *Liberty* incident is discussed:

> There was no evidence that the highest levels of the Israeli government . . . were aware of *Liberty*'s true identity or the fact that an attack was taking place. At the same time, however, no one could prove that they did not know.
>
> The best interpretation from the facts available to me was that there were inexcusable failures on the part of the Israeli Defense Forces.[30]

Shortly after the incident, the U.S. Senate Committee on Foreign Relations held three days of hearings on S. 1872, a bill to amend the Foreign Assistance Act of 1961. "The Israeli Attack on the U.S.S. *Liberty*" was put into question by Senator Bourke Blakemore Hickenlooper of Iowa,[31] who was never considered a supporter of Israel.[32] Secretary of Defense Robert S. McNamara gave the following testimony to the committee:

> In the case of the attack on the *Liberty*, it was the conclusion of the investigatory body headed by an admiral of the Navy in whom we have great confidence that the attack was not intentional. I read the record of the investigation, and support that conclusion. . . . It was not a conscious decision on the part of the Government of Israel.
>
> Senator Hickenlooper: Perhaps not. . . .

Secretary McNamara: There is no evidence that the individuals attacking the *Liberty* knew they were attacking a U.S. ship, and there is some evidence, circumstantial, that they did not know it . . .

Secretary McNamara: Senator Hickenlooper, I don't want to carry the torch for the Israelis. It was an inexcusable error in judgment. . . . And an inexcusable error of professional tactics. I would simply point out to you that, at the same time, I was denying that we had struck a Russian ship in Haiphong Harbor [sic]; and I proved to be in error. These errors do occur. We had no more intention of attacking a Russian ship than Israel apparently did of attacking an American ship.[33]

Contrary to some claims, Congress took the *Liberty* attack quite seriously and looked into the events surrounding the attack a total of five times. On the afternoon of February 1, 1968, in the Old Senate Office Building, a hearing before the Committee on Armed Services of the U.S. Senate again heard from Secretary of Defense McNamara, who was accompanied by Gen. Earle G. Wheeler, chairman of the Joint Chiefs of Staff. They were there to testify about the more recent *Pueblo* incident, in which another U.S. intelligence-gathering ship had been captured by North Korea.[34] Senator Stuart Symington of Missouri asked McNamara about air support for the *Pueblo* in its hour of need. In his response, McNamara compared the *Pueblo* incident to the *Liberty* attack:

The kind of uncertainty you have in that kind of a situation was illustrated by the *Liberty* incident. When the *Liberty* was attacked, we had a task force in the Mediterranean. We received a flash report here in the Pentagon at the time of the attack. We examined the situation. My first reaction—that is the question I immediately posed to the Chiefs and the Joint Staff was: Is it not likely it was attacked by Soviet forces?

We knew the location of certain Soviet forces in the area. Certainly the initial reaction, having known their location, would be to attack those forces. Within a half hour or 45 minutes, however, we concluded that a Soviet attack was unlikely.

The next obvious answer was it had been attacked by Egyptians. Who else would have done it if it were not the Soviets or the Egyptians? Well that too proved in error. It took us a while to find that out.

What I am suggesting to you is that it is very difficult for a commander not on the scene to know what happened and how he should react.[35]

The transcripts of these hearings indicate a genuine bipartisan concern for developing information about military command and control.

The House of Representatives was also interested in the *Liberty* affair. Hearings were held before the Subcommittee on Department of Defense of the Committee on Appropriations, House of Representatives, on April 8, 1968. After Air Force lieutenant general Richard P. Klocko made an opening statement, Congressman Robert Lee Fulton Sikes of Florida indicated that he wished to discuss the worldwide communication system of the Department of the Defense "with emphasis on the USS *Liberty* incident." Sikes began with the comment, "A general conclusion could be drawn from the staff reports that the use and operational capabilities of the Defense Communications system is nothing less than pathetic, and that the management of the system needs to be completely overhauled."[36]

Solis Horowitz, Assistant Secretary of Defense (Administration), commented on an investigation of the *Liberty* incident by the Department of Defense. He testified that the Department of Defense investigation and the House Appropriations hearing had both focused on the defects in the existing system that had left the *Liberty* in harm's way. A great deal of testimony and conversation reviewed not only the *Liberty* incident but also other aspects of Defense communications. Structure, procedures, and equipment as well as problems in Vietnam were on the table, but the discussion seemed to keep coming back to the *Liberty*. The comment of Congressman John Jacob Rhodes of Arizona is noteworthy:

> The record speaks for itself as far as the handling of this message to the USS *Liberty*. It is a comedy of errors. You could not have written it any better if you were writing a musical comedy.
>
> It would be funny if it were not so tragic. Here we are, with the most sophisticated communications system ever known to mankind and maybe it is so sophisticated we do not know how to operate it.[37]

It appears from its printed report that the committee felt that there was some stonewalling by both the JCS and the Navy, and although the committee adopted a "summary of study,"[38] it is apparent that the House Armed Services Committee investigation of worldwide communications in 1971 had its genesis in the dissatisfaction of this committee with the cooperation of the JCS and the Navy with this earlier investigation.

The House Appropriations Committee report was partially published in the *Congressional Record—House* under the heading "Navy Communications

'Foulup' Caused USS *'Liberty's'* Presence off Sinai Coast." One passage read: "Mr. Halpern: Mr. Speaker, I was shocked to learn that a Navy communications 'foulup' led to the presence of the USS *Liberty* of the Sinai coast in June 1967 where it was mistaken for an Egyptian vessel and attacked by Israel torpedo boats and planes."[39]

While almost all other investigations relating to the *Liberty* have been declassified, or partially declassified, a portion of the above report remains highly classified, with a code-name classification. All efforts to have the remainder of this report declassified have been unsuccessful.[40]

In 1971 the House Armed Services Investigating Subcommittee conducted a review of Department of Defense worldwide communications.[41] The House Armed Services Committee investigation of 1971 seems to have been the culmination of the interest in U.S. military communications first developed by the JCS/Russ Report in 1967 and expanded upon by the Senate Armed Services Committee in 1968 and the House Appropriations Committee in 1968. The concern about communications problems had been exacerbated by the losses of the USS *Pueblo* in 1968 and a U.S. Navy EC-l21 intelligence gathering plane in 1969. The investigation sought to deal with inadequacies in U.S. military worldwide communications, as a national interest.

The portion of the text of the report regarding the USS *Liberty* is extremely important and highly instructive. Nevertheless, there are a few mistakes in the report. For example, it states that the *Liberty* suffered seventy-five wounded instead of the correct 171.[42] The report traces each of the five delayed messages, catalogues the specific route of each message, and attributes the reasons for the delays. The report discloses that deletions were made from the report on the recommendation of the Office of the Directorate of Security Review of the Department of Defense.[43] Rear Adm. Francis J. Fitzpatrick, Assistant Chief of Naval Operations for Communications and the number-two person on the Russ Report team, testified extensively before the committee in secret session.[44] The admiral informed the committee on a number of facts and nuances that were ultimately deleted from the published report for security reasons, as indicated above.

The committee was shocked by testimony of Admiral Fitzpatrick that in June 1967 there was no protocol between the Army Communications Station in the Pentagon and the U.S. Navy for sending a message to a ship. The Navy sent messages to fleet broadcast via Navy communications daily. The army rarely sent messages to ships, and on the few occasions when it did, the messages were to ships off Vietnam. This is probably the reason the messages were routed to the Navy Communications Station in the Philippines.

To better appreciate the text of the report, one should be aware that, notwithstanding the fact that the United States has the world's finest navy, for some reason even as recently as the Gulf War the Navy remained woefully inadequate in its routine communications with its deployed ships. Brig. Gen. Roscoe Cougill (Ret.), speaking at Harvard University on the status of naval communications during the Gulf War, said: "Then Desert Storm began. I did have message backlogs when the war started, mainly in the priority and routine area and mainly with the U.S. Navy, which was still locked somewhere in the 17th century with its communications."[45]

In 1967, fleetwide broadcasts and other naval messages were generated by teletype. If the message was classified up to secret, following its being typed in English into the teletype machine, it was automatically encrypted and then transmitted. When received, the message was automatically decoded and printed. This process was known as "on-line encryption." However, if the message being generated was classified top secret, after being typed it was first manually encrypted. The message then had to be decoded manually and printed at the receiving end. This was known as "off-line encryption."

This completely manual procedure (with the built-in factor of greater likelihood of human error) meant that there was a greater possibility of delay in understanding commands in the rare top-secret messages sent over the fleetwide broadcast system to second-level units such as the *Liberty*.

Hence some of the "Findings and Conclusions" of the House Armed Services Investigating Subcommittee Report are noteworthy:

1. Communications systems are only as good as those who operate and use them in the command and decision making process. . . .

   b. The Department of Defense Satellite Communications System will not achieve operational capability for some time. That system has lagged several years behind commercial systems. . . .

   g. The time required for processing of messages, before and after their electronic transmission, has prevented any significant improvement in "writer-to-reader" time, despite installation of automatic switch equipment. Statistics reflect that an average of 70 minutes is required for processing a "flash" message, whereas the average time for electronic transmission of such a message is only 5 minutes.

2. Unresponsive communications systems of the Department of Defense delayed the execution of command decisions and retarded
the transmission of information to command officials in critical
international situations.[46]

In the summary of the report, a colloquy between Rep. Durward C. Hall
of Missouri and Air Force lieutenant general Richard P. Klocko,[47] the director of the Defense Communications Agency, was carried on:

Mr. Hall. The clincher is to ask the General one question: Given another
scenario like the *Liberty,* are you confident in your own mind that now
we would have the necessary communications to promptly and effectively complete the command decision?
    General Klocko. No, sir, I couldn't guarantee that.
    Mr. Hall. Then we are in a hell of a mess Mr. Chairman.[48]

The problem of inadequate communications was not unique to the *Liberty* incident. It should be remembered that in 1812 the war between the
United States and England concluded with the Treaty of Ghent, signed on
December 24, 1814. But because that information couldn't be communicated in a timely way, the Battle of New Orleans was fought on January 8,
1815, fifteen days after the combat had effectively ended, costing seventy-
one U.S. casualties and the loss of 289 lives by the British. Communications
capability has improved over the years to the state described by Vice Adm.
John M. McConnell, deputy director of the CIA, at the U.S. Naval Institute
Military Intelligence Seminar at Suitland, Maryland, on June 27, 1995. Admiral McConnell said: "Today signals that are intercepted on the battlefield
usually are too complex to be handled on the battlefield. It requires a lot of
computer power. It is routine for us now to bring them from the battlefield
back to NSA to do whatever the processing is needed on the signal and then
move it back to the battlefield. In Yugoslavia that takes us twelve seconds. In
some places we do it in as few as three seconds." Unfortunately, in 1967, the
U.S. Navy communications capability was more like that of 1812 than 1995.
    In the late 1970s interest in the *Liberty* attack was revived by the publica-
tion of an article by Richard K. Smith in the June 1978 U.S. Naval Institute
Proceedings and by the James M. Ennes Jr. book *Assault on the "Liberty,"* published in 1979.[49] Certain senators read the material, and in 1979 the *Liberty*
incident found its way to the Senate Select Committee on Intelligence. The

chairman of the committee was Birch Bayh of Indiana; the vice chairman was Barry Goldwater of Arizona. The committee began an investigation by sending staff members to Israel to take testimony and collect material provided by the Israel Air Force and Navy. The investigators were permitted to interview the pilots who attacked the *Liberty*. The pilots sat behind a sheet or screen so they could not be identified by the investigators.[50] This author met with and interviewed the pilots face to face and is the only non-Israeli to have done so. In response to this inquiry, the Israel Defense Force Department of Combat History prepared a report on the *Liberty* incident.[51] The introduction to the report states that "the American Congress appointed a committee, headed by Adlai Stevenson, for the purpose of investigating the affair and publishing the results of the investigation."[52]

What is quite clear is that the committee began an investigation of the *Liberty* incident that involved sending its staff to Israel. It is the only time that an official U.S. investigation did any inquiry or fact-finding in Israel on the *Liberty* attack. The committee heard the allegations and gathered and reviewed evidence. Almost no record or institutional memory of this investigation can be found.[53] There is considerable correspondence between the CIA and various committee members. Various Israel Defense Force officials recall the investigation and visits of committee staff to Israel.[54] After an extensive investigation, the committee apparently did not find sufficient evidence to warrant pursuing Smith's and Ennes's charges, and the investigation was laid to rest without releasing a report,[55] thus leaving undisturbed the official U.S. government position taken by President Johnson and maintained by Presidents Nixon, Ford, Carter, Reagan, Bush (41), Clinton, and Bush (43).

Two other events occurred in this time frame that seem to further support the conclusion. First, the Israel Defense Force Department of Combat History prepared and published an official Israeli version of the *Liberty* attack entitled *The Attack on the* Liberty *Incident*. This document makes specific reference to a U.S. congressional committee created to investigate the *Liberty* incident. Although it remains classified by Israel, the document was delivered to the U.S. government and was the beginning of Israel's relaxation of security and the release of information about the *Liberty* incident.

Second, within this time frame the U.S. Department of State settled the *Liberty* incident with Israel by an exchange of diplomatic notes that acquiesced in the Israeli position that Israel refused to accept total blame for the incident. Did the Department of State receive any data from the Senate Select Committee? State Department documents declassified to date do not indicate such a passage of information from the committee to the Department of State.

The super-secret National Security Agency published a seventy-seven-page document fourteen years after the event. The top-secret document was partially declassified and released in 1983.[56] It was authored by two NSA officials after they had retired. The authors are William D. Gerhard and Henry M. Millington. Though scheduled for declassification review in 2011, the document has been partially declassified more than one time since 1983 and was further declassified pursuant to the FOIA request of this author on July 2, 2003, and then further declassified voluntarily by the NSA on June 6, 2007. Nothing further has been released as a result of the scheduled 2011 review.

Though a great deal of the document remains classified, the unclassified portions disclose a wealth of data. The NSA is very candid in shouldering more than its share of the blame. The foreword to the report, written by Vincent J. Wilson Jr., chief historian and publications staffer at NSA, describes the document: "The passage of time has made it possible for the authors to reexamine the *Liberty* incident objectively and answer a number of persistent questions. The authors accordingly set forth the technical rationale for the *Liberty* mission, the particulars of the Israeli miscalculation, the details of the American communications failures, a narrative of the attack [deleted] and the lessons to be learned from the event."

The unclassified table of contents of the copy of the document in the National Archives indicates that in chapter 5, on page 38, the report sets forth the Israel prosecutor's charges of negligence, but page 38 of the document as obtained from the National Archives remains redacted, with the exception of a picture of an Israeli motor torpedo boat of the class that attacked the *Liberty* and a note that the figure is unclassified. Other unredacted copies of chapter 5 are in the possession of various persons. The document shows unclassified pictures, which were used as the basis for the silhouettes shown on page 161.

The document concludes with respect to the Israelis:

(U[unclassified]) In summation, the judge concluded that in all the circumstances of the case the conduct of the naval officers concerned in the *Liberty* incident could not be considered unreasonable to an extent which would justify committal for trial.

Explanation Reexamined (U)

(U) Reexamination of Israel's explanation of why its air and naval forces attacked the *Liberty* reveals egregious errors in both command judgments and operational procedures.[57]

The NSA was certainly angry with Israel over the death of its own staff member as well as the deaths of thirty-three Navy men on board a platform that NSA had sent to the war zone and was unable to extract in time to avert disaster.[58] Like the Navy, the NSA has an emotional connection with the *Liberty* incident. Its man, a civilian employee, Allen Blue, was killed on board the *Liberty,* and its program was negatively affected. It would be easy to understand if the NSA rejected the Israeli explanation as a result of the direct impact of the event on the agency and the fact that many of its staff members probably knew Allen Blue. Nevertheless, the NSA was not influenced by emotions and concluded in the report that the *Liberty* had been mistaken for an Egyptian ship as a result of miscalculations and egregious errors.[59]

In June 1991, on the twenty-fourth anniversary of the *Liberty* incident, the *Liberty* Veterans Association held its annual reunion in Washington, D.C. The chief of staff to President Bush, John Sununu, arranged to meet the veterans in the Rose Garden of the White House. There was high anticipation that they would have an opportunity to present their grievances about the *Liberty* incident to the president. The president did not join them in the Rose Garden that day. In fact, the president already had a position on the *Liberty* incident, which is set forth in a letter from the White House dated September 5, 1991. Its essence is: "A thorough investigation into the USS *Liberty* incident was conducted and the conclusion was that it was a tragic case of mistaken identity. No real basis exists for reopening the matter."[60]

Through Sununu, the *Liberty* veterans were referred to Congressman Nicholas Mavroules, chairman of the House Armed Services Subcommittee on Investigations, to whom they sent a letter dated July 1, 1991, requesting an investigation of the *Liberty* incident. The letter contained twenty-two specific allegations, many of which have little to do with the issue of whether or not the attack was a mistake—for example, "The American Red Cross refused to honor USS *Liberty* survivors' requests to notify our next of kin as to our condition."[61]

A letter supported by the president's chief of staff clearly carried some political weight. Mavroules obtained the loan of Roy J. Kirk from the General Accounting Office (now the Government Accountability Office), one of Congress's investigating arms, and began an investigation that lasted nearly a year. Warren Nelson, a member of Congressman Mavroules's staff, had code-word security clearance, which is higher than top secret. He personally reviewed the then-still-classified Clifford Report and the NSA document in its unredacted form and confirmed to Kirk that neither report contained any support for an intentional-attack theory.[62] Kirk was able to read the Clifford Report and found it not to be significant. Ultimately the committee concluded that the incident had already been fully investigated and that there was no evidence to support the allegations made by the *Liberty* Veterans Association or any reason for any further investigation. The subcommittee did not issue a report.

In all, then, the attacks were investigated by a naval court of inquiry, the CIA, the NSA, the JCS, and the President's Foreign Intelligence Advisory Board and examined by Congress on five occasions. Each official investigation concluded either that the attacks were a tragic mistake or that there was no evidence that the attacks were anything else. Seven U.S. presidents—three Democrats and four Republicans—have agreed.[63] The official investigations and presidential positions remain consistent. The *Liberty* incident was a tragic mistake. There is no competent evidence to the contrary.

Chapter 13

ISRAEL INVESTIGATES

Israeli military law is based on U.S. and British military law. In the U.S. Navy, a Judge Advocate General (JAG) Manual investigation is required any time a death, injury, or damage to property occurs. The investigation may be conducted by one officer, who need not be a lawyer. The initial Israeli investigation of the *Liberty* incident began with the appointment of Col. Ram Ron as a commission of inquiry to examine the *Liberty* incident under section 537 of the Israeli Military Justice Law of 1955.[1] The initial investigation was comparable to a U.S. Navy JAG Manual investigation.

Ram Ron was born in Poland in 1925 and came to Israel as a baby. He had received some legal training at the University of Jerusalem but was not a judge or a lawyer. He was an infantry officer and paratrooper who had served as a battalion commander and a brigade commander and had been assigned to the planning division at General Headquarters. He spent the 1967 war with Gen. Avraham Joffe in the Sinai. Upon his appointment he began his investigation on June 12, completing his report on June 16, 1967. When asked by this author about command control and what influence or pressure, if any, was put on him in regard to the investigation, Ram Ron responded, "One thing I can tell you for sure, I was totally free to come to any conclusion. Had I come to a conclusion that a crime had been committed, I would have reported it without hesitation."[2] Ron concluded that a chain of battlefield errors resulted in a severe tragedy—for the dead and wounded and their families, for the American people, and for Israel.

The investigation was conducted mainly at naval headquarters in Haifa. Ron considered at least fourteen items of documentary evidence.[3] He took testimony from twelve witnesses, all air force and naval officers, including the commander of the navy, the officer who authorized the torpedo attack, the motor torpedo boat division commander, and the captain of the torpedo boat that launched the torpedo that hit the *Liberty*. He also took testimony of the chief of Air Force Intelligence, the chief of Air Force Operations, and the chief air controller, who selected and dispatched the aircraft to attack the *Liberty*. He did not have communication with, or access to, any U.S. witnesses.

His report contains a number of minor errors that do not bear on the conclusions reached. For example, he reports that four torpedoes were launched, when the number was five. He confirms that a ship was observed and identified as the U.S. ship *Liberty* at 0550 on the morning of June 8. However, he lists her bow marks as "R.T.R.-5," when in fact they were "GTR 5."[4]

He came to the conclusion that the attack resulted from three principal Israeli errors. There were numerous other errors, some of which he mentioned and some not. The three points on which he focused were (1) the erroneous report concerning the shelling of El Arish; (2) the establishment of the *Liberty*'s speed at thirty knots; and (3) the identification of the *Liberty* as the *El Quseir*. He also concluded that "another grave error—no less decisive than the mistakes referred to above—was made by the ship *Liberty* itself." He concludes that the *Liberty* "acted carelessly and placed herself in far reaching peril by approaching so near to the coast of an area known to her to be a war area without giving notice of her presence to the Israeli authorities" and that she tried to conceal her identity and presence in an area that was not a navigation area crossed by maritime routes but rather an area where ships do not usually sail.

Ron made a number of recommendations, including that procedures be established for declaring "danger zones"; that pilots be better trained in the identification of enemy vessels; and that better procedures be established for disseminating information about neutral ships observed in war zones. Ron found a chain of errors, a lot of nervousness on the part of the navy, and a lot of "fog of the battlefield."

The file and the report were forwarded to Col. Meir Shamgar, the military advocate general, on June 18, 1967. After two days' study by Colonel Shamgar, it was submitted to Lt. Gen. Itzhak Rabin, Chief of Staff, with a recommendation to convene a preliminary inquiry under section 283 of the Israel Military Justice Law of 1955.[5]

Why did the military advocate general want a preliminary inquiry, when the commission of inquiry had reported no misconduct or wrongdoing by the IDF? When interviewed in Jerusalem on June 6, 1988, Shamgar, who was then serving as the president of the Supreme Court of Israel, answered that he wanted a full judicial procedure because of the seriousness of the event and the fact that so many people had been killed and injured. He stated that while he never had the slightest suspicion of any malicious intent, he was not satisfied with only a military review, which someone might characterize as sweeping the incident under the rug. He wanted judicial consideration of the errors reported by Ram Ron and judicial determination of whether any of the reported errors constituted negligence or misfeasance that might rise to a level where prosecution was warranted.

So Judge Yeshayahu Yerushalmi, a lieutenant colonel in the IDF, began a procedure as examining judge. Yerushalmi was born in Poland in 1920 and came to Israel in 1935. He graduated from Balfour College in Tel Aviv and went on to study law at the University of Jerusalem. He joined the Haganah and worked as a law clerk and lawyer from March 1942 until 1947, when he joined the army as a private. He was soon transferred to the military advocate general and became JAG to the air force and then JAG to the navy. In 1957 he was appointed as a judge on the Court of Military Appeals, a position he had held for ten years when he was appointed as examining judge in the *Liberty* matter.

Yerushalmi heard thirty-four witnesses and received fourteen documents into evidence in the *Liberty* inquiry. Witnesses included the operations officers of the air force, the navy, and General Headquarters; the persons who were on the motor torpedo boats; and the pilots of the attacking aircraft. The proceedings were closed to the public but were recorded by a court reporter (who was a sergeant in the army at the time but later became a lieutenant colonel and a judge).

The proceeding was conducted using a combination of English and American common law. The rules of evidence were observed, and hearsay was not allowed. As in a U.S. Navy court of inquiry, the proceeding began as a fact-finding procedure and went forward until the judge stopped the proceedings and named parties. Like its U.S. counterpart, the proceeding was then adjourned to allow any named party to obtain counsel and prepare a defense. From that point on, the proceeding was adversarial. The government was represented by Chief Military Prosecutor Yaacov Kedmi, who had the burden of proof. The named party, in this case Avraham "Ramy" Lunz, was represented by Chief Military Defense Counsel Villie Tien, and the inquiry continued with the possibility that the judge could bind over the party for prosecution by court-martial. Defendant Lunz called three witnesses, produced five exhibits, and made a statement under oath.

Judge Yerushalmi did not see the Ram Ron report before starting his inquiry, and his work was totally independent. Recalling the episode, he particularly remembers that he was shown silhouettes of the *Liberty* and the *El Quseir*. They were overlaid, and Judge Yerushalmi found the overlays to be persuasive evidence. He also recalls that at the time, after weeks of waiting for the crisis to develop, there was extreme tension in Israel. There was also a strong concern for the feelings of the United States, as well as gratitude, because no one in the world stood with Israel except the United States.

Yerushalmi made it clear "that it is not my function to determine, in any manner whatsoever, whether the *Liberty* acted properly at any stage prior to the incident or during the incident itself." However, he went on to say that in order to determine the reasonableness of all concerned, it would be necessary for him to examine the conduct of the *Liberty*. He did a thorough job of analyzing the testimony and the facts known on the Israeli side of the equation. He, like Rear Admiral Kidd, was handicapped by lack of input from the other parties to the incident. Yerushalmi told this author that each day he asked the chief military prosecutor, "When are the Americans coming?" Finally he was told that they were not coming. It is amazing that both Yerushalmi and Kidd were able to do such excellent work without input from each other.

Yerushalmi noted in his decision that the incident had occurred in the midst of a war, very close to a coast where battles were still raging, and that the *Liberty* had been in "the naval battles arena," an area that had been declared by the Egyptians as dangerous for shipping,[6] of which he presumed the *Liberty* was aware. He also noted that the site of the attack was not on a recognized shipping lane and that foreign warships, particularly in sensitive zones, announce their approaches to foreign shores.

He entered an interim decision on July 5, 1967, holding: "It appears to me, *prima facie,* that offenses of negligence may have been committed by the Acting Chief of Naval Operations (Avraham Lunz) because he did not report to the Head of the Naval Department, that on the day of the incident the American ship *Liberty* was observed proceeding in the vicinity of and along the Israel coast."[7] The inquiry then reconvened as an adversarial proceeding and was completed on July 21, 1967 (the thirteenth day of Tamuz 5727 on the Hebrew calendar) with the reading of the judge's his decision in the presence of the chief military prosecutor, Major Kedmi; the chief military defense counsel, Lieutenant Colonel Tein; and the Acting Chief of Naval Operations, Avraham Lunz.

When the inquiring judge's decision had been rendered, it was classified and sent to the United States by two different routes. One copy was delivered at the Department of State in Washington, D.C., by Deputy Chief of Mission Ephraim Evron, to the U.S. Under Secretary of State, Nicholas Katzenbach. Katzenbach read the report in Evron's presence and then stated that it was an excellent report except for the last sentence. The last sentence stated, "I hold that there is no sufficient amount of *prima facie* evidence, justifying committing anyone for trial."

As a general rule of appellate review, many cases fall into a category called "fairly debatable." In such cases, the reviewing court allows the decision to stand and does not substitute its judgment for the judgment of the judge who heard the testimony and had the opportunity to observe the demeanor and appearance of the witnesses and deal with the evidence at first hand. Perhaps if the judge had been American rather than Israeli, a decision to prosecute might have been reached. It is always easier for someone conducting a review of actions taken and decisions made under great pressure to calmly and peacefully decide what would have been the best decision. But at the time and place of the event, when the original actors' glands were pumping adrenaline and the fight-or-flight syndrome was affecting their brains, it becomes more a question of whether they acted reasonably than whether they acted perfectly. Judge Yerushalmi put it this way in his decision: "For all my regret that our forces were involved in an incident with a vessel of a friendly state, and its sad outcome, I ought to put the behavior of each of the officers, who had any connection with the incident, to the test of the conduct of reasonable officers during war operations, when the Naval arm of the Israel Defense Force was confronted with maritime forces superior in numbers, and when all involved were conscious of the task before them—to protect the safety of Israel, to identify every enemy threatening from the sea, to attack it and speedily destroy it. The criterion for reasonable conduct under these conditions may possibly differ from that in time of relative quiet."[8]

A copy of the decision was delivered to the U.S. Chief of Naval Operations, Adm. Thomas Moorer, who limited it for dissemination to only four codes in his office: one copy stayed with the CNO, Code 00; one copy went to the Vice Chief of Naval Operations, Code 09; one went to Operations, Code 62; and one went to Intelligence, Code 92. Although the document has never been declassified, it is easily obtainable in the Pentagon and in Israel.

Neither Ram Ron's report nor Judge Yerushalmi's decision was satisfactory to the U.S. Department of State. The position of the State Department had been since the *Liberty* incident occurred that the responsible military persons should be punished. The language of the initial notes from Dean Rusk to the Israeli ambassador stated this in no uncertain language. A note handed personally to Ambassador Avraham Harman of Israel by Under Secretary Eugene V. Rostow contained the language, "The Secretary of State wishes to make clear that the United States Government expects the Government of Israel also to take the disciplinary measures which international law requires in the event of wrongful conduct by the military personnel of a State."[9] The Clifford Report also recommended that Israeli military personnel be punished.[10]

It is quite common for the country of victims harmed to cry out for punishment by another country of individuals responsible for inflicting the harm. It is far less common for countries to take formal disciplinary action against their own personnel. In the Cam Pha Harbor incident, in which U.S. Air Force planes attacked the Soviet ship *Turkestan* by mistake, killing and wounding Soviet sailors, a general court-martial against the pilots who made the attack and the colonel who failed to report, or covered up, the incident resulted in acquittal of the pilots and a six-hundred-dollar fine for the colonel. In the USS *Stark* incident, a court-martial of the *Stark*'s commanding officer was considered, but instead he was allowed to retire at the next lower rank.[11] Although Turkey called for disciplinary action when Sea Sparrow missiles were accidentally launched from the U.S. aircraft carrier *Saratoga* into the bridge of the Turkish destroyer *Muavenet,* killing the captain and others and wounding a large number of crew members, the only punishment was a letter of reprimand placed in the file of one U.S. naval officer. In the Black Hawk helicopter shoot-down, one low-ranking air force officer, Capt. James Wang, was sent to court-martial, where he was promptly acquitted.

Ambassador Evron told this author that the issue of punishment had often been discussed between him and Itzhak Rabin, who on numerous occasions had said to Evron that it was unfortunate that there had been no formal punishment of some military person involved, because people in the United States interpreted the lack of punishment of a lower-ranking person as an indication of a cover-up at a higher level.

While there was no court-martial, punishment within the understanding of the naval service itself was clearly evident in an event that took place about two weeks after the 1967 war, the most successful war in the history of the state of Israel. Capt. Issy Rehav, the second in command of the Israel Navy and the most likely candidate to become the next commander in

Royal Flight Mystere attacking from the stern.

An Israeli torpedo boat passes the port side of USS *Liberty* following its attack.
U.S. NAVY PHOTO

An Israeli torpedo boat passes across the *Liberty*'s bow. Note the ship's 10°
list to starboard. U.S. NAVY PHOTO

Liberty turns to port during the torpedo attack.

Capt. Donald D. Engen, right, with Vice Adm. C. T. "Tommy" Booth, Commander, Naval Air Force, Atlantic Fleet, on the flight deck of USS *America*. On June 8, 1967, Engen was commanding officer of *America*. Before he retired as a vice admiral, he served as deputy commander in chief, Atlantic Fleet. He later served on the National Transportation Safety Board, as president of AOPA Safety Foundation, as administrator of the Federal Aviation Administration, and as director of the Smithsonian National Air and Space Museum. U.S. NAVY PHOTO

An A-4C Skyhawk of VA-64 seconds away from launching from the *America*. On June 8, 1967, *America* launched four of VA-64's Skyhawks armed with AGM-12 "Bullpup" air-to-ground missiles to defend *Liberty*. U.S. NAVY PHOTO

Liberty arrives at Valletta, Malta. Note the torpedo hole on the starboard side. U.S. NAVY PHOTO

In Malta, Cdr. William L. McGonagle, commanding officer of the *Liberty*, surveys the damage to his ship. *Liberty* had arrived safely at Valletta, Malta, on June 14. For his actions on June 8, McGonagle received the Medal of Honor. U.S. NAVY PHOTO

Liberty's superstructure bears mute testimony to the severity of the attack. As a result of the encounter, 34 crewmen were killed and 171 were wounded, many severely. U.S. NAVY PHOTO

Liberty on the day after the attack, with a decided starboard list. The helicopter hovering near the bow is removing casualties to the *America*. The large holiday 7 x 13–foot flag is more than twice the size of the flag that flew at the beginning of the air attack. Even the larger flag appears small in comparison to the size of the ship.

U.S. NAVY PHOTO

America's sailors "man the rail" to observe the scarred and listing intelligence ship. Evident in both photographs is a helicopter working to evacuate *Liberty*'s wounded and dead to the carrier. The guided missile cruiser USS *Little Rock*, flagship of the U.S. Sixth Fleet, passes alongside in the background.

U.S. NAVY PHOTO

chief of the navy, resigned from the service.[12] Had Rehav been fired? When asked, Rear Adm. Shlomo Erell, the commander in chief of the navy in 1967, said no. He also said that he had had a heart-to-heart talk with Rehav and pointed out to him that he had made a serious error in judgment when he authorized the *tesha vuv*, the torpedo attack. Erell pointed out that on the afternoon of June 8, 1967, the burning ship off El Arish had been no threat to Israel or the Israel Defense Forces. There had been many other options, including capturing the ship, that should have been considered. So while most of Israel was rejoicing over the great 1967 victory, a man who had spent his adult life working his way up to a position from which he would probably become commander in chief instead resigned from the navy.

In June 1982 the Israel Defense Forces, History Department, Research and Instruction Branch, published a classified document in Hebrew and English entitled *The Attack on the "Liberty" Incident*. The document says its object is to present an authoritative version of the circumstances and chain of events that led to the *Liberty* incident and to respond to some of the claims made regarding Israel's intentions.[13]

The IDF history report is essentially what was provided to the investigators from the Senate Select Committee on Intelligence. The report itself was written by Lt. Col. Matti Greenberg, head of the Combat Research Branch. It is still classified but is easily obtainable in the United States and Israel. Some of the documentary items listed in the eighty-eight endnotes are far more difficult to obtain. (The original Hebrew version of this document is thirty-two pages; the English translation is forty-two pages.)

The IDF history is probably the most extensive research accomplished in Israel on the *Liberty* incident up to the time of its publication. It was not prepared under serious pressure, and its author had access to all Israeli data. The movements of the *Liberty* to the combat zone are discussed, followed by the details of the "attack."[14] The report then discusses the causes of the errors and Israel's actions following the incident. It ends with a discussion of the revival of the affair. It suggests that the incident has an inherent interest because of the "mystery of a spy ship," "the drama of war," and the "tragedy of the killed and wounded." The report finds two common denominators in the stories put forth by the various doubters: first, the categorical assertion that the *Liberty* was maliciously attacked by Israel with the intention of sinking her; second, weighty-seeming reasons why Israel acted maliciously. These common denominators are linked with "flights of imagination, missing facts, half truths or false conclusions."[15] The report then spends several pages responding to the alleged reasons for malice. The IDF report comes to the following conclusion:

> An examination of the facts in the *Liberty* incident, in their proper context proves beyond any doubt that the attack on the American intelligence ship came about as a result of innocent error by the forces which operated on the spot and the HQs which supervised them.
>
> Though the attack on the armed forces of a friendly nation is a most regrettable and painful occurrence, incidents of this kind do occur in war-time.
>
> It goes without saying that such an incident must be thoroughly investigated, that all causes of the tragic encounter must be examined, conclusions drawn, and proper instructions issued which will prevent the occurrence of such an incident in the future. From Israel's point of view all these steps have been carried out in a most thorough and comprehensive manner. However, it is inappropriate to attribute malicious intent to Israel, when the evidence does not bear out such an attribution.[16]

The carefully worded conclusion leaves the blame on "forces which operated on the spot," which would include the *Liberty* and the "HQs which supervised them," including the U.S. higher command.

> The Israelis make a good point on their two common denominators. Most, if not all, of the doubters start with a conclusion that Israel intentionally attacked a known U.S. ship, without offering any evidence to support the conclusion, instead offering reasons why Israel intentionally attacked.
>
> The *Liberty* incident remains a very sensitive issue with the IDF, and while the Israelis have always insisted that they are entitled to only part of the blame for the tragedy, they go out of their way to be delicate about putting blame on the United States. A good example of this sensitivity is reflected in the letter from the officer in command of the Israel Navy in response to an article published in the *Naval Reserve Association Newsletter*. As gentle as the letter is, it accepts only "humanitarian responsibility" and refers to the diplomatic settlement that left open the issue of blame on both sides:

Commander in Chief of the Navy of Israel

As General Officer in Command of the Navy of Israel, I read with pain and sorrow the article published in the June issue of the *Naval Reserve Association Newsletter*. On June 8, 1967, the U.S.S. *Liberty* sailed into the middle of our Six Day War. That she did so was a mistake on the part of the U.S. Navy, as has been thoroughly established by an extensive investigation of the House Armed Services Committee of the Ninety Second Congress, under authority of H. Res. 201, published by the Superintendent of Documents in 1971. It is undisputed that the Joint Chiefs of Staff and the National Security Agency believed that it would be dangerous for *Liberty* to approach the Sinai Coast, and sent at least five Naval Messages to her directing her to remain clear of the area. These messages were misdirected by the Naval Communications System, and were not received by *Liberty* until after the tragedy had occurred. The next mistakes were ours, and a series of blunders on our part resulted in our attacks on a naval vessel of our best friend in the world at that time.

We immediately accepted humanitarian responsibility, offered our apology and condolences and paid humanitarian reparations to the dead and the wounded in amounts set by the United States government.

Thereafter we settled the remaining issues regarding the *Liberty* with the United States at the diplomatic level.

Mere words can never ease the pain of young lives lost in their prime. We sent you our words of condolence in 1967 full knowing that words are not enough. Still today, twenty five years later, we share your grief and pain. Again I express to you our apology and condolences. I regret the tone of the author of your June 1992 article. I fully understand his bitterness and my sympathy for him and his shipmates is in no way diminished by his perhaps less than objective perspective.

We made the mistake, we admitted it and we remain extremely sorry and distressed.

There have been at least ten official investigations of the incident both in Israel and in the United States. Every official investigation, yours and ours, has concluded that the event was a tragic mistake. There have also been numerous unofficial investigations, such as those conducted by Thames TV, ABC News, and NBC News, to name a few. These unofficial investigations, after examining the evidence, have also concluded that the event was a tragic mistake. The published article confirms this with the words "after filming was completed . . . [the] producers slanted the story to favor the Israeli version." The "story" does not favor Israel. An examination of the facts merely confirms the tragic mistake.

Confirmation of the true version of events is readily available in the record of the U.S. Navy Court of Inquiry or the C.I.A. report, both of which are now declassified and available to you.

Israel and the Navy of Israel have a great debt to the United States and the United States Navy. Our first General Officer in Command of the Navy of Israel, the equivalent to your CNO, was a U.S. Naval Academy graduate. Your traditions are our traditions. In this case, your grief and your loss are also our grief and our loss.

With my deepest respect,
Michael Ram
Commander in Chief
Israel Navy.[17]

Chapter 14

TELEVISION'S PERSPECTIVE

In 1986, a well-known Thames TV producer, Rex Bloomstein, heard of the intentional-attack theory and came to the United States with a team to do the story. His team consisted of himself as producer/director, Adrian Pennink as research editor, Mary Horwood as production assistant, and David Hudson-Millman as film editor.[1] The taping began in Washington, D.C., with the allegations of a number of surviving *Liberty* crew members: Lloyd Painter, George Golden, James Ennes Jr., and Phil Tourney. At the time of the taping, the U.S. Navy court of inquiry record of proceedings and the CIA report had already been declassified, but they were not in the Thames TV research files.[2] The Thames team became very fond of, and sympathetic to, the *Liberty* crew. Early scripts of the program contemplated telling the *Liberty* veterans' story, concluding with a few authenticity shots in Israel and a remark that the Israel Defense Force declined comment, because, until that point, the official Israeli position on the *Liberty* incident had been "no comment."

When the Thames team concluded its shooting in the United States and went to Tel Aviv, the script changed dramatically. It contacted the office of the Israel Defense Force Spokesman, the counterpart of the U.S. Department of Defense public affairs officer, and requested an official comment about the *Liberty*. The Deputy IDF Spokesman was a reserve colonel named Raanan Gissin. Instead of responding "no comment" as expected, Colonel Gissin, along with Israel Air Force major Danny Grossman and army lieutenant colonel Matti Greenberg of the IDF Combat History Branch, took the request directly to the IDF Spokesman and argued that it was time to tell the Israeli side of the story. They won their argument, and suddenly the Thames team found themselves with a very large group of Israeli military personnel who had been authorized to meet with them, answer questions, and cooperate. A high-ranking and highly decorated retired naval officer, Capt. Yaacov Nitzan, was assigned to provide technical assistance. The navy provided documents and pictures. The air force provided gun-camera film, as well as transcriptions and translations of audiotape of the attack. The more Bloomstein and Pennink investigated, the less confidence they had in their original script concept. The producer developed enough doubt to change the program format from the *Liberty* Veterans Association's allegations and an Israeli "no comment" to a presentation of the crew members' story and their evidence followed by the Israeli response. The producer merely reported what each side presented and did not take a position endorsing either. Near the end of the Thames program, Bloomstein, as commentator, made the following statement: "Any examination of the conflicting arguments must first come to terms with motive. 24 hours after the attack on the 'Liberty,' the Israelis took the Golan Heights. Was this a coincidence, or was the assault on the spy ship designed to stop it intercepting plans for the invasion?"[3]

Then followed the comments of Capt. Ernest Castle, the U.S. naval attaché at the U.S. embassy in Tel Aviv in 1967, who strongly endorsed the mistake theory. Then the voice-over by Bloomstein, the commentator, mentioned the allegations that Moshe Dayan ordered the attack: "If there was a high level conspiracy to destroy the 'Liberty,' an inevitable suspect was the Minister of Defense, Moshe Dayan. But on the 8th of June, Dayan was the only voice in the Israeli Cabinet against an attack on Syria. It was not until the next morning, when he learnt that Egypt, Jordan and Syria had agreed to a cease-fire that he gave the order to invade the Golan 16 hours after the 'Liberty' was attacked."[4] The program was aired on Tuesday, January 27, 1987, at 10:30 p.m. on British television.

Just a few weeks after it was broadcast in England, the Thames documentary was aired on Israeli television on February 15, 1987, on an evening program titled *Mabat Shaine*,[5] which is an Israeli magazine-format show similar to *20/20* or *60 Minutes*. The program began with the following introductory comment:

Good evening. The tragedy of the Intelligence Ship *Liberty* left a deep scar on U.S.-Israeli relationship. . . .

[A]s we will shortly see, former Secretary of State Mr. Dean Rusk claims that "Israel's Air Force and Navy intentionally attacked the ship . . . this was a premeditated scheme. . . ." This opinion is shared by many

American Navy men as well as those who served aboard the *Liberty* along with the 171 who were injured and family members of the 34 crew members that were killed. The rest blame Israel and the U.S. for conspiring to keep the records of the incident under complete secrecy.

The film we are about to see was aired by BBC Second Network a few weeks ago. Israeli diplomats in London were concerned at the time that the program will [would] raise anti-Israel feelings, especially after the recent revelation of the Vaanunu affair and the supply of arms to Iran scandal. In retrospect, these concerns were proven uncalled for. The newspaper comment after the broadcast concluded that Israel did not intentionally attack the ship, "It was a mistake." The work of the Thames team proved to be fair and objective and the producer, Rex Bloomstein, coordinated an outstanding investigation that we put on now for you.

Both the *Liberty* crew members who had initiated this production and the IDF Spokesman who changed his position and opened up to the Thames team were disappointed with the production, as each expected it to completely adopt their respective versions of the event.

In May 1987, the Iraqi attack on the U.S. guided-missile frigate *Stark* generated interest in the *Liberty* incident on the part of the producers of the ABC-TV program *20/20*. ABC News bought the rights to the Thames TV program and produced a segment aired on *20/20* that consisted of an edited version of the Thames program, cut from fifty-three minutes seventeen seconds to a little under thirty minutes. The *20/20* segment, produced with voice-overs by Barbara Walters and Hugh Downs, aired on May 21, 1987.

By the time *20/20* acquired the program, Thames producer Rex Bloomstein, who served as a technical adviser for the *20/20* production, had shifted from his neutral position and had become convinced that the attack on the *Liberty* was made in error by the Israelis.[6] Whether Bloomstein's opinion went with the sale of the videotape is unknown, but Barbara Walters opened the program with the remark, "The similarities to this week's attack on the USS *Stark* are uncanny."[7] Certainly the tenor of the program seemed to adopt the mistake theory. Walters and Downs explained and commented on the footage shown and concluded the program with the following colloquy:

Barbara Walters: "You know, there are unanswered questions about the *Liberty*. There will probably be unanswered questions about the *Stark* for years to come, but Hugh, if there is a lesson, couldn't one of them be that in time of war, even if it's not your war, you have to behave as if you might very well be the target, behave that way all the time?"

Hugh Downs: "Somebody once said, 'We learn from history that we do not learn from history.' I hope that's not true and I think there's a deeper lesson here, and that points to the urgent necessity of arms reduction in an age of high-tech weaponry, where a mistake can be so devastating. I think humanity has the potential to accomplish this and owes it to itself...."

Barbara Walters: "Because there are mistakes."

Hugh Downs: "You bet!"[8]

The "Liberty" newsletter reported that "Walters and Downs . . . repeatedly described the attack as a 'terrible accident.'" The article characterized the film as misleading because of what it described as the absence of effective rebuttal to the Israeli arguments and because of other alleged omissions.[9]

Shortly before the twenty-fourth anniversary of the *Liberty* incident, June 8, 1991, the *Liberty* Veterans Association extended an invitation to the NBC program *The Story behind the Story* to attend the association's annual meeting, which was held in Washington, D.C., that year, and to tape a program. Christopher Carlson, a producer working with NBC Television, and his team attended. A number of the *Liberty* crew members were videotaped on the afternoon of June 7, 1991. The producer, on his own, also obtained an on-camera appearance by Michael Shiloh,[10] Deputy Chief of Mission at the Embassy of Israel in Washington, D.C., who responded to each of the association members' allegations. Capt. William McGonagle, U.S. Navy (Ret.), the commanding officer of the *Liberty* at the time of the attack, met with the producer in the suite of George Golden, the president of the association. Captain McGonagle was quite firm in his position that he would go on tape only to talk about the professionalism and heroism of his crew in saving the ship and that he would not discuss theories of the attack.

The final format of the program was a segment of allegations followed by the Israeli rebuttal.[11] The program included Seth Mintz telling a modified version of his story and Cdr. David Lewis giving his account of his conversation with Rear Admiral Geis. James Ennes Jr. also told his story about the *Liberty* having been promised jet air cover overhead in ten minutes in the event of trouble.

The *Liberty* veterans had high hopes for this production, but they were extremely disappointed when the program aired on the evening of January 27, 1992. The program seemed to refute all their claims and support the mistake theory. The program began with the following opening statement by the commentators:

> Jane Wallace: "On the fourth day of the Six Day War, an American ship, the *Liberty*, was patrolling off the coast of the Gaza Strip."
>
> Richard Kiley: "Simultaneously, reports came in that a nearby Israeli position was being shelled from the sea. The Israeli high command believed they were under attack by Arab forces. Naval and Air units were sent to investigate and a counterattack was launched. The USS *Liberty* was in the wrong place at the wrong time."

The program was not fully researched and contained a number of misstatements of fact. Nevertheless, it was a reasonably accurate account and came to the conclusion that the incident was a tragic mistake, much to the distress of the *Liberty* crew members who had initiated the interest of NBC.

In the spring of 1992, an independent producer, Justin Sturken, heard the *Liberty* veterans' story and was very much persuaded by it. He taped the comments of two of the *Liberty* crewmen who told the "intentional attack on a U.S. ship" story. For balance, he taped the public affairs officer of Israel's embassy, Ruth Yaron, at the embassy in Washington, D.C. The program ran seven minutes, forty-eight seconds and was aired on April 14, 1992, on the Geraldo Rivera show *Now It Can Be Told*.[12] Geraldo introduced the tape with the comment:

> The year was 1967, and the tiny state of Israel was in a battle for its very existence. Surrounded by Arab enemies who cut off vital supply routes and then promised to push the Jews into the sea, Israel launched a blitz that became known as the Six Day War. On the fourth day of that intense and bloody conflict, Israeli aircraft and torpedo boats attacked an American spy ship that was located in the Mediterranean Sea. Thirty-four Americans were killed. Scores more were wounded. As our Craig Rivera now reports, many survivors believe this incident has been covered up for political reasons ever since that awful day.

Craig Rivera then commented, "It's been almost a quarter of a century since the USS *Liberty* left American shores and began its fateful voyage to the Middle East . . . and for all those years Israel has maintained that the attack on the *Liberty* was a tragic case of mistaken identity. But now, more than ever, the *Liberty* survivors and their backers think otherwise."

The program does little more than present the unsubstantiated allegations of two crew members, James Kavanaugh and Richard Sturman,
interviewed by Sturken with voice-over by Craig Rivera, and the response of
the Embassy of Israel public affairs officer. Geraldo Rivera's closing remarks
suggest that he leans toward the mistake theory. He concluded the program,
"Israeli officials admit their confusion at the time, including the identification of the *Liberty* at one point as a Russian vessel. Israeli sources also mention the fact that their war planes bombed and strafed their own troops in
an incident just before the *Liberty* attack. This is further evidence of a tragic
mistake that can often occur in the heat and fog of war." Geraldo Rivera's
comments certainly do not coincide with the very strong views held by Justin Sturken, the producer.[13]

On August 9, 2001, at 8:00 p.m. EDT the History Channel aired a program produced by Andrew Rothstein and David Siegel entitled *Cover-Up:
Attack on the USS Liberty.* The producers produced anything but history.
The program is not a professional documentary but rather a professional
hatchet job. The program was produced with inadequate research and is
infected with errors, misrepresentations, and charges not supported by any
evidence. All of the conspiracy theories presented in this program have been
previously refuted, disproved, or discredited.

The program lacks balance, in that the producers interviewed only a
half-dozen of the *Liberty* crew members.[14] The program failed to disclose
that the positions presented are not unanimously supported by the entire
Liberty crew. Not a single Israeli with firsthand involvement in the event was
interviewed. If the producers did not wish to take the necessary time or go
to the expense of such interviews, numerous interviews of Israelis with firsthand knowledge of the event were available on videotape from the Thames
TV or *20/20* programs on the subject. Of course, those programs presented
a very different picture of the event than this production.

The story told by Lloyd Painter, an officer who was on the bridge of the
Liberty at the time she was attacked, was apparently not checked against his
testimony under oath at the U.S. Navy court of inquiry thirty-four years
before. Painter's sworn testimony varies widely from his comments in the
program, but no mention was made of the difference.

Although probably not by design, the production does contain one enlightening sequence of footage looking past a copilot's helmet in a helicopter
slowly flying clockwise around the *Liberty,* first from stern to bow down the
port side and then from bow to stern down the starboard side. This helicop-

ter is flying at only a few hundred feet, permitting the viewer to observe the areas where the flag was hoisted on *Liberty*'s halyard, the letters and numbers on her bow and stem, and the name *Liberty* on her curved stern. It is readily apparent that the flag is not discernible; that the letters *GTR* are almost impossible to read, while the larger number 5 is more discernible; and that the curved stern makes it very difficult to read the name except from close in, directly astern. If these identification points are that difficult to see from a slow-moving helicopter within a few hundred feet of the ship and only a few hundred feet in the air, then it is apparent that a plane flying fast and high at a distance of a quarter of a mile or more would have little chance of identifying the ship from the flag, the hull marks, or the name on the stern.

The narrator, Arthur Kent, talks about, and attributes motives to, the actions of Robert McNamara, the U.S. secretary of defense in June 1967, but he neither interviews McNamara nor discloses his testimony about the event before Congress. Some excerpts from that testimony that conflict with the program's inferences are:

> Secretary McNamara. . . . But I have examined the record of investigation, and I find no intent by the Israeli Government, and no intent by any representative of the Israeli Government to attack a U.S. vessel. . . .
>
> Secretary McNamara. . . . In the case of the attack on the *Liberty,* it was the conclusion of the investigatory body headed by an admiral of the Navy in whom we have great confidence that the attack was not intentional.
>
> I read the record of the investigation, and I support that conclusion, and I think this, therefore . . . It was not a conscious decision on the part of either the Government of Israel . . . [t]o attack a U.S. vessel.[15]

The most outrageous false statement by Arthur Kent is: "Unidentified torpedo boats suddenly began firing. McGonagle sent a man to the ship's machine gun to fire back." The program thus accuses the Israeli torpedo boats of suddenly opening fire on *Liberty* and has the *Liberty* responding by firing back at the torpedo boats. Until this program was aired, it has not been disputed for thirty-four years that the torpedo boats arrived, stopped, and began signaling the *Liberty,* whereupon the *Liberty* opened fire on the torpedo boats. The sworn testimony of Commander McGonagle to that effect is in the record of the U.S. Navy court of inquiry, easily available to, but ignored by, the producers.[16] In addition, this author provided a copy of the Thames TV documentary *Attack on the "Liberty"* to producer David Siegel via a letter dated August 10, 2000. The tape contains footage of Commander McGonagle at a press conference in 1967 on board the *Liberty* with various crew members seated around him. In the tape, McGonagle confirms that the *Liberty* opened fire on the torpedo boats while the boats were "attempting to signal the ship."[17] In his court of inquiry testimony referred to above, Commander McGonagle said, "As far as the torpedo boats are concerned, I am sure that they felt that they were under fire from USS *Liberty*."

Another gross misstatement attacks the quality of the U.S. Navy court of inquiry investigation. Narrator Arthur Kent starts with, "During the formal inquiry aboard ship, it becomes apparent to the crew that the Navy is not interested in conducting an in-depth investigation." Since the court of inquiry was conducted behind closed doors, Kent does not explain how the intent of the Navy became apparent to the crew during the investigation. Next, crew member John Hrankowski appears on screen and comments, without any further explanation, "The Court of Inquiry was a farce." There is no mention of the fact that the court was convened by order of Adm. John S. McCain Jr., the commander of U.S. Naval Forces Europe, and swiftly went into session in London at 2314 London time on the evening of June 10 and took testimony until 0250 the following morning of June 11. The court then left immediately for Valletta, Malta, to meet the *Liberty*.

There is no mention of Admiral Kidd and his counsel flying to the *Liberty* while she was still at sea en route to Malta and boarding her at sea on June 12, or of how the court worked continuously after the *Liberty*'s arrival in Malta, taking testimony on June 14 and 15 and then flying back to London, where it took further testimony until 1645 on June 16. Following deliberations the court's report was presented to Admiral McCain, who endorsed it and dispatched Admiral Kidd to personally rush-deliver it to the Chief of Naval Operations in Washington, D.C. The actions of Admiral McCain, Admiral Kidd, and the Navy do not suggest a lack of interest in conducting the investigation. The record of the court of inquiry is available upon request from the office of the Judge Advocate General of the Navy. It consists of hundreds of pages, including 158 pages of testimony and forty-nine exhibits, many of which are lengthy. It concludes with fifty-two findings. These findings were endorsed by Admiral McCain with the following conclusion: "The foregoing comments by the convening authority lead to an overall conclusion that the attack was in fact a mistake." (See chapter 12 for more detail on the court of inquiry.)

It is respectfully suggested that any reasonable person who reads the record and examines the exhibits considered by the court of inquiry would agree that the quality of the report is outstanding. In fact, over thirty years later this author remains impressed by the vast scope of the investigation and its drafters' ability to gather the facts, deliberate on them, and complete the court's conclusions in the brief time in which the work of the court was accomplished.

Some *Liberty* conspiracy theorists complain that the court of inquiry did not take testimony from any Israeli witnesses. This is not unusual. After the Gulf War, the United States did not permit U.S. military personnel to appear or testify at the British inquiry into the deaths of nine British military personnel killed by U.S. friendly fire.[18] The Israelis did permit their pilots to talk to the U.S. Senate Select Committee on Intelligence (see chapter 12).

Former crew member James Ennes claims in the documentary that no one on the court of inquiry talked to any of the crew. The program fails to mention that the court of inquiry called and took the testimony of nineteen witnesses, of whom fourteen were *Liberty* crew members.[19]

The program does not mention that Ennes was wounded in the first minutes of the air attack and taken below deck, where he remained until he was transferred to the *America* the next day. He was presented on the program speaking in the first person about events that occurred out of his presence with no disclosure that his narrative was pure hearsay. Commander McGonagle remained on the *Liberty*'s bridge commanding the ship and ultimately sailed her out of harm's way to a rendezvous with Sixth Fleet destroyers the following morning. Under such circumstances one would assume that Commander McGonagle observed and knew more of what took place during the air and torpedo-boat attacks than Ennes. But the program does not give the viewer the opportunity of learning what Commander McGonagle saw, testified about under oath, and recorded in an official record.

The program provides a comment by Ennes regarding offers of help from the Israeli torpedo boats: "They claim that they came alongside and immediately offered help. Well, that is the purest of baloney." Neither the producers, the narrator, nor Ennes explain how Ennes knew anything about offers or lack of offers of help from the torpedo boats. When Commander McGonagle was recalled a second time to testify before the court of inquiry on June 14, 1967, less than a week after the event, he read into the record a chronology of events that the court, during his initial testimony the day before, had instructed him to prepare in consultation with his crew. The chronology entry for June 8, 1967, at 1503 was: "One MTB returned to ship and signaled ["Do you need help?" in English] C.O. signaled 'Negative.'"[20]

The *Liberty* deck log for 1503 on Thursday, June 8, 1967 reflects, "One MTB returned to ship and signalled 'Do you need help?' Commanding Officer directed that, 'Negative' be sent in reply."

Obviously, the Ennes account of this event, which he did not personally observe but presented thirty-four years later on the History Channel, and the account given by his commanding officer in sworn recorded testimony six days after the event (and corroborated by the *Liberty*'s log made at the time of the event) are not in agreement on this point. It is one of many times that Ennes has disagreed with the memory or actions of his commanding officer as well as the written official records created within a few days of the event. What kind of research did the producers do on this issue?

Another gross misrepresentation involves *Liberty* crewman Joe Meadors, who states that he signaled the torpedo boats and that he raised a flag after the first flag had been shot away. The sworn testimony at the U.S. Navy court of inquiry given a few days after the event by Ens. David G. Lucas and by Chief Petty Officer Harold Jessie Thompson indicates that Signalman Russell O. David did the signaling to the torpedo boats and that it was also Signalman David who raised the flag after it had been shot down.[21] In a letter dated September 4, 2001, Russell O. David authorized this author to quote him as follows: "I am, indeed, the one that did the signaling to the boats and I am the one who put up the sailing ensign after it was shot down! At that time I was one of only two people, on the ship, who could send and receive light transmissions, and I am the one who received the Bronze Star with Combat V for the actions of that day."

The producers apparently never checked the court of inquiry testimony or the Navy records regarding Signalman David's medal, or if they did, they presented Meadors' tale without disclosing that there was substantial evidence that his claim was false. In regard to why Meadors claimed he did the signaling and hoisting, Signalman David wrote, "I can only surmise that Mr. Meadors didn't want to be left out, for whatever reason."

There are many other significant incorrect statements of fact. There are also just plain misrepresentations, such as showing footage of a destroyer steaming and leading the viewer to believe the destroyer is the *Liberty*. There was other footage of a ship being strafed by a plane and a ship with a plume of smoke drifting off to the side, which was contrary to the actual wind conditions at the time of the air attack. No voice-over or subtitle on the screen discloses that this footage is not of the *Liberty;* the narrative in fact was presented in a manner to mislead the viewer into believing the footage in fact is of the *Liberty*.[22] These deficiencies all lead to the conclusion that the program was produced without adequate research, fact-checking, or attention to detail, which in the past had been the hallmark of programs presented on the History Channel.

A private video was also produced by Sligo Productions, *USS Liberty Survivors: Our Story*.[23] The script was written and the taping directed by Patrick King. The credits list James Ennes Jr. as responsible for research. Rather than a story, it is a series of interviews with the *Liberty* crew members and others who support the intentional-attack conspiracy theory. While it contains some footage of the *Liberty* and some pictures relating to the incident, it does not present, or even refer to, the mistake theory or the many official investigations that concluded that the attack was a tragic mistake. It tells its story from the point of view that the attacks were intentional attacks on a U.S. ship.

Tito "De Nagy" Howard, a self-proclaimed man "at war with the Israelis," had a relationship with the *Liberty* Veterans Association (LVA) going back many years.[24] According to Joe Lentini, the LVA gave Howard "$20,000.00 or $25,000" in order to make a movie about the *Liberty* incident, but for a long period of time the movie was not made, and the money paid was not publicly disclosed or accounted for.[25] In 1983 Howard produced a videotape. The USS *Liberty* newsletter in January 1984 commented on a one-hour tape produced by Tito Howard titled "Massacre and Masquerade.": "We found that only six minutes pertain to the *Liberty*. Most of the rest consists of brief interviews with leading anti-Zionist leaders, all airing their views about Israel."[26]

In 2002 Howard produced a video documentary titled "Loss of *Liberty*," which was presented at Connecticut College on Tuesday, October 29, 2002. The program was sponsored by the Connecticut Chapter of the Council for the National Interest.[27] When Howard finally produced "Loss of *Liberty*," Joe Lentini was asked by Howard to comment on it. He offered what he believed to be constructive criticism. Lentini was then called by Phil Tourney, then *Liberty* Veterans Association president, who said to him, "It was too bad that he wasn't killed by the torpedo with the rest of his buddies."[28]

"'Loss of *Liberty*" is a poor-quality production, poorly researched, poorly produced, and saturated with factual errors. For example, the video is critical of Adm. Isaac C. Kidd Jr., the officer designated by Adm. John McCain to serve as president of the U.S. Navy court of inquiry that investigated the *Liberty* incident. It is amusing that the video shows a portrait of Admiral Isaac C. Kidd Sr., the father of Isaac Kidd Jr.—and represents him as "Isaac, Jr." Howard uses a cut of Cdr. Ramy Lunz from the Thames TV production and identifies him as Lt. Cdr. Pincus Pinchasy.[29] Enlisted *Liberty* crew member James Smith is described as a lieutenant commander. Enlisted crew member Glenn Olipant is described as a "radio man" when in fact he was an ETR, a rate that repaired radios (as well as radars), not operated them.

Howard claims the Navy F-14 Tomcat was named in honor of Adm. Thomas Moorer. In fact the Tomcat was named in honor of Vice Adm. Thomas F. Connolly, Deputy Chief of Naval Operations (Air).[30] Howard claims the Washington-Moscow hotline was used for the first time specifically for the *Liberty* incident. The hotline was used for serious communication between Washington and Moscow for the first time during the 1967 war. Twenty messages were exchanged. There were three messages on June 5, four messages on June 6, two messages on June 7. On June 8 five messages were exchanged, of which three (the eleventh, thirteenth, and fourteenth) related to the *Liberty* incident.[31]

In the video, Phil Tourney tells of Admiral Kidd removing his stars (marks of rank) and then replacing them on "his lapel." Marks of rank are not worn on lapels. The rolling credits mention the "United States *Navel*" archives—that is right, *Navel*. This production does not confuse apples and oranges but rather *navel* oranges and belly buttons. Finally, although all records confirm that the launch of aircraft from the carriers *America* and *Saratoga* to defend the *Liberty* occurred between 3:50 and 4:00 p.m., Howard claims Secretary McNamara recalled the aircraft at 2:35 p.m., about an hour and twenty minutes before they took off.

On July 30, 2008, Military.com carried a story titled "SS *Liberty* sails to Challenge Israel." On August 1, 2008, James Ennes posted the following comment on the Military.com website:[32]

Aug 1, 2008 4:44:16 PM

One of the links above recommended a *Liberty* film. We appreciate the support for our story, but must tell you that most survivors do not recommend this film.

As a survivor of the attack, I have seen all the films, participated in most of them, read all the books, most of the articles and many of the forums and have participated in literally hundreds of radio, television and film interviews in the past thirty years.

The LOSS OF LIBERTY film is probably the worst of several films that have been made on this subject even though it is definitely the most aggressively marketed online. It is not supported by survivors. Survivors sued the producer of this film for breach of contract and other things. I feel it is mostly a collection of film clips, poorly edited and poorly caption[ed], with a lot of enthusiastic rave reviews by Medal of Honor winning senior officers who have no personal knowledge of the circumstances and whose views are essentially irrelevant.

The Howard production has never been aired on network television. It is sold through Howard's organization, "The *Liberty* Alliance," and also offered for sale by Noontide Press. What else can you buy from Noontide Press? They sell "audio and video tapes from the 14th IHR conference." IHR is the Institute for Historical Review, one of the two major Holocaust-denial organizations in the United States. The same 2002 circular offering sale of "Loss of *Liberty*" also offers the remarks of Phillip Tourney, at the time president of the LVA, which he made at the fourteenth Holocaust-denial conference.

On February 2, 2002, John Hadden, CIA Chief of Station, Tel Aviv, on June 1967, was visited by a "TV crew" consisting of Peter Hounam and Chris Mitchel, who claimed to be from a British TV production company working on a production about the Six Day War.[33] They described documents to Hadden, allegedly CIA documents of which he has no memory and that Hadden said he doubts exist. They told him that A Jay Cristol was an Israeli agent and that the book *The* Liberty *Incident* was "a brief for the prosecution."[34] They told Hadden they had spent the previous night at Colebrook, Vermont, interviewing "a crew member."[35] They stressed that the Israeli motive in attacking the *Liberty* was to keep the United States from learning of the Israeli plan to attack Syria. They ignored Hadden's response that Israel had kept the United States fully informed about the impending attack on Syria.

John Hadden was convinced that the "program" about the Six Day War was a cover story, because Hounam and Mitchell remained focused on attacking A Jay Cristol and his *The* Liberty *Incident* and were displeased when he rejected their allegations as untrue. The tapes of Hadden's denials did not appear in the video. Passage of time confirmed Hadden's intuition. Hounam did not produce a video on the Six Day War. He produced a book, *Operation Cyanide: Why the Bombing of the USS* Liberty *Nearly Caused World War III,* together with a video documentary, "Dead in the Water," aired on BBC Four, Sunday August 21, 2004.[36] "Dead in the Water" has not aired on U.S. TV but is available on DVD.

"Dead in the Water" was reviewed with the following comments:

The worst type of story telling
    This production, the foundation for Peter Hounam's book titled "Operation Cyanide," is a prime example of myth creation disguised as "investigative journalism."
    What is most remarkable about the production's theses is that—if it were accurate—then in fact the U.S. was not a non-belligerent in the June 1967 Arab-Israeli war as claimed by outspoken former *Liberty* crewmembers and others, but actually a co-belligerent, and thus the USS *Liberty* was not entitled to the rights of a neutral as a non-belligerent third party.[37]

One needs go no farther than the cover of Peter Hounam's *Operation Cyanide,* on which his video production is based, to be aware of the superficiality of his research on the attack on the *Liberty*. His subtitle is "Why the *Bombing* [emphasis added] of the USS *Liberty* Nearly Caused World War III." The *Liberty* was not bombed but rather strafed and torpedoed. The flawed research and presentations of false information permeate the book and the entire production.

The video is not only a dishonest presentation of fact but presents a thesis so absurd that it is not worthy of serious consideration. The thesis is that the Six Day War was in fact a joint U.S.-Israeli military operation designed to destroy Egypt and that the attack on the USS *Liberty* was simply a pretext for a U.S. aerial strike on Cairo—using nuclear weapons, no less. The attack on the *Liberty* occurred on the fourth day of the Six Day War. By the fourth day Israel had destroyed the Arab air forces, swept through the Sinai and captured the Suez Canal, the West Bank, and Jerusalem. Only a one-day operation against Syria remained unfinished. Under these circumstances, why would Israel or the United States make a nuclear attack on Cairo? What would such an attack accomplish?

The same week in Vietnam, the U.S. lost 187 military personnel, and no one in the U.S. government or military was contemplating a nuclear attack on Hanoi. But Hounam argues that the loss of thirty-four lives on the *Liberty* would support nuking Cairo. Absurd!!

The video is factually inaccurate in many ways. It presents remarks by the *Liberty*'s commanding officer edited out of context. This can be confirmed by viewing and comparing the actual speech quoted by the Associated Press.[38] The video reports the story, first written about by Stephen Green,[39] of one Greg Reight claiming that U.S. Air Force RF-4C aircraft flew reconnaissance for Israel before and during the war, without mention that

Reight was completely discredited by U.S. ambassador Richard Parker in an article published in 1997.[40] Reight is also filmed saying Israel had no reconnaissance aircraft in 1967. A widely published picture taken by an Israeli Mirage IIIC clearly showing the shadow on the ground of the aircraft itself as it approaches three destroyed MiGs on the tarmac was edited to eliminate the shadow and attributed by Reight to a USAF RF-4C.[41]

Ambassador Parker's research elicited denials of a U.S. Air Force RF-4C operation during the Six Day War from the commanding officer of the 38th Tactical Reconnaissance Squadron, a unit in Germany that operated the aircraft; from Col. Thomas Whitlock and the next commander up the echelon; and from Col. Earl A. Butts of the 26th Tactical Reconnaissance Wing (TRW). Colonel Whitlock had a "compelling conviction" that no such operation took place, and Colonels Whitlock and Butts both refuted technical details of the story.

Parker commented further at page 71:

> There is also no knowledge of this operation among officials who were at the working level in the State Department, CIA, and the White House at the time. Alfred Atherton (then director of Arab-Israel affairs), Donald Bergus (director of Egypt affairs), Harold Saunders (Walt Rostow's deputy for the Near East at the National Security Council), and James Critchfield (director of the CIA's Near East division) all say they saw no sign of such an operation. Saunders said that Rostow denied any knowledge of it. Critchfield commented that he was running an ad hoc control group during the 1967 crisis and saw "everything." He saw nothing that would support Green's story and did not know why Green continued to pursue that "dead dog." I have also talked with the man who was the CIA station chief in Tel Aviv in 1967. He had never heard the story and commented that he could not imagine the Israelis letting any foreigners that close to their military operations.
>
> All told, these statements make a convincing set of denials. Supported by the technical problems raised by Colonels Butts and Whitlock, they were enough to persuade me that the story was not true and that Green had been the victim of an intelligence fabricator, perhaps of a Soviet disinformation effort, because I could not conceive of anyone else who might have a motive for planting the story.

Parker received further refutations from personal inquiry to Secretary Robert McNamara, as well as two Israeli generals in positions to know—

Maj. Gen. Shlomo Gazit, head of Israel military intelligence research, and
Maj. Gen. "Motti" Hod, chief of the Israel Air Force in 1967.

The narrator in the video talks of *Operation Cyanide*, the title of the
Hounam book, an "operation" that has never been documented anywhere
except in Hounam's imagination, while the screen displays a memo clearly
marked "FRONTLET 615," which is a memo regarding approval of a U.S.
covert operation in April 1967, months before the beginning of the Six Day
War, and the USS *Liberty* receiving orders diverting her from her African
mission and directing her to the eastern Mediterranean.

The program includes Cdr. David Lewis telling his hearsay story about
Rear Admiral Geis launching and calling back Sixth Fleet aircraft without
mentioning that all records show that the aircraft were launched and recalled
upon order of the Sixth Fleet's commander, Vice Admiral Martin. On the
issue of the recall of aircraft, the narrator muffles the question to Secretary of Defense Robert McNamara so that one must replay the tape several
times to hear and understand it. This appears to be a premeditated action,
designed to obfuscate McNamara's very strong, positive denial. The failure
to check facts and the omission of facts demonstrate Hounam's anti-Israel
bias, which can be independently verified by examining Hounam's history
and other writings.

It is reported that in 1981ABC News prepared a program for *Nightline*.
There was much excitement among some of the *Liberty* crew members when
they were told that their version of the story was going to be told by Ted
Koppel on *Nightline*. The *USS "Liberty" Newsletter*, under the caption "USS
Liberty in the News," carried an article in 1981 that read, "*ABC Nightline*, the
national late-evening news show from ABC studios in New York, has offered
to release Ennes's *Defense Electronics* story about the attack on the *Liberty* to
coincide with the release of the magazine. That broadcast, barring possible
schedule changes, should be aired Wednesday, October 7 [1981]. This will
be the first mention on national television of any crew member's version of
the attack."[42]

The story did not appear on *Nightline*, and in 1982 the *USS "Liberty"
Newsletter* carried the following:

Ted Koppel's *Nightline*
    Thursday afternoon a call came from a producer for Ted Koppel's na-
tionally broadcast late night television news program, ABC *Nightline*. *Nightline* had heard about the reunion and wanted to do a story. Could four of

us come to the ABC Studio at 7:00 p.m.? So that evening Jim Ennes, Don Blalock, Joe Meadors and Mike Schaley spent three hours under television lights answering questions about the attack, the heroism and the cover-up, while ABC collected eleven reels of tape. But that wasn't enough. To round it out they spent the next three days attending reunion activities, interviewing other men at the hotel, tracking down archive films of the ship's battered arrival in Malta, and editing it all into a logical story sequence. It was to be a 30 minute segment which would occupy the entire *Nightline* broadcast on June 7. The schedule was considered firm, but it was not to be.[43]

A few pages later in the same newsletter the following appeared:

What happened to the Nightline Story?
    The story scheduled for Ted Koppel's *Nightline* was to have run on Monday evening, June 7. Unfortunately, Israel invaded Lebanon only hours before that story was to run. The invasion was considered a bigger news story, and so the *Liberty* story was bumped. *Liberty,* in other words, was shot down by Israel again.[44]

The *USS "Liberty" Newsletter* of March 1983 wrote that the *Nightline* tape of the *Liberty* story, which cost more than $100,000 to produce, "had mysteriously disappeared without a trace."[45]

On January 12 and 13, 2004, the U.S. Department of State held a conference in Loy Henderson Auditorium under the auspices of the historian of the State Department titled "The United States, the Middle East, and the 1967 Arab-Israeli War," in conjunction with the release of volume XIX of the *Foreign Relations of the United States.* The conference consisted of seven panels and was carried live on C-SPAN.[46]

This author was invited to participate on the first panel, "War, Intelligence and the USS *Liberty*." The moderator was Dr. Marc Susser, Historian, U.S. Department of State; this author participated along with Dr. David Robarge, Central Intelligence Agency History Staff; and Dr. David Hatch, Technical Director, Center for Cryptologic Studies (National Security Agency).[47]

Following the panel presentation this author was approached by Brooke Runnette, whose business card stated "Producer, ABC News, *Nightline*." Ms. Runnette stated an interest in doing a *Nightline* program about the *Liberty* incident. Time marched on until November 11, 2004, when an e-mail was received from Brooke E. Runnette stating, "Dear Judge Cristol, it's been nearly a year since we met at the State Department in January, but I haven't forgotten about the USS *Liberty* piece I was interested in doing for *Nightline*, and now that the election is over with, I have a correspondent on board, and some real forward momentum!"[48]

Numerous e-mails and telephone conversations followed, and finally, on January 31, 2005, an on-camera interview of about two hours was completed at my office. The correspondent was David Marish; his interview was straightforward and highly professional. Throughout he remained impartial and focused on getting factual answers to his questions.

Following the interview, and off camera, we had a long discussion during which it appeared to this author that David Marish had become fascinated with a series of conspiracy tales told by three persons claiming they had heard transmissions of the Israeli pilots (interesting, since the pilots spoke Hebrew and the three storytellers did not) or that they had received transcripts of Israeli pilots/controllers transmissions on or about June 8, 1967. On that day the three individuals—who I will call the "Three Blind Mice," since they were operating in the blind and only reporting decades-old memories without any supporting documents—were located in:

1. Offutt Air Force Base, near Omaha, Nebraska: Mouse Number One stated, "On the day of the attack [June 8], I read yellow teletype sheets . . . from a variety of sources including the NSA."
2. All Source Reconnaissance Center at Iraklion Air Station, Crete: Mouse Number Two stated he received "direct intelligence" from the air force EC-121 aircraft.
3. Da Nang, Vietnam—Mouse Number Three stated that he received rough transcripts on June 8 and smooth transcripts the next day. Then came a message to destroy all transcripts. Later this individual claimed that after discharge from the Air Force he worked for the NSA and that while working in NSA headquarters he saw an NSA report proving the attack deliberate. (Responding to a Freedom of Information Act request, the NSA confirmed that this individual never worked for that agency.)

This author was concerned about what kind of *Nightline* program would result if the program included the stories of the three individuals who *remembered* receiving top-secret information in June 1967, while they were in Omaha, Crete, and Da Nang, respectively.

Following the interview and meeting with David Marish, Brooke E. Runnette took maternity leave and had a baby girl. Time went by and communication with Ms. Runnette could not be reestablished. On November 22, 2005, Ted Koppel retired from *Nightline*. Soon thereafter it was reported that Koppel had declined an offer of a job with Al-Jazeera but that David Marish had accepted a position there as a correspondent.[49] Nothing has been heard from *Nightline* since early 2005.

The network television treatment of the *Liberty* story has been a substantial disappointment to James Ennes and some members of the *Liberty* Veterans Association. Ennes is convinced that the power of Israel has been able to subvert the television industry against his version of events.[50]

Some members of the *Liberty* Veterans Association are generally dissatisfied with the TV coverage of their story, as indicated by the following statement: "In recent weeks we have heard from *60 Minutes, Good Morning America, Nightline,* and *Larry King.* All have considered and then apparently rejected the possibility of doing live interviews with survivors. *American television, it seems, does not want to tell the* Liberty *story without filters, censorship, and unrebutted Israeli excuses*" (emphasis added).[51]

The statements suggest that Israel controls American (and probably British) TV media and has successfully prevented the true story of the *Liberty* incident from being told. Another analysis might suggest that American and British television are free and independent and not willing to release as fact a version of a story that cannot be verified by normal standards of TV journalism. In Israel, which like the United States and Britain enjoys a free and independent media, it has been stated that what absolutely proves that there is no secret connected with the *Liberty* incident is the fact that the alleged secret was not leaked to, or discovered by, the media within thirty-six hours of the tragic event.

Chapter 15

RED HERRINGS AND MYTHS

Few relevant facts are in dispute regarding the *Liberty* incident. The *Liberty* arrived near the Sinai coast on June 8, 1967, as a result of outdated orders. New orders directing the ship not to approach her original assigned position had been mistakenly dispatched elsewhere. She was attacked by the Israel Air Force and Israel Navy. Thirty-four U.S. crew members died, and another 171 were wounded. There were acts of heroism on board the *Liberty*. There were numerous blunders by both Israel and the United States. The major debate is not about the individual events that took place but about whether the Israeli attackers knew they were attacking a U.S. ship or, in a tragic mistake, identified their target as an enemy ship.

A very important question must be considered before reaching a final conclusion. If Israel attacked a ship known to be American, what was the motive for the attack? Various motives attributed to the Israelis for attacking a ship known to be a U.S. ship have already been discussed. No Israeli has stated or testified that the attack was other than a tragic case of mistaken identity. When considering the issue of motive, one must remember that in 1967 the state of Israel stood alone against its Arab enemies, without a single friendly nation in the world supporting her in any way—except the United States! Assuming that Israel did not want the *Liberty* positioned where she was for any reason, is it reasonable that Israel would commit an act of war against the only nation in the world offering any support? On this point, Ambassador Ephraim Evron was quoted as saying, "I'll take up the challenge of the *Liberty* with your permission. Why would Israel do such a terrible thing? We may be crazy, but we are not fools."[1]

Furthermore, if eliminating the *Liberty* was so important to Israel, is it not reasonable to assume that a military force that four days earlier had destroyed all the air forces of the Arab confrontational states within one day and hundreds of Egyptian tanks in the Sinai and that had routed the Jordan Legion in the West Bank and Jerusalem could not have easily sank an old tub of a ship, lacking any armor and armed with four inadequate machine guns?

An analysis of the air and naval attacks demonstrates that they were neither well planned nor effective. *Kursa* Flight was not armed to attack a ship. The primary standard weapon for attacking a ship was in 1967, as it had been during World War II, the five-hundred-pound conventional iron bomb. In the battle of Midway during World War II, in ten minutes the U.S. Navy sank three heavily armored Japanese aircraft carriers and seriously damaged a fourth using such bombs.[2] *Kursa* was armed with 30 mm cannons and a couple of air-to-air missiles.[3] Although *Kursa's* gunfire was accurate and started multiple fires on the *Liberty*, the ship continued under way and was in no danger of sinking. The attack by Royal Flight, armed with 30 mm cannon and napalm canisters, also lacked the capability to sink the ship. If it was intended to sink the ship, that could have accomplished easily by sending aircraft armed with five-hundred-pound iron bombs, as requested by Royal Flight leader. The air attack terminated without dropping any ship-sinking bombs on the *Liberty*. The two flights of the attacking aircraft were assigned to other missions, for which they were properly armed. *Kursa* had been returning from combat air patrol over the Suez Canal, and Royal had been diverted from armor and infantry interdiction over the Sinai desert.

It is also undisputed that when the Israeli motor torpedo boats caught up with the *Liberty*, they did not attack. They stopped and tried to communicate with her by means of a flashing light. Why did they stop and try to communicate if they already knew the identity of the ship and their mission was to attack and sink her? They were faster than the *Liberty*, and the ship's ability to maneuver was extremely limited by the shallow water to the south. The three MTBs had all the time necessary to bracket the ship, one MTB to one side and two on the other, without concern for shallow water, and to launch all their torpedoes in a pattern that would have ensured the destruction of the *Liberty*. Instead they performed an uncoordinated attack in which 80 percent of their torpedoes missed and one was not even launched.

There is disagreement as to what signals each side flashed and when, as well as what each side received or thought it received. Nevertheless, there is no dispute that as the MTBs were signaling, *Liberty* responded by commencing firing at them. Under such circumstances, the MTBs were entitled, even under the most stringent rules of engagement, to return fire. If this was a carefully preplanned attack as alleged, why was it not better coordinated so that more than one of the five torpedoes launched hit the target? It is frequently claimed that the torpedo strike in the National Security Agency compartment of the *Liberty* was a precise, intentional act to put the NSA capability on the ship out of action. A number of persons who do not accept the fact that the attack was a tragic mistake in identification remain convinced that that particular hit was an intentional part of the overall plan to sink the ship. If the plan was to sink the ship, why the need to separately target the NSA compartment? Also, if the Israelis were so accurate with their torpedoes that they could precisely hit the NSA compartment, why did they not sink the *Liberty* altogether, and why how did they manage to miss the ship entirely with four of the five torpedoes they launched?

The nearest U.S. aircraft was stationed more than an hour's flight away, and the nearest U.S. ship was almost a day's steaming away. How is it, then, that under such conditions the military force that had just destroyed billions of dollars' worth of sophisticated enemy hardware was unable to accomplish the destruction of a ship? Any analysis of these facts must conclude that if Israel had really wanted to sink the *Liberty,* it would have done just that. The underlying logic of the argument against Israel is that if it was capable of such infallible planning, the same logic must be applied to the execution of the plan. On the other hand, if the plan was so poorly executed, maybe the planning was not that sinister either.

Various doubters of the tragic-mistake explanation have presented a number of ideas that can only be classified as red herrings. Even if any of these stories, which are summarized below, are true, they have no bearing on the issue of whether the attack was a case of mistaken identity as opposed to an attack on a ship known to be American.

There is a dispute over whether Israel inquired of the United States prior to the attack whether any U.S. ships were in the area. In his memoirs, Itzhak Rabin states that such an inquiry was made. Capt. Ernest Castle, the U.S. naval attaché in Tel Aviv in 1967, reported that no such inquiry was made to him prior to the attack. (There has been no accounting of other Israelis who may have inquired of U.S. military or diplomatic personnel, either formally or informally.) But this begs a question: Why would Israel have made such an inquiry? No U.S. Navy ship had made a port call in Israel since November 1963. The war was between Israel and the Arabs. Why would anyone contemplate a U.S. ship sailing close to the combat zone without advising a friendly country (if not all parties concerned) about the ship's presence?

This is especially puzzling in light of the U.S. public pronouncement at the UN Security Council just days before that no U.S. ships or planes were within hundreds of miles of the combat zone.

But assuming no inquiry was made by anyone in Israel, it would seem that this tends to prove a mistake occurred more than it proves otherwise. The idea that Israelis had no idea that a U.S. ship was in the area and never inquired about that possibility would tend to support rather than controvert the explanation that the *Liberty* was mistaken for an enemy.

Did Egypt declare the waters off Sinai a combat zone closed to neutral traffic days prior to the attack? The initial Israeli explanation said yes.[4] But let us assume Egypt did not. The NSA and the Joint Chiefs of Staff knew that the area was well within a combat zone and were concerned for the safety of the *Liberty*. They sent numerous misdirected messages trying to keep her from entering the area. The *Liberty* knew of the war, and the shore explosions visible to the *Liberty*'s crew members made her aware of fighting was going on within eyesight. Whether Egypt did or did not declare the area a combat zone has nothing to do with proving that the attack was not a mistake.

Another dispute concerns whether or not the Israeli aircraft fired rockets or missiles at the *Liberty*. The evidence, supported by the tests performed by the U.S. Navy laboratories, seems to establish that they did not. If they did, what does the firing or nonfiring of rockets or missiles show about the intent of the attackers?

Some of the *Liberty* crewmen claim that a great deal of surveillance by aircraft took place prior to the attack. Therefore, they argue, the Israelis knew the identity of the ship before the attack. The Israelis admit that the early-morning reconnaissance Nord 2501 flight identified the *Liberty* and that reports were made about a ship off El Arish by aircraft passing near throughout the morning. The Israelis claim that all of these aircraft except the early-morning naval reconnaissance were on combat-related missions against Egyptian military targets. Some aircraft reported a ship near El Arish, and some apparently had no interest in the *Liberty* whatsoever—they never even bothered to report about her. Israel never denied identifying the ship early in the morning. No data can be found that indicates that any other position report on the *Liberty* ever reached naval or other headquarters. The thought that such evidence, if it ever existed, was destroyed does not make sense either, because in such a case all evidence, including the morning sighting, would have been destroyed.

There are several conflicting stories about how many launches of aircraft were made by the Sixth Fleet in an attempt to defend the *Liberty* while it was under attack. Whether a launch of aircraft to protect the *Liberty* was made and recalled and then a second launch made or only one, what bearing do these disputes about U.S. naval flight operations, entirely within the control of U.S. Navy commanders, have on the Israelis in regard to whether they knew they were attacking a U.S. ship?

Some conspiracy theorists claim that the *Liberty* and her crew were betrayed by coconspirators President Lyndon Johnson; Secretary of Defense Robert McNamara; the Chief of Naval Operations, David McDonald; the Commander in Chief, U.S. Naval Forces Europe, John McCain; Commander Sixth Fleet, William Martin; and the president of the U.S. Navy court of inquiry, Adm. Isaac Kidd. The claims actually insinuate treason. If we are to believe that this distinguished group, or even several of members of it, were acting in concert against the national interest of the United States in order to confer some benefit on Israel in connection with the attack on the *Liberty* by participating in a conspiracy or a cover-up, several questions need to be answered.

First, any one of the alleged conspirators (with the exception of Admiral Kidd, who arrived on the scene several days after the event) could have issued an order early on that would have prevented the *Liberty* from entering the combat zone. If the conspirators did not want the *Liberty* there, why did they send her there in the first place?

Second, if one believes that President Johnson and Secretary McNamara had some political motive for the alleged conspiracy, is it really believable that Admiral McDonald, Admiral McCain, Admiral Martin, and Admiral Kidd, or any of these distinguished officers, would betray his country and conspire against a U.S. Navy ship and its crew? The suggestion that these officers were involved in such a conspiracy is ludicrous.

Third, why would the president of the United States, the secretary of defense, the commander of the Sixth Fleet, or any of them, betray a U.S. Navy ship and its crew by lying about the availability of air cover to defend a U.S. ship or by denying it available air cover when the U.S. ship was actually under attack?

These red herrings have no bearing on the issue of whether the Israeli forces that attacked the *Liberty* were aware before or during the attack that it was a U.S. ship. Some of the claims may be interesting, but none of them is relevant to the question under review. In addition to the red herrings, however, there are a number of myths that have been repeated and repeated until they have developed lives of their own. They are, however, absolutely without substance.

The stories of President Johnson, Secretary McNamara, and Admiral McDonald talking to the Sixth Fleet over a secure voice radio in 1967, as discussed earlier, are simply not in the realm of the possible. No such capability existed in 1967.

Stephen Green's story of U.S. Air Force RF-4C reconnaissance aircraft from Germany flying to Israel before the 1967 war began and supporting the Israelis against the Arabs was completely debunked by Ambassador Richard Parker. Parker established that no record existed to support the tale and that the source was one person who had been totally discredited by numerous contemporaries who had served with the source and absolutely denied the story (see chapter 9).

The myth floated by President Nasser and King Hussein about U.S. and British carrier aircraft participating in the initial Israeli air strikes on Egypt on June 5, also discussed in chapter 9, has been fully exposed by numerous sources and was not believed even by the Soviets.

Some *Liberty* crewmen still insist that it should have been perfectly safe to sail into a combat zone where major armed conflict was in progress. The ship's commanding officer, other ships' officers, the NSA, the JCS, and other senior commanders all held contrary opinions.

The story of a promise of air cover in ten minutes from the Sixth Fleet, based on Ennes's memory of a message that does not exist in any record, is a totally undocumented myth, simply a physical impossibility. The nearest U.S. aircraft carriers were over five hundred miles away, much more than an hour's flight time for their jets and almost three hours for their propeller aircraft.

The myth of F-4B Phantom aircraft armed with nuclear weapons being launched from the U.S. carriers, as described in the Ennes book (and supported by Admiral Moorer), is an impossibility. In 1967 there were no U.S. Navy or Marine F-4s configured and wired to carry nuclear weapons. Even if the F-4s had been so configured, authorization for a launch of nuclear-armed aircraft, as Admiral Moorer should know, could be issued only by presidential authority (and in some rare cases by theater commanders), and launch required three to four hours of advance preparation. There is no record of such authorization or launch.

The story of a submarine in the area working with the *Liberty,* propounded by Pearson, Eveland, and Ennes is not supported by any record. The logs of the submarines allegedly involved do not reflect such activity, and the commanding officer of the submarine *Amberjack* denies the submarine was there (see chapter 17). The myth lingers on.

The claim that Moshe Dayan, Israel's minister of defense, personally ordered the attack is based on a single piece of unevaluated raw intelligence (obtained via the Freedom of Information Act). The CIA publicly denied the veracity of this story on several occasions (see chapter 11).

Although the logs and records created on June 8, 1967, by both the U.S. Navy and the Israel Defense Force show that the air attack lasted from 1358 to 1412 (approximately fourteen minutes) and the naval attack lasted from about 1430 to 1440 (approximately ten minutes), the myth persists that the attack continued for hours.

The pièce de résistance of these myths is the bold claim by *Liberty* survivor David Lewis that the president of the United States betrayed the United States and a U.S. Navy ship and its crew because he did not want to embarrass our ally, Israel. Any claim of evidence suggested to support this myth has been thoroughly and completely discredited. First, any student of history is aware that in 1967 Israel was not yet a close ally of the United States. Those who make the argument are guilty of anachronism. President Johnson was a strong and controversial president with whom many Americans disagreed on many subjects, but to charge him with betrayal, as Lewis does, suggests incredible audacity.

The most far-reaching myth is the unmitigated falsehood propounded by author James Bamford denying that there has ever been an investigation of the *Liberty* incident by the U.S. government. In an interview with Geoff Metcalf for *World Net Daily,* an Internet site, on Sunday June 24, 2001, on page 10 of 17, Bamford unequivocally states the need to "call on the U.S. government to do an investigation—which is what they have never done in the past. . . . [T]hey never did an investigation on the *Liberty.*" Bamford somehow overlooked, or chose to ignore, at least ten official U.S. investigations, discussed in detail in chapter 12.

All but the Senate Select Committee on Intelligence and the House Armed Services Investigations Subcommittee reports are available upon written request. Most are free. A few require payment but just to defray the cost of copying. Some sources also include the Naval Security Group Report of 1967 as an additional investigation. There are also four official Israeli reports (see chapter 13).

In dealing with myths, one is frequently faced with the impossibility of proving a negative. How does one prove one does not have a sister? In the case of the *Liberty*-related myths, the problem is not a lack of records. There are thousands of pages of authentic records relevant to the event. Most of them were created at or near the time of the event. When faced with a photograph or recorded sworn testimony or a message that tends to prove a point, it is common for conspiracy theorists to claim that the photograph, record of testimony, or message was altered. Unfortunately, the hunger for theories of conspiracy, cover-up, or intrigue often results in the rejection or dismissal of fact and the acceptance of myth as fact without any effort to find out what the truth is, from the evidence available. In the formation of opinions the true story is too often ignored.

Perhaps this is so because to search for the truth by checking all the evidence requires significantly more work and effort than inventing a story. This author has made a diligent effort to collect and review all the evidence.

Chapter 16

CONFIRMATION

National Security Agency Intercepts

On June 8, 1967, a Navy EC-121M electronic surveillance aircraft (Bureau No. 135757) assigned to a Fleet Air Reconnaissance Squadron 2 (VQ-2) detachment took off from Athens, Greece, and flew to a patrol site clear of, but within radio surveillance distance of, the war that had been raging in the Middle East since June 5. On board, in a restricted area referred to as "the tent," was a National Security Agency (NSA) electronic communications surveillance compartment that was sophisticated for its day. The tent was staffed with a team of communications technicians (CTs)—NSA linguists. There were Arabic linguists and two Hebrew linguists: Chief Petty Officer Marvin Nowicki,[1] the supervisor, and a second Hebrew linguist, Petty Officer Michael Prostinak. The CTs were busy identifying, recording, and monitoring Arabic and Hebrew radio transmissions when, at about 1430 Sinai (1230Z, GMT), Prostinak heard something that caused him to call Nowicki, "Listen to this." The Hebrew transmissions of interest were monitored and recorded until 1528 Sinai (1328Z).

At 1559 Sinai (1359Z), Vice Adm. William Martin, Commander U.S. Sixth Fleet, who was monitoring the situation and had ordered U.S. Navy aircraft from the carriers *America* and *Saratoga* to the scene of the attack on the *Liberty*, sent a message to VQ-2 in Athens requesting that all VQ-2 flights launched from Athens be recalled and no further flights be launched until advised.[2] Shortly thereafter the EC-121M turned for a straight line course back to Athens. On the ground at Athens, Nowicki and Prostinak made a rough translation of the tapes. The tapes were then sent by courier to NSA headquarters at Fort Meade, Maryland, where a smooth translation was made by NSA Hebrew linguist Richard W. Hickman,[3] who briefed the NSA's director, Army lieutenant general Marshall Carter, on their contents. The translations were classified top secret, code words Savin and Crayon.

The top-secret information gleaned from the tapes by the NSA was shared with the Central Intelligence Agency (CIA), the Defense Intelligence Agency (DIA), the White House, and Clark Clifford, chair of the President's Foreign Intelligence Board. The tapes remained highly classified because of the concern of the Department of Defense over compromising the means and methods of the SIGINT collection, and those of the Department of State over U.S. relations with Arab countries that had accused the United States of fighting, or being involved in, the Six Day War on the side of Israel. The State Department concern was especially sensitive because the United States had stated on the floor of the United Nations on June 6, 1967,[4] that it had no ships or planes within several hundred miles of the war zone and had then been embarrassed by the USS *Liberty* popping up in the middle of the combat area. It would have been a further embarrassment to admit that U.S. aircraft had also been close to the war zone.

When the U.S. government made the statement "no U.S. ships were within several hundred miles," the *Liberty* was actually still in the western Mediterranean sailing toward a point off the Gaza Strip. Then she was ordered to stay clear of the combat zone by at least five messages that she did not receive and thus sailed into the combat zone.[5] However, the presence of the Navy EC-121M aircraft was specifically and intentionally ordered.

As a result of the web of secrecy cast over the incident, dozens of conspiracy stories developed. By some estimates there are as many conspiracy stories about the *Liberty* incident as about the assassination of John F. Kennedy. The conspiracy stories vary greatly, from notions that the *Liberty* was there fighting with the Arabs against Israel to her fighting with Israel *against* the Arabs. Over the years, stories developed about the existence of audiotapes of intercepts of Israel radio transmissions. The story of these tapes was told again and again, claiming was that these audiotapes would prove that the Israeli air and naval forces intentionally attacked the *Liberty* with full knowledge that she was a U.S. ship.

For example, as described earlier, George Golden, the engineering officer on the USS *Liberty* on June 8, 1967, believed the *Liberty* had recorded intercepts of Israeli aircraft communications. He said in an interview: "Some of that could have counted also for the fact that Lieutenant [Maurice] Bennett brought some information and gave it to me. He said they had taped it, concerning the planning of the attack and I gave that to a member of

Admiral Martin's staff the next morning and nothing came of that. I wish I was in a position to make a copy of it myself."[6] It should be noted that neither Bennett nor anyone else on the *Liberty* on June 8, 1967, was a Hebrew linguist. Ultimately the NSA did provide a definitive confirmation. The NSA 1981 report "Attack on a SIGINT Collector" confirms that "the *Liberty* had no specific mission against Israeli communications" and that "Hebrew language tapes produced by USN-855 the NSA detachment on *Liberty* . . . did not contain information on the forthcoming Israeli attack."[7] The NSA, however, kept this portion of the 1981 report classified until July 2, 2003, when it was declassified and released as a result of this author's Freedom of Information Act lawsuit.[8]

A lead to the actual existence of the EC-121M tapes was given to author James Bamford by Nowicki, the Navy Hebrew linguist who had been the supervisor on the EC-121M surveillance aircraft. Although Nowicki clearly told Bamford the tapes showed that the attack was an accident, Bamford insisted that the tapes proved the attack was intentional and that the leadership of NSA was unanimous in that belief.[9] An almost unprecedented press release by the NSA stated, "Mr. Bamford's claim that the NSA leadership was 'virtually unanimous in their belief that the attack was deliberate' is simply not true."[10] Nowicki himself responded to Bamford's claim with a letter to the *Wall Street Journal* stating that the tapes proved that the Israeli attack was a gross error. Nowicki closed his letter with the question, "How can I prove it? I can't, unless the transcript/tapes are found and released to the public."[11]

This author's Freedom of Information Act appeal to NSA for the tapes dated July 6, 2001, was denied,[12] and this author then filed a federal district court lawsuit to obtain them.[13] This suit resulted, on July 2, 2003, in the release of the NSA EC-121M audiotapes and translations of transcripts of intercepts. Along with the transcripts of the tapes, a secret message of the National Security Agency to the White House dated June 22, 1967, titled "Aftermath of Israeli Attack on USS *Liberty,* 8 June 1967," was also released. It contained the following opening paragraph: "1. General. The following activity is based on Israeli plain language VHF/UHF voice communications intercepted on 8 June 1967 between 1229Z and 1328Z. This activity deals solely with the aftermath of the attack of Israeli jet aircraft and torpedo boats on the USS *Liberty* (GTR 5). *There are no COMINT reflections of the actual attack itself* " (emphasis added).

The NSA also declassified and released the English translations and the audiotapes in Hebrew and further declassified a portion of the NSA 1981 report that reads: "While these reports revealed some confusion on the part of the pilots concerning the nationality of the ship, they tended to rule out any thesis that the Israeli Navy and Air Force deliberately attacked a ship they knew to be American."[14]

On September 19, 2005, in response to another of this author's FOIA requests, the oral history of Richard W. Hickman, the NSA Hebrew linguist who translated the tapes at NSA headquarters, was released and *further confirmed* that the tapes show the attack was a mistake.[15] Hickman's interviewer (William Gerhard) stated, "The transcripts tend to show that the Israelis were confused as to the nationality." Hickman replied, "That's right . . . I would tend to say that the Israelis did not know they had attacked a U.S. vessel."

In 1986, at the request of Thames Television,[16] the Israel Air Force released transcripts of tapes of their communications during the attack that showed considerable confusion about the *Liberty*, what she was, and where she was. The Israeli Hebrew transcripts and rough English translations of the tapes were released to this author in 1993 and are presented in appendix 2, along with the NSA EC-121 tape translations.

In the past, skeptics have claimed that the Israel Air Force tapes cannot be relied upon, alleging that they were manufactured by the Israelis after the fact.[17] This could have been a challenge to the authenticity of the Israel Air Force tapes prior to the release of the NSA tapes, which dovetail with and confirm the veracity of the Israeli tapes. It must be remembered that when the Israel Air Force tapes were released, the existence of the NSA tapes was not generally known.

The Israel Air Force tapes are a combination of VHF/UHF radio transmissions between aircraft and their controllers, aircraft and motor torpedo boats, and closed-line telephone conversations between Israel Air Force controllers. The NSA EC-121M intercepts begin at 1430 Sinai (1230Z) with the Israeli control tower at Hatzor air base (call sign "Tribune") telling Super Frelon helicopter 815 by radio, "Pay attention. There was a warship there which we attacked [one word garbled] the men jumped from it into the water, you will try to rescue them." The Israeli tapes of a few minutes earlier contained a report by Royal Flight leader that "people are jumping into the water" and an order by air control to send search and rescue helicopters to the scene.

At 1432 Sinai (1232Z) the NSA intercept records Tribune telling helicopter 815, "Pay attention. This ship is now identified as Egyptian . . ." Two

minutes later at 1434 Sinai (1234Z) the Israeli tape has Israeli air control reconfirming, "Robert . . . it's an Egyptian supply ship." At 1459 Sinai
(1259Z) on the NSA tapes helicopter 815 informs Tribune that he has "visual contact with a vessel straight ahead 12 miles." At 1501 Sinai (1301Z) air
control tells IAF headquarters on the Israeli tapes "He is 12 miles from them
now. He has eye contact with the ship."

At 1506 Sinai (1306Z) NSA tapes, "It's not men in the water it's boats." At
1510 Sinai (1310Z) Israel Air Force tapes give, "There are no people. He sees
boats but no people." Finally, and most conclusive, at 1512 Sinai (1312Z)
the NSA tapes have Tribune asking helicopter 815, "Check once more if this
is really an American flag," and the Israeli tapes at 1512 Sinai (1312Z) have,
"Kislev, there is an American flag on board."

An examination of the NSA tapes and the Israeli tapes shows that the identical events are being described on both sets of tapes at near or exactly the same
time. Minor discrepancies of a few minutes between other segments of the tapes
are easily accounted for, by not only different clocks or watches and different
translators of Hebrew to English but also by the natural time lag of information
being passed either up or down the Israeli chain of command.

A careful, attentive comparison of the NSA tapes and the Israel tapes
authenticates the accuracy of the Israel Air Force tapes. Israeli officials were
not aware of the existence of the NSA tapes until thirty-five years after the
attack. If the veracity of the Israeli tapes is not accepted and the Israel Air
Force tapes are disregarded, then the only tape-intercept evidence remaining is that of the NSA tapes, which state that the American flag was not
identified until 1512 Sinai (1312Z), approximately forty-four minutes after
the attack was over. The NSA concluded, without any reference whatsoever
to the Israeli tapes, that "the tragedy resulted not only from Israeli miscalculation but also from faulty U.S. communications practices."[18] The NSA tapes
"tended to rule out any thesis that the Israeli Navy and Air Force deliberately
attacked a ship they knew to be American."[19]

Specifically, a Central Intelligence Agency intelligence memorandum of
June 13, 1967, stated, "None of the communications of the attacking aircraft
and torpedo boats is available, but the intercepted conversations between the
helicopter pilots and the control tower at Hatzor leave little doubt that the Israelis failed to identify the *Liberty* as a U.S. ship before or during the attack.[20] A
CIA memorandum of June 21, 1967, stated, "The Israelis presumably thought
the vessel they were attacking not to be the *Liberty* for it is also clear that when
the initial attack took place the ground controllers and the pilots believed the

ship to be belligerent."[21] The CIA restated its official position in 1978: "It remains our best judgment that the Israeli attack on the USS *Liberty* was not made in malice toward the United States and was a mistake."[22]

The Defense Intelligence Agency, in a June 13, 1967, top-secret memorandum for the chairman of the Joint Chiefs of Staff (code word Trine) concluded, "There is no available information which would conclusively show the Israelis made a premeditated attack on a ship known to be American," and, "NSA advises that additional COMINT bearing on this subject will be available. Meanwhile, the weight of the evidence is that the attacking force believed their target was Egyptian." On June 28, 1967, in a top-secret addendum to the memorandum for the chairman, the DIA reported, "Further information has been received concerning the *Liberty* incident which clarifies the sequence of events surrounding the attack. . . . This evidence fails to show that the Israelis made a premeditated attack on a known American ship. . . . [A] completed NSA translation and analysis of the intercept of transmissions between Israeli ground control and helicopters near the Liberty after the attack . . . tends to bear out the analysis offered on pages 2 and 3 of the initial memorandum."[23]

After studying the NSA tapes, Clark Clifford reported to the president, the secretary of defense, and the secretary of state, by means of the President's Foreign Intelligence Advisory Board report: "The weight of the evidence is that the Israeli attacking force originally believed their target was Egyptian," and, "The information thus far available does not reflect that the Israeli high command made a premeditated attack on a ship known to be American."[24]

Independently, and without any access to the NSA tapes, the U.S. Navy court of inquiry presided over by Adm. Isaac C. Kidd Jr. concluded, on June 18, 1967, "Available evidence combines to indicate the attack on *Liberty* was in fact a case of mistaken identity . . . There are no available indications that the attack was intended against a U.S. ship."[25] Adm. John McCain, Commander in Chief, U.S. Naval Forces Europe, in June 1967, also without access to the tapes, endorsed Admiral Kidd's conclusions with the comment, "The foregoing comments by the convening authority lead to an overall conclusion that the attack was in fact a mistake."[26]

After almost four decades, the release of the NSA tapes confirms the independent conclusions of Admirals Kidd and McCain. Although a profusion of propaganda alleging dozens of conflicting conspiracy stories continues to this day, the NSA tapes confirm the official position of the United States. The attack was a tragic case of mistaken identity.

Chapter 17

CONFIRMATION

The Mythical Submarine

National Security Council Note NSC 5412/1 created a special group 5412, a directive on covert operations.[1] On June 2, 1964 by a top-secret memo designated "National Security Action Memorandum No. 303," the name of Special Group 5412 was changed to the 303 Committee.[2] A secret-eyes-only, typed document of that body, dated April 10, 1967, states:

.... 10 April 1967
MEMORANDUM FOR THE RECORD
    SUBJECT: Minutes of the Meeting of the 303
        Committee 7 April 1967
    PRESENT: Mr. Rostow, Ambassador Kohler, Mr. Vance
        and Admiral Taylor
    General Ralph D. Steakley was present for Item 1.[3]
    Mr. William Broe was present for Item 2.[4]
    1. *DOD Proposal*
General Ralph D. Steakley briefed the committee on a sensitive DOD project known as FRONTLET 615. After a number of questions exploring alternative methods of satisfying the requirements and assessing the mission's current priority, the proposal was approved by the committee principals.[5]

Submarine within UAR waters [Hand-written]

Although the memorandum refers to Item 1 and Item 2, only item 1, "DOD Proposal," appears. A line is drawn around the text of the DOD Proposal, and handwritten across the page, as indicated above, are the words "Submarine within UAR waters." The person who wrote these added words and the date the words were written are unknown.

Assuming that "FRONTLET 615" was an authorization on April 10, 1967, to covertly insert a submarine into UAR (Egyptian) territorial waters, this approval occurred forty-five days before the USS *Liberty* received orders in Abidjan, Ivory Coast, to proceed to the eastern Mediterranean, fifty-seven days before the start of the Six Day War, and sixty-one days prior to the attack of June 8, 1967. Nevertheless, the submarine-conspiracy believers rely on the words "submarine within UAR waters" as proof not only that a U.S. submarine was present but that it photographed the attack and that these photographs prove the attack was deliberate.

A number of stories have grown over the years, first initiated by James Ennes claiming a U.S. submarine was within periscope sight of the *Liberty* during the attack. Ennes tells it this way:

> Quickly poking a periscope above the surface of the water, American submariners watched wave after wave of jet airplanes attacking *Liberty*. Strict orders prevented any action that might reveal their presence. They could not help us, and they could not break radio silence to send for help. Frustrated and angry, the commanding officer activated a periscope camera that recorded *Liberty*'s trauma on movie film. He could do no more.[1]
>
> [Ennes's Footnote 1] This story first came to me from an enlisted crew member of the submarine, who blurted it out impulsively in the cafeteria at Portsmouth Naval Hospital a few weeks after the attack. The report seemed to explain the marks I had seen on the chart in the coordination center, as well as reports of periscope sightings that circulated in the ship on the day of the attack. Since the attack, three persons in positions to know have confirmed the story that a submarine operated near *Liberty*, although no credible person has confirmed the report that photographs were taken.[6]

In 1997 Ennes published an article titled "USS *Liberty*: Periscope Photography May Finally Reveal Truth,"[7] in which he identified the submarine as the *Amberjack*, based on "a relatively senior member of the crew of the submarine, but he was unwilling to give his name or to talk to us except through a third party." Through third-party hearsay Ennes claims *Amberjack* was only one of five submarines in the Gaza Strip area, the others being the USS *Trutta*, the USS *Requin,* a French submarine, and an Italian submarine.

Various other stories claim that the submarine was the *Amberjack* (SS 522), the USS *Andrew Jackson* (SSBN 619),[8] the *Trutta* (SS 421),[9] or *Requin* (SS 451).[10] Assuming that a U.S. submarine was indeed in the area at the time of the attack, what could a submarine have seen or heard that could have contributed evidence on the issue of whether or not the attack was a deliberate attack on a ship known to be American? Ennes writes, "Submarine photography can prove what happened." He quotes four unnamed submarine crew members as all saying the *Amberjack* was "very close to" or "almost directly under" the *Liberty*.[11] He also says, "None of these four was certain that pictures were taken." If pictures were taken, what kind of view was available from "almost directly under" the *Liberty*? And if such submarine evidence exists, where is it?

Today's submarine technology has come a long way since 1967. In those days only one person could look through the periscope on the submarine, observing only a limited field of vision of the surface of the sea or a patch of the sky. There was limited capability to take pictures (possibly movie film) through the periscope. There was no capability to listen through the periscope to noise on the surface or to intercept radio transmissions. Possibly the submarine could have projected above the sea surface an antenna that might have intercepted some VHF or UHF radio transmissions within a very limited and finite distance,[12] but how a submerged submarine would have known to listen to a specific tactical channel, out of the many available,[13] on which Israeli aircraft pilots were talking in Hebrew to the controllers, who were located far out of range of any possible reception capability at sea level, is not explained by the submarine storytellers. Furthermore, the water depth in the vicinity of El Arish and near to the point of attack makes it an area where a submarine captain would not operate his submarine; the court of inquiry record contains testimony of a depth of thirty-one or thirty-three fathoms, approximately 186 to 198 feet.[14]

What about the various submarines alleged to have been there? Their logs for June 8, 1967 reflect:

Amberjack	Position "Special Operations"
	1–8 June Special Operations[15]
Andrew Jackson	1–13 June Special Operations[16]
Trutta	Position in Port
	Moored port side to starboard side
	USS *Tidewater* (AD-31)[17]
Requin	8 June 1967—in port
	Moored to buoy no. 7 in anchorage at
	Souda Bay, Crete[18]

Since the *Amberjack* was in the Mediterranean and had the distinction of being identified as the mystery sub by the largest number of submarine-conspiracy supporters, this author contacted Capt. Augustine E. Hubel, who commanded the USS *Amberjack* on June 8, 1967, to determine if he would confirm the claim of the unnamed *Amberjack* sailor mentioned on page 64 of the Ennes book. Captain Hubel provided an affidavit that states:[19]

Augustine Hubel, U.S. Navy (Ret) who after first being duly sworn, deposed and said:

1. Affiant makes this affidavit based on his own personal knowledge.
2. In June 1967 he was on active duty with the United States Navy serving as Commanding Officer of the USS *Amberjack* (SS-522) operating in the Mediterranean in accordance with CTF69 (Commander Submarine Flotilla Eight) message 061140Z June 67.
3. He is aware of the incident which occurred on the afternoon on June 8, 1967 when the USS *Liberty* was attacked by Israeli forces at a position near the Sinai coast off El Arish, approximately 31-23 N, 33-25 E.
4. That on June 8, 1967 the USS *Amberjack* (SS-522) was not within 100 miles of the USS *Liberty* or its approximate position 31-23 N, 33-25 E.

If, as Captain Hubel says, the *Amberjack* was not there, then could it have been another U.S. submarine?

In 1967 all U.S. submarine operations in the Mediterranean were under the control of Submarine Flotilla 8 (COMSUBFLOT 8), commanded by Vice Adm. Marmaduke Gresham Bayne. He provided an affidavit that stated:

Marmaduke G. Bayne, U.S. Navy (Ret) who after first being duly sworn, deposed and said:

1. Affiant makes this affidavit based on his own personal knowledge.
2. In June 1967 he was on active duty with the United States Navy and as Commander of Submarine Flotilla 8 (COMSUBFLOT 8) in which capacity he commanded and controlled all United States submarines operating in the Mediterranean.
3. He is aware of the incident which occurred on the afternoon on June 8, 1967 when the USS *Liberty* was attacked by Israeli forces at a position near the Sinai coast off El Arish, approximately 31-23 N, 33-25 E.
4. To the best of his recollection, there was not assignment of any United States submarines in *Liberty*'s vicinity on June 8, 1967.[20]

On August 26, 1998, many years before this author contacted Vice Admiral Bayne, the latter gave an oral history to Dr. David Winkler at the U.S. Naval Historical Center (now known as the Naval History and Heritage Command). Comments on pages 74 and 75 are enlightening:

It was during that time LIBERTY was attacked by the Israelis. SUB-FLOTEIGHT had the most complete operational plot in the whole Mediterranean, including Commander Sixth Fleet, simply because we had to let the missile boats know of all maritime traffic. This was after Ellis had left. I think Vice Admiral Bill Martin was then COMSIXTHFLT. We knew where the LIBERTY was and we knew what LIBERTY was. So everybody was coming to SUBFLOTEIGHT to view our plot. Admiral Griffin, Admiral Martin assorted operational people from Sixth Fleet, all trying to get an idea about what could have happened. It was kind of a surprise to me that that big screen it was as big as the side of this room . . . was the one place in the Mediterranean where everything was displayed. It gave us problems, too, for before we could display the plot [page 75] we had to remove the symbols showing positions of the missile submarines or we would have violated our own operational policy.

I will believe always that the attack on LIBERTY was a mistake. It was not deliberate. I am not a great admirer of the conduct of the Israelis today; they are far too internal and unreliable in their international cooperation, but what happened with LIBERTY was a mistake made during the change of an operational commander watch.[21]

On January 13, 2003, in a letter to this author, Vice Adm. (retired) Marmaduke Bayne wrote the following:

> I was Commander Submarine Flotilla Eight in the Mediterranean for two years ending in July, 1967, just after the *Liberty* incident. This was early in our deployment of Polaris (later called SSBN's) submarines into the area. The operational policy for moving the submarines around that relatively restricted body of water was to inform the submarines of everything possible about the movement of other ships, and to tell others nothing about the movement of the submarines. In that way the Commanding Officers could be given the maximum opportunity to remain undetected during their time in the Mediterranean Sea. As a consequence ComSubFlot Eight maintained the most complete US operational plot of maritime activities in the region. The physical size of the plot covered an entire wall, about 15 by 12 feet. We were informed of the *Liberty's* movements, knew what she was, and marked her on our plot with a special symbol.

In a Freedom of Information Act lawsuit dated January 21, 2003, *A. Jay Cristol v. National Security Agency,* paragraph 2 of the complaint requests three specific items. Specifically, plaintiff filed a request with the NSA pursuant to FOIA by letter dated April 26, 2001, a copy of which is attached as Exhibit "A." Plaintiff's request sought access to tapes, recordings, or other electronic or paper recordings of surveillance of common voice radio transmissions made or intercepted on June 8, 1967 by the USS *Liberty,* the USS *Amberjack,* and a U.S. EC-121 aircraft during a deployment in the eastern Mediterranean. Importantly, plaintiff did not seek the disclosure of information pertaining to the type of equipment used in, or the manner of making, the documented transmissions. Rather, plaintiff's requests were exclusively limited to identifying and reviewing transmissions that either had already been disclosed to the public through the open radio and/or materials that demonstrate the existence of such transmissions—neither of which are exempt from disclosure.[22]

The answer to plaintiff's complaint filed by the United States Attorney on behalf of the National Security Agency on July 3, 2003, confirmed release of the "actual recordings and English translations (including summaries of those translations) that relate to the USS *Liberty* incident" and responding to the other two requests, stated:

21. Defendant admits that the USS *Liberty* did not locate, receive, or record on June 8, 1967, any transmissions to which Plaintiff refers . . .

25. Defendant admits that the NSA has no tapes, recordings, or other electronic or paper records of surveillance of VHF/UHF or high frequency voice transmissions made or intercepted on June 8, 1967 between 1100Z and 1300Z and collected by the USS *Amberjack*.[23]

Is it possible that the periscope was on a Soviet submarine? There is a published story that there was a Soviet submarine hull number K-172 (NATO classification Echo II) in the eastern Mediterranean.[24] The writer is Nikolai Cherkashin, who is described as a captain in the Russian navy and a marine writer. The article format is that of an interview with reserve Vice Adm. Nikolai Shashkov, described as the commander of the submarine, who is quoted as placing his submarine "near the shores of Syria that was my main positioning area." The "shores of Syria" are almost two hundred miles from the site of the *Liberty* incident, which would exclude Captain Shashkov's submarine from being on the scene. He further stated that the Americans "were looking for an entire underwater Soviet screen, while in fact all there was my one *K-172*."

Shashkov's story raises more questions than it answers. He said he was near the shores of Syria and dangerously close to three U.S. aircraft carriers—the *America*, the *Forrestal*, and the *Enterprise*, all of which he describes as nuclear carriers.[25] In fact, in June 1967 the carriers of the Sixth Fleet were five to six hundred miles west of the "shores of Syria," and neither *Forrestal* nor *Enterprise* were there. Only *America* and *Saratoga* were in the Mediterranean at that time. He can perhaps be excused for believing the carriers were "nuclear," although in fact neither USS *America* nor USS *Saratoga* were nuclear powered. Nevertheless, he described his mission as to launch eight P-6 (SS-N-12) missiles with nuclear warheads into Israel and destroy Israel with "a minimum of eight Hiroshimas" in the event of an American or Israeli attack on "friendly Syria." On June 10, 1967, Israel did attack Syria and captured the Golan Heights, but obviously Shashkov did not launch eight nukes into Israel.

Also, the writer, Cherkashin, describes the events as occurring "on the eve of or during Passover 1968."[26] This is almost a year after the 1967 war. Is it possible that Cherkashin is remembering an event from the 1973 war? He describes 1967–68 as "then the most troubled region of the planet, the eastern Mediterranean, scene of the Arab-Israeli conflict."[27] It is thus respectfully suggested that the Shashkov story does not provide evidence that a Soviet submarine was in sight of the *Liberty* on June 8, 1967. It is difficult, if not impossible, to prove a negative, namely, that there was no U.S. submarine in the area. It is respectfully suggested that the burden of proving that a submarine was actually there, and the burden of producing the "evidence"—tapes, pictures, videos, intercepts—is upon the proponents of this claim, which over the last forty years has been supported only by hearsay stories. To date, the only credible piece of documentary evidence on the subject is the single-page Committee 303 memo, which falls far short of proving anything. All available evidence establishes that there was no submarine in the area of the attack on the *Liberty* on June 8, 1967.

Chapter 18

CONFIRMATION

Department of State

Less than six months after the release of the NSA tapes, the U.S. Department of State released *Foreign Relations of the United States, Volume XIX*, which declassified the last known significant American documents relating to the *Liberty* incident. The separate State Department summary of the volume shows the evolution of the U.S. position from the initial outrage to a final conclusion that the tragedy had been a mistake.

On October 1, 2003, the State Department announced a conference titled "The United States, the Middle East and the 1967 Arab-Israeli War" and invited proposals for original papers on topics including "The USS *Liberty* Incident and Role of Intelligence."[1] Beginning on the morning of January 12, 2004, the conference took place at the Department of State in the Loy Henderson auditorium. It lasted two days and included seven panel discussions. This author was invited to participate on Panel 1, titled "War, Intelligence, and the USS Liberty." A paper coauthored with Capt. Ernest Castle (who served as U.S. naval attaché at the U.S. embassy in Tel Aviv in 1967) and John Hadden (the CIA chief of station in Tel Aviv in 1967) was submitted. None of the papers submitted for the conference have been published in hard copy by the Department of State, allegedly for budgetary reasons, but the above paper "The USS *Liberty* and the Role of Intelligence," may be viewed at www.thelibertyincident.com/docs/liberty-intelligence.pdf.

Included on the panel were Dr. Marc Susser, the historian of the Department of State, Dr. David Robarge, Central Intelligence Agency history staff, and Dr. David Hatch, the historian for the National Security Agency. The *Liberty* panel was scheduled for 10:00 a.m. until noon, while the release of volume XIX of *Foreign Relations of the United States* was scheduled for noon. Therefore this author was not aware during the time of the panel whether any material in volume XIX would conflict or contradict his presentation.

The entire conference was broadcast live on C-SPAN.[2] Following the keynote address by David Satterfield, Deputy Assistant Secretary, Bureau of Near Eastern Affairs, Harriet Schwar, the editor of *Foreign Relations of the United States, Volume XIX,* read (at 9:45 a.m.) a summary of the volume which contained the following:

The Attack on the U.S.S. *Liberty*

On June 8, at 8:03 a.m. Washington time, Israeli planes and patrol boats attacked the U.S.S. *Liberty*, an electronics intelligence ship, in international waters, causing severe damage to the ship and numerous casualties. The Joint Chiefs of Staff had dispatched the *Liberty* to the eastern Mediterranean on May 23, when Nasser's closure of the Gulf of Aqaba greatly increased the likelihood of hostilities in the area. The *Liberty* reached its location off the Sinai coast early on June 8. Meanwhile, the UAR charges of U.S. participation in Israel's air operations had prompted the JCS to send new orders instructing the *Liberty* to remain at least 100 miles from Egypt and Israel. Due to a series of errors, the message never reached the ship. *(192, 199, 217)* [Italicized numerical references are to documents in volume XIX][3]

At 9:50 a.m. on June 8, Walt Rostow informed the President that the *Liberty* had been attacked and that the attacker was unknown, and that reconnaissance aircraft from the Sixth Fleet had been sent to the scene. (In fact, the planes had been sent with orders to defend the *Liberty* and destroy its attackers.) *(205–207)* About an hour later, word reached Washington that the Israelis had informed the U.S. Naval Attaché in Tel Aviv that Israeli planes and torpedo boats had attacked a U.S. ship in error. *(211)* The Sixth Fleet aircraft were promptly recalled.

President Johnson ordered a thorough investigation of the facts surrounding the attack. *(269–70, 284)* After extensive investigation, the Central Intelligence Agency and the National Security Agency concluded that there was "little doubt" that the attacking Israeli units "failed to identify the *Liberty* as a US ship before or during the attack" and that they had mistakenly identified the ship as Egyptian. Subsequently the Central Intelligence Agency repeated the conclusion that the Israeli attack was a mistake although it was "both incongruous and indicative of gross negligence." Clark Clifford also examined the evidence at Walt Rostow's request and concluded that there was no evidence that the attack was intentional. *(284–85, 317, 373)*

Only commentator Dr. Charles Smith of the University of Arizona and author James Bamford contradicted the conclusions of this author's paper and the conclusions of the State Department. Smith referred to a book he had written in 1988 claiming "The Israelis attacked probably in order to sink the *Liberty* and forestall American awareness of their plans to expand to the Jordan River on the West Bank, or, more likely, to move against Syria."[4] This author's response to Dr. Smith's thesis was first, that on June 8, 1967, the Israelis had already advanced on the West Bank to the Jordan River. More significant, the move against Syria has long been discredited by a State Department cable from Ambassador Wallace Barbour to Secretary of State Dean Rusk advising that at 1130 a.m. on June 8, 1967, Gen. Aharon Yariv, then chief of IDF Intelligence, had advised both Barbour and the president's special representative, Harry McPherson, of the impending attack on Syria.[5] Telling the United States of the impending attack on Syria at 11:30 a.m. and then attacking the USS *Liberty* at 2:00 p.m. to keep the United States from learning of the impending attack defies logic.

James Bamford challenged the validity of the U.S. Navy court of inquiry findings, which concluded among fifty-four findings: "1. Available evidence combines to indicate the attack on *Liberty* on 8 June was in fact a case of mistaken identity . . ."; and "6. There are no available indications that the attack was intended against a U.S. ship."[6] Bamford alleged the National Security Agency tapes released pursuant to this author's Freedom of Information Act lawsuit (see chapter 16) were false and claimed, without any supporting basis, that the NSA had other tapes that it had not released.

Chapter 19

CONFIRMATION

Court of Inquiry Audiotapes

On June 8, 1967, Ens. John D. Scott was the USS *Liberty*'s damage control officer. He testified under oath at the court of inquiry proceedings held on board the *Liberty* on June 14, 1967.[1]

Fast-forward to 2006/2007, when journalist James Scott, the son of Ensign Scott, was enrolled at Harvard as a Neiman fellow. James Scott decided to write a book about the *Liberty* incident. For his research, he visited the U.S. Naval Historical Center (which became the next year the Naval History and Heritage Command), in the Washington Navy Yard, on May 4, 2007. There he conducted research in the public archive of declassified Navy documents, which included copy number four of the U.S. Navy court of inquiry record concerning the *Liberty* incident.[2] The keen-eyed journalist noted eleven IBM "dictaphone" belts attached to the record. He asked to hear them and was advised that the Naval Historical Center did not have the equipment to play them and did not know what they contained. On May 7, 2007, James Scott filed a Freedom of Information Act request that the tapes be converted to a usable form that would allow researchers to utilize them.

The center staff was taken by surprise. As they had told Scott, they had no idea of the content of the tapes and did not have the IBM equipment that could play the tapes. Although the court of inquiry record had been declassified and released on April 21, 1976, some thirty-one years earlier, because the tapes were from an obsolete and long-discarded IBM recorder the center staff had no way to listen to or transcribe the tapes. So, in an abundance of caution, they denied Scott's request and sent the tapes to the Navy Judge Advocate General for review and instructions.

On August 29, 2007, Scott filed a Freedom of Information Act lawsuit in the U.S. District Court for the District of South Carolina.[3] In his complaint Scott alleged that the center had "retaliated" by referring this matter to the Navy's Office of the Judge Advocate General (OJAG).[4]

The tapes were sent to the Navy Judge Advocate General's office in Norfolk, Virginia, where equipment was located to play them. They were then recorded onto CDs and reviewed by the OJAG. The tapes are not a part of the official transcribed record of testimony taken by the U.S. Navy yeoman, YNC Joeray Spencer, during the June 1967 court of inquiry proceedings,[5] although they do contain partial testimony of witnesses Capt. L. R. Raish, USN, taken in London; Lt. (later Cdr.) M. H. Bennett, USN; Cdr. E. A. Platzek, USN; and Capt. R. L. Arthur, USN. As far as this author could identify, no testimony of James Scott's father, Ens. John D. Scott, USNR, is on the tapes. Belt seven contains the official opening of the court of inquiry and, though the two are not identical word for word, the tape essentially tracks with the official transcript taken by and prepared under the supervision of Chief Spencer. At times Spencer is heard on the tapes saying, "You are going a little too fast." The tapes also contain some off the record conversations during the court of inquiry proceedings, but they do not add anything new to the court of inquiry record.[6]

After review of the tapes by the OJAG, they were released to James Scott. He then stipulated to dismissal of his FOIA lawsuit against the Naval Historical Center.[7] The United States Attorney for the District of South Carolina filed a Notice of Voluntary Dismissal in the case, dated January 3, 2008.[8]

When the destroyer USS *Davis* reached the *Liberty* on June 9, 1967, Lt. Paul Tobin, USN, came on board the *Liberty* leading a damage control party and—it stands to reason—worked with Ensign Scott to control the damage, restore the ship's electrical power and engines, and steam the *Liberty* under its own power to Malta. Lieutenant Tobin, as we saw above, was awarded the Bronze Star for his contribution. Some forty years later, retired rear admiral Paul Tobin was serving as the Director of Naval History and therefore of the Naval Historical Center, the organization sued by Ensign Scott's son, James.

The opening of the court of inquiry includes the voice of Admiral Kidd: "Do you, Captain Ward Boston, Jr., U.S. Navy, swear that you will faithfully perform the duty of Counsel for the Court, so help you God?," followed by the voice of Ward Boston saying, "I do."[9] At the conclusion of the court of inquiry the record was signed by Admiral Kidd and Captains Atkinson, Lauff, and Boston.[10] Thirty-nine years later, on October 22, 2003, Capt.

Ward Boston signed an affidavit prepared for him by James Ronald Gotcher, a conspiracy-theory supporter, claiming the court of inquiry findings had been falsified.[11]

This author tried to locate court member Capt. Bernard J. Lauff, USN, but could not. In 1992, Capt. Bert Atkinson, USN, responded to a query by this author that everything in the record of the court of inquiry was proper and correct, except that he had some reservations as to whether the *Liberty* had actually been over fourteen miles offshore or inside twelve miles; the court had given the *Liberty* the benefit of the doubt.[12] In 1991, Adm. Isaac Kidd Jr. commented to this author, "Nothing you told me, wrote to me or provided by way of documentation has been inconsistent with what we had to work with at that time. This has been reassuring to me—even after so many years. You have done a splendid job. . . . With high esteem, Isaac C. Kidd, Jr."[13] The findings of the court of inquiry were approved by endorsement of Adm. John S. McCain Jr.,[14] Commander in Chief, Naval Forces Europe, who wrote, "The foregoing comments by the convening authority lead to an overall conclusion that the attack was in fact a mistake." The findings of the U.S. Navy court of inquiry were endorsed a total of seven times.[15] None of the official endorsers have ever amended, modified, or withdrawn their endorsement. Capt. Ward Boston completed his career in the U.S. Navy and retired. As an officer and a lawyer it is strange that he should close his record with an act that dishonors him, claiming to have violated his oath to "faithfully perform his duty of Counsel for the Court" by filing a false report in a U.S. Navy court of inquiry.

In the legal arena, lawyers struggle to impeach (destroy the credibility of) witnesses' testimony. Impeachment is accomplished by establishing a prior inconsistent statement made by the witness and then asking the witness, "Were you lying then or now?" The testimony of an impeached witness is given little consideration by courts, because it has been established that the witness is a liar. Why did Ward Boston sign an affidavit impeaching himself? Why did a man who had sworn under oath to faithfully perform his duties and who had remained silent for over thirty years suddenly swear under oath that he had not faithfully performed his duty?

James Scott continued to work on his book. In the fall of 2007 he traveled to Israel with his father, John D. Scott, to do further research on the subject. The Scott book, *Attack on the* Liberty,[16] was released by Simon and Schuster on June 2, 2009. It was reviewed by John Lancaster in the *Washington Post* on July 12, 2009. Lancaster concluded, "Scott clearly had his own suspicions, though he produces no smoking-gun evidence to support the charge of a deliberate attack, perhaps because none exists."

Lt. John Scott is a U.S. naval officer. On June 8, 1967, he went through a terrible ordeal. He described the ordeal most vividly to his son, and James Scott details the horror well in his book. It is understandable how, having been on the receiving end of the attack, Lieutenant Scott is unable to accept the fact that the attack was the result of a tragic mistake. As a victim of the tragedy, he is not unique in that feeling. For instance, as we have seen in earlier chapters, when, on June 2, 1967, just six days before the attack on the *Liberty*, U.S. Air Force planes strafed the Soviet ship *Turkestan* in Vietnam, reportedly killing and wounding Soviet sailors, the Soviets refused to accept the U.S. explanation that the attack was a mistake.[17] On May 7, 1998, when NATO forces bombed the Chinese embassy in Belgrade, the Chinese refused to accept the explanation that the attack was a mistake, and they still claim it was deliberate.[18] The families of the Canadian soldiers killed and wounded in April 2002 by a U.S. Air National Guard F-16 strike in Afghanistan still refuse to believe their loved ones died as the result of a mistake.[19]

Initially, on January 11, 1990, when this author interviewed General Mordechai ("Motti") Hod, in 1967 the chief of the Israel Air Force, the general did not wish to talk about the *Liberty* incident. He said that the families of those lost and the surviving crew members had suffered enough and that it was not appropriate to disturb old wounds. His initial words were, "If it gives them some comfort to believe the attack was not a mistake, then let them so believe." After hearing some of the conspiracy stories, however, General Hod changed his mind. He said that because the conspiracy stories were so distorted, they continued to create pain rather than comfort; the truth was better than the false stories. He then cooperated with this author's research.

Not every *Liberty* survivor believes the attack was deliberate. Cdr. Maurice Bennett, who was awarded the Silver Star and Purple Heart for saving lives on the *Liberty*, wrote to this author: "From the viewpoint of one who was on board . . . your account leaves little doubt that the attack was the result of a series of confused decisions made in a war setting. . . . Perhaps your account may lay to rest the many conspiracy theories which have plagued us these last 30 years. . . . I must confess that through the years I had convinced myself that the attack was deliberate. . . . You have put a lot of ghosts to rest."[20]

What was the response to that declaration? After this author published the above, a former *Liberty* crew member called Commander Bennett a traitor.[21] For this reason, this author has not disclosed any further names of other *Liberty* crew members who have expressed their agreement with Commander Bennett or reject the conspiracy stories.

James Scott should be commended for carrying out the fifth biblical commandment, "honor thy father and mother," and writing a book in support of his father's belief. As a talented writer with a Harvard master's degree in journalism, he writes well. He does *not* resort to falsehoods. Additionally, to his credit, he does not resort to vicious attacks on U.S. naval officers or the U.S. government, as have some of the purveyors of the *Liberty*-related conspiracy stories. However, his book is flawed by misleading his readers through the presentation of partial information and selective facts while omitting other important, undisputed material facts that do not support his thesis.

For example, one of the most compelling pieces of evidence confirming that the Israeli attackers believed they were attacking an Egyptian target is the set of NSA EC-121 intercepts. They clearly establish that the Israelis did not see a U.S. flag on the *Liberty* until 3:12 p.m., forty-four minutes after the attack was over. This is confirmed by the Israel Air Force audiotapes. In James Scott's book, on page 83, he writes that a Navy spy plane "dubbed the Willy Victor," with NSA Hebrew linguist Michael Prostinak on board, was flying over the Mediterranean when Prostinak "heard something that shocked him. He flipped on the secure intercom to his supervisor. 'Hey Chief. I've got really odd activity, . . . *They mentioned an American flag*'" (emphasis added).

James Scott leaves it at that. He fails to mention anywhere in his book that this transmission occurred and was intercepted forty-four minutes *after* the attack was over, thus misleading the reader into thinking that the flag sighting occurred during or before the attack, rather than confirming that it was only after the attack that the flag was sighted.[22]

What did Mike Prostinak conclude from the Israel Air Force radio transmission he intercepted and recorded? On September 25, 2009, he wrote to this author:

FROM: Michael Prostinak
To: A Jay Cristol
RE: Israeli intercepts I recorded on 8 June 1967
Sorry, I am unable to join you at the NSA Symposium on 16 Oct. 2009. I agree with Marvin Nowicki that the intercepts clearly show the attack on the U.S.S. *Liberty* was a mistake.
Mike

James Scott refers to Michael Prostinak's supervisor as being addressed "Hey Chief" but does not mention the supervisor by name. The supervisor was Dr. Marvin Nowicki, then a chief petty officer who retired as a lieutenant and later earned a PhD in international studies. Nowicki and Prostinak both heard the Israeli transmissions. Together they made preliminary translations of the Hebrew intercepts after the EC-121 returned to Athens. and then sent the tapes by courier to NSA headquarters in Maryland. In 2004, Nowicki disclosed the existence of the tapes to James Bamford, who wrote in his book that Nowicki had told him the tapes confirmed the attack was deliberate.[23] Nowicki reacted, following the publication of Bamford's book, with a letter to the *Wall Street Journal* that concluded, as we have seen earlier: "My position, which is opposite of Mr. Bamford's, is that the attack . . . was a gross error. How can I prove it? I can't unless the transcripts/tapes are found and released to the public."[24] This author sued the National Security Agency for the release of the above tapes, and the NSA released them on July 8, 2003.[25] For this author's conclusions based on the release of the NSA tapes, see chapter 16.

James Scott did contact two Americans who were on the ground in Israel on June 8, 1967. The first was then Capt. Ernest Castle, the U.S. naval attaché at the U.S. embassy in Tel Aviv. Castle was advised of the attack on the *Liberty* by the Israel military liaison officer, Lt. Col. Michael Bloch. Castle sent at 1414Z a message to the White House and the Sixth Fleet informing them of Israel's report of the attack. He was the first U.S. Navy person to reach the *Liberty* after the attack. He coordinated the transmission of questions and information back and forth to the U.S. Navy court of inquiry and the Chief of Naval Operations.

James Scott does mention Castle seven times in his book but never mentions Castle's conclusions about the attack. Initially Castle had been furious, "*mad as hell*," about the attack, but as the investigation developed he concluded it was not premeditated. Ernest Castle and this author went to Israel together on the twenty-fifth anniversary of the *Liberty* tragedy. This author flew Captain Castle out to the exact spot, by GPS, where Castle had flown over the *Liberty* on June 8, 1967. We dropped thirty-four flowers in a circle around the spot to commemorate the U.S. naval men who died.[26] Here, again, are a few lines of what Captain Castle told Thames TV on camera in 1982:

> Let us presume that the Israeli High Command was so fearful that the United States would learn of what was an evident Israeli plan to take the Golan or any other plan on the part of the Israelis, when they say, "My

golly, that will irritate the United States, our great friend, we better not do that or let that happen so let's sink their ship instead."

Let us presume it was a premeditated plan for whatever reason to get rid of a United States ship that was a threat to Israel. Then, the nation that had just, in 22 minutes, destroyed an entire Egyptian air force, and captured all the Egyptian armor in the Sinai, if they had decided they had to sink the United States ship, I believe they would have done so.[27]

The other American whom James Scott contacted was John Hadden, the CIA chief of station in Tel Aviv. After his assignment in Israel, Hadden returned to CIA headquarters, where he ran the Israel desk and then the Middle East desk. Hadden was deeply involved in the CIA investigation of the *Liberty* incident. He had many contacts in Israel; he and Castle are probably the two most knowledgeable Americans about the *Liberty*, having been on the ground in Israel in June 1967. Hadden told this author that he had told James Scott that the evidence established that the attack was a tragic mistake. Yet neither Hadden's name nor Hadden's conclusions are mentioned anywhere in the Scott book. Prior to Scott's visit to Israel he was provided by Hadden with names of persons in Israel who might assist him in his research. There is no indication in the Scott book of any contact with those sources.[28]

Another example of Scott's technique of selective omission is on page 236 of his book, where he quotes a passage from a highly respected syndicated columnist, James J. Kilpatrick, published on August 1, 1967: *"Syndicated columnist James Kilpatrick urged reporters to 'keep digging'"* (emphasis added).[29] Apparently Kilpatrick did keep digging and on September 5, 1967, he published an article in the *National Review* that summed up his conclusions from his digging to date:

> *Press service interviews with survivors of the attack have turned up a uniform conviction that the attack was deliberate* [emphasis added]. Sailors point to the morning-long aerial surveillance; the presence of the flag; the known configuration of the *Liberty;* her name in English on the stern (Egyptian naval ships carry their names in the cursive Arabic script); her slow progression in international waters. All of these factors support the crew's conclusion that the assault was no accident.
>
> *Opposed to this argument is the line of reasoning which holds that the Israeli government was heavily dependent upon the goodwill of the United*

States; that it would have been utterly irrational for the Israeli navy know-
ingly to have launched an attack on a U.S. ship; and that the only reason-
able explanation is that the incident was a mistake arising from the natural
tensions and fallible judgments of a hot war [emphasis added].[30]

On page 141 of his book James Scott claims that President Johnson believed that the attack was deliberate: "The president handed a great scoop to
the magazine reporter, but with conditions. Attribution had to be indirect
with references only to senior or high-ranking administration officials. The
president told Charles Roberts of *Newsweek* that the United States had accepted
Israel's apology, but had rejected its explanation of how the attack occurred.
Israel's assault on the *Liberty,* he told the reporter, was deliberate. The Jewish state's motive was to prevent the American ship from eavesdropping on
Israeli transmissions during the war." His only support for this claim is a
cable sent by the then-spokesman at the Israeli embassy in Washington, Dan
Pattir, to the Israel Foreign Ministry in Jerusalem, and it directly contradicts
President Johnson's own written statement, "At eleven o'clock we learned
that the ship had been attacked in error."[31]

Presumably, Scott's source for his claim was page 568 of Tom Segev's book
1967: Israel, the War and the Year That Transformed the Middle East,[32] because
Segev's English translator misspells Pattir's name as "Patir" and so does Scott.
Dan Pattir has advised this author that Scott never spoke to him. This author
spoke to Dan Pattir several times in September, October, and November 2009.

Pattir's cable was in Hebrew, except for two English words. An English
translation of the full text is:

No. 155

To: The Ministry Jerusalem   [illegible word] 111220
                                              June 67
From: Mem Israel [Embassy] Washington   Typed: 120330
Top Urgent—Handle
[word illegible Maybe: Foreign Ministry/U.S. Department?
abbreviated] SECRET.
Very reliable press source told me last night:

1. Briefing by the President and his press secretary George Christian
    given separately on Thursday and Friday to representatives of "News-

week" and "Time" which included references intended for indirect publication on the subject of the ship incident.

2. Following these conversations, a news report will be published tomorrow to be attributed to top Administration sources that the U.S. accepted the apology from the Israeli government on the incident, but rejected its explanations. The news report will say that according to the Administration sources the Israelis perpetrated(?) A DELIBERATE ATTACK because the Liberty was intentionally involved in electronic spying on Israeli and Egyptian transmitters close to the area of the land and aerial battles.

3. "Newsweek" adds that this claim from the top Administration derives from a clear intention to free the President from being tied by pro-Israeli moves and public opinion that is so all encompassing and energetic all over the U.S., and will enable him [to take] more convenient steps in renewed conversation with Arab countries.

Pattir

[TO] Foreign Minister [abbreviated]; Prime Minister [abbreviated]; [Moshe]

Dayan; Director General 2 [abbreviated]; Vice Director General [abbreviated]; Foreign

Ministry-U.S. Department [abbreviated]; or [rosh Mossad?]

Yod yod/yod bet yod.[33]

While James Scott relies on this cable, it is in fact double hearsay. "*Charles Roberts had said* that *President Johnson had said*." Both President Johnson and Charles Roberts are deceased (Johnson died on January 22, 1973, and Roberts on January 15, 1992), and no written document is known to exist anywhere to confirm that President Johnson believed the attack was premeditated. In fact, the third paragraph of the above cable states that the news leak about the *Liberty* was motivated by the political consideration of giving the U.S. president more flexibility in establishing renewed conversations with Arab countries, many of which had broken diplomatic relations with the United States as the war started.

It is true that President Johnson gave interviews to two journalists on the late evening of June 9, 1967.[34] The interview with Charles Roberts is mentioned in the White House log without any notation regarding the substance of the interview. We do not know whether Johnson told Roberts that he believed the attack *was* deliberate, or that the attack *might have been* deliberate, or that some persons believed the attack was deliberate. What is interesting is that the second interview of President Johnson that evening, with Hugh Sidy of *Life* magazine, which is noted in detail in the White House log, does not mention or even suggest that Johnson believed the attack was deliberate.[35] When this author interviewed him, on April 18, 1994, Sidy had no recollection of Johnson telling him the attack was deliberate. Rather, he recalled Johnson handing him a document about the *Liberty* incident and watching him read it and asking him what he thought.

Johnson's memoir, *The Vantage Point*,[36] infuriated some *Liberty* survivors by stating that the death toll was ten, with one hundred wounded. These numbers were from the first reports received about the attack and do not accurately reflect the final official numbers: thirty-four dead and 171 wounded.[37] President Johnson also stated in his memoir that "the ship had been attacked in error";[38] he later referred to "the tragic accident involving the *Liberty*."[39] It is conceivable that Johnson, like others, may have suspected that the attack was deliberate thirty-six hours after first word of the incident reached Washington. But his final opinion, after multiple investigations, was clear. His own investigation was conducted by Clark Clifford, chair of the Foreign Intelligence Advisory Board, who, as we have seen, researched the incident and reported on July 18, 1967 (five weeks and four days after the attack) to Johnson that "the information thus far available does not reflect that the Israeli high command made a premeditated attack on a ship known to be American" and that "the weight of the evidence is that the Israeli attacking force originally believed their target was Egyptian."[40]

The Scott book quotes a cadre of U.S. government officials as believing the attack was premeditated but fails to provide any evidentiary basis for those opinions. Scott also quotes a book that Richard Helms, the CIA director, published in 2003,[41] where Helms states that the attack was premeditated but at the same time concedes that he "had no role in the Board of Inquiry that followed [the attack]." Nor does Scott mention the official public position of the CIA that "the Israelis were apparently not aware that they were attacking the *Liberty*. The attack was not made in malice toward the U.S. and was by mistake."[42]

The Scott book may be an appropriate tribute from a son to a father, but it does not substantiate the theory that the attack on the *Liberty* was anything but the outcome of a set of tragic mistakes by the United States and Israel.

Chapter 20

CONFIRMATION

NSA 1995 Historian's Analysis

D r. Thomas R. Johnson served for many years as historian for the National Security Agency. He came to the agency in 1964. In 1992 he was tasked with writing a history of it. He completed the work in 1998 and retired in 1999.[1] Johnson authored a six-document series for the NSA titled "American Cryptology during the Cold War 1945–1989."[2] The history has been criticized for telling only the agency's failures and not its many successes.[3]

The history consists of a series of six documents:

Document 1: *American Cryptology during the Cold War, 1945–1960*, pp. 1–155

Document 2: *American Cryptology during the Cold War, 1945–1989*, pp. 157–287

Document 3: *American Cryptology during the Cold War, 1960–1972*, pp. 289–494

Document 4: *American Cryptology during the Cold War, 1945–1989*, pp. 495–652

Document 5: *American Cryptology during the Cold War, 1945–1989*, pp. 1–116

Document 6: *American Cryptology during the Cold War, 1945–1989*, pp. 117–262.

In response to a request by Matthew M. Aid of the National Security Archive at George Washington University, the first three documents were released on July 9, 2007. Matthew Aid posted them on the Internet on

November 14, 2008. The posted material may be viewed at www.gwu
.edu/~nsarchiv/NSAEBB/NSAEBB78/docs.htm.[4]

Of interest regarding the *Liberty* incident are 8 pages (432 through 439)
of Document 3, captioned "The Attack on the USS *Liberty*," which include
the following statements:

> The Johnson administration was properly outraged. The State Depart-
> ment, in a scathing statement highly unusual for diplomats, called the
> attack "quite literally incomprehensible. As a minimum, the attack must
> be condemned as an act of military recklessness reflecting wanton disre-
> gard for human life." But Clark Clifford, who was appointed by the presi-
> dent to render a final judgment, called it an identification error. Clifford
> relied heavily on COMINT reports showing Israeli confusion about the
> identification; these would have been difficult to fake. Going into it with
> a preconceived notion that the Israelis must have known [that they were
> attacking an American ship], he concluded that what was involved was
> "a flagrant act of gross negligence . . ." rather than a deliberate act. . . .
>
> The attack on the *Liberty* should not be viewed as a bizarre, or even
> an especially unusual, identification error. Even in peacetime such errors
> are made all too frequently—the Soviet shootdown of Korean Airlines
> Flight 007 and the American shootdown of an Iranian Airlines Flight
> IR 655 on July 3, 1988 are good examples. When a country is at war, the
> possibility of error is compounded by haste and fear. Losses to friendly
> fire always represent a substantial percentage of the casualties. And the
> Israeli agreement to compensate should not be taken as proof of guilty
> knowledge, but rather as an attempt to retain the friendship of a bene-
> factor wronged. (Page 438)

The entire text of Dr. Johnson's segment on the *Liberty* follows. (Several
comments by this author on minor points are inserted in square brackets in
Johnson's text. For instance, he mentions the launch of A-4 Skyhawks but
fails to mention that A-1 Skyraiders and F-4 Phantoms were also launched.
He also states that two torpedoes were launched against the *Liberty*, when in
fact five were launched.)

> The *Liberty*, NSA's choice as the TRS (Technical Research Ship) deploy-
> ment to the Middle East, was a reconditioned World War II Victory ship,
> converted to an AGTR (Auxiliary Technical Research Ship) in 1964. The

vessel already had five cruises under its belt. It had 20 intercept positions, 6 officers, a SIGINT crew of 125 and an overall complement of 172 men. With TRSSCOM, ship-to-shore radiotelephone circuits, and two receive terminals for fleet broadcasts, the *Liberty* was one of the best equipped ships in the TRS inventory. The Navy approved NSA's request, and the *Liberty*, off the west coast of Africa, steamed for Rota, where it took aboard an additional 9 linguists, including 3 NSA civilians, and more keying material for its communications circuits. On the second of June, it set off for the eastern Mediterranean.

The *Liberty*'s sailing order specified that it was to stay at least 12.5 miles off the coast of the UAR [United Arab Republic, i.e., Egypt] and 6.5 miles from Israel. When war broke out on 5 June, the Sixth Fleet, to which the *Liberty* had been temporarily attached, was directed to remain at least 100 miles off the coasts of Lebanon, Syria, Israel, and the UAR, but the *Liberty*'s instructions were not changed. When it arrived in its operating area late on 7 June, Captain McGonagle, the vessel's commander, still had written instructions that brought the Liberty close into the coast.

Nasser's charge on 6 June that the U.S. and Britain were providing air cover for the Israelis, and the possibility that the Soviets might intervene, brought new orders to the Sixth Fleet to stand off at least 200 miles from the eastern Mediterranean littoral. The next day the JCS [U.S. Joint Chiefs of Staff] decided to pull the *Liberty*, the only U.S. naval vessel still in the far eastern Mediterranean, back to at least 20 nautical miles from the UAR and 15 from Israel. Later that day JCS changed again, this time to 100 nautical miles from both countries.

The first JCS message never reached the *Liberty*—an Army communications center misrouted it to a naval communications station in the Pacific. When, an hour later, the Joint Reconnaissance Center of the JCS decided to pull the *Liberty* back to 100 nautical miles, a series of communications fiascos occurred which stretched on into the night. Message misroutings, delays occasioned by the press of other business, refusals by the Navy to transmit based on a verbal order, all combined to delay the message receipt until after the attack. It was a repeat of the warning message to Pearl Harbor on 7 December 1941, and there was blame aplenty.

The *Liberty* was reconnoitered by several unidentified aircraft during the morning hours of 8 June. That afternoon it was about twenty-five nautical miles north of the Egyptian city of Al Arish when, at about 1400 local, two French-built Israeli Dassault fighters veered toward the ship and began strafing it with cannon and rockets. The attack put some 821 rounds into the hull and superstructure, wounded McGonagle, and killed 8 crewmembers. The *Liberty* managed to get off a desperate message to Sixth Fleet before the power to the radio equipment went out, and Admiral Martin, the Sixth Fleet commander, launched 4 armed A-4 Skyhawks for air cover. [NOTE: 4 armed A-1 Skyraiders and 4 F-4 Phantoms were also launched. Estimated time of arrival over *Liberty* was 1715 Sinai.] Since his flagship was 450 nautical miles away from the *Liberty*, however, the aircraft did not arrive before 3 Israeli torpedo boats launched 2 torpedoes [NOTE: Actually, five torpedoes were launched. One hit the *Liberty*.] at about 1430. The torpedoes tore through the SIGINT spaces, killing 25 men and putting a hole in the hull 39 feet across. As the crew of the *Liberty* scrambled to keep the vessel afloat, one more crewmember was killed by machine-gun fire from 1 of the torpedo boats.

Once the torpedo boats departed, McGonagle directed his vessel to Malta. Sixth Fleet escorts reached the *Liberty* sixteen hours after the attack and trailed the vessel, picking up classified and cryptographic keying material escaping from the hole in the hull. The *Liberty* limped into Malta on 14 June after a heroic struggle to stay afloat that eventually earned McGonagle the Medal of Honor. In all, thirty-four crewmembers were killed, including one NSA civilian Arabic linguist, Allen Blue. The men lost their lives in a war in which the U.S. was not a combatant because of errors in a military communications system that, by 1967, could no longer do the job.

At NSA, word of the attack reached [NSA] Director [General] Marshall Carter at 0915 Washington time. The telephone began ringing almost at once, as word of the attack spread through Washington. While Carter was directing intercept coverage reallocation, Secretary of Defense McNamara called him (at 1015) to ask for details on the vessel and the voyage so that he could make a statement to the press. Deputy Director [of the NSA] Louis Tordella took charge of devising a cover story. Carter diverted many of the queries to NSG (Naval Security Group). At one point during the day the director got a call from the Joint Reconnaissance Center suggesting that the vessel be sunk. Carter replied that this was the worst thing they could do—heaps of classified documents and equipment would end up in shallow water. He was right, and McGonagle's heroic piloting of his vessel to moorage in Malta saved what could have become a much worse situation.

Lyndon Johnson got word at 0949. At the time the U.S. still did not know the identity of the attackers, but the White House soon found out through a Defense Attaché Office message from Tel Aviv that the Israeli navy had admitted the error. This presented the president with a very touchy dilemma. Because of Arab charges that the U.S. had assisted the Israelis, the Sixth Fleet was standing far away from the conflict in the central Mediterranean. Yet here, unannounced, was an American naval vessel only a few miles off the coast of Israel, in the middle of a war zone. Johnson's first concern was about Soviet reaction. He had Walt Rostow send a message to Kosygin [premier of the USSR] stating that the Israelis had apparently fired on a U.S. ship in error and that the Sixth Fleet was sending ships and planes to investigate (he repeated it twice). Kosygin replied that he had passed the message to Nasser.

Meantime, the Pentagon had released a statement about the attack, indicating that the *Liberty*'s mission was to "assure communications between U.S. Government posts in the Middle East and to assist in relaying information concerning the evacuation of American dependents and other American citizens from countries in the Middle East." This was the cover story that NSA had devised under hurried circumstances. It didn't work, but like the [American] U-2 [downed by the Soviets] incident in 1960, no cover story would have worked in the situation. The press very quickly sniffed out the truth, which was attributed to an anonymous military officer that the *Liberty* was a "spy ship." According to this source, "Russia does the same thing. We moved in close to monitor the communications of both Egypt and Israel. We have to. We must be informed of what's going on in a matter of minutes." The assertion was denied by official sources, but the true mission of the *Liberty* was never in doubt again. (The vessel did not, in fact, have an Israeli mission because linguists were too scarce.)

How did the incident happen? Was it a deliberate attack by Israel, as has been alleged countless times by many people? (Even General Carter believed it to have been deliberate.) If it was an accident, how could the Israelis have possibly misidentified the ship? The *Liberty* was flying an American flag, was clearly marked on the hull "AGTR-5," [NOTE: The ship was actually marked GTR 5.] and when the first flag was shot down by the attacking fighters, McGonagle hoisted the largest flag he had on board, a holiday ensign seven by thirteen feet. This enormous flag was flying above the *Liberty* when the torpedo boats executed their attack.

The idea that the attack was deliberate turned out to be wrong. Although there was no SIGINT bearing directly on the attack, there was a [redacted] report shortly after the incident dealing with the aftermath. It reported air/ground conversations between a ground controller at Hatsor [Israel Air Force base] and two Israeli helicopters which reconnoitered the *Liberty* as it was turning toward Malta. Hatsor first identified the vessel as Egyptian, but later became unsure, and requested that the helicopter crews "verify the first man that you [bring up] as to what nationality he is." A few minutes later Hatsor instructed: "Pay attention; if they speak Arabic and are Egyptians take them to Al Arish. If they speak English and are not Egyptians, take them to Lydda . . . the first thing is for you to clarify what nationality they are." Two minutes later Hatsor asked, "Did it clearly signal an American flag?" And a minute later, "Requesting that you make another pass and check again whether it is really an American flag."

One can imagine the panic at Israeli naval headquarters at the time. They had apparently attacked a vessel of their closest ally. [NOTE: It is a bit of a stretch to refer to the U.S. and Israel as "allies" in 1967. U.S.-Israeli relations would blossom into a close friendship—never a formal alliance—only later.]

Based on this report, Rostow told Johnson that the Israelis appeared to be confused about the nationality of the vessel, and he suggested that there might have been some breakdown within the Israeli military which resulted in the attack.

The official Israeli court of inquiry concluded on 21 July [1967] that it had in fact been an identification error. When the *Liberty* was first discovered by an Israeli spotter plane on the morning of the eighth, it was unidentified but possibly hostile, and a red marker was placed on the map in the naval war room. Later in the morning, the identification was tentatively changed to friendly (American), and a green marker replaced the red one. But the Israeli navy then went a period of time without a location, and someone, instead of retaining the green marker with a question mark, pulled it off the map entirely.

The [Israeli navy] shift changed at 1100 Israeli time, and the new shift knew nothing about the American vessel, which was no longer designated on the map. What they did know was that Israeli army units in the Sinai coastal town of Al Arish were reporting artillery bombardment from an unknown source. (It later turned out to be the explosion of an ammunition dump.) The Israelis began searching the Sea for a possible hostile ship, and they found the *Liberty*. The crew of the vessel that did the identification claimed that its radar showed the ship to be heading at twenty-eight knots toward Suez (an impossible speed for the *Liberty*—an error by the radar operator), and Israeli naval control ordered an air attack. Two Mirage fighters on their way home from an air patrol over the Suez Canal were diverted to the spot where the supposed hostile [ship] was. After a quick pass, the pilots claimed that the ship was not displaying a flag (another error) and were ordered to execute an attack.

The torpedo boats arrived in the area at 1418. A low-flying aircraft had just radioed to its controller that he had seen a marking "CPR-5" on the hull. The naval controller told the torpedo boats to attempt a better identification, but the captain of one of the boats claimed that when he requested identification, the ship requested him to identify himself first. Based on identification aids available on board, it appeared to him to be the Egyptian supply vessel *El-Kasir,* and with this information in hand Israeli naval control again ordered an attack. After the first torpedo hit the boat the markings "CTR-5" were observed on the hull. Control immediately terminated the attack, just before the torpedo boats were about to launch additional torpedoes that would have sunk the *Liberty.* An Israeli helicopter flying over the ship after the attack finally noticed an American flag, and the Israeli navy realized what it had done.

An Israeli court of inquiry, whose findings were kept secret at the time (but which were uncovered and published by two Israeli journalists in 1984), condemned the confusion, incompetence, and interservice rivalry that contributed to the attack. There was no finding of a deliberate attack, but there was plenty of blame for all the Israelis associated with the incident.

The Johnson administration was properly outraged. The State Department, in a scathing statement highly unusual for diplomats, called the attack "quite literally incomprehensible. As a minimum, the attack must be condemned as an act of military recklessness reflecting wanton disregard for human life." But Clark Clifford, who was appointed by the president to render a final judgment, called it an identification error. Clifford relied heavily on COMINT reports showing Israeli confusion about the identification; these would have been difficult to fake. Going into it with a preconceived notion that the Israelis must have known, he concluded that what was involved was "a flagrant act of gross negligence . . ." rather than a deliberate act.

This did not, of course, quiet the press. Journalists, both reputable and disreputable, supported the "deliberate attack" theory, and the legend arose, without basis in fact, that the Israelis wanted to blind American SIGINT sensors to their communications, both to keep them from finding out that Israel actually started the war and to keep secret a plan to launch an attack on Syria. (As was stated already, the vessel was not tar-geting Israeli communications and had no Hebrew linguists on board.) All these charges were repeated and embellished by James M. Ennes, a lieutenant on board the *Liberty* who published a book on the subject in 1980. Most of the crew still believes that the attack was deliberate.

Many of the journalists properly questioned the position of the ves-sel at the time. Clifford, too, made a special point of this. The *Liberty* was clearly not where it should have been. The original plan was formulated before war broke out. Once the eastern Mediterranean became a battle-ground, it was decided to hold the *Liberty* out of the area, but the mes-sages never reached McGonagle. The U.S. communications system was approaching breakdown; war sufficed to push it over the edge.

The crew, on the other hand, performed magnificently, and they and their vessel deserved better. NSA wanted to refurbish the ship and use it again, but the price tag of over $10 million was too high. The *Liberty* was decommissioned a year after the attack, and in 1973 it was cut up for scrap in Baltimore's Curtis Bay Shipyard. An abashed Israeli govern-ment paid $13 million in compensation for the loss of life and damage to the vessel.

The attack on the *Liberty* should not be viewed as a bizarre, or even an especially unusual identification error. Even in peacetime such errors are made all too frequently—the Soviet shootdown of KAL 007 and the American shootdown of an Iranian airliner are good examples. When a country is at war, the possibility of error is compounded by haste and fear. Losses to friendly fire always represent a substantial percentage of the casualties. And the Israeli agreement to compensate should not be taken as proof of guilty knowledge, but rather as an attempt to retain the friendship of a benefactor wronged.

Dr. Johnson's comment that "the Israeli agreement to compensate should not be taken as proof of guilty knowledge" is fully supported by facts. When the incident occurred the Israelis were shocked and horrified at what had happened and initially assumed that the mistake was all on the Israeli side. As more facts became available it became apparent that there were multiple mistakes by both Israel and the United States—a "perfect storm" that had compounded to bring about the tragedy.

Within about a year, the Israelis tried to make amends by paying hu-manitarian reparations to the wounded and the families of the deceased.

Under international law and most national legal systems, such payments for human suffering are considered humanitarian gestures and not admissions of guilt or liability. However, under both international and most local law, payment for property damage is considered an admission of guilt or fault. For that reason Israel refused to pay for damage to the ship until it was finally agreed by exchange of diplomatic notes on December 17, 1980, that payment by Israel to the U.S. for damages to the USS *Liberty* was "without prejudice to the legal position of the Government of Israel and to the question of liability for the tragic event."[5]

Chapter 21

FINAL ANALYSIS

There are many important lessons that can be learned from this tragic story. One important one is that field commanders need to know what they are doing and why. The better briefing a participant in a military operation receives, the more likely it is that the participant will exercise discretion in the face of unforeseen events or changes in conditions or circumstances on the scene. Not every sailor on the *Liberty* needed to know the details of the *Liberty*'s mission, but the commanding officer most certainly should have been fully briefed on the purpose of his ship's mission. Since the purpose of the mission had been overtaken by events, there was no need for the *Liberty* to remain in harm's way. If Commander McGonagle had been informed of the purpose of the ship's mission, perhaps he would have withdrawn his ship from a position of potential danger. He clearly had that inherent authority, and the U.S. Joint Chiefs of Staff certainly confirmed his authority to exercise discretion by virtue of orders transmitted on June 7: "1. In view of present situation east Med, operating area specified ref for guidance only and may be varied as local conditions dictate."[1]

Sending insufficiently armed military units either into, or close to, areas controlled by friendly or hostile forces where major wars are raging is risky at best. Today, it is neither prudent nor necessary to collect electronic intelligence in this manner. With the advent of modern satellite technology, the National Security Agency became aware that satellites are a more effective, far safer way to collect the electronic intelligence (ELINT) that the *Liberty* and her sister ships had been designed to collect.

246

Less than a year after the tragedy of the *Liberty*, on January 23, 1968, the U.S. Navy lost another ELINT ship, the USS *Pueblo*. The reference to history repeating itself printed on the cover of Trevor Armbrister's book on the *Pueblo* affair is uncanny: "A combat-oriented naval bureaucracy sends an unfit intelligence ship commanded by an ill-informed officer on a confused mission into dangerous waters."[2] Following the tragedy of the *Liberty*, the loss of the *Pueblo* in the Sea of Japan and of a U.S. Navy EC-121 reconnaissance aircraft shot down by North Korea over the Sea of Japan on April 15, 1969, the ELINT ships were decommissioned; since then the same and better data has been collected by satellite, without risk to life.[3]

Another lesson, not new, is even more important. Truth and candor are best when it comes to national policy. Misleading the public by issuing false press releases (as, for the *Liberty*, the U.S. Department of Defense did on April 14, 1969) and keeping the facts classified (as both the United States and Israel did for ten years in this incident) only feeds conspiracy theories and tall tales. While the plain and simple facts of the *Liberty* tragedy, perhaps embarrassing to some, remained classified, a wide-ranging literature developed, with a spectrum of conspiratorial explanations running from the interesting to the bizarre. No useful purpose was accomplished by this governmental nondisclosure. Moreover, the image of the United States was damaged by the initial false statement and subsequent failure to disclose the whole truth.

The *Liberty* incident, in its externals—occurring as it did during an armed conflict with the loss of thirty-four U.S. lives—is similar to the cases of the *Stark*, in which thirty-seven died; the *Mayaguez* incident, with forty-one fatalities;[4] and the Black Hawk incident of April 14, 1994, over northern Iraq, with twenty-six killed. Unlike the *Liberty* case, the investigations of the *Stark*, *Mayaguez*, and Black Hawk incidents were all completed quickly and transparently. Perhaps it is for that reason these incidents did not seem to have the lasting allure of the *Liberty* incident. Certainly they have not become the hot-button political issue that the *Liberty* incident has become. Probably the biggest mistake made, after the event, by both the United States and Israel was the failure to quickly and publicly disclose the contents of their numerous official investigations for so many years.

With the National Security Agency releases of July 2, 2004, and June 6, 2007, and the State Department release of *Foreign Relations of the United States, Volume XIX*, essentially all of the known significant data is now declassified or obtainable, but the stories and theories of the conspiracy theorists and doubters have had at least a ten-year head start. It is easy to read a letter to the editor or a newspaper or magazine article and form an opinion without making a complete examination of the many details of the official investigations that put more light on the subject. In addition, as has been discussed, many of the conspiracy theorists have their own agendas, which do not always coincide with precise factual presentation or even with a need to be truthful. The Israeli factor plays a role here, in that so many Muslim organizations and Arab countries have special reasons to attack the U.S.-Israeli relationship. They know the answer before they investigate the issue. They then select or twist the facts to support their advance conclusion, ignoring the facts that undermine, let alone negate, their thesis.

This investigation began as a quest to answer on question: Did the Israelis knowingly and deliberately attack a U.S. naval vessel? This author did not decide the answer in advance of the investigation. The initial effort began with a search for a "smoking gun." That search proved fruitless. Adm. Isaac Kidd, the president of the U.S. Navy court of inquiry held on the incident, when asked by this author if the court had found any smoking guns, replied "We didn't even find a water pistol."

This author's twenty-seven year research effort fully corroborates the findings of the U.S. and Israeli official investigations, with which the network television programs on the subject generally agree. The facts are by now clear, and the totality of the evidence establishes that while in port in Abidjan, Ivory Coast, on May 24, 1967, the *Liberty* received orders to proceed at her best speed to a point in the Mediterranean near Port Said, Egypt. The *Liberty* sailed promptly and reached the U.S. naval base at Rota, Spain, on June 1, 1967; there she underwent hurried repairs and took on board several Arabic and some Russian linguists for duty in the National Security Agency compartment of the ship. On June 2, 1967, the *Liberty* sailed from Rota for an assigned patrol station off the coast of the Sinai peninsula. On her patrol, assigned before the 1967 war began, *Liberty*'s closest position to the pre 1967 war Israel border was beyond the range of her VHF/UHF listening capability.[5]

While the *Liberty* was en route to her patrol area, three significant events took place. First, the United States publicly announced to the world on June 6 at the UN Security Council that it had no carriers or aircraft within hundreds of miles of Egypt or Israel.[6] This was clever, because it was only true on the day of the announcement. On that day, *Liberty* was still two days away, sailing across the Mediterranean toward Point Alpha.

Second, at 0745 on Monday, June 5, the 1967 war began. Third, on June 7, almost three days after the commencement of fighting, the U.S. National

Security Agency determined it was not safe for the *Liberty* to be fourteen miles from the beach of the Sinai, in the midst of a major combat area, and requested that a message be sent to the *Liberty* ordering her not to approach her originally assigned patrol path.[7] Although ultimately five such messages were sent, none of those messages reached the *Liberty* until after the Israeli air and naval attacks. Some never reached her at all.

At El Arish on June 8, 1967, the Israel Army observed explosions around its positions and a gray ship on the horizon, which the Israel Defense Forces correctly assumed was a warship. Since the IDF controlled the air and the land, its forces erroneously concluded that they were being bombarded from the sea and referred the matter to the navy through the IDF High Command Headquarters in Tel Aviv.

By the fourth day of the war all branches of the IDF had scored major victories except for the navy, which was eager to get some of the combat action. The Israeli navy headquarters was located in Haifa and thus physically isolated from the Tel Aviv headquarters of the other branches of the IDF. When the navy was told that El Arish was being bombarded from the sea, several assumptions were appropriate. First, it was assumed that the warship bombarding El Arish was a destroyer, because no Arab navy had any other types of ships capable of shore bombardment. Second, it could be inferred the destroyer could steam at thirty knots per hour, as destroyers are generally capable of that speed. Third, the destroyer would be Egyptian, because Egypt had six destroyers and no other Arab combatant had any. The assumption that the ship off El Arish was a destroyer was further reinforced by the erroneous calculation of the target speed by the Israel Navy MTB combat information center officer. The assumption that the target was Egyptian was further reinforced by its heading westward in the general direction of the Egyptian port of Port Said. When an Israeli motor torpedo boat commander calculated that he would not be able to overtake the target, because at the speed he thought the target was steaming it would reach the safety of Port Said before he could overtake it, he asked for air support. Anyone with knowledge of the rivalry between the Israel Navy and the Israel Air Force would agree that the navy would never have asked for air support if it had even the slightest chance of catching up with the target on its own.

After the attacking aircraft realized they were not attacking an Arab warship and had been withdrawn and the MTBs arrived near the smoking, burning vessel, the *Liberty* was still under way and at this point probably moving faster than five knots. It also apparently became clear that the ship was not a destroyer, as had been previously suspected; it had the hull of a freighter or merchant ship and no large gun mounts typical of a destroyer. However, when the *Liberty* opened fire on the MTBs, it was reasonable for the MTB commander to assume that she was foe rather than friend.

Whether the torpedo attack should have been authorized by Capt. Issy Rehav is a judgment call—one with which, incidentally, the commander of the Israel Navy, Rear Adm. Shlomo Erell, disagreed (after the fact). However, it was reasonable to assume that the ship, which had opened fire on the MTBs, was an enemy ship.

All of the foregoing is relevant evidence in support of the explanation that the attack was carried out in the mistaken belief that the target was an enemy ship. The facts are beyond dispute. If one questions the explanation and the assumptions and chooses to believe that the assumptions were not made and that the explanations were not true, then the evidentiary scale is empty—there is no evidence on the issue. That leads one to the second conclusion, which every single official investigation has taken—that is, that there is no evidence whatsoever that the attack was *not* a case of mistaken identity.

History cannot be properly reconstructed by looking backward after the actual results of an action are known. History must be constructed by going back in time and looking forward into the as yet unknown before the action took place. What seems clear in hindsight is usually quite obscure when looking forward. It is essential to examine what was known at the time, what was learned thereafter, and when it all was learned. Judging history through hindsight usually results in conclusions that are out of context; it subjects history to a slant according to the judging historian's a priori position.

This author—having applied to his research an initial investigative question ("Did the Israelis know?") and his know-how and experience as a U.S. naval aviator and a U.S. federal judge—firmly concludes that there is substantial competent evidence that the Israeli attack was made as a result of a mistaken belief that an enemy ship was being attacked. He concurs with the second position of the official reports, that there is no evidence to be found that the attack was made on a target that the Israelis knew to be a U.S. ship. The argument that lack of evidence is a lame excuse not to find Israel guilty is itself a lame argument under the American system of justice, where there is a presumption of innocence until guilt is proven.

After more than five hundred interviews, conducted in Israel, the United States, England, and Egypt, with persons connected with all aspects of the event; review of hundreds of articles and books and of thousands of pages of official investigations; and collection and study of close to 3,100 original documents—this author has reached the following conclusions:

1. The sympathy of the United States must go out to the crew of the *Liberty* and the NSA detachment and NSA civilians on board. They deserve gratitude for their heroism and sacrifice.

2. That fact of having been on a ship under attack does not make the victim really aware of the broader picture of what happened, nor does it qualify the victim to make statements based on conjecture, hearsay, or plain wishful thinking.

3. The best evidence of whether a U.S. flag hoisted on the *Liberty* was extended and thus easily seen by the Israeli pilots is the gun-camera photographs on page 81 of this book and in the gun-camera film that this author personally investigated. The film shows smoke billowing straight up from the ship at the precise time of the attack. This is further corroborated by a picture showing smoke going straight up, taken on the *Liberty* by Commander McGonagle (or the ship's photographer) at about the same time. It therefore proves that there was no wind and thus that the much-talked-about flag was drooping straight down.

4. The Israelis were smart enough to know that there could be no benefit from the attack on a U.S. naval ship, even if it might have provided some immediate tactical advantage, which it did not.

5. There was neither a conspiracy nor a cover-up concerning the attack. It was not preplanned. That the attack involved a mistake in identity was announced by Israel immediately and accepted by the United States. The more than a dozen investigations thereafter by both the United States and Israel confirmed there was no credible evidence that the attack had been made against a ship known to be American, let alone a ship known to the Israelis as the USS *Liberty* (GTR 5). There is in fact substantial credible evidence that the attack was indeed a case of mistaken identity. No one has been able since 1967 to show a piece of real evidence to prove otherwise.

6. The *Liberty* incident involved a long list of unfortunate bad mistakes on the part of both Israel and the United States. These mistakes snowballed and converged to the point where the stage was set for tragic disaster. Unfortunately, the disaster did occur, and on the Israeli side the responsibility falls mainly on the Israel Navy. The Israel Air Force participated in the action but only at the request of the navy and on the basis of a

representation that the navy had identified a target. Thus the Israel Air Force has the burden of secondary responsibility. The eagerness of navy personnel to get into combat action removed the last safety net that might have prevented the disaster. It is easy to place blame when one is warm and dry, with no one shooting at one or expected to; or when one is not involved in the heat and fog of a major war; or with hindsight. The governments of Israel and the United States finally resolved the diplomatic aspects of the incident by an exchange of diplomatic notes on December 17, 1980, without either country accepting responsibility.[8]

7. The failure by the Israeli and U.S. governments to make more of the details of the official investigations public for between ten and twenty-five years after the incident greatly contributed to the likelihood that detractors with agendas would cry "cover-up," and it led to much speculation and many conspiracy theories, some bordering on the bizarre. Some critics went as far as to conclude that the *Liberty* had been there to spy on Israel for the Arabs, while others concluded that she was there to spy on the Arabs for Israel. Later speculation was that the *Liberty* was there to monitor the Israel nuclear facility at Dimona.[9] Most recently, it has been speculated that the *Liberty* was there to listen and determine if Soviet pilots were flying aircraft of the Egyptian air force.[10] Finally, thirty-four years after the incident, by letter to this author dated June 14, 2001, about FOIA Case 40039, the National Security Agency admitted that "the NSA has publicly acknowledged that the USS *Liberty* was deployed on a SIGINT (electronic signal intelligence) collection mission on June 8, 1967." If there was a cover-up, it related to the reason the NSA had sent the *Liberty* to the eastern Mediterranean and not to the issue of whether the Israelis knew they were attacking a U.S. ship.

To the best of this author's knowledge, all the significant documents and reports have now been declassified, with the exception of an accurate and *detailed* statement on why the *Liberty* was sent by the United States to the eastern Mediterranean in the first place.

There is an old U.S. Marine Corps adage that is perhaps appropriate here: "Never attribute to malice that which can be explained by stupidity." Recall from an earlier chapter that when this author first met Gen. Mordechai "Motti" Hod, who had been the general in command of the Israel Air Force during the 1967 war, General Hod was reluctant to discuss the *Liberty* incident. He said that the families of those lost and the surviving crew members of the *Liberty* had suffered enough and that it was not appropriate to disturb old wounds: "If it gives them some comfort to believe the attack was not a mistake, then let them so believe."[11] After hearing from this author some of the conspiracy theories, as we have seen, however, Hod changed his mind—because the stories were not true, he felt, they created pain rather than provided comfort. To anyone who takes comfort in the conspiracy theories, this author says, "So be it." Unfortunately, the survivors of the *Liberty,* their families, and the families of the fallen are subjected to the cruelty of persons and organizations who pursue various conspiracy theories for their own political, financial, or personal objectives and agendas without regard for the distress, pain, and suffering they continue to inflict. Detractors of U.S.-Israel friendly relations and collaborations have continuously fueled mot of the conspiracy theories. Sensationalists have used the latter to promote their own interests.

To those who are interested in reviewing the facts, this book is an honest effort to list and study all the sources of information so that they may be reviewed and considered, together with conclusions of the official investigations. Additional documentary data may be found on the website *The Liberty Incident,* at www.thelibertyincident.com. This author, after almost three decades of studying the matter, concurs with those conclusions.

Unless their minds were made up prior to reading this book, readers will, I hope, by now agree with this author that the totality of the evidence establishes that the attack on the *Liberty* was a tragic case of mistaken identity and friendly fire, a tragedy that resulted from a compounding of bad mistakes perpetrated by both the United States and Israel, and nothing more.

EPILOGUE TO THE FIRST EDITION, BY ERNEST C. CASTLE

O n June 8, 1992, a plane departed Sde Dov Airport, just north of Tel Aviv, twenty-five years to the day—at the hour, almost the minute, of my takeoff in the Super Frelon helicopter provided to me by Israel in my capacity as naval attaché at the U.S. embassy in Tel Aviv. In 1967 my mission had been to try to assist the USS *Liberty*.

The 1992 flight was in memory of the 1967 event. airborne, Judge Jay Cristol, the author of this book, set a course to the point where the Super Frelon had overflown the *Liberty* on the late afternoon of that fate-blemished day. Also in the small aircraft was my wife, Dr. Jeanie Castle; Maj. Danny Grossman, an Israel Air Force flyer (and former U.S. Air Force flyer); and Grossman's young son, Akiva. Cristol flew the aircraft, with the aid of the Global Positioning System, to the precise point where I had observed the *Liberty* twenty-five years before. As the plane circled the point, Judge Cristol dropped thirty-four pink carnations into the sea, one in the name of each American who had lost his life. The aircraft's flight path and the laws of gravity caused the flowers to fall in an approximate circle around the ship's position twenty-five years earlier.

I asked a blessing upon the souls of the dead and on their surviving loved ones. The U.S. Navy hymn was recited. Major Grossman intoned the Kaddish, the Jewish prayer for the dead. The event was sufficiently moving to bring tears.

In silence the little plane broke away from the site and returned to Tel Aviv. It was a small tribute paid to the gallant sailors who had died in the tragedy—tragedy for them, their loved ones, their country, and Israel. The sorrow-filled event is now over four decades behind us. I have waited all that time for the emergence of this book. It is, for the first time, the complete, accurate, and evenhanded report of the *Liberty* incident. It is now time to turn this final page and to close the book.

Ernest C. Castle
Captain, USN, Retired
U.S. Naval Attaché, Tel Aviv
November 1965–November 1967

Captain Castle was awarded the Silver Star during the Korean conflict.

IN MEMORIAM

Lieutenant James Cecil Pierce, USN
Lieutenant Stephen Spencer Toth,
   USN
Chief Petty Officer Raymond E. Linn
Chief Petty Officer Melvin D. Smith
Petty Officer William B. Allenbaugh
Petty Officer Francis Brown
Petty Officer Ronnie J. Campbell
Petty Officer Jerry L. Converse
Petty Officer Robert B. Eisenberg
Petty Officer Jerry L. Goss
Petty Officer Curtis A. Graves
Petty Officer Warren E. Hersey
Petty Officer Alan Higgins
Petty Officer Richard W. Keene
Petty Officer James M. Lupton
Petty Officer Duane R. Marggraf
Petty Officer Anthony P. Mendle
Petty Officer John C. Smith Jr.
Petty Officer John C. Spicher

Petty Officer Alexander N.
   Thompson
Petty Officer Thomas R. Thornton
Petty Officer Phillipe C. Tiedtke
Petty Officer Frederick J. Walton
Seaman First Class Gary R.
   Blanchard
Seaman First Class Lawrence P.
   Hayden
Seaman First Class Carl L. Hoar
Seaman First Class James L. Lenau
Seaman First Class David W.
   Marlborough
Seaman First Class Carl C. Nygren
Seaman First Class David Skolak
Sergeant Jack L. Raper
Corporal Edward E. Rehmeyer
National Security Agency civilian
   Allen M. Blue

Appendix 1

OFFICIAL REPORTS OF THE *LIBERTY* INCIDENT

U.S. Reports

U.S. Navy Court of Inquiry, June 18, 1967

Conclusion: Available evidence combines to indicate the attack on *Liberty* on June 8 was in fact a case of mistaken identity.

CIA Report, June 13, 1967

Conclusion: "It remains our best judgment that the Israeli attack on the U.S.S. *Liberty* was not made in malice towards the United States and was a mistake."

Joint Chiefs of Staff (Russ Report), June 9–20, 1967

Conclusion: General Russ did not make any findings about the actual attack. The report compiled all message traffic and contains no evidence that the attack was not a mistake.

Clifford Report, July 18, 1967

Conclusion: The information available does not reflect that the Israeli high command made a premeditated attack on a ship known to be American.

Senate Committee on Foreign Relations, June 12, July 14, July 26, 1967

Conclusion: "The attack was not intentional."

Senate Armed Services Committee, February 1, 1968

Conclusion: Very difficult for a commander not on the scene to know what happened.

House Appropriations Committee, April and May 1968

Conclusion: "The use and operational capabilities of the Defense Communications system is nothing less than pathetic, and the management of the system needs to be completely overhauled."

House Armed Services Committee Investigation, May 10, 1971

Conclusion: "[The] Navy remains in the dark ages insofar as routine communications with its deployed ships."

Senate Select Committee on Intelligence, 1979/1981

Conclusion: No merit to the claims of intentional attack.

National Security Agency, 1981
> Conclusion: *Liberty* was mistaken for Egyptian ship as a result of miscalculation and egregious errors.

House Armed Services Committee, 1991/1992
> Conclusion: No support for theory of intentional attack.

United States Department of State, 2004, *Foreign Relations of the United States, 1964–1968, Volume XIX, Arab-Israeli Crisis and War, 1967*
> Conclusion: After extensive investigation, the Central Intelligence Agency and the National Security Agency concluded that there was "little doubt" that the attacking Israeli units "failed to identify the Liberty as a US ship before or during the attack" and that they had mistakenly identified the ship as Egyptian.

Israeli Reports

Ram Ron Commission of Inquiry, June 16, 1967
> Conclusion: "The attack on the ship by the Israeli Defense Forces was made neither maliciously nor in gross negligence, but as a result of a bona fide mistake."

Preliminary Inquiry, July 21, 1967
> Conclusion: No sufficient amount of prima facie evidence justifying committing anyone for trial.

State of Israel—IDF History, June 1982
> Conclusion: Attack on American intelligence ship came about as a result of innocent error.

Israel Air Force Report—2002
> (This report was released to the Author by the IDF spokesperson as a Hebrew document. There is no official translation and was translated for the author by a person not a certified translator.)
>
> Conclusion: There is only one new item of information in the report, which is the disclosure of meetings between the Israel Air Force and the Israel Navy in 1968 to establish protocols for better communication between the services to prevent a repetition of the tragedy. Pages 2, 3, 27, and 31 are redacted.

Appendix 2

ISRAEL AIR FORCE AND NSA AUDIOTAPES: COMPARED

The NSA tapes and the Israel Air Force (IAF) tapes coincide or dovetail with respect to multiple reported events. Both confirm that the target (or ship) was presumed to be Egyptian until an American flag was first observed—at 1512 on the NSA tapes and 1512 on the IAF tapes—forty four minutes after the attack was over.

Israel Air Force Tapes

During the 1967 war, Israel Air Force headquarters, at the Kirya in Tel Aviv, routinely made audiotape recordings of radio transmissions by Israel Air Force pilots on UHF frequencies. It also made audiotape recordings of telephone conversations, including one between the chief air controller, Col. Shmuel Kislev, at headquarters and controllers at Air Control Central, Air Control South, and Air Control North. To provide continuity and understanding of the two tapes, this author has integrated them into one continuous transcript and added bracketed explanatory comments. Portions of the tapes on unrelated subject matter have been omitted.

The IAF tape states in the background, in a female voice speaking Hebrew, the time of speaking. Voice transmissions block the time announcement. The tapes can thus be compared to a chronograph, and this sequence is accurate to the second.

This author first obtained access to the IAF transcripts and translations on June 18 and 19, 1990, and had the opportunity to listen to the tapes on those days together with two Hebrew language speakers, one a native-born Israeli and the other an American fully qualified in Hebrew, as well as six of the original air controllers. The transcripts and translations had previously been released by the IAF to Thames TV in 1987.

In September 2001, the Israel Air Force provided access to the tapes of the air controller's telephone conversations (commencing at 1342 Sinai time) and pilots' transmissions on the attack channel frequency (commencing at 1329 Sinai time), as well as a transcription of the air controllers' telephone conversations. An additional listening session took place on September 7, 2001, which this author attended together with three Hebrew speakers, two native-born Israelis and one American. All emphasis is by this author.

Key players in the Israel Air Force tapes are:

Air controllers
    "Homeland": Call sign of the air controllers
    Kislev: Shmuel Kislev, chief air controller at the Kirya, in Tel Aviv
    Giora: deputy chief air controller at the Kirya
    Robert: chief air controller at Air Control Central, twenty-five
        miles south of Tel Aviv
    Shimon: deputy chief air controller at Air Control Central
    Menachem: chief air controller at Air Control South, near the
        Sinai border
    Yigal: deputy chief air controller at Air Control South
    L.K.: a weapons system officer.
Aircraft
    Kursa: Two Mirage IIICJs that made the initial air attack run
    Royal: Two Super Mystères that made the second air attack run
    Menorah: Flight of four Mirage IIICJs, armed with five-hundred-pound
        iron bombs
    Nixon: Flight of two Mystères loaded with five-hundred-pound iron bombs
    Chalon: One Mirage IIICJ
    Ofot: Helicopters, referred to as "*Ofot* 1," "*Ofot* 2," etc.
Watercraft
    "Pagoda": MTB Division 914, consisting of MTBs 203, 204, and 206 and led by
        Lt. Cdr. Moshe Oren
    Migdal: MTB 206, the only MTB with a working UHF radio.

All times are Sinai times unless otherwise indicated. 1343 Sinai = 1143 GMT = 0743 in Washington, D.C. There were no NSA intercepts until 1430, and therefore the IAF tapes are presented, to that time, without comparisons.

Author's Note
A careful examination of the transcripts of translations of the NSA tapes suggests that some of the text describing which source broadcast a transmission to the receiving entity were either incorrectly transcribed or incorrectly attributed.

The NSA tapes show for each transmission the sender and the receiver. For example, Tribune to 810: Tribune is the Hatzor Air Base controller broadcasting to Israel Air Force helicopter number 810.

Several examples are:

At 1438:810 to Tribune: "Where are you?" 810 to Tribune: "Where are you now?" It seems unlikely that a helicopter in flight and moving would be asking Hatzor Air Base, a fixed point on the ground, "Where are you?" Much more likely Hatzor was asking the moving helicopter, "Where are you?" "Where are you now?"

This is supported by the answer: Tribune to 810: "Ashdod, altitude 1000 feet." It is difficult to imagine that Hatzor Air Base was at an altitude of one thousand feet over the Port of Ashdod; it is more likely that this was an answer of helicopter 810 advising Tribune (Hatzor) that it, helicopter 810, was at an altitude of one thousand feet over the Port of Ashdod, approximately twenty-five miles south of Hatzor.

Likewise, directions from the helicopter telling the Hatzor air controller, "You will try to take the men from the water," was much more likely an order from Hatzor to the helicopter.

Again at 1441 the order from helicopter 810 to Tribune to "Take the men to El Arish" and the reply by Tribune, "Roger, okay," was also more likely a reversal of transmitter and receiver.

At 1502 the request of helicopter 815 located miles out to sea near the USS *Liberty* to have the controller at Hatzor tell the helicopter the nationality of the ship or to have the controller at Hatzor telling the helicopter about the size of the ship, the status of the smoke, the three small vessels nearby—it seems more likely that the helicopter was passing this information to the controller and that this was a typographical reversal of the transmissions sources.

At 1503 the controller at Hatzor transmits to helicopter 815, "I'm heading for the big one [LIBERTY]." Surely it was helicopter 815 advising the controller that the helicopter was heading for the ship, [The big one], not the controller at Hatzor, heading for the ship.

There are numerous other places throughout the NSA transcript of translation where it is obvious that the transmitter and receiver described in the text are reversed. These misprints in no way detract from the value of the voice transmission intercepts but merely reflect errors in translating or constructing the transcript.

1343

Unknown: The navy received a report that two miles at sea, off El Arish, there is something that's pounding El Arish. Their torpedo boats are going towards there.

Giora: I heard. I took helicopter from El Arish. I spoke with him. He went out to have a look and says he doesn't see a thing.

Unknown: There's contact with the [El Arish] field but not with the city. [El Arish airport is located inland several miles south of the city of El Arish. At this time the airport was in Israeli hands.]

Kislev: Yigal, have *Chalon* take a look.

Yigal: *Chalon.*

Kislev: Clear.

Shimon: Robert, have him take a look. He's circling the same area.

Kislev: Can you see him, Shimon?

1344

Shimon: Yeah. Sure, Yigal, can you see route 4? Have you informed him of 20,000 feet of altitude?

Unknown: Do you have *Tiyeh* 39 10? [*Tiyeh* is phonetic for *tet,* the ninth letter of the Hebrew alphabet. The numbers are grid coordinates.]

Unknown: *Tiyeh* 39 10, one moment.

1345

Kursa: We're switching to military power. Affirmative, northern direction. [*Kursa* has just been given a vector to a target.]

Kursa: Fuel okay, 3,000 [liters].

1349

Yigal: Robert, where is Menorah now?

1350

Kislev: Forget about Menorah. Yigal, you have a ship at 26 [A site designation.] Take *Kursa* over there. If it's a warship, then blast it. [At this point, the air force has a request from the navy to assist the chase of the vessel and, on urging from General Hod, via Cdr. Pinchas Pinchasy, has obtained authority from Capt. Issy Rehav, who has tactical command of the navy at headquarters at Stella Maris, Haifa, to attack the ship "if it's a warship." Attack is thus conditionally authorized by Kislev at 1350, subject to *Kursa* identifying the ship as a warship.]

Yigal: Clear.

1351

Unknown: Wait a minute, Kislev. The navy says that there are two [*sic;* there were three] torpedo boats of ours in the area, called Pagoda. They are on frequency 186. [A minute later the navy warns of its own boats in the area. There appears to be more concern for preventing the aircraft from attacking the Israeli navy boats than for further identification of the target, which has been identified as enemy under existing Israel Navy rules of engagement (ROE). The Israel Navy ROE were quite similar to those of U.S. Navy ROE for 1967.]

Kislev: If it's a warship, you can throw [attack]. There are two torpedo boats of ours. They want to know. They want [the pilots) to see them or call them on 86. Robert, do you have Royal?

[Kislev knows that Royal has already taken off from an air base in the north.]

Robert: Royal?

Shimon: He's at *Hava* 16 10 [*Hava* is phonetic for *het,* the eighth letter of the Hebrew alphabet. Again, grid coordinates.] That's track 15.

Kislev: Robert, take Royal along the coast so that if *Kursa* identifies, he can go in. [Kislev positions Royal to prepare to follow *Kursa* on the attack.]

Robert: Okay.

Kislev: Menachem, how much fuel does *Kursa* have?

Menachem: He's got a lot. A minute ago he had 3,000 [liters].

1352

Kursa: What is the range? Seven turns. 040 degrees. Roger. [*Kursa* asks the distance to the target. Confirms a slight right turn to point at the target.] I'll stay on 19 and 9 [two radio frequencies, or channels.] How do you call the torpedo boats? Pagoda? *Kursa* 9 and 3.

1353

Kursa: Homeland, keep on directing me to the place.
Homeland: 045[°], 20 miles. Ah, can you see them at the moment?

1354

Kursa: Affirmative, it looks longer [i.e., more distant] by eyesight.
L.K.: What is that? Americans? [No one had any data on the location for Americans. Without hard data, the subject was not pursued further. Following the tragedy, L.K. was called on July 4, 1967, before the examining judge and testified in the second Israeli investigation. On October 1, 2001, this author obtained the declassification of L.K.'s testimony before the examining judge. The following is his sworn response to a question asking why he mentioned Americans:

> I was on duty and I was on the [communications] line K.M.NK. (Weapons Systems Officer).
> . . . It is clear to me that I threw in [i.e., posed] the question—a shout which is written [in the transcript?]. It does not relate to the conversation that was conducted on the line at that same moment. Since at the time the conversation was about an attack on missile bases.
>
> In relation to this there are two possibilities:
>
> It is possible that this question was asked during a conversation with Lieut. [——] of his [probably a typo for "my"] unit with whom I spoke about the ship that purportedly was shelling El Arish, and the air force was about to attack it jointly with the navy. I at that time expressed an opinion that we had taken only one action, that is to say, we had ascertained it was not an Israeli ship, and we did this through the naval representatives who were sitting with us.
>
> The hour was approximately 1350.
>
> I was not the officer who would have been able to decide on an attack, but it was my duty to be as a passive party on the line in order to absorb information that might have helped, but like any officer I wanted to help, and therefore I wanted to suppose to the ears of [i.e., alert] those [officers] who were managing the war to a possibility—supposition that it was an American ship. That was only my supposition, since it was my assessment that it was not [an] Egyptian [ship], for they would not dispatch a solitary ship to our coast, and therefore I thought there was such a possibility.
>
> All those who were connected on this line were able to hear me. Of course, all of them were overcome by this and they began to ask [questions] and then I did not want to delay the attack on the ship [because] they said it was shelling El Arish. And since the supposition was not based on data but on an assessment—supposition— therefore I did not want to delay the thing. Therefore I immediately retracted. Today

I understand that had I persisted in my supposition, it would have been possible to prevent the tragedy. I did not know about the existence of an American ship in the morning.]

Shimon: What Americans?
Kislev: Robert, what did you say?
[No one answers.]
Unknown: I'm putting Squadron *(Palga)* 116 on alert. [Squadron 116 is a reference to Nixon Flight.]
Kislev: Okay.
Kislev: Does he see more torpedo boats north of him?

1355

Kislev: Menachem, if there are three torpedo boats, it's a possibility that they are ours. [Note that Kislev now has the correct number of torpedo boats, three rather than two, as stated incorrectly above at 1351, four minutes earlier.]
Shimon: Pay attention, *Kursa.*
Kursa: Pagoda from *Kursa.* Are you *Migdal?* [Because *Migdal,* MTB 206, possesses the only functional UHF radio in Pagoda, MTB Division 914, *Kursa* must relay communication to division commander Moshe Oren, on board MTB 204, through *Migdal.*]
Migdal: Affirmative.
Kursa: Are you attacking some ship now?
Migdal: We're on our way to one.
Kursa: Okay . . . I'll come and give you a hand. Where are you?
Kursa: Migdal from *Kursa,* are you three? [*Kursa* sees the three MTBs and asks if they are a formation of three.]
Kursa: There's no need. Bring yourselves up some 10–15 kilometers from the boat. Is it in the direction of your (garbled) home?
Kursa: I see you on a right turn. Why are you turning? It's not in that direction.
Migdal: Okay, all right. Affirmative. . . . Affirmative.

1356

Migdal: Kursa, can you identify the target? [At 1351, *Kursa* was authorized to attack the ship "if it's a warship."]
Kursa: Can you identify his target, *Migdal?* [The MTBs and the aircraft are each asking the other to identify the ship.]
Kursa: She's running from you in the direction of El Arish, excuse me, Port Said. What is it? What is it? A destroyer? A patrol boat? What is it?
Migdal: Kursa, can you manage to identify it?
Kursa: I can't identify it, but in any case it's a military ship.
Migdal: Okay, what is it?
Kursa: It has one mast and one smokestack.
Migdal: Roger.

Kursa: It has one mast up front.

Shimon: Menachem, *Kursa* is calling you.

Shimon: He says he is starting strafing them.

Menachem: I told him that if it's a warship, he can start to attack. That was the last command.

Kislev: Menachem.

Menachem: Does he have authorization to attack?

Kislev: He does. If this is a warship, then yes. Royal is to be turned there.

Menachem: Okay.

Kislev: Send Royal over there with bombs [*ptzatzot*—Hebrew for bombs]. [Kislev believes at this point that Royal has iron bombs.]

Robert: On what frequency are you attacking?

Shimon: She's running away from them. [At this point Shimon apparently sees the ship on his radar.]

Kislev: Menachem, after he attacks have him explain to Royal how to find her.

Shimon: She's running fast.

Kislev: Okay, attack.

Shimon: Robert, have Royal call us on 19. [At this time Royal is on another channel or frequency. Royal is arguing with his controller about the fact that he is carrying napalm, not iron bombs.]

Robert: Royal to you on 19.

1357

Shimon: Just a minute, Kislev, we see the ship. [Shimon sees the ship on his radar scope.]

Shimon: That's one hell of a ship. [Shimon commenting on the radar signature of the ship.]

Robert: Menachem, I'm passing [code words for Royal Flight] to you on 19. Royal. El Arish at 20,000.

Kislev: Menachem, have them tell us if there is *Nun Mem* [the Hebrew letters for NM, representing *neged metosim,* meaning antiaircraft fire].

1358

Kursa: . . .

Kislev: Menachem, *nu?* [An idiom, "So or well, what is happening?"]

Menachem: We're asking him. She's not shooting back.

Kislev: Not shooting? Give me 19. [Kislev is puzzled by the report that the ship is not shooting at the attacking aircraft.]

1359

Kursa: We've hit her a lot. . . . But maybe she is doing it [putting out smoke] on purpose, I don't know. Oil is spilling out into the water. I'm in eye contact. Great, wonderful. She's burning. She's burning.

Royal: What ship, *Kursa?*

Menachem: Did you hear? He's hit her a lot. There's a lot of black smoke. There's an oil leak into the water. [This was more likely a gasoline leak from the fuel cell that was near the motor whale boat located on the deck of the *Liberty.*] He's continuing.

Kislev: Was there any *Nun Mem* on him?

Menachem: She's burning. The warship is burning.

1400

Royal: [Apparently we miss a transmission from *Kursa* to Royal where *Kursa* asks Royal the traditional "How do you hear me?" Royal responds with "five by five," or "5X5," the traditional aviator's idiomatic response "I hear you perfectly."] 5X5, eye contact with the target. [Royal sees the *Liberty*.] Eye contact with *Kursa*. [Royal sees *Kursa* Flight attacking the target.] Royal requests 15,000 feet. [At 1357 Royal was at El Arish at 20,000 feet and wants to come down to set up for attack.]

Kursa: Okay, *Kursa* is coming in . . . you a bit further in. I'll go in the direction . . . Okay? [*Kursa* seems to be telling Royal he is going in on another run and also talking to his wingman.] *Kursa* Wing: . . . I think she is putting out smoke on purpose, it's coming out of the chimney, Okay, I'm finished too. . . . [*Kursa* exhausts its ammunition on the third pass and pulls off at about 1401.]

Menachem: Shmulik [a diminutive for Shmuel, Kislev's first name], she's burning. [Menachem is obviously excited.] The minute *Kursa* is finished, we're sending in Royal.

Kislev: Right. Sink her.

Menachem: Sink her. Okay.

1401

Kursa: The ship is really burning. There is a large fire and a lot of black smoke.

Kursa: Royal, your altitude? We're at 5,000 feet.

Royal: You're east, right?

Kursa: We're south of the ship.

Royal: . . . [Apparently Royal's transmission was blocked by someone's transmission. It was probably an inquiry of whether *Kursa* was clear of the target, as the answer from *Kursa* is "Affirmative."]

Kislev: Menachem.

Menachem: We're sending in Royal.

Kislev: Okay.

1401:52

Robert: . . . This ship?

Kislev: Menachem, if Royal has napalm, it will make things easier.

1402

Kursa: Affirmative.

Royal: Not ours?

Royal: Homeland, can you hear? Call Homeland on 19. Ask if it's allowed to go in.

Royal: Homeland from Royal. Is it permitted to go in?

Royal: I understand, do not go in. Fine, we're circling above the ship at 15,000 feet. Tell him the navy will be arriving before us, I can see.

Kursa: 5 and 3. I've got him. [*Kursa* is apparently relaying to control for Royal.]

Royal: Does Royal have permission?

Kursa: Affirmative, you have permission Royal.

Shimon: Menachem, Royal is calling you.

Menachem: He got off the line.

1402:11

Shimon: Kislev, there is doubt about the identification. [Note, about nineteen seconds have elapsed since Robert came on the loop at 1401:52. At this point, the lack of return antiaircraft fire and some questions from naval headquarters at Haifa, possibly received by the naval liaison officer with Robert, as a result of communication with Haifa, raised some doubts.]

Kislev: If there is a doubt, then don't attack. [Again Kislev, the skilled professional, does not take over the tactical situation at the scene but puts a restriction on the attacking aircraft.]

Shimon: Don't attack, Menachem. Robert, pay attention. There is doubt as to the identification.

Kislev: What does that mean? [Kislev, ever vigilant, wants an explanation. He is asking Robert, who has a naval liaison officer, Yehoshua Barnai, at his side.]

Robert: Okay, you may attack. [Apparently he has resolved the identification issue either with the naval liaison officer or through him with naval headquarters at Stella Maris, Haifa.]

Kislev: You may attack.

1402:32

Royal: Sausages, [napalm canisters] in the middle and up . . . in one pass. Two together. [Royal Flight leader tells his wingman to drop both of the napalm canisters on the first run.] We'll come in from the rear. Watch out for the masts. Don't hit the masts, careful of the masts. I'll come in from her left, you come behind me.

Shimon: Next formation—get a briefing on what took place.

Robert: Authorized to sink. [This comes from the naval liaison officer who is with Robert.]

Kislev: You can sink it.

Shimon: Royal started chatting.

Robert: One eight [most likely referring to sector coordinates], that is not the ship. Wait a minute.

Kislev: Menachem, is he hitting *(dofek)* her?

Menachem: He's going low with napalm.

Unknown: No, Robert, it is not worthwhile.

Kislev: You don't need any more for the ship. Enough.

Menachem: There's no need. Our forces are there. So is the navy.

Shimon: It's worth it just for insurance.

Kislev: But napalm went there. [Kislev, an air force officer, apparently does not understand the effect of napalm against a ship. It may have some value in the suppression of antiaircraft fire. Here there was no antiaircraft fire.]

Unknown: What can napalm do [to a ship]?

1404
Royal: . . . on the right side of the stern . . .
Royal Wing: You've missed by an undershot. [Referring to the napalm.]
Royal: . . . a deep gash . . .

1405
Kislev: What is *Kursa* reporting? Was there any *Nun Mem?*
Menachem: I passed him to 33 and asked for a report.
Kislev: Robert, ask *Kursa* if there was any *Nun Mem.* [Kislev is still concerned about the lack of antiaircraft fire.]
Robert: Kislev, the navy asks not to sink her completely; they want to get close and have a look.
Shimon: Have them rescue the people with the torpedo boats to help.
Robert: Okay, finish with this formation. The torpedoes are coming up to them.

1406
Kislev: Robert, what does *Kursa* say?
Robert: I'm telling you already. "This is easier than MiGs." [The comment suggests that shooting at a surface target on the water is easier than dogfighting with a MiG.]
Kislev: What's the situation now?

1407
Royal: Fine, pull up.
Royal: . . . I'm behind you. Careful of her antennas.
Unknown: I don't know. Number Two [Royal Wing] hit [with a napalm bomb] . . . and now he's strafing.

1408
Royal: Homeland from Royal, how do you hear me? She has some kind of marking, P30 and something.
Kislev: Robert, take 116 Flight out there, too. [Nixon Flight. An attack by this flight with iron bombs would very likely have sunk the *Liberty* in the next seven or eight minutes.]
Robert: Okay.
Menachem: Her marking . . . [cut off by Kislev]
Kislev: Yes, I heard. We're checking.
Shimon: Robert, take 116 Flight to . . .

1409
Royal: Homeland, if you had a two-ship formation with bombs, in ten minutes before the navy arrives, it will be a *mitzvah.* Otherwise the navy is on its way here. [*Mitzvah,* a good or worthwhile deed based on a commandment. The old competition between navy and air force clearly rears its head.]
Shimon: Before the navy arrives, it will be a *mitzvah.* [Shimon wants the target for the air force, with the navy left out.]

Kislev: Take 116 Flight in the meanwhile. Who is checking this? [Kislev is still concentrating on identification, while Shimon is enraptured at the prospect of beating the navy to the target.]

Shimon: Royal reported that it will be a *mitzvah*, before the navy comes.

Kislev: Look for a flag if they can see one. Have Royal look. See if they can identify with a flag. [The *Liberty*'s flag was shot from the halyard on the first pass by *Kursa*. It is about ten minutes later, and the second flag has not yet been hoisted.]

1410

Royal: (unintelligible)

Royal: Twelve o'clock . . . look higher. Now left, slowly, slowly . . . a bit faster so it will stay external, okay?

Robert: Kislev, They're [the navy] asking us here [at the Radar Air Control Central, where Robert sits with the naval liaison Yehoshua Barnai] not to do anything else about her. They want to take her. I want to receive an answer.

Kislev: No, no. They're [the navy] . . .

1411

Robert: Menachem, is Royal leaving?

Menachem: Wait a minute, he's reporting something.

Kislev: Okay, attack, Menachem. [Apparently Kislev is about to send in Nixon Flight.]

Royal: Homeland from Royal, do you read me? Pay attention, this ship's markings are Charlie Tango Romeo 5. Pay attention, Homeland, Charlie . . .

1412

. . . Tango Romeo 5. There is no flag on her! She looks like a minesweeper with that marking. Roger, I'm leaving her. I'm staying around one more minute. [Royal misread GTR 5 as "CTR 5." At this point, both he and control are alerted to the fact that she is not marked like an Arab ship.]

Robert: Menachem, has Royal come out? [Robert is making sure that it is clear for 116 Flight to go in.]

Menachem: Not yet.

Robert: What height? What height is Royal reaching [descending to]?

Menachem: Charlie Senator Romeo. [Menachem relays even more incorrect markings: CSR.]

Kislev: Leave her! [There is a dramatic change on the audio tapes in the tone of Kislev's voice. Kislev knows that Egyptian ships are marked in Arabic script. English or roman letters are not used and arabic numerals are not used. Approximately sixty seconds before, Kislev had authorized Nixon Flight to attack, and now he cancels the air operation with the terse "Leave her."]

Robert: Leave her? What ship is this?

Kislev: Leave her! Menachem, report the approximate damage. Nixon Flight to her [i.e., Nixon's original] mission.

1413

Royal: Homeland, 5X5 [advising control that he hears perfectly], there's external fire on her, a lot of hits on her upper parts. People are jumping into the water. [This was not correct. No one jumped into the water; life rafts were thrown into the water, and this may be what Royal saw.] She's

not shooting at all. She has hardly any armaments on her. She's going full steam toward the north.
Kislev: Shimon, Robert, we're sending two helicopters to them. [Kislev moves to a rescue mode.]
Robert: Okay, clear. I'm sending helicopters.
Menachem: Kislev, what country? [Menachem has become concerned.]
Kislev: Possibly American.

1415

Shimon: Kislev, maybe you know which countries are around here. If it's possible to take them, they are taking care of it. [Shimon still believes that the ship is Egyptian. He is concerned about rescue operations if the seamen are Egyptian.]

1417

Robert: There is no contact yet with Menorah. He's around the canal at low altitude. I don't have any contact with him yet. [The war goes on. Menorah Flight must be monitored and controlled.]

1419

Royal: I'm in the direction . . .
Kislev: Robert, do you have contact with *Ofot* 1 and 2? [Two Super Frelon helicopters, numbers 810 and 815]
Robert: Okay, I'm trying. None yet.
Shimon: Kislev, I have *Ofot* 2 in Teiman Field. [Teiman is an air base in the south near Beer Sheba.]
Robert: Okay, I'm trying. None yet.
Shimon: Kislev, I have [*Ofot*] 2 in Teiman Field.
Kislev: Not him.

1425

Kislev: Robert, Two [*Ofot,* a Super Frelon 807] is in Teiman Field?
Shimon: Yes, with the Minister of Defense. [Defense Minister Dayan had driven to the Cave of Machpelah at Hebron in the late morning and returned to the Kirya by helicopter from Beersheva in the early evening. See chapter 11, *Did Dayan Order It?*]
Shimon: Frelon from Air Force Base 8 [Tel Nof, located south of Tel Aviv] is ready to leave for the ship. Shall I send him out? Operations notified Base [censored].
Kislev: Okay.

1429

Kislev: Robert, is there any contact with the Super Frelons?
Shimon: Yes.

1434

Robert: Kislev, *it's an Egyptian supply boat.* My "admiral" is next to me. I'm touching him. [Robert is referring to the naval liaison officer Yehoshua Barnai. Robert is elated. The navy MTBs on the scene had identified the ship as Egyptian.]

Kislev: Is that true or not? [Kislev is extremely excited, but still the same precise professional.] Where did he get it positive identification from?

Robert: The helicopter went away from there. That is what he [Yehoshua Barnai] says.

Kislev: If so, then have the helicopter get out of there. [Kislev has become concerned about the safety of the helicopter that was sent to rescue Americans and is near the ship now identified as Egyptian.]

Robert: The torpedo boat is taking care of it. *It's an Egyptian supply ship.* They're torpedoing it now.

1435

Robert: Where are the helicopters you sent?

Kislev: The helicopters are back.

Robert: Tell them to go away.

Kislev: Just a minute. Robert, get the guys out of there.

[The air force tries to conduct rescue operations in the midst of the naval attack.]

Kislev: Just a minute, Robert, for . . .

Shimon: I'm keeping them aside; I just want to see.

Kislev: On the side until he will identify.

Robert: Have him stay on the side, they're putting torpedoes into it. You can get the guys out later.

Menachem: Kislev, air force commander is arriving in ten minutes. I've informed him and told him to bring the helicopters because we have torpedo boats in the area. He said okay.

Shimon: What's the call sign of the torpedo boats?

Unknown: Pagoda.

1436

Robert: The air force has no identification problems. I won't have anyone telling me again that the air force has any identification problem. [Robert became incensed at the suggestion that the air force might have any problem with identification.]

Menachem: Now, listen, I've also told the air force commander that this ship was finally identified as Egyptian. I told him we're transferring the helicopters. We're not sending them, because we have torpedo boats. We'll keep them aside, to pull the survivors out of the sea. They're putting another torpedo into her. Just in case. I hope this torpedo will hit. [Menachem's understanding of the events at sea is inaccurate. A single torpedo attack was made with five torpedoes launched. One torpedo, the last launched from the last boat, T-203, hit the ship at about 1435.]

1437

Robert: The torpedo hit.

1438

Robert: *You can send in the helicopter in order to get the people out of the water. Tell the helicopters they are not Americans, they're Egyptians.* [The navy has now convinced the air force that the ship is Egyptian.]

Shimon: Who'll guard the guys in the helicopters?

Robert: I hope there are more people in the helicopters. [Robert is concerned about security and hopes there are more than just the pilot and copilot on the helicopters.]

Shimon: I think it is better the torpedo boats should take them. They should sit on the torpedo boats who'll put them ashore.

Robert: I told the air force commander we're not sending the helicopters because we have torpedo boats. He said, fine.

1439

Menachem: *If there is a helicopter nearby, have him start getting them out of the water* and take them to El Arish. Air force commander is not in the picture and doesn't know what's going on, but I don't have time to run over and tell them the whole story.

Robert: Just tell me what to do with the helicopter.

Shimon: . . . *said get the people out of the water.*

Robert: You can pick them up and hit them over the head. [Robert's solution to the rescue of the Egyptians.]

Unknown: Robert, did you hear my theory? Just when the navy saw we're getting them off, they began shouting.

1440

Robert: Kislev shouted "Americans." [It was Kislev at 1414.]

Unknown: How many helicopters are on their way?

Shimon: Super Frelon. [Not responsive to the question that was how many, not what kind.]

Menachem: *Giora, they went to El Arish to tell them that Egyptian sailors are arriving, from the sea. From a boat they sank.*

Kislev: I said so. Have the helicopters take them out slowly, slowly. And inform El Arish.

Menachem: Robert, I don't think they managed to sink her.

Robert: They took her apart (garbled).

1451

Robert: There is another ship. Can you see her? [Robert probably sees the image of the *Liberty* on his radar screen and identifies it as another ship, because he believes that the *Liberty* was sunk.]

1454

Robert: Shimon, does Yami have contact with the helicopter? The identification is not clear yet.

1456

Kislev: Robert, what do you say about the identification?

Robert: The navy says that even though they sent a torpedo, there is a part which is unclear. Soon I'll ask what language these guys talk, then we'll know for sure. [The air force controllers are still unsure of the identification of the ship nineteen minutes after the torpedo attack.]

Kislev: Have they taken them [the survivors] out yet?

Robert: I have no idea.

Kislev: What about the Super Frelon?

Robert: Immediately.

1457

Shimon: *The Super Frelon has no contact with the torpedo boats.* Can he go in alone and get them out?

Kislev: Can he see people in the water? [There are none to see. At this point, with the Super Frelon hovering nearby and the torpedo boats lying nearby, the *Liberty* survivors are bracing for another attack and have no idea that the operations are now devoted to rescue.]

Shimon: He's getting closer.

1501

Kislev: *Shimon, what about the Super Frelon?*

Shimon: *He is 12 miles from them now. He has eye contact with the ship.* He's asking for relays in the air. Between him and the torpedo boats, it's being taken care of.

1504

Shimon: *Kislev, first, Giora said before that if they're Arabs, take them to El Arish. They're not Arabs.*

Kislev: *Take them to Lod.* [Lod was Israel's international airport, later renamed in honor of Ben-Gurion.]

Robert: Is there any identification yet?

Shimon: None yet.

Menachem: Is it American after all?

Shimon: That's still not clear, Menachem.

Menachem: Why did they blast a torpedo?

Shimon: They [the navy] probably can't read English.

1505

Kislev: Shimon, well, what about the helicopters?

Shimon: He's still three miles away. He's going to start. He's above them, and he'll give a report any minute now.

1509

Kislev: It's not clear what's happening here. I don't understand.

1510

Shimon: *Kislev, there are no people. He sees boats* [probably the life rafts] *but no people.*

Kislev: *The navy also reports that there are no people. He sees boats but no people.*

Shimon: They have three more torpedo boats around. He's coming in low in order to see better. The Mirage pilot [*sic;* it was the Super Mystère pilot, Royal Flight leader] reported people jumping.

Kislev: *Robert, have the helicopters come home. Both of them, and without picking anyone up.*
Robert: Okay.

1512

Shimon: *Kislev, there is an American flag on board.*
Kislev: *Sure or not sure?*
Shimon: *He'll check again. He reported it. He'll check a second time.*
Kislev: *Have him get a good look at the flag.*

1513

Kislev: *Nu?*
Shimon: *Here, he's reporting in a second.*

1514

Shimon: *Kislev, it's an American flag, People keep hiding every time he flies over.*
Kislev: I understand. Okay, come home.

1515

Kislev: Shimon, do you have contact with the helicopter in Sinai?
Shimon: None.

1516

Kislev: *Shimon, doesn't the Super Frelon have gas?*
Shimon: *He reported that he's short.*
Kislev: *One of them should go to El Arish.*
Shimon: Okay.
Kislev: *One to El Arish and the other home.* Is there QL there?
Shimon: Nothing.

1519

Kislev: Shimon, try to find the helicopter in the Sinai.

1604

Shimon: Kislev, the ship hasn't sunk yet. She's getting farther and farther away. She's going north. [North would have been out to sea and away from the coast.]

1605–1724

No transmissions relating to the *Liberty* during this time period.

1725

Robert: Is there contact with the helicopter? I returned the second helicopter too. Answer, you're the only one left.

1742

Shimon: 36 Super Frelon searching for the damaged ship. What shall he do? Should he save the people?

Unknown: Shimon, the air force commander [Gen. Mordechai "Motti" Hod] wants you. Is someone answering there?

Unknown: Answering, yes.

1743

Shimon: Wait a minute, I'm picking up the phone.

1751

Kislev: I'm not sure. He's bringing the American ambassador over there. [In fact it was Cdr. Ernest E. Castle, the U.S. naval attaché from the embassy in Tel Aviv, and the assistant naval attaché, Lynn Blasch.]

Shimon: Is he afraid they'll open fire on him?

1819

Shimon: They're going home.

Kislev: In the area, I understand.

Shimon: Kislev, the Super Frelon asks what to do with the ship.

Kislev: He landed there. He has to try and land it on the ship.

1820

Kislev: Shimon, tell him not to take any people because of flight safety.

Shimon: Okay.

1821

Shimon: He asks, if there are wounded on board, if he can take them.

Kislev: If his passenger wants it, yes.

Shimon: So I'll tell him according to the considerations of his passenger.

Kislev: Okay.

1834

Kislev: Shimon, what about this *Ofot?*

Shimon: *Ofot* 2 ? He's got a lot. Forty miles by sea to the ship.

1840

Shimon: Kislev, he's very close to the ship, he'll try to let him [Cdr. E. E. Castle] down soon.

Kislev: Is he trying to land?

Shimon: He is close and is starting to organize above her.

1857

Shimon: Kislev, the ship didn't want to stop. The passenger [Cdr. Ernest Castle, USN] didn't manage to persuade her. They threw a note. They said in return that there . . . is no

. . . (unintelligible) [believed to be "casualties." This was in error. There were many dead and many more wounded.]

Kislev: Okay, the helicopter is coming back.

2130

[The tape continues to 2130. There are no other transmissions relating to the *Liberty*.]

National Security Agency Tapes

The U.S. Navy EC-121 aircraft carrying the NSA communications equipment and technicians heard and recorded only radio transmissions beginning at 1430 Sinai time (1230Z GMT) and ending at 1528 Sinai time (1328Z GMT).

The NSA tapes and translations were released on July 3, 2003, as a result of a Freedom of Information Act lawsuit, *Cristol v. National Security Agency,* U.S. District Court, Southern District of Florida, Case No. 03–20123-CIV-HUCK.

The following translations were released to this author by the NSA and may be viewed on the NSA website www.nsa.gov. They are transcribed as released to this author by the NSA. All emphasis is by author.

Key players on the NSA tapes are:

> "Tribune": Call sign of air controllers at Hatzor air base.
>
> 810: Israel Air Force Super Frelon helicopter 810
>
> 815: Israel Air Force Super Frelon helicopter 815
>
> "Pagoda": Israel Navy MTB Division 914 commander on board MTB 204
>
> "Thorn": Israel Navy MTB 203
>
> "Crisis": Israel Navy MTB 206
>
> "Jewel": Not identified—possibly Haifa [navy headquarters]
>
> "The Big One": USS *Liberty.*
>
> "The Small Ones": Israel MTBs

NSA intercept tapes begin at 1429 Sinai time. The NSA translations show the transmitting entity to the receiving entity. For example Tribune + Hatzor air controller to 815, IAF Super Frelon helicopter 815.

1429

I understand the course from Ashdod [31-55 N 34-39 E] is 215.

Negative [The course is] 250.

Goger. [*sic* for Roger]

Tribune to 815: to What altitude are you climbing?

815 to Tribune: I'm now at 500 feet.

1430

Five by.

Tribune to 815: Pay attention: There was a warship there which we attacked [one word garbled—hereafter, 1 WD G] The men jumped from it [the ship] into the water, you will try to rescue them.

815 to Tribune: Roger, I understand it was hit and unable to fire.

Tribune to 815: no fire was seen from her and those onboard did not fire, heavy smoke is rising from her.

815 to Tribune: Roger.

815 to Tribune: Crossing the coast now at a course of 250.

Tribune to 815: Roger, over. What location [are you]

815 to Tribune: Over Ashdod.

Tribune to 815: Roger, what's your altitude?

815 to Tribune: 500 feet

Tribune to 815: Are you able to climb to an altitude of [1,000 feet]?

815 to Tribune: Roger, I'm climbing.

1432

815 to Tribune: Altitude 1 [1,000], course 250.

Tribune to 815: Roger.

Tribune to 815: Are you at sea now?

815 to Tribune: About 2 or 4 miles.

Tribune to 815: Roger.

Tribune to 815: Visual [radar] contact with you.

815 to Tribune: Roger.

815 to Tribune: [Calling] [Repeats].

Tribune to 815: At the moment she [the *Liberty*] is straight ahead at a distance of about 50 miles.

815 to Tribune: Roger.

810 to Tribune: [Calling].

815: Five by, 810 is calling you.

Tribune to 815: [Calling]

815 to Tribune: Five by.

Tribune to 815: Pay attention: *the ship is now identified as Egyptian,* you can return home now.

815 to Tribune: Roger.

1435

815 to 810: Establish communications with you also.

Tribune to 815: Did you receive?

815 to Tribune: Affirmative, receive, I'm returning.

Tribune to 815: Roger.

810 to Tribune: [Calling].

815 to Tribune: [Calling].

810 to Tribune: Am I to return also?

Tribune to 810: I'll let you know shortly.

810 to Tribune: Roger.

1436

Tribune to 810: [Calling].

810 to Tribune: Roger, I'll let you know shortly.

Tribune to 810: OK.

Tribune to 810: [Calling] [REPEATS]

810 to Tribune: You remain meanwhile in communications with me.

Tribune to 810: Roger, what am I to look for?

Tribune to 815: [Calling].

810 to Tribune: Where are you?

Tribune to 810: I'm close to Ashdod.

810 to 815: Roger, I'm also close to Ashdod, on the seaward side.

1438

Tribune to 810: Did you receive?

810 to Tribune: What did 815 request?

810 to 815: What's your altitude?

815 to 810: Altitude 500 feet, near Ashdod.

810 to 815: Roger, we're at altitude 1200 feet over Ashdod.

815 to 810: Roger.

810 to Tribune: [CALLING].

Tribune to 810: five by.

810 to Tribune: pay attention: you will continue meanwhile on a course of 250 from Ashdod. The both of you [1–2 WD G] will head toward the ship.

815 to Tribune: [CALLING.]

Tribune to 815: Five by.

815 to Tribune: Roger, you will continue [at a course] of 250 from Ashdod. The both of you
will head for the ship, for the time being the both of you will be at altitude 1 [1,000 feet].

810 to Tribune: Do you see us?

Tribune to 810: Affirmative, affirmative.

810 to Tribune: Where are you?

810 to Tribune: Where are you now?

Tribune to 810: Ashdod, altitude 1 [1,000].

Tribune to 810: Did you receive?

810 to Tribune [CALLING].

Tribune to 810: Five by.

Tribune to 810: Altitude is 1 [1,000], at Ashdod.

810 to Tribune: Roger.

Tribune to 810: Going to course 250 together with 815.

810 to Tribune: Are the two of you together?

Tribune to 810: Affirmative, we're together.

810 to Tribune: Roger.

810 to Tribune: Pay attention: you ——— nonetheless are heading for the ship.

810 to Tribune: *You will try to take the men from the water.*

Tribune to 810: Roger, okay.

810 to Tribune: For your information: the ship is ——— apparently burning.

810 to Tribune: [1 WD G] *It is an Egyptian cargo ship.*

Tribune to 810: Roger.

810 to Tribune: Visual [radar] contact with both of you.

Tribune to 810: Roger.

1440

810 to Tribune: I understand that you [1–2 WD G] both of you?

Tribune to 810: Affirmative.

810 to Tribune: Roger.

1441

810 to Tribune: [CALLING].

Tribune to 810: Five by.

810 to Tribune: *Take the men to El Arish.*

Tribune to 810: Roger, okay.

815 to 810: Did you receive?

810 to 815: I received, affirmative.

1442

810 to 815: How much fuel do you have?

815 to 810: Two and a half tanks.

810 to 815: I have 1,700 [liters].

815 to 810: This isn't good.

810 to 815: [1 WD G] to El Arish.

815 to 810: Roger.

810 to Tribune: The ship is located no straight ahead at a range of 50 miles.

Tribune to 810: Roger.

——— Are you first in line?

——— Affirmative.

——— Roger.

Tribune to 815: [2 WD G] From the coast of El Arish.

1448

Tribune to 810: [CALLING] [REPEATS].

1450

Tribune to 810: About how many men are there?

815 to Tribune: [CALLING].

Tribune to 810: How many men are there?

815 to Tribune: Turn right to [course] 260.

Tribune to 815: Repeat.

815 to Tribune: Turn right to course 260.

Tribune to 815: [COURSE], they want to know how many men are there?

815 to Tribune: at the present time, it still isn't known, the distance to you is now 33 miles.

Tribune to 815: Roger.

Tribune to 815: What is the distance from it [the *Liberty*] to El Arish?

815 to Tribune: The distance is approximately 30 miles.

Tribune to 815: Roger.

Tribune to 810: [CALLING].

810 to Tribune: Five by.

Tribune to 810: It's noteworthy that it [1 WD G].

810 to Tribune: Roger.

Tribune to 815: [CALLING].

815 to Tribune: Five by.

Tribune to 815: What is the distance?

815 to Tribune: the distance is now 23 miles.

Tribune to 815: Roger.

815 to Tribune: Pay attention: call on 86 or on 186 Pagoda

[TR NOTE: 186 and 86 refer to a uhf frequency]

Tribune to 815: Roger.

Tribune to 815: I'm going over to 186.

815 to Tribune: Roger.

Tribune to 810: I'm also [going over to 186].

815 to Tribune: Is someone calling [me] Tribune?

Tribune to 815: Affirmative, I don't have contact with Pagoda.

815 to Tribune: Roger, clear, the ship is now at a distance of 19 miles.

Tribune to 815: Roger, is Pagoda located near [the *Liberty*]?

815 to Tribune: Apparently it's located near it [the ship].

Tribune to 815: Roger.

1457

815 to Tribune: *If you are able, try to call her [Pagoda] on 86.*

Tribune to 815: *I tried.*

Tribune to 815: *I didn't c val get anything [make contact].*

815 to Tribune: Roger.

Tribune to 815: [CALLING].

815 to Tribune: Do you have visual contact? Straight ahead, a distance of 18 miles.

Tribune to 815: I have visual contact with [1 WD G] smoke or it could be [1–2 WD G].

815 to Tribune: Roger, is there much smoke rising from it?

Tribune to 815: Roger.

Tribune to 815: *I don't have contact with Pagoda.*

815 to Tribune: Roger.

810 to 815: [CALLING].

815 to 810: Five by.

810 to 815: *Do you have contact with Pagoda?*

815 to 810: *Negative.*

810 to 815: *Roger, I don't either.*

815 to Tribune: [CALLING].

Tribune to 815: Five by.

815 to Tribune: When you begin bringing up the men, clarify by the first man that you bring up, what nationality he is.

1459

815 to Tribune: and report to me immediately, it's important to know.

Tribune to 815: Roger.

815 to Tribune: What is your altitude now?

Tribune to 815: Altitude is 1 [1,000 feet].

815 to Tribune: Roger

Tribune to 815: I have [visual] contact with a vessel straight ahead [at a distance of] 12 [miles] a little from the right, smoke isn't rising; qt [*sic*] the north isn't smoking.

815 to Tribune: The distance is now 13 miles.

Tribune to 815: Roger.

815 to Tribune: Do you see the ship?

Tribune to 815: I see the ship, a little to the right of the smoke, the smoke the smoke isn't rising.

815 to Tribune: Roger, it's possible that [the smoke] is from one of ours.

Tribune to 815: Roger.

Tribune to 815: It's worth clarifying.

815 to Tribune: Roger.

Tribune to 815: Roger, what I see —— now is ours, this is clear.

815 to Tribune: Roger

815 to Tribune: 10 miles is the distance now.

Tribune to 815: Roger, I understand at 12 o'clock [1 WD G].

815 to Tribune: Affirmative, a little on the right side.

Tribune to 815: Voger [*sic*, Roger].

1501

815 to Tribune: The distance is now 9 miles.

1502

Tribune to 815: I'm going over to 86.

815 to Tribune: Roger, I request to receive a report, tell me the nationality.

Tribune to 815: [CALLING].

815 to Tribune: Go ahead.

Tribune to 815: Roger, there is a large ship, smoke isn't rising. At the present time smoke is a little to the right on its left side [XG] [*sic*]. I see a small vessel.

Tribune to 815: Three small vessels.

1503

815 to Tribune: Are you calling me?

Tribune to 815: Five by.

815 to Tribune: Did you call me?

Tribune to 815: Affirmative.

815 to Tribune: Roger, what's the matter?

Tribune to 815: There is a large vessel, near it are 3 small vessels, could this be it, at a distance of a mile from me?

815 to Tribune: Roger, clear.

815 to Tribune: Roger, apparently the small vessels are ours.

Tribune to 815: Roger.

815 to 810: [CALLING].

810 to 815: Five by.

815 to 810: What's the matter?

810 to 815: Don't you see it yet?

815 To 810: I'm behind you, I still don't see the ship [1 WD G] on the right side of us.

810 TO 815: Roger, exactly in front of me, there are the small vessels.

815 TO 810: What's with them, what's going on?

810 to 815: It appears that they are ours.

815 to 810: On our right side?

810 to 815: Yes.

815 to Tribune: All 3 of them are ours.

Tribune to 815: Roger, the small ones, right.

815 to Tribune: Affirmative.

Tribune To 815: Roger, I'm heading for the big one [the *Liberty*].

815 to Tribune: Are you going for the big one?

Tribune to 815: Affirmative.

1504

815 to Thorn: Roger, wait.

———— Five by.

———— Roger transmit.

———— Yes.

———— With you

[TR NOTE: Last 4 transmissions are one way communications—All 4 are from same source—other terminal is on different frequency]

185 [*sic*] to Thorn: We search around and didn't find anyone.

[TR NOTE: It is believed that Thorn made an error and wanted to call 815. The call sign 185 however has been used by an Israeli jet aircraft (either a Mirage or a Mystère). It is of course possible that Thorn had previously been in contact with 185, but if this was the case there are no COMINT reflections of this activity.)

Thorn to 815: Roger.

815 to Thorn: The big one [the *Liberty*] is not ours.

185 [*sic*] to Thorn: How do you read me?

[TR NOTE: Again thorn says 185 vice 815]

Thorn to 815: [CALLS].

815 to Thorn: *We searched around and didn't find anyone.*

Thorn to 815: Roger.

———— to Pagoda to 810: Roger.

———— to Tribune: I understand and for the big one [the *Liberty*]

Tribune to Pagoda: Don't speak on the channel now [REPEATS].

———— to Pagoda: Five by. It appears to me that I found the men.

———— to Pagoda: Affirmative?

———— to Pagoda: Roger, that's clear.

———— to Pagoda: Roger.

———— to Pagoda: Negative, it's not men, it's boats, it's not men.

Tribune to 810: [CALLING].

810 to Tribune: Go ahead

815 to 810: [CALLING].

810 to 815: Five by.

815 to 810: What's going on?

810 to 815: I don't know anything [1 WD G] [about them] I'll try to contact them on 186.

[TR NOTE: 815 is trying to get in touch with the 3 small ships on 186 frequency]

815 to 810: Are the small ones ours?

815 to Tribune: [CALLING].Tribune to 815: Five by.

815 to Tribune: *pay attention: if any of them are speaking, and if they are speaking Arabic [Egyptian] you tak [sic] them to El Arish [31-03 N 33-45 E] if they are speaking English, not Egyptian, you take them to Lod (31-58 N 34-54 E) Is this clear?*

Tribune to 815: Roger.

815 to Tribune: *Do you see the men?*

815 to Tribune: To whom does the big one [ship] belong?

Tribune: We hear you excellently.

Pagoda to 810: [CALLS].

810 to Pagoda: Transmit.

Pagoda to 810: What are you saying?

810 to Pagoda: Send your report.

Pagoda to 810: What has to be done here?

Pagoda to 810: [CALLS].

810 to Pagoda: *Search to see if there are men in the water.*

1506

Pagoda to 810: Roger.

——————— to Tribune: I understand and for the big one [Liberty]

Tribune to Pagoda: Don't speak on the channel now [REPEATS].

——————— to Pagoda: *Five by. It appears to me that I found the men.*

——————— to Pagoda: Affirmative?

——————— to Pagoda: Roger, that's clear.

——————— to Pagoda: Roger.

——————— to Pagoda: *Negative, it's not men, it's boats, it's not men.*

Tribune to 810: [CALLING].

810 to Tribune: Go ahead

815 to 810: [CALLING].

810 to 815: Five by.

815 to 810: What's going on?

810 to 815: I don't know anything [1 WD G] [about them] I'll try to contact them on 186.

[TR NOTE: 815 is trying to get in touch with the three small ships on 186 frequency]

815 to 810: Are the small ones ours?

815 to Tribune: [CALLING].

Tribune to 815: Five by.

815 to Tribune: *Pay attention: if any of them are speaking, and if they are speaking Arabic [Egyptian] You tak [sic] them to El Arish* [31-03 N 33-45 E] *if they are speaking English, not Egyptian, you take them to Lod* (31-58 N 34-54 E) *is this clear?*

Tribune to 815: Roger.

815 to Tribune: *Do you see the men?*

815 to Tribune: To whom does the big one [ship] belong?

1507

815 to 810: [CALLING] [REPEATS].

810 to 815: Five by.

815 to 810: Don't leave the vicinity, if you do leave, report [to me].

810 to 815: I'm not monitoring this channel, I'm speaking on 186 with thorn. This is the small ones [sic].

815 to 810: Roger. What should be done?

810 to 815: *Search for survivors (whether you find them or not).*

Pagoda to 815: [CALLS].

815 to Pagoda: Transmit

1508

815 to 810: Roger.

810 to Tribune: Are you able to go up a little higher in order to see the situation better?

Tribune to 810: Roger.

810 to Tribune: [CALLING] [REPEATS].

815 to Tribune: [CALLING].

815 to Tribune: Are you over whatever you located?

[TR NOTE: It should be noted here that helicopters 810 and 815 are now answering control on another frequency]

815 to Tribune: Roger, *the first matter to clarify is to find out what their nationality is.*

815 to TRIBUNE: Report to me immediately.

1510

815 to Tribune: Roger this is clear.

815 to Tribune: Roger, you watch our [*sic*] for the masts there.

815 to Tribune: [CALLING].

Pagoda to 815: I understand that the ship is not in danger.

815 to Pagoda: I am not sure that it [the *Liberty*] is not in danger. Are you suggesting the seriousness of it [the situation], by [saying] this?

[TR NOTE: As heard].

Pagoda to 815: Negative, G.T.R.-5 is written [on it].

[TR NOTE: Letters G.T.R. sent in English]. 815 to Pagoda: Roger. [STOPS].

Pagoda to 815: Does this mean something?

815 to Pagoda: Negative, it doesn't mean anything.

Pagoda to 815: *From behind it [the* Liberty*] several uninflated boats were seen.*

815 to Pagoda: Roger.

815 to Tribune: You take 810 with you and return home, bearing) 070, distance of 6 miles.

815 to Tribune: Five by.

1512

815 to Tribune: *Roger, this is clear, did you clearly identify an American flag?*

815 to Tribune: *Thanks, remain meanwhile over the area.*

810 to 815: [CALLING].

815 to Tribune: *We request that you make another pass and check once more if this is really an American flag.*

Tribune to 815: Roger.

[TR NOTE: Do not hear from 815 until 1327Z]

———— to Tribune: Five by.

815 to Tribune: *Roger, this is clear, what kind of flag is it?*

815 to Tribune: Roger, this is clear.

815 to Tribune: Five by, remain meanwhile in waiting and we'll report to you immediately.

815 to Tribune: Is this clear?

815 to Tribune: Take 810, and return home.

815 to Tribune: [Course] 065, distance of 65 miles.

815 to Tribune: Roger, this is clear.

 815 to Tribune: Roger, I received. I will notify you immediately as to what to do.

815 to Tribune: Roger.

1516

———— to Tribune: Pay attention

815 to Tribune: *Roger, this is clear. According to the instruction, whoever has the 60st [sic] fuel.*

1517

815 to Tribune: Roger, I'm checking on it.

815 to Tribune: *Pay attention: whoever has the most fuel between you will return home, the one with the least will go to El Arish.*

815 to Tribune: Not at the present time. Qpparently [sic] the one who is going to El Arish will return later.

815 to Tribune: Qhich [sic] one of you is going home?

815 to Tribune: Who is going home?

815 to Tribune: OK.

815 to Tribune: Roger, this is known. I Received the notice and it's known that these orders came from above.

1521

———— Go over to 170 on the way home.

810 to Tribune: He says over to 170 on the way home.

Tribune to 810: Roger.

1527

Jewel to 815: [CALLS] [REPEATS].

[TR NOTE: 815 calls Jewel until 1328Z]

[end of radio telephone conversation]

Comment: This activity had been reported in a condensed version by USA-556 IN ITS 2/J5 /R23067, 082015Z, and follow ups.

Appendix 3

MEMO, DIRECTOR NSA: BRAVO "CRAYON" REPORT, NR2149

This message was sent by the director of the National Security Agency to the White House on June 22, 1967.

Released by NSA on 2 July 2003 pursuant to the Freedom of Information Act Case #40039

22 June 67, 1011.

FM DIRNSA [Director, National Security Agency]
TO OSCAR/PAPA ALFA
WHITE HOUSE

S E C R E T SAVIN

SIGINT READINESS BRAVO "CRAYON" REPORT NR. 2149
AFTERMATH OF ISRAELI ATTACK ON USS LIBERTY, 8 JUNE 1967

1. GENERAL

THE FOLLOWING ACTIVITY IS BASED ON ISRAELI PLAIN LANGUAGE VHF/ UHF VOICE COMMUNICATIONS INTERCEPTED ON 8 JUNE 1967 BETWEEN 1229Z AND 1328Z. THIS ACTIVITY DEALS SOLELY WITH THE AFTERMATH OF THE ATTACK BY ISRAELI JET AIRCRAFT AND TORPEDO BOATS ON THE USS LIBERTY (GTR5). *THERE ARE NO COMINT REFLECTIONS OF THE ACTUAL ATTACK ITSELF.* [Emphasis added]

2. SUMMARY

AT 1230Z, TWO ISRAELI HELICOPTERS 810 AND 815, WERE DIS-PATCHED BY HATSOR TO THE AREA OF THE INCIDENT TO CHECK FOR SURVIVORS OF AN UNIDENTIFIED "WARSHIP." APPROXIMATELY AT 1234Z,

THE AIR CONTROLLER AT HATSOR CLARIFIED THE IDENTITY OF THE SHIP
TO THE TWO ISRAELI HELICOPTERS BY INFORMING THEM THAT IT HAD
BEEN IDENTIFIED AS EGYPTIAN. AT 1239Z, HATSOR TOLD THE HELI-
COPTERS THAT IT WAS AN EGYPTIAN CARGO SHIP.

AT 1307Z, HATSOR TOLD HELICOPTER 815 TO TAKE ANY SURVIVORS
THAT SPOKE EGYPTIAN TO AL ARISH ((31-08N 34-54E)), BUT IF THEY
SPOKE ENGLISH TO TAKE THEM TO LOD ((31-58N 34-54E)).

AT 1312Z, THE ISRAELI HELICOPTER 815 APPARENTLY INFORMED
HATSOR ON A DIFFERENT FREQUENCY THAT IT HAD SIGHTED AN AMERICAN
FLAG ON THE SHIP. HATSOR THEN ASKED THE HELICOPTER TO MAKE
ANOTHER PASS TO CHECK "IF THIS IS REALLY AN AMERICAN FLAG."

THE HELICOPTERS AND THE MTBS WERE COMMUNICATING ON A UHF
FREQUENCY WHEREAS THE HELICOPTERS AND THE AIR CONTROLLER AT
HATSOR WERE USING VHF THROUGHOUT. AT 1310Z, HELICOPTER 815 IN-
FORMED THE MTB USING CALLWORD "PAGODA" THAT THE SHIP WAS NOT IN
DANGER. THE SAME HELICOPTER THEN REPORTED THAT G.T.R.-5 WAS
WRITTEN ON THE SHIP AND INQUIRED IF THIS MEANT ANYTHING. THE
MTB REPLIED IN THE NEGATIVE.

THROUGHOUT THIS INTERCEPT, THE USS LIBERTY IS REFERRED TO AS
THE "BIG ONE" WHILE THE THREE ISRAELI MOTOR TORPEDO BOATS ARE RE-
FERRED TO AS THE "SMALL ONES". THE HELICOPTERS USED CALLSIGNS
810 AND 815. THE AIR CONTROLLER AT HATSOR AIR BASE USED CALL WORD
"TRIBUNE". THE MTBS USED CALLWORDS "THORN," "PAGODA," AND "CRISIS."
THE CALLWORD "JEWEL" IS NOT IDENTIFIED, BUT MAY BE
HAIFA.

3. DETAILS

TIME Z=GMT S=Sinai time	TO	FROM	TEXT
			——I UNDERSTAND THE COURSE FROM ASHDOD ((31-55N 34-39E)) IS 215.
			——NEGATIVE ((THE COURSE IS)) 250.
			——ROGER.
	815	(TRIBUNE)	TO WHAT ALTITUDE ARE YOU CLIMBING?
	(TRIBUNE)	(815)	I'M NOW AT 500 FEET.
	(815)	(TRIBUNE)	
1230Z/1430S	—		FIVE BY.

TIME	TO	FROM	TEXT
	(815)	(TRIBUNE)	PAY ATTENTION: THERE WAS A WARSHIP THERE WHICH WE ATTACKED ((1 WD G)), [1 word garbled] THE MEN JUMPED FROM IT ((THE SHIP)) INTO THE WATER, YOU WILL TRY TO RESCUE THEM.
	(TRIBUNE)	(815)	ROGER, I UNDERSTAND IT WAS HIT AND UNABLE TO FIRE.
	(815)	(TRIBUNE)	NO FIRE WAS SEEN FROM HER AND THOSE ____ ONBOARD) DID NOT FIRE; HEAVY SMOKE IS RISING FROM HER.
	(TRIBUNE)	(815)	ROGER.
	(TRIBUNE)	(815)	(__ CROSSING THE) COAST NOW AT A COURSE OF 250.
	(815)	(TRIBUNE)	ROGER, OVER. WHAT LOCATION (ARE YOU)
	(TRIBUNE)	(815)	OVER ASHDOD.
	(815)	(TRIBUNE)	ROGER, WHAT'S YOUR ALTITUDE?
	(TRIBUNE)	(815)	500 FEET.
	(815)	(TRIBUNE)	ARE YOU ABLE TO CLIMB TO AN ALTITUDE OF ((1,000 FEET))?
	(TRIBUNE)	(815)	ROGER, I'M CLIMBING.
1232Z/1432S	(TRIBUNE)	(815)	ALTITUDE 1 ((1000)), COURSE 250.
	815	(TRIBUNE)	ROGER.
	(815)	(TRIBUNE)	ARE YOU AT SEA NOW?
	(TRIBUNE)	(815)	ABOUT 3 OR 4 MILES
	(815)	(TRIBUNE)	ROGER.
	(815)	(TRIBUNE)	VISUAL ((RADAR)) CONTACT WITH YOU.
	(TRIBUNE)	(815)	ROGER.
	(TRIBUNE)	(815)	((CALLING)). ((REPEATS)).
	(815)	(TRIBUNE)	AT THE MOMENT SHE ((LIBERTY)) IS STRAIGHT AHEAD AT A DISTANCE OF ABOUT 50 MILES.
	(TRIBUNE)	(815)	ROGER.
	TRIBUNE	810	((CALLING))

TIME	TO	FROM	TEXT
	815	(815)	FIVE BY,810 IS CALLING YOU.
	815	TRIBUNE	((CALLING))
	(TRIBUNE)	(815)	FIVE BY.
	(815)	(TRIBUNE)	PAY ATTENTION: THE SHIP IS NOW IDENTIFIED AS EGYPTIAN, YOU CAN RETURN HOME NOW.
	(TRIBUNE)	(815)	ROGER.
1235Z/1435S			
	810	(815)	ESTABLISH COMMUNICATIONS WITH YOU ALSO.
	815	(TRIBUNE)	DID YOU RECEIVE?
	(TRIBUNE)	(815)	AFFIRMATIVE, RECEIVE, I'M RETURNING.
	(815)	(TRIBUNE)	ROGER.
	(TRIBUNE)	(810)	((CALLING)).
	(TRIBUNE)	815	((CALLING)).
	(TRIBUNE)	810	AM I TO RETURN ALSO?
	(810)	(TRIBUNE)	I'LL LET YOU KNOW SHORTLY.
	(TRIBUNE)	(810)	ROGER.
1236Z/1436S			
	TRIBUNE	810	((CALLING)).
	(810)	(TRIBUNE)	ROGER, I'LL LET YOU KNOW SHORTLY.
	(TRIBUNE)	(810)	OK.
	(TRIBUNE)	(810)	((CALLING)) ((RPTS))
	810	(TRIBUNE)	YOU REMAIN MEANWHILE IN COMMUNICATIONS WITH ME.
	(TRIBUNE)	(810)	ROGER, WHAT AM I TO LOOK FOR?
	(TRIBUNE)	815	((CALLING)).
	810	(TRIBUNE)	WHERE ARE YOU?
	(TRIBUNE)	(810)	I'M CLOSE TO ASHDOD.
	(810)	(815)	ROGER, I'M ALSO CLOSE TO ASHDOD, ON THE SEAWARD SIDE.
1238Z/1438S			
	TRIBUNE	(810)	DID YOU RECEIVE?
	(810)	(TRIBUNE)	WHAT DID 815 REQUEST?
	810	(815)	WHAT'S YOUR ALTITUDE?
	(815)	(810)	ALTITUDE 500 FEET, NEAR ASHDOD.
	810	(815)	ROGER, WE'RE AT ALTITUDE 1200 FEET OVER ASHDOD.

TIME	TO	FROM	TEXT
	(815)	(810)	ROGER.
	810	TRIBUNE	((CALLING)).
	(TRIBUNE)	(810)	FIVE BY.
	(810)	(TRIBUNE)	PAY ATTENTION: YOU WILL CONTINUE MEANWHILE ON A COURSE OF 250 FROM ASHDOD. THE BOTH OF YOU ((1-2 WD G)) [1-2 words garbled] WILL HEAD TOWARD THE SHIP.
	815	(TRIBUNE)	((CALLING)).
	(TRIBUNE)	(815)	FIVE BY.
	(815)	(TRIBUNE)	ROGER, YOU WILL CONTINUE ((AT A COURSE)) OF 250 FROM ASHDOD. THE BOTH OF YOU WILL HEAD FOR THE SHIP, FOR THE TIME BEING THE BOTH OF YOU WILL BE AT ALTITUDE 1 ((1000 FEET)).
	810	(TRIBUNE)	DO YOU SEE US?
	(TRIBUNE)	(810)	AFFIRMATIVE, AFFIRMATIVE.
	(810)	(TRIBUNE)	WHERE ARE YOU?
	(810)	(TRIBUNE)	ASHDOD, ALTITUDE 1 ((1000)).
	(TRIBUNE)	(810)	DID YOU RECEIVE?
	810	TRIBUNE	((CALLING)).
	(TRIBUNE)	(810)	FIVE BY.
	(TRIBUNE)	(810)	ALTITUDE IS 1 ((1000)), AT ASHDOD.
	(810)	(TRIBUNE)	ROGER.
	(TRIBUNE)	(810)	GOING TO COURSE 250 TOGETHER WITH 815.
	(810)	(TRIBUNE)	ARE THE TWO OF YOU TOGETHER?
	(TRIBUNE)	(810)	AFFIRMATIVE, WE'RE TOGETHER.
	(810)	(TRIBUNE)	ROGER.
	(810)	(TRIBUNE)	PAY ATTENTION: YOU __ NONETHELESS ARE HEADING FOR THE SHIP.
	(810)	(TRIBUNE)	YOU WILL TRY TO TAKE THE MEN FROM THE WATER.
	(TRIBUNE)	(810)	ROGER, OKAY.
	(810)	(TRIBUNE)	FOR YOUR INFORMATION: THE SHIP IS APPARENTLY __ BURNING.

TIME	TO	FROM	TEXT
	(810)	(TRIBUNE)	((1 WD G)) [1 word garbled] IT IS AN EGYPTIAN CARGO SHIP.
	(TRIBUNE)	(810)	ROGER.
	(810)	(TRIBUNE)	VISUAL ((RADAR)) CONTACT WITH BOTH OF YOU.
	(TRIBUNE)	(810)	ROGER.
1240Z/1440S			
	(810)	(TRIBUNE)	I UNDERSTAND THAT YOU ((1-2 WD G)) [1 - 2 words garbled] BOTH OF YOU?
	(TRIBUNE)	(810)	AFFIRMATIVE.
	(810)	(TRIBUNE)	ROGER.
1241Z/1441S			
	810	TRIBUNE	((CALLING)).
	(TRIBUNE)	(810)	FIVE BY.
	(810)	(TRIBUNE)	TAKE THE MEN TO EL-ARISH.
	(TRIBUNE)	(810)	ROGER, OKAY.
	(815)	(810)	DID YOU RECEIVE?
	(810)	(815)	I RECEIVED, AFFIRMATIVE.
1242Z/1442S			
	(810)	(815)	HOW MUCH FUEL TO YOU HAVE?
	(815)	(810)	TWO AND A HALF TANKS.
	(810)	(815)	I HAVE 1,700 ((LITERS)).
	(815)	(810)	THIS ISN'T GOOD.
	(810)	(815)	((1 WD G)) [1 word garbled] TO EL ARISH.
	(815)	(810)	ROGER.
	(810)	(TRIBUNE)	THE SHIP IS LOCATED NOW STRAIGHT AHEAD AT A RANGE OF 50 MILES.
	(TRIBUNE)	(810)	ROGER.
			———ARE YOU FIRST IN LINE?
			———AFFIRMATIVE.
			———ROGER.
	TRIBUNE	815	((2 WD G))[2 words garbled] FROM THE COAST OF EL ARISH
1248Z/1448S			
	TRIBUNE	810	((CALLING)) ((REPEATS)).

TIME	TO	FROM	TEXT
1250Z/1450S			
	(TRIBUNE)	810	ABOUT HOW MANY MEN ARE THERE?
	815	TRIBUNE	((CALLING)).
	TRIBUNE	810	HOW MANY MEN ARE THERE?
	815	TRIBUNE	TURN RIGHT TO ((COURSE)) 260.
	(TRIBUNE)	(815)	REPEAT.
	(815)	(TRIBUNE)	TURN RIGHT TO COURSE 260.
	(TRIBUNE)	(815)	((COURSE)). THEY WANT TO KNOW HOW MANY MEN ARE THERE?
	(815)	(TRIBUNE)	AT THE PRESENT TIME, IT STILL ISN'T KNOWN, THE DISTANCE TO YOU IS NOW 33 MILES
	(TRIBUNE)	(815)	ROGER.
	(TRIBUNE)	(815)	WHAT IS THE DISTANCE FROM IT ((THE LIBERTY)) TO EL ARISH?
	(815)	(TRIBUNE)	THE DISTANCE IS APPROXIMATELY 30 MILES.
	(TRIBUNE)	(815)	ROGER.
	TRIBUNE	810	((CALLING)).
	(810)	(TRIBUNE)	FIVE BY.
	(TRIBUNE)	(810)	IT'S NOTEWORTHY THAT IS ((1 WD G)). [1 word garbled]
	(810)	(TRIBUNE)	ROGER.
	TRIBUNE	815	((CALLING)).
	(815)	(TRIBUNE)	FIVE BY.
	(TRIBUNE)	(815)	WHAT IS THE DISTANCE?
	(815)	(TRIBUNE)	ROGER.
	815	(TRIBUNE)	PAY ATTENTION: CALL ON 86 OR ON 186 PAGODA. ((TR-NOTE: 186 AND 86 REFER TO A UHF FREQUENCY))
	(TRIBUNE)	(815)	ROGER.
	(TRIBUNE)	(815)	I'M GOING OVER TO 186.
	(815)	(TRIBUNE)	ROGER.
	(TRIBUNE)	810	I'M ALSO ((GOING OVER TO 186)).
	(815)	(TRIBUNE)	IS SOMEONE CALLING ((ME)) TRIBUNE?
	(TRIBUNE)	(815)	AFFIRMATIVE, I DON'T HAVE CONTACT WITH PAGODA.

TIME	TO	FROM	TEXT
	(815)	(TRIBUNE)	ROGER, CLEAR, THE SHIP IS NOW AT A DISTANCE OF 19 MILES.
	(TRIBUNE)	(815)	ROGER, IS PAGODA LOCATED NEAR ((THE LIBERTY))?
	(815)	(TRIBUNE)	APPARENTLY IT'S LOCATED NEAR IT ((THE SHIP)).
	(TRIBUNE)	(815)	ROGER.
1257Z/1457S			
	815	(TRIBUNE)	IF YOU ARE ABLE, TRY TO CALL HER ((PAGODA)) ON 86.
	(TRIBUNE)	(815)	I TRIED.
	(TRIBUNE)	(815)	I DIDN'T (C VAL [probably the hebrew word "kebel" which means "get".] GET ANYTHING) ((MAKE CONTACT))
	(815)	(TRIBUNE)	ROGER.
	TRIBUNE	815	((CALLING)).
		815	TRIBUNE DO YOU HAVE VISUAL CONTACT? STRAIGHT AHEAD, A DISTANCE OF 18 MILES.
	TRIBUNE	815	I HAVE VISUAL CONTACT WITH ((1 WD G)) [1 word garbled] SMOKE OR IT COULD BE ((1-2 WD G))[1-2 words garbled].
		815	TRIBUNE ROGER, IS THERE MUCH SMOKE RISING FROM IT?
	TRIBUNE	815	ROGER.
	TRIBUNE	815	I DON'T HAVE CONTACT WITH PAGODA.
		815	TRIBUNE ROGER.
	810	815	((CALLING)).
	815	810	FIVE BY.
	810	815	DO YOU HAVE CONTACT WITH PAGODA?
	815	810	NEGATIVE.
	810	815	ROGER, I DON'T EITHER.
		815	TRIBUNE ((CALLING)).
	TRIBUNE	815	FIVE BY.
	815	TRIBUNE	WHEN YOU BEGIN BRINGING UP THE MEN, CLARIFY BY THE

TIME	TO	FROM	TEXT
			FIRST MAN THAT YOU BRING UP, WHAT NATIONALITY HE IS.
1259Z/1459S			
	815	TRIBUNE	AND REPORT TO ME IMMEDIATELY, IT'S IMPORTANT TO KNOW.
	TRIBUNE	815	ROGER.
	815	TRIBUNE	WHAT IS YOUR ALTITUDE NO?
	TRIBUNE	815	ALTITUDE IS 1 ((1000 FEET)).
	815	TRIBUNE	ROGER.
	TRIBUNE	815	I HAVE ((VISUAL)) CONTACT WITH A VESSEL STRAIGHT AHEAD ((AT A DISTANCE OF)) 12 ((MILES)) A LITTLE FROM THE RIGHT, SMOKE ISN'T RISING; QT THE NORTH IT ISN'T SMOKING.
	815	TRIBUNE	THE DISTANCE IS NOW 13 MILES.
	TRIBUNE	815	ROGER.
	815	TRIBUNE	DO YOU SEE THE SHIP?
	TRIBUNE	815	I SEE THE SHIP, A LITTLE TO THE RIGHT OF THE SMOKE, THE SMOKE THE SMOKE ISN'T RISING.
	815	TRIBUNE	ROGER, IT'S POSSIBLE THAT ((THE SMOKE)) IS FROM ONE OF OURS.
	TRIBUNE	815	ROGER.
	TRIBUNE	815	IT'S WORTH CLARIFYING.
	815	TRIBUNE	ROGER.
	TRIBUNE	815	ROGER, WHAT I SEE ___ NOW IS OURS, THIS IS CLEAR.
	815	TRIBUNE	ROGER.
	815	TRIBUNE	10 MILES IS THE DISTANCE NOW.
	TRIBUNE	815	ROGER, I UNDERSTAND AT 12 O'CLOCK ((1 WD G)) [1 word garbled].
	815	TRIBUNE	AFFIRMATIVE, A LITTLE ON THE RIGHT SIDE.
	TRIBUNE	815	[R]OGER.

TIME	TO	FROM	TEXT
1301Z/1501S			
	815	TRIBUNE	THE DISTANCE IS NOW 9 MILES.
1302Z/1502S			
	TRIBUNE	815	I'M GOING OVER TO 86.
	815	TRIBUNE	ROGER, I REQUEST TO RECEIVE A REPORT, TELL ME THE NATIONALITY
	TRIBUNE	815	((CALLING)).
	815	TRIBUNE	GO AHEAD.
	TRIBUNE	815	ROGER, THERE IS A LARGE SHIP, SMOKE ISN'T RISING. AT THE PRESENT TIME SMOKE IS A LITTLE TO THE RIGHT ON ITS LEFT SIDE ((XG)) I SEE A SMALL VESSEL.
	TRIBUNE	815	THREE SMALL VESSELS.
1303Z/1503S			
	815	(TRIBUNE)	ARE YOU CALLING ME?
	TRIUNE	815	FIVE BY.
	815	TRIBUNE	DID YOU CALL ME?
	TRIBUNE	815	AFFIRMATIVE.
	815	TRIBUNE	ROGER, WHAT'S THE MATTER?
	TRIBUNE	815	THERE IS A LAR[G]E VESSEL, NEAR IT ARE 3 SMALL VESSELS, COULD THIS BE IT, AT A DISTANCE OF A MILE FROM ME?
	815	TRIBUNE	ROGER, CLEAR.
	815	TRIBUNE	ROGER, APPARENTLY THE SMALL VESSELS ARE OURS.
	TRIBUNE	815	ROGER.
	815	810	((CALLING)).
	810	815	FIVE BY.
	815	810	WHAT'S THE MATTER/
	810	815	DON'T YOU SEE IT YET?
	815	810	I'M BEHIND YOU, I STILL DON'T SEE THE SHIP ((1 WD G)) [1 word garbled] ON THE RIGHT SIDE OF US.

TIME	TO	FROM	TEXT
	810	815	ROGER, EXACTLY IN FRONT OF ME, THERE ARE THE SMALL VESSELS.
	815	810	WHAT'S WITH THEM, WHAT'S GOING ON?
	810	815	IT APPEARS THAT THEY ARE OURS.
	815	810	ON OUR RIGHT SIDE?
	810	815	YES.
	815	TRIBUNE	ALL 3 OF THEM ARE OURS.
	(TRIBUNE)	(815)	ROGER, THE SMALL ONES, RIGHT?
	815	TRIBUNE	AFFIRMATIVE.
	TRIBUNE	815	ROGER, I'M HEADING FOR THE BIG ONE ((LIBERTY)).
	815	TRIBUNE	ARE YOU GOING FOR THE BIG ONE?
	(TRIBUNE)	(815)	AFFIRMATIVE.
1304Z/1504s			
	815	THORN	ROGER, WAIT.
			———FIVE BY.
			———ROGER, TRANSMIT.
			———YES.
			———WITH YOU.
			((TR-NOTE: LAST 4 TRANSMISSIONS ARE ON WAY COMMUNICATION— ALL 4 ARE FROM SAME SOURCE — OTHER TERMINAL IS ON DIFFERENT FREQUENCY))
	185 ((SIC))	THORN	WE SEARCH AROUND AND DIDN'T FIND ANYONE. ((TR-NOTE: IT IS BELIEVED THAT THORN MADE AN ERROR AND WANTED TO CALL 815. THE CALLSIGN 185 HOWEVER HAS BEEN USED BY AN ISRAELI JET AIRCRAFT (EITHER A MI RAGE OR A MYSTERE). IT IS OF COURSE POSSIBLE THAT THORN HAD PREVIOUSLY BEEN IN CONTACT WITH 185,

TIME	TO	FROM	TEXT
			BUT IF THIS WAS THE CASE THERE ARE NO COMINT RE FLECTIONS OF THIS ACTIVITY.))
	(THORN)	(815)	ROGER.
	(815)	(THORN)	THE BIG ONE ((LIBERTY)) IS NOT OURS.
	185	((SIC))THORN	HOW DO YOU READ ME? ((TR NOTE: AGAIN THORN SAYS 185 VICE 815))
	(THORN)	815	((CALLS)).
	815	THORN	WE SEARCHED AROUND AND DIDN'T FIND ANYONE.
	THORN	(815)	ROGER. —TRIBUNE WE HEAR YOU EXCELLENTLY.
	PAGODA	810	((CALLS))
	810	PAGODA	TRANSMIT.
	(PAGODA)	(810)	WHAT ARE YOU SAYING?
	(810)	(PAGODA)	SEND YOU REPORT.
	(PAGODA)	810	WHAT HAS TO BE DONE HERE?
	PAGODA	810	((CALLS)).
	(810)	(PAGODA)	SEARCH TO SEE IF THERE ARE ME[N] IN THE WATER.
1306Z/1506S			
	(PAGODA)	(810)	ROGER.
		—(TRIBUNE)	I UNDERSTAND AND FOR THE BIG ONE ((LIBERTY)).
	(TRIBUNE)	(PAGODA)	DON'T SPEAK ON THE CHANNEL NOW ((RPTS)).
		—(PAGODA)	FIVE BY, IT APPEARS TO ME THAT I FOUND THE MEN.
		—PAGODA	AFFIRMATIVE?
		—(PAGODA)	ROGER, THAT'S CLEAR.
		—(PAGODA)	ROGER.
		—(PAGODA)	NEGATIVE, IT'S NOT MEN, IT'S BOATS, IT'S NOT MEN.
	TRIBUNE	810	((CALLING)).
	810	TRIBUNE	GO AHEAD.
	815	810	((CALLING)).
	810	815	FIVE BY.
	815	810	WHAT'S GOING ON?

TIME	TO	FROM	TEXT
	810	815	I DON'T KNOW ANYTHING ((1 WD G)) [1 word garbled] ((ABOUT THEM)) I'LL TRY TO CONTACT THEM ON 186. ((TR NOTE: 815 IS TRYING TO GET IN TOUCH WITH THE 3 SMALL SHIPS ON 186 FREQUENCY))
	815	810	ARE THE SMALL ONES OURS?
	815	TRIBUNE	((CALLING)).
	TRIBUNE	815	FIVE BY.
	815	TRIBUNE	PAY ATTENTION: IF ANY OF THEM ARE SPEAKING AND IF THEY ARE SPEAKING ARABIC (EGYPTIAN), YOU TAKE THEM TO EL ARISH ((31-03 N 33-45E)) IF THEY ARE SPEAKING ENGLISH, NOT EGYPTIAN, YOU TAKE THEM TO LOD ((31-58N 34-54E)) IS THIS CLEAR?
	TRIBUNE	815	ROGER.
	815	TRIBUNE	DO YOU SEE THE MEN?
	815	TRIBUNE	TO WHOM DOES THE BIG ONE ((SHIP)) BELONG?
1307Z/1507S			
	815	810	((CALLING)) ((REPEATS)).
	810	815	FIVE BY
	815	810	DON'T LEAVE THE VICINITY, IF YOU DO LEAVE, REPORT ((TO ME)).
	810	815	I'M NOT MONITORING THIS CHANNEL, I'M SPEAKING ON 186 WITH THORN. THIS IS THE SMALL ONES ((SIC)).
	815	810	ROGER, WHAT SHOULD BE DON?
	810	815	SEARCH FOR SURVIVORS___ WHETHER YOU FIND THEM OR NOT).
	PAGODA	815	((CALLS)).
	815	PAGODA	TRANSMIT.

TIME	TO	FROM	TEXT
1308Z/1508S			
	(815)	(810)	ROGER.
	810	TRIBUNE	ARE YOU ABLE TO GO UP A LITTLE HIGHER IN ORDER TO SEE THE SITUATION BETTER?
	(TRIBUNE)	(810)	ROGER.
	810	TRIBUNE	((CALLING)). ((REPEATS)).
	815	TRIBUNE	((CALLING)).
	815	TRIBUNE	ARE YOU OVER WHATEVER YOU LOCATED? ((TR-NOTE: IT SHOULD BE NOTED HERE THAT HELICOPTERS 810 AND 815 ARE NOW ANSWERING CONTROL ON ANOTHER FREQUENCY))
	815	TRIBUNE	ROGER, THE FIRST MATTER TO CLARIFY IS TO FIND OUT WHAT THEIR NATIONALITY IS.
	(815)	(TRIBUNE)	REPORT TO ME IMMEDIATELY.
	(815)	(TRIBUNE)	ROGER THIS IS CLEAR.
	815	TRIBUNE	ROGER, YOU WATCH OUT FOR THE MASTS THERE.
	815	TRIBUNE	((CALLING)).
	(PAGODA)	(815)	I UNDERSTAND THAT THE SHIP IS NOT IN DANGER.
	(815)	PAGODA	I AM NOT SURE THAT IT ((THE LIBERTY)) IS NOT IN DANGER. ARE YOU SUGGESTING THE SERIOUSNESS OF IT ((THE SITUATION)), BY ((SAYING)) THIS?((TR-NOTE: AS HEARD)).
	(PAGODA)	(815)	NEGATIVE, G.T.R.-5 IS WRITTEN ((ON IT)). ((TR-NOTE: LETTERS G.T.R. SENT IN ENGLISH))
	(815)	(PAGODA)	ROGER ((STOPS)).
	(PAGODA)	(815)	DOES THIS MEAN SOMETHING?
	(815)	(PAGODA)	NEGATIVE, IT DOESN'T MEAN ANYTHING.

TIME	TO	FROM	TEXT
	(PAGODA)	(815)	FROM BEHIND IT ((LIBERTY)) SEVERAL UNINFLATED BOATS WERE SEEN.
	(815)	(PAGODA)	ROGER.
	815	TRIBUNE	YOU TAKE 810 WITH YOU AND RETURN HOME, ____ BEARING) 070, DISTANCE OF 6 MILES.
	(815)	(TRIBUNE)	FIVE BY.
1312Z/1512S			
	815	TRIBUNE	ROGER, THIS IS CLEAR, DID YOU CLEARLY IDENTIFY AN AMERICAN FLAG?
	815	TRIBUNE	THANKS, REMAIN MEANWHILE OVER THE AREA.
	810	815	((CALLING)).
	815	TRIBUNE	WE REQUEST THAT YOU MAKE ANOTHER PASS AND CHECK ONCE MORE IF THIS IS REALLY AN AMERICAN FLAG.
	(TRIBUNE)	(815)	ROGER. ((TR-NOTE: DO NOT HEAR FROM 815 UNTIL 1327Z))
	—	(TRIBUNE)	FIVE BY.
	(815)	(TRIBUNE)	ROGER, THIS IS CLEAR, WHAT KIND OF FLAG IS IT?
	(815)	(TRIBUNE)	ROGER, THIS IS CLEAR.
	(815)	(TRIBUNE)	FIVE BY, REMAIN MEANWHILE IN WAITING, AND WE'LL REPORT TO YOU IMMEDIATELY.
	(815)	(TRIBUNE)	IS THIS CLEAR?
	(815)	(TRIBUNE)	TAKE 810, AND RETURN HOME.
	(815)	(TRIBUNE)	((COURSE)) 065, DISTANCE OF 65 MILES.
	(815)	(TRIBUNE)	ROGER, THIS IS CLEAR.
	(815)	(TRIBUNE)	ROGER, I RECEIVED. I WILL NOTIFY YOU IMMEDIATELY AS TO WHAT TO DO
	(815)	(TRIBUNE)	ROGER.
1316Z/1516S			
	—	(TRIBUNE)	PAY ATTENTION:

TIME	TO	FROM	TEXT
	815	TRIBUNE	ROGER, THIS IS CLEAR. ACCORDING TO THE INSTRUC-TION, WHOEVER HAS THE [MO]ST FUEL.
1317Z/1517S			
	(815)	(TRIBUNE)	ROGER, I'M CHECKING ON IT.
	815	TRIBUNE	PAY ATTENTION: WHOEVER HAS THE MOST FUEL BETWEEN YOU WILL RETURN HOME, THE ONE WITH THE LEAST WILL GO TO EL ARISH.
	815	TRIBUNE	NOT AT THE PRESENT TIME. [A]PPARENTLY THE ONE WHO IS GOING TO EL ARISH WILL RETURN LATER.
	(815)	(TRIBUNE)	[W]HICH ONE OF YOU IS GOING HOME?
	(815)	(TRIBUNE)	WHO IS GOING HOME?
	(815)	(TRIBUNE)	OK.
[TIME?]			
	815	TRIBUNE	ROGER, THIS IS KNOWN. I RECEIVED THE NOTICE AND IT'S KNOWN THAT THESE ORDERS CAME FROM ABOVE.
1321Z/1521S			
			———GO OVER TO 170 ON THE WAY HOME.
	810	TRIBUNE	HE SAYS OVER TO 170 ON THE WAY HOME.
	(TRIBUNE)	(810)	ROGER.
1327Z/1527S			
	JEWEL	815	((CALLS)) ((RPTS)).

((TR-NOTE: 815 CALLS JEWEL UNTIL 1328Z/1538S))

((END OF RADIO TELEPHONE CONVERSATION))

XXXMENT: THIS ACTIVITY HAD BEEN REPORTED IN A CONDENSED VERSION
BY USA-556 IN ITS 2/JL5_/R23-67, 08205Z, AND FOLLOW-UPS.

NOTES

Chapter 1. Roll In on Target

1. It is customary for military aircraft flights to be assigned radio call signs. During the June 1967 war, Israel Air Force Mirage IIIGJ flights were designated by radio call signs in Hebrew named after household items. The flight that first attacked the *Liberty* was designated *Kursa*, which means "armchair." Another Mirage IIIGJ flight call sign was *Menorah*, meaning "lamp." The Super-Mystère B2 aircraft flights were assigned call signs named after cigarettes. The second flight to attack the *Liberty* was a flight of Super-Mystère B2 aircraft call-signed "Royal." The Mystère IV aircraft flights were call-signed after world leaders, "Churchill," "Roosevelt," "Nixon," etc.

   The full name of the *Kursa* lead pilot remains classified under Israeli policy, although part of his name has been inadvertently disclosed. This author personally interviewed the pilot. The Mirage IIIC was developed in France by Dassault with substantial assistance from Col. Danny Shapira, the chief test pilot for Israel Aircraft Industries. Many modifications resulted from his recommendations. Bernard Wacquet, the sales director at Dassault, designated the Mirage IIIC aircraft sold to Israel as Mirage IIICJ. The *J* stood for *Juif*, the French word for Jew. Aside from the letter designation and the replacement of the SEPR 844 rocket motor facilities with two 30 mm cannons, the J aircraft were essentially the same as the French Mirage IIIC. Bill Gunston, *An Illustrated Guide to the Israeli Air Force* (New York: Arco, 1982), 88.

2. The author has been criticized by some jet pilots for writing that the Mirage flew at "nearly 600 miles per hour" in the strafing run. The critics claim strafing runs are conducted at between 450 and 500 knots. As a pilot who primarily flew propeller powered aircraft and never flew a strafing run in a jet supersonic aircraft, I may have overstated the speed of the run. If the run was at 450 rather than 600 it changes the rate of closure from a half mile every three seconds to a half mile every four and a half seconds and increases the margin for error from three seconds to four and a half seconds. I have spoken with Mirage IIIC pilots who confirm that when flying an attack run, they fly as fast as they are able, to minimize the time the enemy has available to shoot at them, and that some have strafed at speeds in excess of 550. It is suggested that the one-and-one-half-second differential has no important effects on the facts of this event.

3. The ammunition load for each gun was about 125 rounds. The total firing time to expend all the ammunition was about seven seconds. Each plane could fire a little over

two seconds in each of its three runs. In that time the plane would move almost a half-mile over the earth's surface and then break away. If firing started just inside a mile from target, it ceased and the plane broke away about a half mile from the target.

Data on the guns and planes from Gunston, *Illustrated Guide,* 86, and Peter B. Mersky, *Israeli Fighter Aces: The Definitive History* (North Branch, Minn.: Specialty Press, 1997), 47.

4. Military time is on a twenty-four-hour clock. 1358 is 1:58 p.m.

5. The Incidents at Sea Agreement is unique in that it is not a treaty between nations but an agreement between the U.S. Navy and the Soviet Navy.

6. The 1967 cruise book of the *America* shows a picture of Rear Adm. L. Geis at a news conference on board the *America* on June 9, 1967, together with a picture of the briefing board used by the admiral for his briefing. The board indicates Soviet surveillance on June 5, 1967, by DLG 381, a Kashin-class guided-missile destroyer. This destroyer was mentioned in a message from COMSIXTHFLT 022032Z June 67: "3. Soviet Kashin-Class DLG-381 021700 posit 34-24N, 23-37E, course 270, speed 18."

See also Neil Sheehan, "A Larger Soviet Vessel Follows U.S. Carrier in Mediterranean," *New York Times,* June 4, 1967, 4. Sheehan, writing on board the USS *America,* described no. 381 as a large guided-missile destroyer (six thousand tons) of the Kashin class that had appeared on the scene on Friday, June 2, 1967.

On June 6, the Soviet surveillance was again by DLG 381. On June 7 the Soviet surveillance was by DLG 383, which was identified in *Life* magazine, June 16, 1967, as a Kashin-class guided-missile destroyer. *Life* reported that two days before the fighting in the Middle East broke out, DLG 383 sailed through the Bosporus past Istanbul en route to the eastern Mediterranean.

In 1967 the U.S. Navy used the designation *DLG* (guided-missile frigate) to indicate a large, missile-armed destroyer. In 1975 the U.S. Navy belatedly dropped the confusing *DLG* designation and began using *DDG* (guided-missile destroyer).

7. The USS *America* 1967 cruise book quotes this message in full. See CVA-66 News Release, no. 29–67. The book contains several pages of pictures of various Soviet warships in tight formation with the USS *America* task group.

8. Phil G. Goulding, *Confirm or Deny: Informing the People on National Security* (New York: Harper & Row, 1970), 146–48; and Jack Broughton, *Going Downtown: The War against Hanoi and Washington* (New York: Pocket Books, 1990), 193–210.

9. Goulding, *Confirm or Deny,* 137–67.

10. Ibid., 145.

11. Ibid., 144.

12. Ibid., 152.

13. The summit meeting did in fact take place shortly thereafter, on June 23 and 24, 1967, at Glassboro, N.J.

14. There are many excellent accounts of the June 1967 war. See, e.g., Randolph S. Churchill and Winston S. Churchill, *The Six Day War* (Boston: Houghton Mifflin, 1967); Brig.

Gen. S. L. A. Marshall, *Swift Sword: The Historical Record of Israel's Victory, June 1967* (New York: American Heritage Publishing, 1967); Associated Press, *Lightning Out of Israel: The Six Day War in the Middle East* (New York: Associated Press, 1967); Raphael Bashan, *The Victory: The Six-Day War of 1967* (Tel Aviv: E. Lewin-Epstein, 1967); J. N. Westwood and Edgar O'Ballance, *The Third Arab-Israeli War* (Hamden, Conn.: Archon Books, 1972); J. W. Westwood, *The History of the Middle East Wars* (New York: Exeter Books, 1984), 80–107.

15. See Benjamin Franklin Cooling, ed., *Case Studies in the Development of Close Air Support*, Air Force History (Washington, D.C.: Government Printing Office, 1990). Brereton Greenhous wrote the section titled "The Israeli Experience." Greenhous comments on the 1956 Suez campaign, "During Operation *Kadesh,* the Israelis claimed a sortie rate of better than four per day for their jets and about two and one-half per day for their propeller-driven aircraft. It seems unlikely that the Egyptians achieved a rate of one sortie per day" (p. 501).

This author believes that the Israel Air Force improved its turnaround time between 1956 and 1967 and that the Arab air forces did not. It is noted: "The Egyptian Air Staff had planned that in the event of war with Israel it would have its attacking aircraft over Israeli targets about once every three hours; this allowed comfortably for a turn around time of two hours, with which Egyptian ground staff and pilots could cope; and for aircraft to make two or three sorties a day." Westwood and O'Ballance, *The Third Arab-Israeli War,* 79–80. Other experts believe that the Jordanian air force was well trained and capable of more than one sortie a day in 1967. This may be so, but there is no evidence confirming these assessments. One explanation of why the Egyptians claimed that U.S. and British aircraft participated against Egypt was that the Egyptian leadership could not conceive that Israel turned its aircraft around so many times in one day. The conception was based on their own capability, and therefore they believed that other aircraft were involved.

16. Churchill and Churchill, *The Six Day War,* 89–90.

17. Prior to 1948 there were various military and paramilitary Jewish forces in Palestine. See Zeev Schiff, *History of the Israeli Army (1870–1974)* (San Francisco: Straight Arrow Books, 1974).

18. Ezer Weizman's distinguished career culminated in his serving as president of Israel from 1993 to 2000.

19. *Ibrahim al-Awwal,* meaning "Abraham the First," was built in Great Britain as a Hunt-class destroyer. It was acquired by Egypt and named in honor of the son of Muhamed Ali, the founder of the royal dynasty that ruled Egypt until the Egyptian revolution of 1952.

20. Martin van Creveld, *The Sword and the Olive: A Critical History of the Israeli Defense Force* (New York: Public Affairs, 1998), 147. The *Kersaint* is listed in *Jane's Fighting Ships* of 1956–57 as D622.

21. See Sherry Sontag and Christopher Drew with Annette Lawrence Drew, *Blind Man's Bluff: The Untold Story of American Submarine Espionage* (New York: Harper

Paperbacks, 1999), 54, where the authors state that "the Soviets signaled 'Able, Able'—international Morse code for 'Who are you? Identify yourself.' *Gudgeon* sent back, 'Able, Able.'" See also Trevor Armbrister, *A Matter of Accountability: The True Story of the Pueblo Affair* (New York: Coward-McCann, 1970), 121: "Now a destroyer on his port bow flashed 'Alpha Alpha'—identify yourself."

22. Interview of Moshe Oren by this author on January 11, 1990, in Tel Aviv, Israel.

23. Interview of Capt. Shmuel ("Samek") Yanay, commanding officer of the Israel Navy destroyer flotilla during the 1956 Sinai campaign, by this author on January 16,1990, in Tel Aviv, Israel.

24. Van Creveld, *The Sword and the Olive,* 147.

25. Interviews of Rear Adm. Shlomo Erell by this author: August 16, 1989, Haifa, Israel; January 13, 1990, Caesaria, Israel; June 16, 1990, Caesaria; August 16, 1991, Caesaria; June 7, 1992, Caesaria; June 6, 1993,Caesaria; and October 20, 1994, Haifa.

26. According to *Jane's Fighting Ships, 1966–67* (London: Jane's Publishing), 146–47, in 1967 the Israel Navy consisted of twenty-nine warships: four submarines; three destroyers (*Eilat* [formerly HMS *Zealous*] and *Jaffa* [formerly HMS *Zodiac*], both Z-class destroyers, and *Haifa* [formerly Egyptian destroyer *Ibrahim al-Awwal,* before that the Chinese *Lin Fu,* originally HMS *Mendip,* a British Hunt-class destroyer); nine motor torpedo boats; two high-speed gunboats; five patrol vessels; and six amphibious craft.

27. Abraham Rabinovich, *The Boats of Cherbourg: The Secret Israeli Operation That Revolutionized Naval Warfare* (New York: Seaver Books/Henry Holt, 1988). The Israel Navy has a very important role on a day-to-day basis in guarding Israel's coastline against terrorist intrusions. It continues to accomplish this mission in a very effective manner.

28. From this author's annotated English translation of a Hebrew transcript of the Israel Air Force audiotapes of pilot/controller transmissions on June 8, 1967.

29. Interviews of Aharon Yifrach by this author: January 15, 1990, Ashkelon, Israel; January 4, 1993, Ashkelon; April 1, 1997, telephone conversation from Miami, Fla., to Ashkelon; April 7, 1997, telephone conversation from Miami to Ashkelon.

30. Rabinovich, *Boats of Cherbourg,* 69.

31. JCS message 011545Z June 67.

32. See *Report of House Armed Services Subcommittee of the Committee on Armed Services,* House of Representatives, 92d Cong., 1st sess., under authority of H. Res. 201, May 10, 1971 (Washington, D.C.: Government Printing Office, 1971).

Chapter 2. The Two-Month Crisis

1. The critical time period from April 7, 1967, through June 4, 1967, is covered in detail in several excellent sources. See Richard B. Parker, introduction to *The Six Day War: A Retrospective,* ed. Richard B. Parker (Gainesville: University of Florida Press, 1996); L. Carl Brown, "Origins of the Crisis," chap. 1 in *The Six Day War,* ed. Parker; Ahron Bregman and Jihan El-Tahri, *The Fifty Years War: Israel and the Arabs* (New York: TV Books, 1998, 1999), chaps. 7–10.

2. *New York Times*, April 8, 1967, 1.

3. See "USS *Liberty* Command History Report, 1967," available at the Naval Historical Center, Navy Yard, Washington, D.C. Why was the *Liberty* off Africa? The ship may have been sent in part to monitor the deteriorating situation in Nigeria following the breakaway of the short-lived Republic of Biafra. In addition, from May 2 to June 2, 1967, a team of Naval Oceanographic Office (NAVOCEANO) scientists were on board studying the unique application of the Navy Navigation Satellite System to problems of precise positioning in equatorial areas. Their mission was canceled, and the team left the ship at Rota, Spain, on June 2; "USS *Liberty* Command History Report, 1967," 27–28 of enclosure 1.

4. Richard B. Parker, *The Politics of Miscalculation in the Middle East* (Bloomington: Indiana University Press, 1993), 3.

5. Parker, *Politics of Miscalculation*, 79, quoting Egyptian vice president Zakaria Muhieddin: "He [Nasser] acted like a man playing poker. He was bluffing, but a successful bluff means your opponent must not know which cards you are holding. In this case Nasser's opponent could see his hand in the mirror and knew he was only holding a pair of deuces."

6. Interview of Maj. Gen. Ahmed H. Halim by this author, October 18, 1994, at the National Center for Middle East Studies, Cairo, Egypt.

7. Parker, *Politics of Miscalculation*, 41.

8. Ibid., 43.

9. Ibid., 44.

10. Parker, *Six Day War*, xviii.

11. Randolph S. Churchill and Winston S. Churchill, *The Six Day War* (Boston: Houghton Mifflin, 1967), 36; Parker, *Six Day War*, 189. The United Arab Republic (UAR) was a union of Egypt and Syria into a single country formed in 1958 and from which Syria withdrew in 1961, thus dealing a severe blow to Nasser's dream of becoming the leader of a "progressive" revolutionary Arab world and of Pan-Arabism. Egypt continued to use the UAR flag and the term "UAR" in reference to itself until January 1, 1972.

12. Parker, *Politics of Miscalculation*, 47.

13. Israel mobilized 438,000 men in less than forty-eight hours without a public announcement.

14. Numerous reports confirm complete Egyptian control of Sharm al-Shaykh by May 22, 1967.

15. Message from JCS [Joint Chiefs of Staff] to USCINCEUR [U.S. Commander in Chief Europe] 201910Z May 67: "1. (S) Confirming reftelcon [most likely refers to telephone conversation as opposed to teletype conference] it is understood that elements of SIXTHFLT are being moved to Eastern Med. Center of Gravity of area of operations will be within two days steaming of the Eastern Shore with Eastern edge no more than one days time."

16. Max Frankel, "Hammarskjold Memo on Mideast Disclosed," *New York Times*, June 19, 1967, 1.

17. Under this international maritime treaty, signed in 1936, the Soviets were required to give ten days' notice of sending warships from the Black Sea through the Bosporus and into the Mediterranean.

18. Commander, Service Squadron Eight (COMSERVRON EIGHT) message 240020Z May 1967. At the time, the *Liberty* was under the operational control of COMSERVRON EIGHT, a component of Commander in Chief, Atlantic Fleet (CINCLANTFLT).

19. The Foreign Broadcast Information Service is a part of the Central Intelligence Agency, under the direction of the deputy director for science and technology. It records radio broadcasts in original languages around the world. It then translates the text, prints it in booklet format by region, and distributes the information.

20. James Bamford, *The Puzzle Palace: A Report on America's Most Secret Agency* (New York: Penguin Books, 1982/1983), 280.

21. Message from *Liberty* 241732Z, May 1967. 0530Z = Greenwich mean time (GMT). This was 0730 Sinai time, 0030 eastern standard time, and 0130 eastern daylight time.

22. This meeting was described to this author by Eugene V. Rostow during an interview in Washington, D.C., on April 29, 1992. Another account of the meeting was presented by Ambassador Ephraim Evron in Ambassador Parker's book *The Six Day War: A Retrospective*. On page 134 of the book there is a picture captioned "Foreign Minister Abba Eban calling on President Lyndon Johnson, May 26, 1967." The picture shows Assistant Secretary of State Joseph P. Sisco, Israeli ambassador Avraham Harman, and Minister Counselor Ephraim Evron as also in attendance at the meeting. The accounts of the meeting are similar.

23. Interview of Eugene V. Rostow by this author on April 19, 1992, in Washington, D.C.

24. There is a disagreement among reports on whether a vote was taken at this meeting on whether to attack or to allow the time the Americans had requested to achieve an international solution to the navigation problem.

25. CINCUSNAVEUR message to COMSIXTHFLT 270152Z May 67: "A. Routine training operations may be conducted North and West of the line connecting 36–00N9, 28–30E3 and coast of Libya at 23–00E5. B. No air ops auth within one zero zero miles of the UAR."

26. *New York Times*, May 30, 1967, 2. The article with dateline Beirut, Lebanon, referenced Damascus radio and went on: "The radio said that Brigadier General Mahmoud Ereim signed for Iraq and Major General Adel Sheik Amin signed for the Syrian Defense ministry. General Ereim arrived in Damascus, Syria's capital, last Wednesday with the first Iraqui [*sic*] troops for stationing on the Syrian border facing Israel."

27. At this time the *Liberty* came first under the operational control of Commander in Chief, European Command (USCINCEUR) and then immediately was assigned to Adm. John S. McCain Jr., Commander in Chief, U.S. Naval Forces, Europe (CINCUSNAVEUR). See JCS message 291602Z May 67 and USCINCEUR message 300932Z May 67. Thus as of June 1, the *Liberty*'s chain of command was from JCS to USCINCEUR to CINCNAVEUR.

28. Bamford reports that the *Liberty* "carried only French linguists" (*Puzzle Palace*, 281). This is contrary to what Staff Sgt. Bryce Lockwood, USMC, is reported to have told Maury Maverick of the *San Antonio Express-News*.

29. Conversation between Sergeant Lockwood, USMC, and this author on June 8, 1991, in Washington, D.C. To the question "Were there any Hebrew linguists aboard?," Sergeant Lockwood replied, "Nope, just Arabic and Russian, we were interested in the Russkies." This is corroborated by an interview of Lockwood reported by Maury Maverick in his article "Marines Met Death on *Liberty*" in the *San Antonio Express-News*, August 11, 1996.

    Conspiracy theorists have alleged that there were or may have been Hebrew linguists on board. In particular Communications Technician First Class Richard K. Baker, now Communications Technician Chief Baker, retired, is alleged to have been a Hebrew linguist. Chief Baker has not participated in the discussions of his linguistic qualifications and could not be found for an interview.

    This author believes that there were no Hebrew linguists on the *Liberty*, primarily because the ship's preassigned patrol pattern would not have been in the receiving range of any Israeli land-based VHF or UHF transmissions.

30. As a result of the start of the war on June 5, 1967, the ceremony for presentation of Nolte's credentials was canceled. *New York Times*, June 6, 1967, 17.

31. *Liberty*'s sailing orders, transmitted in JCS message 011545Z June 67, directed her to proceed from Point Alpha to Point Bravo, 31-22.3° N, 33-42° E; thence to Point Charlie, 31-31° N, 33-00° E. At the time these orders were issued, Egypt controlled the Gaza Strip. The closest point of approach to Israel-controlled territory, which was located northwest of Point Alpha and across the Gaza Strip, was more than twenty-five miles from Point Alpha on the day the orders were issued.

32. Interview of Gen. Mordechai Hod, commander of the Israel Air Force in 1967, on January 11, 1990, at Tel Aviv. General Hod told this author that only four planes were held back on the ground. Nadav Safran, *From War to War: The Arab-Israeli Confrontation, 1948–1967* (New York: Pegasus, 1969), 325, suggests that twelve aircraft were held back, with four on the ground and eight flying combat air patrol over Israel. See also Edgar O'Ballance, *The Third Arab-Israeli War* (Hamden, Conn.: Archon Books, 1972), 66.

33. A "back-channel" message is a message sent by other than the regular or formal or official communications network. The message from Israel to Jordan was sent through Swedish general Odd Bull, at the United Nations.

34. Personal interview with (name withheld by request) on January 14, 1990, at Tel Aviv. He was the commanding officer of Israeli *MTB 206* on June 8, 1967.

35. Arthur Lall, *The UN and the Middle East Crisis, 1967* (New York: Columbia University Press, 1968), 57.

36. Churchill and Churchill, *Six Day War*, 161.

37. Interview of Aharon Yifrach, who was combat information center officer on *MTB 204* on June 8, 1967, by this author on January 15, 1990, at Ashkelon, Israel.

38. House Armed Services Committee Report of May 10, 1971. There is substantial controversy over the exact time that operational control of the *Liberty* was changed to the Sixth Fleet. According to the *Liberty* deck log, her position at 2000Z on June 5, 1967, was 35-47.7° N and 17-37.3° E (about 125 nautical miles [nm] WSW of the eastern tip of Sicily). On June 6, 1967, at 0800Z her position was 34-49° N and 21-37.8° E (about 95 nm WSW of the western tip of Crete). The Tuesday, June 6,1967, deck log entry, signed by Ens. M. M. Watson, USNR, reads: "00–04 Steaming independently on course 111, speed 17 knots. Enroute from Rota, Spain, for operations in the eastern Mediterranean Sea in accordance with CINCUSNAVEUR MOVORD 7–67. Condition of readiness III modified and material condition Yoke are set. 0136 c/c 106."

By interpolation or by dead reckoning, her position at 0001Z on June 6, 1967, was about 35-25° N, 18-57° E. This position was close to the Sixth Fleet and about 210 nm west of the western tip of Crete. Today, with modern military global positioning systems, it is possible to determine location on the face of the earth to within a few yards. In 1967, even state-of-the-art navigation on ships was not nearly so precise. It is therefore possible that the positions reported in the *Liberty* deck log were not exact. Therefore, the positions and locations indicated herein should be considered approximate positions. However, variations of even a few miles are not significant to the story being told.

39. See CINCUSNAVEUR message to COMSIXTHFLEET and *Liberty* 061357Z June 67 acknowledged by the *Liberty* in 062000Z June 67 and 062036Z June 67. Now a fourth level of reporting was added to the chain of command that controlled *Liberty*'s operations: JCS to USCINCEUR to CINCUSNAVEUR to COMSIXTHFLT.

40. "The UN: Egypt Refuses to Agree to Council Truce Deadline," *Washington Post,* June 8, 1967, 1. "Israelis Rout Arabs, Approach Suez, Break Blockade, Occupy Old Jerusalem; Agree to UN Cease-Fire; UAR Rejects It," *New York Times,* June 8, 1967. Office of Public Information, United Nations, "Adoption of Second Cease-fire Resolution," *Year Book of the United Nations: 1967* (New York: United Nations, 1969), 177–78.

41. House Armed Services Committee Report of May 10, 1971.

42. JCS top secret message to USCINCEUR 080ll0Z June 67. Although the *Liberty* was an information addressee on this message, which was intended to keep her one hundred miles off the coast of Sinai, the message could not be received by the *Liberty* as a normal message over the fleet broadcast system because of its top-secret classification.

43. U.S. Navy Court of Inquiry, testimony of Ens. John D. Scott, USNR, 59.

44. In 1967 Uri Meretz was an intelligence officer with the rank of lieutenant commander in the Israel Navy, on a program of study at Tel Aviv University. When the 1967 war began, he was assigned as naval intelligence representative to general headquarters. Later he was promoted to the rank of commander and served as deputy chief of naval intelligence.

45. Israel Defense Forces, History Department, Research and Instruction Branch, *The Attack on the "Liberty" Incident,* June 1982, 6 [hereafter cited as IDF History]. The aircraft used for these reconnaissance missions was a standard Transport Command

Nord 2501 Noratlas, which was flown by an air force crew with a naval officer on board as an observer.

46. IDF History, 7, confirms: "Later at 0603 hours, an additional report arrived from the plane, which described the vessel as a supply ship of the US Navy."

47. Thames TV, *Attack on the "Liberty,"* aired on British television on Tuesday, January 27, 1987, script 26, items 127 and 128.

48. Interview of Uri Meretz by this author on June 11, 1992, at Tel Aviv. Meretz was not certain whether he spoke to the chief of naval intelligence or to a naval intelligence officer named Moshe Barnea when passing this information.

49. Stella Maris, or Star of the Sea, was the name given to an underground bunker atop Mount Carmel in Haifa originally constructed by the British armed forces during the Mandate period. It was used by the Israel Navy as its command-and-control center during the 1956 Suez campaign and during the 1967 war. It contained a large room where the naval commanders sat on an elevated platform and looked out over a large tabletop painted to display the seas around Israel. Enlisted personnel placed colored wedges on the map table to indicate the tactical situation. This was done World War II–style, with wooden rods or bridges to push the wedges about the board. The facility is located over sixty miles north of the Kirya, where Israel's Ministry of Defense and military general headquarters, except for the navy, were located.

50. Interview of Uri Meretz by this author on June 16, 1990, at Tel Aviv, and interview of chief of naval intelligence [name not to be disclosed] by this author on January 12, 1990, at Haifa.

51. House Armed Services Committee Report of May 10, 1971.

52. CINCUSNAVEUR message to COMSIXTHFLT 080455Z June 67. The message instructed Vice Admiral Martin to "take for action" JCS 080110Z.

53. Thames TV script, 28, items 135 and 136.

54. COMSIXTHFLT secret message to *Liberty* 080917Z June 67.

55. House Armed Services Committee Report of May 10, 1971, and Joint Chiefs of Staff Fact Finding Team Report (the Russ Report).

Chapter 3. Why Was the *Liberty* in Harm's Way?

1. Robert Silverberg, *If I Forget Thee, O Jerusalem* (New York: William Morrow, 1970), 577.

2. Interview with former Secretary of State Dean Rusk by this author, April 5, 1989, in Athens, Georgia.

3. Interviews with Ambassador Ephraim Evron by this author on June 7, 1988; August 15, 1989; and January 16, 1990; all in Tel Aviv.

4. Interview of Ambassador Richard B. Parker by this author on March 17, 1997, in Washington, D.C., and telephone interviews and exchanges of correspondence. Parker was a political counselor assigned to the U.S. embassy in Cairo in June 1967.

5. Interview of the CIA station chief assigned to Tel Aviv during 1967 by this author, conducted in the United States in 1988. Confirmed by interview of Ephraim Evron,

Israel's deputy chief of mission in Washington during 1967, on June 7, 1988, in Tel Aviv. See also Silverberg, *If I Forget Thee,* 574–99.

6. In 1967 the U.S. satellite program was known as "Corona"; it had an imaging capability but no listening capability and no real-time capability. Likewise, the U-2, which was operating in the area, had certain imaging capability but no listening capability, and it too was not real-time. The SR-71, which first flew in 1964 and which observed the first detonation of a hydrogen bomb by the People's Republic of China in June 1967, was not yet operating in the Middle East in 1967, and it too was not a real-time electromagnetic-spectrum listener. There is no record of the United States operating RC-135 aircraft in the Middle East at that time. There is new evidence that NSA was also operating EC-121 intelligence-gathering aircraft in the area during the 1967 war.

7. James M. Ennes Jr., *Assault on the "Liberty"* (New York: Random House, 1979), 20 n. l.

8. Ibid., 8.

9. Department of the Navy, Chief of Naval Operations, *Law of Naval Warfare,* NWIP 10–2 (Washington, D.C., 1955).

10. Ibid., see para. 430, 4–6: "430 The Areas of Naval Warfare: a. The General Area of Naval Warfare. The general area within which the naval forces of a belligerent are permitted to conduct operations includes: the high seas, the territorial sea and internal waters of belligerents. b. The Immediate Area of Naval Operations. Within the immediate area or vicinity of naval operations, a belligerent may establish special restrictions (see, for example, paragraph 520a) upon the activities of neutral vessels and aircraft and may prohibit altogether such vessels and aircraft from entering the area. Neutral vessels which fail to comply with a belligerent's orders expose themselves to the risk of being fired upon."

There is doubt as to whether Israel declared the area off El Arish an "immediate area of naval operations." President Nasser declared, "I am going back to the pre-1956 rules governing the Gulf of Aqaba," in a speech on May 21, 1967, which was published in *Al Ahram* on May 22, 1967. In a letter to this author dated November 27, 1994, this declaration has been interpreted by Abdel Monem Said Aly, director of the Centre for Political and Strategic Studies, Cairo, Egypt, as a "declaration of Egypt on the waters off the Sinai as a war zone." A translation of the declaration from Arabic (supplied by a professor of Arabic at the University of Miami, Abla Kahlil) does not seem to relate to the waters off the Sinai. Nevertheless, the area was in fact a war zone, and thus any neutral vessel entering the area exposed itself to the risk of being fired upon under U.S. Navy doctrine in effect at the time, as well as under the international law of naval warfare.

11. NWIP 10–2 of 1955, para. 501 (p. 5–3) provides that even "neutral merchant vessels acquire enemy character and are liable to the same treatment as *enemy warships and military aircraft* (see paragraph 503a) when . . . taking a direct part in the hostilities on the side of the enemy [or] acting in any capacity as a naval or military auxiliary to an enemy's armed forces." Para. 503 (p. 5–5) provides that "enemy warships and military aircraft (including naval and military auxiliaries) may be attacked and destroyed outside neutral jurisdiction."

12. Even following the *Liberty* incident, the listening potential of the type of equipment the *Liberty* carried was almost unknown outside of U.S. intelligence circles. Not until the United States had a sky full of satellites was it deemed prudent to relax the classification of the capabilities of technical research ships, and even then some classification was deemed prudent.

13. In some circumstances VHF/UHF radio waves bounce off the ionosphere or channel and can be heard beyond the horizon. See Joseph F. Bouchard, *Command in Crises* (New York: Columbia University Press, 1991), 141 n. 10. See also R. C. Shearer and Jay Rosenthal, "Don't Fall in the Radar Hole," U.S. Naval Institute *Proceedings* (December 1973), 55.

14. The range is extended if the transmitter or receiver is elevated. Under normal conditions aircraft can receive VHF and UHF transmissions over greater distances while flying at high altitudes. The extension of reception is directly related to increased altitude of the aircraft or the elevation of the transmitting antenna. Under certain conditions on clear, dry days, a phenomenon called "channeling" occurs that allows the straight-line radio waves to be received at a longer distance.

15. Bruce Edwards, "When Friends Look Like Foes," *Rutland Herald, Vermont Sunday Magazine,* March 11, 2001, 3–11.

    The NSA operation on board *Liberty* has been generally referred to as a "department," which would indicate it was within the structure of the ship's command. It is likely that it was in fact a "cryptologic detachment," which would explain the ability of Commander Lewis to originate messages to the detachment's command at NSA without going through the ship's commanding officer, although not directly to any U.S. naval authority. (This distinction will become important later in the story.)

16. Francis A. "Frank" Raven, the former chief of GENS (General Soviet), had been responsible for analyzing and deciphering the medium-level cipher systems and reading the unencrypted traffic of the Soviet Union at NSA. In June 1967, Raven was chief of G Group, the former ALLO, or "ALL Others," and was responsible for electronic intelligence (ELINT) intercepts of more than a hundred nations. He held this position until 1975. See James Bamford, *The Puzzle Palace: Inside the National Security Agency, America's Most Secret Intelligence Organization* (Harmondsworth, England: Penguin, 1983), 125, 269, and 273. "'Now frankly,' recalled Raven, 'we didn't think at that point that it was highly desirable to have a ship right in the Middle East; it would be too explosive a situation'"(Bamford, p. 280). According to the original NSA plan, the *Liberty* was scheduled to depart that same day and steam for the eastern end of the Island of Crete, where she would remain "parked" (p. 281).

17. Ennes, *Assault on the "Liberty,"* 13.

18. Message from COMSERVRON EIGHT to *Liberty*, date/time group 240020Z May 1967 (May 24, 1967, at twenty minutes past midnight GMT. This was 7:20 p.m. EST and 8:20 p.m. EDT.) See the Russ Report.

19. Message from COMSIXTHFLT to *Liberty*, 062349Z June 1967. See the Russ Report.

20. See the Russ Report, tab 24, annex C: "10. (C) The COMSIXTHFLT message on June 1967, [062349Z] instructed USS *Liberty* to change operational control to COMSIXTHFLT and provided instructions regarding threats of attack, logistical requirements, contact reports with unidentified or hostile ships/aircraft and emergency action procedures. Specific instructions regarding communications procedures were also given. This message was probably undelivered to the USS Liberty since she shifted to the Asmara broadcast on 7 June 1967 as originally scheduled by her 2 June 1967 movement order."

     See also U.S. Navy Court of Inquiry, *Liberty Incident, Record of Proceedings,* app. 1, which shows that the message was transmitted on fleet broadcast from Asmara at approximately 070532Z, and, for some unknown reason, not recorded in *Liberty*'s radio logs as having been received.

21. E-mail message from Maurice Bennett to this author, March 14, 2001, 11:10:47 a.m. EST.

22. House Committee on Armed Services, Armed Services Investigating Subcommittee, *Review of Department of Defense Worldwide Communications, Phase 1,* 92d Cong., 1st sess., May 10, 1971, 9 n. 3.

23. House Armed Services Committee, *Worldwide Communications.* See also the Russ Report.

24. There is substantial evidence of back-channel communication between CINCUSNAVEUR and the Sixth Fleet.

25. Phil G. Goulding, *Confirm or Deny: Informing the People on National Security* (New York: Harper & Row, 1970), 100.

26. Ibid., 102.

27. Ibid.

28. Ibid., 93.

29. Ibid., 102; Department of Defense news release no. 542–67.

30. The document remains partially classified and may be obtained only in "sanitized" form. The parentheses indicate the text obliterated on the sanitized document. It still bears the legend "Not Releasable to Foreign Nationals" and the notation "Contents of this publication should not be reproduced, or further disseminated outside the U.S. Intelligence Community, without permission of the Director."

31. National Security Agency, Central Security Service, "Attack on [deleted] the USS *Liberty* (S)-[deleted]," 1981, vii.

32. *Webster's New World Dictionary* and *New Webster's Dictionary,* s.v. "cover-up."

33. Goulding, *Confirm or Deny,* 137.

34. Telephone interview of Dr. Harold Saunders, the incumbent of the Near East Desk on the National Security Council in June 1967, by this author on March 28, 1991. When the question of the false press release was put to Dr. Saunders, he replied, "For every covert operation there has to be a cover story. That's our story."

35. Dean Rusk was interviewed by Thames TV for its documentary *Attack on the "Liberty."* The program aired on British television on Tuesday, January 27, 1987; script, 55, items 255 and 256. Dean Rusk died on December 20, 1994.

Chapter 4. The *Liberty* Targeted

1. The *Liberty* deck log indicates that the ship arrived at Point Alpha at 0849. The findings of the U.S. Navy court of inquiry concur with the deck log. The *Liberty* combat information center (CIC) log indicates 0835, and other sources cite other times. The Israel Defense Forces, History Department, Research and Instruction Branch, report *The Attack on the "Liberty" Incident*, June 1982, states 0843 [hereafter cited as IDF History]. These discrepancies are not significant for this study.

2. Message from USDAO Tel Aviv Israel to DIA, 082100Z June 67. Paragraph 4 refers to DAO 0812 reporting, "Egyptian shelling attack from sea in Gaza area reported by IDF yesterday."

3. The *Liberty* deck log of June 8, 1967, reports the explosions. Also, Commander McGonagle testified about the explosions before the naval court of inquiry, 33–34.

4. James M. Ennes Jr., *Assault on the "Liberty"* (New York: Random House, 1979), 56.

5. Whether the report of shelling from the sea on June 7, 1967, was the result of the sapper activity is not known.

6. Following the 1967 war, the IDF recognized this weak link in its command-and-control system and moved navy headquarters to the Kirya. One can only speculate on whether or not an earlier consolidation of navy command and control with the existing headquarters at the Kirya would have prevented the *Liberty* tragedy.

7. Interviews of Cdr. Moshe Oren, the MTB division commander; Ahron Yurach, the CIC officer on boat 204; Gil Keren, the commanding officer of boat 204; Uri "Chera" Tsur, a junior officer in training on board boat 206; and the commanding officers of boats 203 and 206 (who requested not to be identified), between January 11 and 18, 1990, in Tel Aviv and Ashkelon, Israel.

8. Israel naval headquarters war log, June 8, 1967, 081205 entry. See also war log of Division 914: "DIV 914 sailed out of Ashdod." June 8, 1967, 1120, entry.

9. Although *Jane's Fighting Ships* rated these motor torpedo boats at forty-two knots, interviews with the officers in command of the boats on June 8, 1967, and other Israeli naval officers familiar with the boats established that the boat engines were "high time"—that is, almost at the end of their useful lives and in need of overhaul. The boats' bottoms were encrusted, and thirty-six to thirty-eight knots was the best they could do on that day. The boat most recently out of overhaul was 203. It was the fastest of the three.

10. Israel naval headquarters war log 081330 entry.

11. MTB Division 914, war log, 081341. There is a slight discrepancy between the Israel naval headquarters war log, which reflects contact at 1343, and the air traffic controllers' audiotape, which reflects the vector to the target at 1345. Radars are "line of sight." Therefore, exactly on the surface of the earth or the sea they can "see" a target on the earth's surface at a range of nineteen statute, or 16.5 nautical, miles, because of the curvature of the earth. The radar antennas on the MTBs were mounted on their masts, about eighteen feet above the surface of the sea. In addition, the *Liberty*'s hull, superstructure, and masts projected about seventy feet

above the surface of the sea. These minor elevations would have slightly increased the reception range of the radar. Whether the MTBs' radar could "paint," or see, a reflected radar image at twenty-two miles or whether the *Liberty* and the MTBs were actually closer together is unknown. According to the positions reported by the *Liberty*'s commanding officer, the motor torpedo boats were about twenty miles away from the ship at the time of contact. If they were farther apart than normal radar range, then the ability of the radar to see over the horizon may be explained by channeling. It is known that the destroyers *Davis* and *Massey* reported radar contact with the *Liberty* the following morning at substantially more than twenty miles. See R. C. Shearer and Jay Rosenthal, "Don't Fall in the Radar Hole," U.S. Naval Institute *Proceedings* (December 1973).

12. "Gulli" is the nickname for Gullivir. He was either nineteen or twenty years of age at the time and was a regular navy sailor, with the rank of *samal*, which is equal to sergeant in the U.S. Army or third-class petty officer in the U.S. Navy.

13. Rounded to twenty-four miles.

14. For example, the Decca Bridgemaster radar now available for commercial ship navigation. The radar is integrated with GPS and gives a constant digital readout of the ship's latitude and longitude as well as course over the ground (COG) and speed over the ground (SOG). Placing the cursor on a target will give the target an automatic identification number and provide a digital readout of the target's course, speed, position, and distance. It will also instantly calculate and display the target's true bearing and relative bearing, as well as its closest point of approach.

15. Osa or Komar missile boats could have conducted shore bombardment with Soviet Styx SSM missiles. This type of shore bombardment did not occur during the 1967 war, and the full capability of these Soviet missile boats did not become known to the Israel Navy until many months after the war.

16. See Shearer and Rosenthal, "Radar Hole," 55.

17. The same procedure is followed today between the U.S. Air Force and the U.S. Navy. This was confirmed to this author by U.S. Air Force officers at the Kennedy School of Government, Harvard University, on April 5, 1995, and can be independently confirmed by merely consulting an experienced U.S. Air Force communications officer.

18. The 1300 position interpolated from the 1200 position in the *Liberty* deck log, 31-22.2 N, 33-41.1 E, moved forward on the course line five nautical miles, is 31-22.2 N, 33-36.1 E. This position for the *Liberty* is shown on the map in the IDF History. According to the *Liberty*'s commanding officer, the ship's position at 1300 was 31-25 N, 33-38 E. The positions do not agree. They are about five miles apart. That is why the term "approximate" is used. The five-mile difference is not significant. However, the IDF History indicates that the *Liberty* turned to the north when the air attacks began and continued due north until the torpedo attack was over. While it appears the initial turn to the north took place, Commander McGonagle testified that he held 283 degrees during the torpedo attack, though he conceded that he may have zigzagged.

19. Israel naval headquarters war log 081347 entry.

20. When the Thames TV producer was interviewing Rear Admiral Erell, Erell made several references to "the plot." Erell was referring to the plotting board, but the Thames TV producer thought that Erell was referring to "a plot." After several minutes, they got on the same wavelength, but for a short time Thames TV thought that Erell was making a confession.

21. The same procedure is followed in U.S. Navy court of inquiry procedures.

22. This author first heard this story during an interview of Rear Adm. Shlomo Erell in Israel on August 16, 1989. The general outline of this incident is mentioned by Randolph S. Churchill and Winston S. Churchill in their book *The Six Day War* (Boston: Houghton Mifflin, 1967), 100. See also Shearer and Rosenthal, "Radar Hole," 56. A similar false-image problem occurred on the night of August 4, 1964, in the Gulf of Tonkin, when radar operators on board the USS *Maddox* (DD 731) and *Turner Joy* (DD 951) saw echoes they evaluated as attacking boats. There were no attacking boats. The "ghosts" were very likely caused by anomalous propagation of radar energy resulting from unusual atmospheric conditions.

23. Interview of Pinchas Pinchasy by this author on January 12, 1990, at Technion University, Haifa.

24. *Menorah* (Hebrew for "lamp"), which was the call sign for a flight of Mirage IIICJ aircraft during the 1967 war.

25. Point Boaz was a geographic point in the Mediterranean at 31°36.5 N, 33°15 E, that the IAF designated as a point of entry and departure for Israel Air Force planes going into and out of the Suez and Egypt. The points on the *Liberty*'s patrol pattern were: Point Alpha, 31-27.2 N, 34-00 E; Point Bravo, 31-22.3 N, 33-42 E; and Point Charlie, 31-31 N, 33-00 E. Point Bravo is less than fifteen miles south and twenty-seven miles east of Point Boaz, a direct line distance of less than thirty-one nautical miles.

Point Charlie is less than six miles south and fifteen miles west of Point Boaz, a direct line distance of less than sixteen nautical miles.

26. Israel Air Force transcript of communications between air force headquarters and *Kursa* Flight, time 1351.

27. Interview of *Kursa* Flight leader by this author on June10,1990, at Tel Aviv; and interview of the *Kursa* wingman by author on June 17, 1990, at Tel Aviv. Corroborated by Israel Air Force audiotape of conversations between *Kursa* Flight and air control. (Names not released, by request.)

28. "Blue Max" was the nickname, or code name, that the Israelis used for the mark they put on their ships and armor to identify them as Israeli. In 1967 the Blue Max was a red background with a white cross on it, resembling the Swiss flag. This mark was used until well after 1973.

29. Interview of *Kursa* Flight leader by this author on June 10, 1992, at Tel Aviv.

30. There are many different accounts of the *Liberty* incident, and the times of the start of the first air attack vary from 1358 to 1405 local time. The *Liberty*'s "smooth" deck log, which was prepared after the attack, reflects the attack at

1400. The quartermaster log, which was usually written as events occurred, has 1358. At Israel Air Force headquarters all communications between air control and the pilots are recorded. The recording equipment has a woman's voice in the background repeating the time (hours and minutes) in Hebrew. When a voice transmission is made, the transmission blocks or records over the woman's voice citing the time. The Israel Air Force audiotape shows the *Kursa* flight leader commencing his dive at 1357.

31. Testimony of Cdr. William McGonagle at the U.S. Navy court of inquiry (record p. 37, JAG pagination p. 141).

32. These pictures form part of the exhibits to the U.S. Navy court of inquiry record. See U.S. Navy Court of Inquiry, *Liberty Incident, Record of Proceedings*, exhibit 9, pictures 16, 22, 27, and 29.

33. Testimony of Radioman Chief Smith, U.S. Navy Court of Inquiry transcript, 94. See also message NAVCOMUNIT Naples to CNO and CINCUSNAVEUR 112310Z July 67.

34. Message from USS *Saratoga* to COMSIXTHFLT 081358Z June 67: "This station received attack report from station Rock Star [*Liberty*] at 1210Z." See U.S. Navy Court of Inquiry exhibits 23 and 24, *Liberty*'s radio logs.

35. The *Liberty* rough and smooth radio logs reflect the first transmission of the distress call at 1158Z/1358 Sinai time and the first response from the *Saratoga* two minutes later, at 1200Z/1400 Sinai time. The time noted for the entry about switching transmitters was 1204Z/1404 Sinai. There is no question that the first report of the attack was received from the *Liberty* by the *Saratoga*. It seems doubtful that the first transmission from the *Liberty* occurred at the instant the first gun fired at the ship, 1358 Sinai time. Although the substance of the log entries is correct, it appears the times of the entries are not. This is quite obvious from the fact that the torpedo strike occurred at 1235Z/1435 Sinai, but it is reflected in the log as occurring at 1218Z/1418 Sinai. U.S. Navy Court of Inquiry exhibits 23 (rough log) and 24 (smooth log).

Chapter 5. The Air and Sea Attacks

1. According to William Green, *The World Guide to Combat Planes*, vol. 1 (Garden City, N.J.: Doubleday, 1967), the Mirage could have carried two air-to-air missiles, one each on the outer wing pylons. The inner wing pylons normally carried a 137-imperial-gallon (164 U.S. gallons) drop tank on a combat air patrol mission. Whether any other missile was hung on the center line pylon is unknown.

   There is a debate over whether the aircraft fired rockets or missiles at the *Liberty*. The pilot of the first aircraft, the *Kursa* Flight leader, told this author that his aircraft was armed with a couple of air-to-air missiles. If the aircraft had missiles, they were most likely AIM-9 Sidewinders, which are heat seekers. The use of this missile against a surface-ship target is questionable. Gun-camera film shows two distinct gunsights. *Kursa* Flight leader explained that one was for the 30 mm cannon and one was for the missiles.

Several persons who went on board the *Liberty* after the attack, including Rear Adm. (then Lt. [jg]) Paul E. Tobin Jr., USN (Ret.), have advised this author that they saw no sign of missile or rocket hits. Also, an Israeli naval officer, Capt. Yaacov Nitzan, advised this author that the Israel Air Force was concerned about its 30 mm shells passing through enemy aircraft without exploding and that to resolve this concern it employed a proximity fuse, which exploded the shells near, rather than upon, impact with the target. It is likely that some of the large holes attributed to rockets, or missiles, were in fact due to the 30 mm proximity-fuse explosions. It should also be remembered that the MTBs fired 20 mm and 40 mm cannons.

Capt. R. L. Arthur, fleet material officer, Service Force, COMSIXTHFLT, reported in a message from COMSIXTHFLT to COMSERVFORSIXTHFLT 091954Z June 1967, "H. Cannon holes from 2 inches to one foot in diameter throughout topside area, with associated cable damage in way of holes." Arthur made no mention of missile or rocket damage in his message.

2. The *Kursa* Flight leader went on to become a squadron commander then a base commander and ultimately achieved the rank of general in the Israel Air Force. He became the ace, with the second-highest number of victories of all Israeli fighter pilots.

3. U.S. naval officers who went on board the *Liberty* the following day reported little or no sign of any serious fire damage. The damage caused by the gasoline fires was limited, owing largely to the timely manner in which her crew brought the fires under control. The Israelis thought that one napalm canister struck the *Liberty*, but it may be that none actually hit. It is possible that one napalm canister hit the *Liberty* a glancing blow to the starboard bridge structure, forward of where the motor whaleboat was stored. Commander McGonagle makes no mention of being hit by a napalm canister. In fact, he does describe what may have been a napalm canister missing the ship. U.S. Court of Inquiry testimony of Commander McGonagle, beginning at p. 35: "On what appeared to be the last air attack on the ship, I observed a cylindrical object dropped from one of the aircraft as it was passing from port to starboard ahead of the ship. This object landed in the water an estimated 75 to 100 yards directly ahead of the ship. There was no explosion from this object, but it shattered into several pieces. It appeared to me that it might have been an empty wing tank."

Dr. Richard F. Keifer, the ship's doctor, in his testimony said, "But I didn't treat anyone that I would think of as having a napalm burn." U.S. Navy Court of Inquiry, *Liberty Incident, Record of Proceedings,* testimony of Dr. Keifer, p. 86.

4. COMSIXTHFLT to COMSERVFORSIXTHFLT 091954Z June 1967.

5. Royal Flight leader described the attacks by Royal Flight in an interview with this author on July 2, 1992, in Tel Aviv. At p. 39 of the testimony to the U.S. Navy court of inquiry by Commander McGonagle, he said he elected to steer 283° during the torpedo attack. He also testified that during the air attacks, "I do not recall whether I ordered any course changes to have the ship zig zag or not." It is suggested that the ship did turn during the air attacks. A turn to port would not have been prudent, as it would have taken the ship

toward the shore and shallow water. Thus a turn to starboard was no doubt made. This is further supported by the picture McGonagle took of the Super-Mystère flying from stem to bow across the ship. This coincides with the description given by Royal Flight leader. It also fits his description of making a 270° turn to west and crossing the ship from west to east with the sun behind him and the enhanced light on the bow that permitted him to read the bow marks. If *Liberty* had remained on the 283° heading during the air attack, then Royal Flight would have been attacking into the sun, which is a very unlikely choice when all the options were with the attacking aircraft.

6. Interview of Royal Flight leader on July 2, 1992, at Tel Aviv.

7. Official press release of the U.S. Department of Defense, June 28, 1967.

8. Thames TV transcript, *Attack on the "Liberty,"* item 194, 36, 39, 40.

9. During the 1967 war, Israel Air Force Mystère IV aircraft were assigned two-syllable radio call signs named after world leaders, such as Churchill, Roosevelt, Nixon.

10. The straight-line distance from Tel Nof Air Base to the vicinity of EL Arish is about 138 nautical miles. The Mystère IV had a maximum speed of 696 miles per hour and a cruise speed of 488 mph. A Mystère could easily have flown to the *Liberty* in this time. Bill Gunston, *An Illustrated Guide to the Israeli Air Force* (New York: Arco, 1982), 62.

11. James M. Ennes Jr., *Assault on the "Liberty"* (New York: Random House, 1979), 51, 52.

12. Immediate confidential message from CINCUSNAVEUR to COMDESRON ONE TWO 132335Z June 67.

13. Immediate confidential message from USS *Liberty* to SECNAV 140306Z June 67.

14. Message from SECNAV to CINCUSNAVEUR 192026Z June 67.

15. Message from NAVCOMUNIT NAPLES to CNO 061222Z July 67.

16. Testimony of Commander McGonagle at U.S. Navy Court of Inquiry, 39.

17. Secret message from USDAO Tel Aviv to CINCUSNAVEUR 191200Z June 67, sequence no. 0933 June 1967.

18. This press conference is reported in Clifford Hubbard, "*Liberty* Brings in Memories," *Norfolk Virginian-Pilot,* July 30, 1967, 1, 4. The Thames TV production *Attack on the "Liberty"* erroneously indicates that this press conference took place on board the aircraft carrier *America* a few days after the court of inquiry.

19. Thames TV, *Attack on the "Liberty,"* script, item 94, p. 19.

20. There is testimony in the U.S. Navy court of inquiry that one unoccupied gun tub was burning and the heat from the fire caused the ammunition to detonate and the gun to fire.

21. Division 914 war log, 8.

22. Israel Defense Forces, History Department, Research and Instruction Branch, *The Attack on the "Liberty" Incident,* June 1982 [hereafter cited as IDF History], 16.

23. Testimony of Commander McGonagle, U.S. Navy Court of Inquiry, 39–40.

24. See U.S. Department of the Navy, Hydrographic Office, *International Code Signals,* U.S. ed., pub. 102 (Washington, D.C.: Government Printing Office, 1968).

25. The Red Book got its name because it was first printed and bound with a red cover. Since then, the book has been reissued with a dark-green cover, but it is still called the Red Book. U.S Navy message from USDAO to CINCUSNAVEUR 191200Z refers

to the book by the color of its cover, Green Book. When this author obtained copies of the contents of the book from Israel Navy headquarters at Tel Aviv, it had a green cover but was still referred to as the Red Book.

26. The name of the commanding officer of MTB 203 is not disclosed per agreement with Field Security, Israel Defense Forces.

27. Interview of Uri "Chera" Tsur by the author on January 18, 1990, in Tel Aviv.

28. Israel Navy headquarters war log, June 8, 1967.

29. Telephone conversation with Cdr. Moshe Oren on August 31, 2001. This author was in Miami, and Oren was in Tel Aviv.

30. U.S. Navy Court of Inquiry, 39.

31. Interview of MTB 203 commander by this author on January 11, 1990, at Tel Aviv.

32. During the 1973 war the Israel Navy sank eighteen Syrian missile boats without the loss of a single Israeli missile boat. The navy is also reported to have sunk a few neutral ships and a Soviet resupply ship.

33. The Israeli ship that was struck by it own torpedo was the *Nogah*, a patrol vessel that was a former U.S. patrol vessel (submarine chaser) of the steel-hulled PC type. It is identified in *Jane's Fighting Ships*, 1966–67, as the former *PC 16* and in the 1968–69 edition as former *PC 1188*. The date of the event is not established.

34. Testimony of Lt. (jg) Lloyd Painter at U.S. Navy Court of Inquiry, 57: "We then filed out to our life rafts which were no longer with us because they had been strafed and most of them were burned, so we knocked most of them over the side. All during this time in Repair Three, my men were fighting fires and knocking burning life rafts, etc."

35. *Liberty* deck log, June 8,1967, and Israel Navy Division 914 war log, June 8, 1967.

36. Interview of the pilot (name not to be disclosed) by this author on April 29, 1998, in Israel. The helicopter was an SA-321K Super Frelon. It arrived on the scene following the air and torpedo attacks.

37. Translation of transcript of Israel Air Force audiotape of conversations of air controllers re: *Liberty*, June 8, 1967, Channel 14, time entry 1512. Shimon says to Kislev, "There is an American flag on board."

38. USDAO TEL AVIV message 151615Z June 67, U.S. Navy Court of Inquiry document 45, exhibit 48.

39. *Sde* is Hebrew for "field."

40. The Super Frelon helicopter flew from Sde Dov 230° a distance of forty-nine miles to 31-31.11° N latitude and 34-06.32° E longitude. This position was calculated from the bearing and distance information reported by Commander Castle in 1967. This author and Castle repeated the flight twenty-five years later within minutes of the 1967 times. On the 1992 flight a global positioning system, which is accurate to within a few hundred feet, was used for navigation. The 1967 position was computed by dead reckoning and therefore may have been less accurate than if calculated by the more precise navigational aids available in 1992.

41. Interview with Cdr. (now Capt.) Ernest Castle on January 14–15, 1989, at Columbia, S.C., telephone conversations between Castle and the author in March 2001, and a letter from Castle to this author dated March 10, 2001.

42. See U.S. Navy Court of Inquiry document 45, exhibit 48, message 151615Z June 67, from USDAO TEL AVIV ISRAEL to CINCUSNAVEUR: "7.(C) On return Embassy, ALUSNA informed that Genl Getty of NMCC requested phone report which was made at approx 082100Z. Substance of phone con same as para 5 above."

Chapter 6. In the Aftermath

1. Word was passed to the NSA at 0915 EDT (1515 Sinai time).

2. National Security Advisor W. W. Rostow, as was his custom, made a memo of the conversation, which he marked Thursday, June 8, 1967, 9:50 a.m. See also COMSIXTHFLT message 081250Z June 1967.

3. Telephone interview of George Christian by this author on July 19, 1991. Christian was in Austin, Texas.

4. Ultimately, four hotline messages were sent on June 8, 1967: at 0948, from Kosygin to Johnson, on the status of the Middle East cease-fire; at 1100, from Johnson to Kosygin, about the aircraft en route to the *Liberty;* at 1135, from Johnson to Kosygin, about the cease-fire; and at 1220, from Kosygin to Johnson, about the *Liberty.* All times are EDT.

5. Hotline message from President Johnson to Chairman Kosygin on June 8, 1967. Received by the Soviets at 1124 Washington time.

6. Tom Johnson came to the Washington as a White House fellow in 1965. In 1966 he was hired as assistant press secretary to President Johnson. In 1967 he became deputy press secretary and ultimately, in 1928, became special assistant to the president.

7. Marvin Watson served as special assistant to President Johnson from January 1965 to April 1968. During this period he was appointments secretary, political adviser, and chief of staff. In April 1968 Johnson appointed him postmaster general.

8. White House Daily Log, June 8, 1967.

9. Phil G. Goulding, *Confirm or Deny: Informing the People on National Security* (New York: Harper & Row, 1970), 97.

10. About twenty Soviet intelligence gatherers of the *Mirnny* class were built between 1962 and 1967 (Norman Polmar, *Guide to the Soviet Navy,* 5th ed. [Annapolis, Md.: Naval Institute Press, 1991], 290–91), and 4th ed. (1986), 333–35. Many pictures of these ships taken after 1967 show hull marks as "CCB," which is the Cyrillic for their designation, "SSV." This author has not been able to locate a picture taken in 1967, but numerous IDF officers have advised him that the Soviet intelligence gatherers were marked thus in 1967.

11. MTB Division 914 war log: "1520—Identification of the vessel—American. Lying on its right [starboard] side."

12. Interviews of Lt. Col. Michael Bloch by this author on August 14, 1989; January 14, 1990; June 16, 1990; June 10, 1992; and June 6, 1993—all at Tel Aviv.

13. From Castle to the White House and others, 081414Z (1614 Sinai/1014 Washington).

14. Interview of Dean Rusk by this author on April 5, 1989, at Athens, Georgia.

15. JCS flash message 081529Z June 1967. The text of the message states that before the message was generated, a transatlantic telephone call had been placed from the Vice Chief of Naval Operations to Deputy USCINCEUR. It can be assumed that the purpose of this call was to convey the first word down the chain of command that force was no longer needed and that a confirming message would follow. It is also likely that the Vice CNO learned that COMSIXTHFLT had already issued the recall orders for the aircraft.

16. COMSIXTHFLT flash message to CINCUSNAVEUR 081439Z June 1967.

17. It is more likely that this memory was of a day other than June 8, 1967, as none of the interviewed A-1 pilots recall doing Soviet destroyer (DD) overflights on June 8 (a scheduled nonflying day), while there are other reports of the A-1 aircraft conducting this type of countering the Soviet DDs on other days.

18. There is no documentation indicating that the Sixth Fleet or the Soviet ships went to general quarters (battle stations) when word was received regarding the *Liberty*. It is known that the fleet increased its readiness status to Condition III when the fighting broke out on June 5 and that the situation had become more relaxed by June 8. The *America* had resumed training operations, including a Single Integrated Operational Plan (SIOP) drill (an exercise involving training for delivery of nuclear weapons) that had been in progress when first word of the attack on the *Liberty* was received.

19. Interview with Francis Snyder on April 6, 1995, in Cambridge, Massachusetts.

20. Interview of Ambassador Richard B. Parker by author on September 8, 1997, in Washington, D.C.

21. Goulding, *Confirm or Deny,* 102, 103.

22. Department of Defense news release 550–67 of June 6, 1967.

23. Incoming telegram, Department of State 101415Z June 67 from American embassy, Madrid, to Secretary of State, Washington, D.C. (author's collection of State Department documents no. 452 and repeated as no. 458). The telegram is signed "Walker." At the time, the U.S. ambassador to Spain was Angier Biddle Duke. In the absence of the ambassador, the deputy chief of mission or chargé d'affaires would normally sign messages. It has not been possible to identify the "Walker" who signed this message.

24. The National Security Council held a special committee meeting at 6:30 p.m. on June 9, 1967, in the Cabinet Room of the White House. A typewritten memorandum for the record is supplemented by handwritten minutes of the meeting scribbled on the memo. The document is no. 100 National Security Council Document from the Lyndon Baines Johnson Library, Austin, Texas. Clark Clifford is recorded as saying, "My concern is that we're not tough enough. Handle as if Arabs or USSR had done it." Dean Rusk is recorded as saying, "Do what is normal."

25. Interview of Eugene V. Rostow by this author on April 29, 1992, at Washington, D.C.

26. W. W. Rostow (who died on February 13, 2003) and Eugene V. Rostow (died November 25, 2002), were brothers.

27. Interview of Dean Rusk by this author on April 5, 1989, at Athens, Georgia.

28. The name is transliterated from Arabic and is spelled many ways. A more accurate spelling is Zakaria Muhyi al-Din.

29. Department of State, incoming telegram, 081545Z from American Embassy, Cairo, to Secretary of State, Washington, D.C., flash precedence.

30. Confidential DOD Message 081517Z June 67 from Commander in Chief, U.S. Naval Forces Europe to Commander Sixth Fleet.

31. Goulding, *Confirm or Deny,* 124.

32. Ibid. See also part of press release authorized by Secretary McNamara, ibid., 130. This release was termed by reporter Fred Farrar of the *Chicago Tribune* "one of the most intriguing pieces of prose that ever came out of the Department's Press Office." *Chicago Tribune,* June 18, 1967, 16.

33. James E. Akins, "The Israeli Attack on the USS *Liberty,* June 8, 1967, and the Thirty-Two-Year Cover-up That Has Followed," *Washington Report on Middle East Affairs,* (December 1999), 28–34. *Liberty* crew member Phillip F. Tourney told this author a similar story in a telephone conversation on November 3,1997, and James Bamford repeats the story in *Body of Secrets* (New York: Doubleday, 2001), 228.

34. Interview of retired ambassador Mahmoud Kassem by author on October 18, 1994, at the National Center for Middle East Studies, Cairo.

35. "Periscope," *Newsweek,* June 26, 1967, 12.

36. "Periscope: Ahead of the News, Sinking the *Liberty:* Accident or Design?," *Newsweek,* June 19, 1967, 21.

37. Five days after the attack, on June 13, 1967, it was reported on page 1 of *Al-Ahram* in Cairo, in an article headlined, "The task of the American ship which Israel *hit by mistake* [emphasis added] near Sinai was to intercept messages from the operation room in cipher, uncode them, and transmit them immediately." The article said: "It has been proven that the mission of the American ship *Liberty* which was sailing 15 miles away from the coast of Sinai, was to intercept the wires which were issued from the operation room of the Sinai front, uncode them and transmit them. The ship is the most modern 'spy ship' of the American Sixth Fleet and is equipped with electronic installations and can connect with any place in the world via satellites."

    The presence of the ship was not discovered until it was hit *by accident* [emphasis added] by Israeli torpedo boats."

38. "Armed Forces: Finis," *Newsweek,* July 3, 1967, 24.

39. "Periscope: Inside Story," *Newsweek,* August 28, 1967, 14.

40. "Periscope: Ahead of the News," *Newsweek,* September 4, 1967, 11.

41. Goulding, *Confirm or Deny,* 101.

42. Ibid., 137.

43. Ibid., 102.

44. Telephone interview of Dr. Harold Saunders by this author March 28, 1991. Dr. Saunders was in Washington.

45. The simplest explanation of the difference between the two types of intelligence gatherers is that an AGTR was subject to national tasking, while an AGER was tasked by the Navy. For a more detailed explanation of the differences between the *Pueblo* and *Liberty*, see Trevor Armbrister, *A Matter of Accountability* (New York: Coward McCann, 1970), chap. 10.

46. Some reports say the *Liberty* was moving at about two or three knots, but if, as also reported, she was out of water for steam, dead in the water is more likely.

47. In the 1973 war, one of three flights of Israeli F-4 Phantoms made its way, by dead reckoning above overcast, to the vicinity of Damascus, the capital of Syria. The other two flights of F-4 aircraft with the same assigned target aborted their missions. The persistent flight dove down through the clouds, and the pilots found themselves near the Syrian military headquarters. They released their bombs, pulled up through the clouds, and returned to home base. The bombs hit the upper floors of the headquarters. Unbeknownst to the attackers, the Syrians had brought some captured Israeli prisoners of war into their headquarters, and at the time of the attack the Israeli prisoners were in the basement of the building. Many Syrian air force personnel insist to this day that the bombs were directed specifically at the upper stories of the building so as not to harm the Israeli prisoners in the basement. See Merav Halperin and Aharon Lapidot, *G-Suit: Combat Reports from Israel's Air War* (London: Sphere Books, 1990), 106. This story, like the story of the Israeli torpedo being intentionally aimed at the NSA compartment, has its genesis in the legend of Israeli military infallibility. Those who want to believe these stories will probably never be persuaded otherwise.

48. Paul Tobin was ultimately promoted to the rank of rear admiral. He served as Oceanographer of the Navy before his retirement in 1998.

49. At this point the U.S. Navy was unaware that those code keys had probably already been compromised, having been sold to the Soviets by the Walkers, a U.S. naval family that included Chief Warrant Officer John A. Walker Jr.; his brother, Lt. Cdr. Arthur J. Walker; and his son, Yeoman Third Class Michael Walker. Norman Polmar and Thomas B. Allen say, "The Walker case was probably the largest and most damaging spy episode in the history of the U.S. Navy." See Norman Polmar and Thomas B. Allen, *The Spy Book* (New York: Random House, 1997), 516, 585–88, 609.

50. Paul E. Tobin, "Comment and Discussion: The Violation of the *Liberty*," U.S. Naval Institute *Proceedings* (December 1978), 104–107.

Chapter 7. Friendly Fire Kills

1. Charles R. Shrader, *Amicicide: The Problem of Friendly Fire in Modern War* (Fort Leavenworth, Kans.: U.S. Army Command and General Staff College, 1982).

2. James Ennes Jr., *Assault on the "Liberty"* (New York: Random House, 1979), 51, 52.

3. Ibid., 51.

4. Excerpt from enclosure 3 attached to letter dated March 3, 2000, to Mr. James Bamforth [*sic*] Washington, D.C., from Marvin E. Nowicki, Ph.D. Copy provided to this author by Nowicki via e-mail, April 28, 2001.

5. The formula for visual acuity is included here, although it may not mean much to the average lay person. It may be used to confirm the distance conclusions used in this study. Any competent mathematician or physicist can confirm the validity of the conclusions by applying the formula to the data.

   A person with 20/20 vision is able to distinguish visual targets with an angular separation of one minute (1/60th of a degree) of arc. If the targets are closer than one minute of arc, they are visually indistinguishable.

   To understand the calculation, imagine lines extending from the observer's eyes to the two edges of the target. For a small (compared to the distance) distant target, we can assume that the imaginary lines are the same length, r. These lines intersect at the center of a circle with radius r. The target forms an isosceles triangle with the lines. Call the small angle by the observer *theta*. Then, for a small distant target, the length of the target equals the distance r times *theta* (measured in radians). Thus, for a target of size s, the distance (r) at which it subtends one minute of arc and can be distinguished can be calculated:

   $r = s / theta$

   If the target is a five-by-eight-foot U.S. flag, it may be distinguished at 17,194 feet. Knowing that one minute of arc is 0.0002908 radians (2 x ϖ x 1/360 x 1/60 = 0/0002908), the limit of distinguishability is

   $r = 5$ ft. / 0.0002908 $=17,194$ ft.

   This does not mean that it could be identified at this distance, only that it would appear as a distinct spot, indicating that something is there but not necessarily recognizable as a flag.

   For a five-by-eight-foot U.S. flag, the stripes are 0.3846153 feet. Thus, the limit of distinguishability for this identifying feature of the U.S. flag is 1,323 feet:

   $r = 0.384615$ ft. / 0.0002908 $= 1,323$ ft.

   Similarly, for a seven-by-thirteen-foot U.S. flag, the limit of distinguishability for the stripes is 1,852 feet for a person with 20/20 vision.

   These computations are for static pictures. Movement of the target or the viewer would adversely affect the result.

   An aircraft flying at 1,000 ft/s (600 mph) would have a little less than two seconds to see and identify a flag before reaching it, in optimum conditions.
6. U.S. Navy Court of Inquiry, *Liberty Incident, Record of Proceedings*, Finding no. 2. See also message from CINCUSNAVEUR (Admiral M Cain) to SECNAV, 142148Z June 67.
7. English translation of pilot debriefing report filed by *Kursa* Flight leader at 1500 Sinai time on June 8, 1967. Copy in this author's files.

8. Joseph Lentini, a *Liberty* crew member, believes that pictures were also taken by the *Liberty*'s photographer's mate. The photos were taken on board the ship during the attacks and are a part of the record of the U.S. Navy court of inquiry, where Commander McGonagle testified that he took pictures with the ship's camera while additional pictures were taken by others. The pictures in the court of inquiry record are not identified by photographer.

9. U.S. Navy Court of Inquiry, exhibit 9.

10. Frederick D. Mullenin, *Handbook of the Law of War for Armed Forces* (Geneva: International Committee of the Red Cross, 1987), 96.

11. U.S. Department of the Navy, Office of the Chief of Naval Operations, *The Commander's Handbook on the Law of Naval Operations*, NWP 9 (Washington, D.C.: Naval Warfare Publications, 1989), 12–1.

12. Samuel Eliot Morrison, *John Paul Jones: A Sailor's Biography* (Boston: Little, Brown, 1959), 229.

13. David Howarth, *Famous Sea Battles* (London: Artus, 1981), 131.

14. Dudley Pope, *The Battle of the River Plate* (New York: Avon Books, 1956), 71.

15. See Graham Rhys-Jones, *The Loss of the "Bismarck": An Avoidable Disaster* (Annapolis, Md.: Naval Institute Press, 1999), 182–85, for a detailed description of the attack on HMS *Sheffield* by British Fleet Air Arm pilots. See also Howarth, *Famous Sea Battles,* 138–149; Oliver Warner, *Great Sea Battles* (New York: Exeter Books, 1981), 272–81; and Geoffrey Regan, *Blue on Blue: A History of Friendly Fire* (New York: Avon Books, 1995), 219.

16. The *Bismarck*'s actual length was 792 feet, two inches at the water line and 813 feet, eight inches overall.

17. The basic displacement of the *Liberty* was 7,190 tons. With a full load of stores and fuel she would displace up to 10,680 tons.

18. Indar Jit Rikhye, *The Sinai Blunder: Withdrawal of the United Nations Emergency Force Leading to the Six-Day War of June 1967* (London: Frank Cass, 1980), 96–97.

19. Regan, *Blue on Blue.* The incident became known as the Dogger Bank incident; see 202–207.

20. Ibid., 207–208.

21. Ibid., 209.

22. Ibid., 215–18.

23. Danny Shapira was one of the first Israeli pilots in the Israel Air Force. He became the chief test pilot for the IAF and flew combat in every war fought by Israel until his retirement in 1992. He was assigned to Dassault in France, where he worked on the development of a new Dassault jet fighter and became known as the father of the Mirage IIIC. He personally flew fifty-three of the seventy-six Mirage IIICJs acquired by Israel from France to Israel. He was the ninth person in France to break the sonic barrier. He was the first Western pilot to fly a MiG-21. After checking out the aircraft for Israel in 1966, he checked out an American pilot and turned the MiG-21 over to the U.S. Air Force. (The plane was returned to Israel many years later and may be seen at the Israel Air Force Museum at

Hatzerim Air Force Base.) In 1995 Shapira was inducted into the International Association of Experimental Test Pilots at a ceremony at the Beverly Hilton, in Hollywood, California. In 1997 he was still flying demonstration flights at the Paris Air Show. This author has had the privilege of flying with him on numerous occasions, including a flight to the site of the attack on the *Liberty*.

24. Destroyers of the Z, or Zed, class were manufactured by Great Britain. The Egyptian navy in 1956 was composed of Zed-class and Hunt-class destroyers, both of British manufacture. Prior to 1967 the Egyptians also obtained Skory-class destroyers from the Soviets.

25. Interview of Danny Shapira by this author on June 21, 1990, at Hatzerim Air Force Base, Israel. Shapira was one of four graduates of the first class of pilots in the Israel Air Force. Among his classmates was Mordechai Hod (commander of the Israel Air Force during the 1967 war).

   See also Joseph F. Bouchard, "Accidents and Crises: *Panay*, *Liberty*, and *Stark*," *Naval War College Review* (Autumn 1988), 87–102. Martin van Creveld, in *The Sword and the Olive: A Critical History of the Israeli Defense Force* (New York: PublicAffairs, 1986), 150, cites as his source Y. Steigman, *Me-atsmaut le-kadesk Chel Ha-Avir ba-shanim* (Tel Aviv: Ministry of Defense, 1990), 281–82.

26. George M. Gawrych, *Key to the Sinai: The Battles for Abu Ageila in the 1956 and 1967 Arab-Israeli Wars* (Fort Leavenworth, Kans.: U.S. Army Command and General Staff College, 1990).

27. John McCain and Mark Salter, *Faith of My Fathers* (New York: Random House, 1999), 79–80.

28. Regan, *Blue on Blue*, 219.

29. Interview of Cdr. Tom Krupp by this author at the U.S. embassy, Tel Aviv, August 16, 1989.

30. Krupp interview.

31. As a further example of thoughts like the ones expressed by Lt. Col. Grossman (Ret.), see the *20/20* ABC News broadcast "Friendly Fire," aired July 14, 1995, which tells of the suffering of the parents of Cpl. Lance Fielder, killed on February 27, 1991, by American friendly fire during the Gulf War of 1991.

Chapter 8. Survivors' Perceptions

1. Twenty-five died in the National Security Agency compartment, twenty-four Navy men and one civilian. The other nine fatalities were members of the crew of the *Liberty*. Although there is a technical distinction between the crew and the NSA detachment personnel, in most instances all personnel are referred to as *Liberty* crew.

2. On that day he held the rank of commander. As commanding officer, he was referred to as the "skipper" or the "captain" of the ship. He was promoted to the rank of captain on August 3, 1967.

3. Testimony of Cdr. William L. McGonagle, commanding officer of the *Liberty*, on June 13, 1967, before U.S. Navy court of inquiry. Transcript of testimony, 39.

4. The first meeting occurred on June 7, 1991, in Washington, D.C.; a second meeting occurred on June 9, 1991.

5. Letter from Capt. William L. McGonagle to this author dated August 20, 1998.

6. *New York Times,* March 9, 1999, C27.

7. According to the *USS "Liberty" Newsletter,* August 1981.

8. *USS "Liberty" Newsletter,* November/December 1981, 5.

9. Interview of Brig. Gen. Oded Erez, IAF (Ret.), by this author on June 5,1988, at Tel Aviv. Erez was a lieutenant colonel on June 8,1967, and flew over the *Liberty* at noon at thirty thousand feet in a Vatour. His log book reflects that he reported a ship with "no wake."

10. Interview of Thames TV producer Rex Bloomstein by this author on September 16, 1991, in London. A follow-up telephone interview was conducted on June 25, 1992, with Rex Bloomstein in London.

11. The *USS "Liberty" Newsletter* was published until September 1986. The next issue, in December 1986, was renamed the *"Liberty" News.*

12. John Hrankowski, "Post-Traumatic Stress Disorder," *"Liberty" News* 14, no. 2/3, 1996, 7.

13. Interview of George Golden by this author on March 11, 1991, by telephone. Mr. Golden was in Norfolk, Virginia.

14. The most senior chief petty officer is called the "leading chief."

15. Interview of Chief Machinist Mate Richard J. Brooks by this author on June 7, 1991, in Washington, D.C.

16. Interview of Seaman Steven Richards by this author on June 8, 1991, in Washington, D.C.

17. James M. Ennes Jr., *Assault on the "Liberty": The True Story of the Israeli Attack on an American Intelligence Ship* (New York: Random House, 1979).

18. Ibid., 62.

19. Ibid., 137 [emphasis added].

20. Ibid., 206.

21. Ibid., fn 5.

22. Telephone interview of Adm. David L. McDonald by this author on June 29, 1990. Admiral McDonald was in Jacksonville, Florida. He died on December 16, 1997.

23. Interview of Sen. J. William Fulbright by this author at Coral Gables, Florida, on December 6, 1988. Senator Fulbright died on February 9, 1995.

24. E-mail from Commander Bennett to this author, March 14, 2001.

25. 0800 June 5, 1967; Ennes, *Assault on the "Liberty,"* 38.

26. James Ennes Jr., "The USS *Liberty:* Back in the News," *American-Arab Affairs,* no. 15 (Winter 1985–86), 26 fn 18 [emphasis added].

27. Bill Gunston, *An Illustrated Guide to the Israeli Air Force* (New York: Arco, 1982), 86–89. See also William Green, *The World Guide to Combat Planes* (Garden City, N.Y.: Doubleday, 1967), vols. 1 and 2.

28. Hard points are specially strengthened fittings, usually on the wings or fuselage of aircraft, where ordinance, fuel tanks, and other accessory items may be attached and, in most cases, released during flight. For an explanation of hard points and their

locations on the Israeli Mirage CIII, see Shlomo Aloni, *Mirage III vs. MiG 21: Six Day War 1967* (Oxford, U.K.: Osprey, 2010), 9.

29. "Documentation," *American-Arab Affairs* 15 (Winter 1985–86), 104.

30. Ennes, "*Liberty*: Back in the News," 19.

31. In 1967 the title of the number-two person in the Department of State was "Under Secretary." In 1972 it was changed to "Deputy Secretary."

32. Ennes, "*Liberty*: Back in the News," 24–26.

33. Ibid., 26.

34. Reinforced to this author by Joseph Lentini, a *Liberty* survivor, at a meeting in Washington, D.C., on June 21, 1998.

35. Interview of CIA chief of station, Tel Aviv, in June 1967 by this author. Name and date and place of interview not disclosed, by agreement.

36. Interview of former Secretary of State Dean Rusk by this author on April 5, 1989, in Athens, Georgia. Dean Rusk died December 20, 1994.

37. Abba Eban, television documentary *Israel: A Nation Is Born*, program 4, part 1, Tele Cine, London, England, October 6, 1992. According to Eban, this call was from McGeorge Bundy, special adviser on the Middle East to President Lyndon Johnson. See also Ahron Bregman and Jihan El-Tahri, *The Fifty Years War: Israel and the Arabs* (New York: TV Books, 1998), 110.

38. Incoming telegram, Department of State telegram, from American Embassy, Tel Aviv, to Secretary of State, Washington, D.C. Date/time group 081604Z June 1967, State Department number 4020, declassified by Freedom of Information Act appeal of this author in 1999. The telegram reports: "1. Following is summary of IDF Intelligence Chief's briefing of McPherson of White House June 8, 11:30 a.m." It is signed by the U.S. ambassador to Israel, Walworth "Wally" Barbour. In addition to the comments on Syria, it gave a detailed brief on all IDF activities of the past few days.

39. Thames TV documentary *Attack on the "Liberty,"* script VTR/THS/37733, prod. no. N. 1005, transmission, Tuesday, January 23, 1987; script ref 245, and script ref 251, 52.

40. Ennes, *Assault on the "Liberty,"* 164.

41. Ibid., 77.

42. James M. Ennes Jr., Prodigy, account DRNV11F, July 22, 1992. This was before the Internet as it exists today. In 1992 Prodigy was operated by Sears and was an interactive computer service forum. It was available to computer owners for a monthly charge. The Ennes postings were in an area called "Art Club-Books-Non-Fiction-Assault on the *Liberty*." The *Liberty* Veterans Association reported "*Liberty* On-Line with Prodigy."

43. Letter dated September 28, 1989 to the *Keene (N.H.) Sentinel*, signed by James M. Ennes Jr. and republished in the *"Liberty" Newsletter*, September/December 1989, 20.

44. *Colebrook (N.H.) News and Sentinel*, January 27, 1988. The article cites: "Reprinted from 'Christian News.' Dale Crowley Jr. is a Christian evangelist with his own radio program, *The King's Business*.

45. Telephone interview of Mrs. Lawrence Geis by this author on March 14, 1994. Mrs. Geis was in Jacksonville, Florida.
46. Interview with Capt. Joseph M. Tully Jr., USN (Ret.), June 8, 1991, *Liberty* Veterans Association annual meeting, Washington, D.C.
47. Ibid.
48. Telephone interview of former Secretary of Defense Robert McNamara by this author, December 17,1993. McNamara was in Washington, D.C.
49. Yoichi Okamoto was the official White House photographer in 1967. Pictures from the rolls of film shot by Okamoto on June 8, 1967, are available through the Lyndon Baines Johnson Library, Austin, Texas.
50. McNamara interview.
51. Secret message from Vice Admiral Martin to Admiral McCain on the subject "Press Briefing Covering Damage to USS *Liberty* and Heroic Actions of Crew." Paragraph 5 of that message states: "In general questioning, I acknowledge that *I had ordered aircraft airborne* quote to protect, and only to protect USS *Liberty* as soon as I was convinced that a U.S. ship was really under attack, and *called back the aircraft when I became aware that they were not required* unquote. The press was also informed that *senior commanders had been fully informed of my actions and received copies of all my messages*" [emphasis added].

Five days later a twenty-one-page message was sent from USS *America* to CINCUSNAVEUR (Admiral McCain in London) transmitting the transcript of COMSIXTHFLT's (Admiral Martin's) meeting with the press. The message stated that "A tape of the interview has been air mailed to CHINFO [Chief of Naval Information]." On pp. 19 and 20 the following colloquy was reported (emphasis added):

> Q. After you found out the *Liberty* was under attack, did you inform Washington?
> A. About the very first thing I did was to get the aircraft moving to protect that ship. That's the first thing to do, is to protect the ship.
> Q. And then having done that.
> A. And the steps that I took to do that were sent to my superiors. Immediately, they were information [i.e., included as information addressees] on every message in connection with this that I sent to the task force commander.
> Q. Sir, were you on the phone to the White House today?
> A. No.
> Q. Were you talking to the Joint Chiefs in Washington on the phone?
> A. No.
> Q. This was all radioteletype messages that you used. *Did you get any instructions from them in Washington at any time?*
> A. *No.*
> Q. Did you know who was? Did you have any idea at the time who was attacking that ship when you did get the word and you sent out?
> A. None whatsoever.

52. Letter from USS *Liberty* Veterans Association to Cong. Nicholas Mavroules: "Neither Capt. Joseph Tully, Commanding Officer of the USS *Saratoga* nor his Executive Officer, Max Morris [*sic;* Morris was the navigator, not executive officer] have ever been contacted by the U.S. Navy to provide testimony concerning their launch of two flights of rescue aircraft. *Indeed, the U.S. Navy denies two flights were launched*" [emphasis added].

53. See column by John Omicinski, national defense correspondent of Gannett News Service, *USA Today,* June 7, 2001. Omicinski, relying upon the allegations of James Bamford, suggested that the supposed recall of the first flight of aircraft was grounds to impeach President Johnson.

54. John Borne, *USS "Liberty"* (Brooklyn, N.Y.: Reconsideration Press, 1995), 41, 42 fn.

55. Patrick King, producer, *U.S.S. "Liberty" Survivors: Our Story* (Los Angeles: Sligo Productions, 1991). No known TV airing.

56. NBC Television, aired January 27, 1992. Producer Christopher Carlson.

57. E-mails from Cdr. Maurice H. Bennett to this author, March 14, 2001.

58. Interview of Joseph Lentini by this author.

Chapter 9. Conspiracy Theories

1. Interview of McGeorge Bundy by this author on April 19, 1993, New York City.

2. Ye. Primakov, "How Israel Began the Aggression," *Pravda,* July 27, 1967, 4. Translated from the Russian by Gregory Koldys.

3. I. Belyayev, T. Kolesnichenko, and Ye. Primakov, *The "Dove" Has Been Released (Soviet Review of the Israeli-Arab June 1967 Conflict)* [*"Golub" Spushchen*] (Moscow: Molodaya Gvardiya Publishing House, 1968). An English translation was published by the U.S. Department of Commerce, Joint Publications Research Service, Clearinghouse for Federal Scientific & Technical Information, Springfield, Va., JPRS 45466, May 23, 1968.

4. Belyayev, Kolesnichenko, and Primakov, *The "Dove,"* 50.

5. Ye. Primakov and I. Belyayev, "Lessons of the 1967 Middle East Crises," *International Affairs* (Moscow) 3 (March 1968), 41.

6. Ibid., 41.

7. This author was invited by the Egyptian armed forces to visit the National Center for Middle East Studies in Cairo. The visit occurred on October 18, 1994, and he conferred with Maj. Gen. Ahmed Fakhr, the director of the center; Dr. Ali Sadek, the deputy director of the center; Maj. Gen. Ahmed M. Abdel Halim, the head of the military unit of the center; Ambassador Mahmoud Kassem, a retired Egyptian ambassador; and Amin Huwaydi, the director of Egyptian intelligence during the 1967 war and minister of war after the death of Field Marshal Abdul al-Hakim Amer. An entire day was spent discussing the *Liberty* incident. At the meeting this author learned that he is not strong enough to drink Egyptian coffee.

8. Chapter 3 of unpublished manuscript by Ambassador Mahmoud Kassem.

9. Interview of Ambassador Mahmoud Kassem on October 18, 1994, at the National Center for Middle East Studies, Cairo.

10. Anthony Pearson, *Conspiracy of Silence* (London: Quartet, 1978), 319.

11. Anthony Pearson, "The Attack on the USS *Liberty*: Mayday! Mayday!" *Penthouse*, May 1976, 54–58, 137–47; Pearson, "Conspiracy of Silence," *Penthouse*, June 1976, 60–64, 147–51.

12. Pearson, *Conspiracy of Silence*, 30; see also 88.

13. Ibid., 30.

14. Report of Armed Services Subcommittee of the Committee on Armed Services, House of Representatives, 92d Cong., 1st sess., Under authority of H. Res. 201. May 10, 1971 (Washington, D.C.: U.S. Government Printing Office, 1971).

15. Pearson, "Conspiracy," 62.

16. Randolph S. Churchill and Winston S. Churchill, *The Six Day War* (Boston: Houghton Mifflin, 1967), 161.

17. Various reports fix the *Liberty*'s arrival at Point Alpha between 0832 and 0849. The exact time of arrival within sixteen minutes is not significant.

18. Pearson, *Conspiracy of Silence*, 33.

19. Ibid., 1.

20. Ibid., 75, 76.

21. Richard K. Smith, "The Violation of the *Liberty*," U.S. Naval Institute *Proceedings* (June 1978), 62–70.

22. Ibid., 64.

23. On December 12, 1937, Japanese naval aircraft bombed and strafed the USS *Panay*, a river gunboat engaged in evacuating American civilians from Nanking during the Japanese invasion of China. In the attack three Americans were killed and forty-eight wounded.

24. Smith, "Violation of the *Liberty*," 70.

25. Secret message from American Embassy, Tel Aviv, to Secretary of State, number 4014, 081510Z June 67.

26. Department of State, Memorandum of Conversation, June 28, 1967; Subject: Attack on the U.S.S. *Liberty*; Participants: H. E. Avraham Harman, Ambassador of Israel, Mr. Ephraim Evron, Minister, Embassy of Israel, Acting Secretary Katzenbach, Donald R. Morris, and James K. Matter.

27. Alfred Friendly, comment on "The Violation of the *Liberty*," by Robert K. Smith, U.S. Naval Institute *Proceedings* (January 1979), 88.

28. Wilbur Crane Eveland, *Ropes of Sand: America's Failure in the Middle East* (London: W. W. Norton, 1980), 325.

29. Prior to the 1967 war the United States had never provided Israel with any offensive weapons, except for a few M-48 tanks. Israel had no ballistic missiles in 1967.

30. Eveland, *Ropes of Sand*, 325.

31. Richard B. Parker, *The Six Day War* (Gainesville: University Press of Florida, 1996), 257.

32. Rowland Evans and Robert Novak, "Remembering the *Liberty*," *Washington Post*, November 6, 1991.

33. "The use of VHF/UHF radio waves is limited by the position of the receiver in relation to the transmitter. . . . When using airborne VHF/UHF equipment, it is of the utmost importance that this limitation be understood. The range of VHF/UHF transmission increases with altitude, and may be approximately determined by the following simple method: Multiply the square root of the aircraft altitude in feet by 1.23 to find the VHF/UHF transmission range in nautical miles." See U.S. Department of Transportation, Federal Aviation Administration, *Instrument Flying Handbook*, AC 61–27C (Washington, D.C.: Superintendent of Documents, 1980), 112–113.

34. See ibid.

35. Telephone interview of Ambassador Dwight Porter by this author on November 20, 1991. Ambassador Porter was at his home in Silver Spring, Maryland. The tape is in this author's possession.

36. Letter from Ambassador Dwight Porter to this author dated December 14, 1991. The letter is handwritten and confirms that it responds to this author's letter dated December 6, 1991, which the ambassador received on December 13, 1991.

37. The State Department document (Incoming Telegram Department of State Z 061021Z June 67, FM AMEMBASSY BEIRUT TO RUEMC/SECSTATE WASHDC FLASH) established that the mob gathering outside and threatening the U.S. embassy in Beirut occurred on June 6, 1967, two days before the attack on the *Liberty*. See also Hirsh Goodman, "Messrs. Errors and No Facts," *Jerusalem Report,* November 21, 1991, 42.

38. Stephen Green, *Taking Sides: America's Secret Relations with a Militant Israel* (New York: William Morrow, 1984).

39. In 1992, an Israeli writer repeated Stephen Green's tale about the U.S. Air Force assisting Israel against the Arabs while Israel prepared for the 1967 war. Apparently Katz did no independent research and relies solely on Green as the source for the story. It is careless research like this that nurtures and perpetuates conspiracy theories. Samuel M. Katz, *Soldier Spies: Israeli Military Intelligence* (Novato, Calif.: Presidio Press, 1992).

40. Ambassador Richard B. Parker served after 1967 as U.S. ambassador to Algeria, Lebanon, and Morocco. He retired from the Foreign Service in 1980. He edited the *Middle East Journal* from 1981 to 1987 and served as scholar in residence at the Middle East Institute in Washington, D.C.

41. Richard B. Parker, "USAF in the Sinai in the 1967 War: Fact or Fiction?," *Journal of Palestine Studies* 27, no. 1 (Autumn 1997), 67–75.

42. Parker, *The Six Day War,* 239.

43. John E. Borne, *The USS "Liberty": Dissenting History vs. Official History* (Brooklyn, N.Y.: Reconsideration Press, 1995), 55.

44. This is clearly reflected in the White House Diary of June 8, 1967, at 0838 a.m. It is further corroborated by Harold Saunders in the "Middle East Crisis Chronological Guide, May 12–June 20," National Security Council Document file at the Lyndon Baines Johnson Library, Austin, Texas, 27.

45. Paul Findley, *They Dare to Speak Out: People and Institutions Confront Israel's Lobby* (Westport, Conn.: Lawrence Hill, 1985). Findley was elected to the U.S. House of Representatives in 1960 and lost his seat in the election of 1982.

46. Ibid., 167.

47. Ibid., 168.

48. Ibid., 167.

49. Interview of Adm. Donald D. Engen by this author on May 3, 1990, in Washington, D.C.

50. "Several authors have written about the attack on the *Liberty*. One or two have been highly emotional and have written less than factual books that failed to understand the why or to explore factually the actions of the Sixth Fleet and its aircraft carriers. For those interested in the full story, the most scholarly and factual treatise is the doctoral thesis of A. Jay Cristol." Donald D. Engen, *Wings and Warriors: My Life as a Naval Aviator* (Washington, D.C.: Smithsonian Institution Press, 1997), 322.

51. Findley, *They Dare to Speak Out,* 168.

52. Donald Neff, *Warriors at Suez: Eisenhower Takes America into the Middle East* (New York: Amana Books, 1981).

53. Donald Neff, *Warriors for Jerusalem: The Six Days That Changed the Middle East* (New York: Linden Press/Simon & Schuster, 1984).

54. Ibid., 220. It is claimed that this message was sent on Tuesday, June 6, 1967.

55. James Ennes, *Assault on the "Liberty:" The True Story of the Israeli Attack on an American Intelligence Ship* (New York: Random House, 1979), 38–39. The Neff quotation is exactly the same as the Ennes quotation. In footnote 3 Ennes admits: "The message exchange comes from the recollections of the author and several ship's officers. Like so many others, *the messages can not be found in the message files preserved by the Court of Inquiry or by various Washington agencies*" [emphasis added].

56. Neff, *Warriors for Jerusalem,* 391. The note relating to page 209 of his book reads, "209 The crew of: Ennes, *Assault on the 'Liberty.'* Also Ennes to author, letter."

57. Modern military jet engines can generate substantial increased power and therefore substantial additional speed through the use of a system called an "afterburner." In this mode of operation, fuel is consumed at an enormous rate. Military jets use afterburner only for takeoff and when engaged in combat. Such use is limited to minutes, since more than that will exhaust the jet's fuel supply.

58. Neff, *Warriors for Jerusalem,* 259–60.

59. Ibid., 263.

60. Ibid., 266.

61. Central Intelligence Agency, Directorate of Intelligence, 8 June 1967, Intelligence Memorandum, Arab-Israeli Situation Report, As of 9:00 a.m. EDT. Lyndon Baines Johnson Library, declassified February 26, 1990.

62. John Loftus and Mark Aarons, *The Secret War against the Jews: How Western Espionage Betrayed the Jewish People* (New York: St. Martins, 1994).

63. Ibid., 268.
64. Ibid., 259–86.
65. Although the *Liberty* "chopped"—that is, was assigned to the Sixth Fleet—after her entry into the Mediterranean, she in fact was tasked by NSA and operated independently under orders issued by NSA. Effectively, she was not being controlled by the Sixth Fleet in the same manner as other Sixth Fleet ships.
66. James Taylor, *Pearl Harbor II: The True Story of The Sneak Attack by Israel upon the U.S.S. "'Liberty,'" June 8, 1967* (Washington, D.C.: Mideast Publishing, 1980).
67. Adm. Thomas Hinman Moorer was born February 9, 1912, in Mount Willing, Alabama. He graduated from the U.S. Naval Academy and was commissioned ensign on June 1, 1933. He served as Commander in Chief, Atlantic Fleet, from 1965 until August 1, 1967. On June 3, 1967, he was named by President Johnson as Chief of Naval Operations. He became the eighteenth CNO on August 1, 1967. He was appointed chairman of the Joint Chiefs of Staff by President Nixon, effective July 1, 1970. He served in that capacity until July 1974. Admiral Moorer was interviewed by this author on February 10, 1989, and on May 3, 1990, in Washington, D.C. He told this author he had no personal knowledge regarding the attack on the *Liberty*.
68. Under U.S. law, only the president may order a nuclear attack. Adm. Jerome L. "Jerry" Johnson was interviewed by this author on April 19, 1991, at his office in the Pentagon. In 1967 Johnson was strike operations officer on board the *Saratoga*. He directed the arming and fueling of the attack aircraft launched from the *Saratoga*. He said there were no nuclear weapons on the aircraft. Rear Adm. (retired) Max Morris, who was navigator of the *Saratoga* at that time, confirms the armament was not nuclear. This author also interviewed two of the A-4 pilots launched from the *America*—K. C. Spayde, August 7, 1991, and James E. Kneale, August 8, 1991—who both confirmed they carried only Bullpup missiles, not nuclear weapons.

    In addition, the oral history of Vice Adm. Don Engen, the commanding officer of the *America* on June 8, 1967, confirms that the aircraft launched from *America* were not nuclear armed and further that the F-4B Phantom aircraft on *America* were not even wired to carry nuclear weapons. The oral history is on file with the U.S. Naval Institute.
69. Admiral Moorer had extensive experience during World War II as a Navy patrol bomber pilot. He flew many combat missions in PBY Catalinas.
70. Intelligence Memorandum, Central Intelligence Agency, June 13, 1967, 4.
71. The last U.S. Navy ship visit to Israel prior to the 1967 war occurred in November 1963.
72. Interview of Admiral Moorer by this author on February 10, 1989, in Washington, D.C. at the Center for Strategic Studies. The admiral told this author that as CNO he moved then in much lower circles and it was only in later years when he became chairman of the Joint Chiefs of Staff (JCS) that he talked directly to the president or to the secretaries of state or defense on a one-on-one basis. This author interviewed Admiral Moorer a second time on May 3, 1990, at the Army-Navy Club in Washington, D.C.

73. Interview of Dan Schueftan by this author on June 20, 2001, in Jerusalem. The comment was thereafter confirmed by facsimile on July 25, 2001. Dr. Schueftan is a senior research fellow at the National Security Studies Centre at Haifa University and a senior fellow at Shalem Centre in Jerusalem. He specializes in the study of the Arab-Israeli conflict and has published extensively on the June 1967 Arab-Israeli War, as well as *A Jordanian Option: Israel, Jordan, and the Palestinians* (Tel Aviv: Ha'kibbutz Ha'meuchad, 1986), in Hebrew; *Attrition: Egypt's Post War Political Strategy 1967–1970* (Tel Aviv: Ma'arachot, 1989), in Hebrew; and *Disengagement: Israel and the Palestinian Entity* (Tel Aviv: Haifa University Press & Zemora-Bitan, 1999), in Hebrew.

Chapter 10. Tall Tales vs. Reality

1. *USS "Liberty" Newsletter,* May 1984, 4. The *USS "Liberty" Newsletter* was published until September 1986. The next issue, in December 1986, was renamed the *"Liberty" News.*

2. Jim Anderson, "New Light Shed on Israeli Attack on U.S. Ship," United Press International, Washington, March 18, 1984.

3. No one in the IDF could identify a general with this name.

4. Roland Evans and Robert Novak, "Remembering the *Liberty,*" *Washington Post,* November 6, 1991.

5. A. M. Rosenthal, "Anatomy of a Scoop," *New York Times,* November 8, 1991, A-27.

6. Seth Mintz, "Attack on the *Liberty:* A Tragic Mistake," *Washington Post,* November 9, 1991, A-26.

7. Jonathan Schachter, "Source: I Was Misquoted about '67 *Liberty* Attack," *Jerusalem Post,* November 13, 1991. Schachter wrote: "But in an interview with *The Jerusalem Post,* Mintz said he had been 'badly burned' by the columnists who 'distorted' his remarks into a 'lie.'"

   The article also states: "In an apparent attempt to justify their story, the two columnists yesterday quoted an article in the [leading Israeli morning newspaper] Ha'aretz, written after their original column appeared, in which Mintz reportedly expressed 'grave anxiety over the media interest in him,' adding: 'Everyone is after me now and that is what I'm afraid of. I don't need the Mossad and Shin Bet knocking at my door.'"

   Schachter's concluding comment: "At no time during his interview with *The Jerusalem Post,* however, did Mintz speak of any fears of danger or reprisals, but he did complain about the unwanted publicity the Evans and Novak column had thrust upon him."

8. Roland Evans and Robert Novak, "The *Liberty* Quotes," *Washington Post,* November 11, 1991.

9. Hirsh Goodman, "Messrs. Errors and No Facts," *Jerusalem Report,* November 21, 1991, 42.

10. Stephen Green is the author of *Taking Sides: America's Secret Relations with a Militant Israel* (New York: William Morrow, 1984).

11. Goodman, "Messrs. Errors and No Facts," 41.

12. Fax dated August 6, 1992, from Maj. Gen. (Res.) Daniel Matt to this author in response to a detailed letter to the general dated June 26, 1992. The fax said:

Dear Judge Cristol,

I would like to inform you that a General by the name of Benni Matti is not known to me and that I myself am not the person in question, for the reasons raised in your letter dated 26 June 1992.

May I add that I do not know Messers. Mintz and Dagan.

Yours faithfully,

Major-General (Res.) Daniel Matt.

13. *USS "Liberty" Newsletter*, May 1984, 4.
14. Interview of Adrian Pennink by this author on August 30, 1989, in London.
15. Undated transcripts of the Stephen Green interviews of Seth Mintz ultimately came into the hands of Pennink of Thames TV, probably from David Walsh, and then passed from Pennink to this author.
16. Green, *Taking Sides*.
17. This author called Seth Mintz at his listed telephone number on November 8, 1991, and requested an interview. The man who answered the telephone identified himself as Seth Mintz but declined to be interviewed.
18. Interview of Seth Mintz aired on NBC, *The Story behind the Story*, January 27, 1992.
19. Telephone conversation between Rich Bonin and this author on March 10, 1992, in Miami, Florida.
20. This author requested the search through Col. Raanan Gissen (Res.), Deputy IDF spokesman.
21. The U.S. Medical Center for Federal Prisoners opened in 1933. It is a federal detention facility located at 1600 West Sunshine, Springfield, Missouri.
22. Judge Thomas P. Griesa was appointed to the U.S. District Court for the Southern District of New York by President Richard M. Nixon and was sworn in on September 22, 1972. He took senior status on March 13, 2000.
23. This author communicated with Shimon Nachama of Israel TV Channel 1 on July 26, 2001, and was advised that the search for Tavni was still in progress but that the trail was cold.
24. Hamermish was flying a Tsukit twin-engine jet trainer aircraft and attempted a slow roll too close to the ground.
25. Interview of *Kursa* Wing by this author on June 17, 1990, in Israel; interview of Royal Flight leader by this author on July 2, 1992, in Israel.
26. Interview of *Kursa* Flight leader by this author on June 10, 1992, in Israel.
27. Ronald M. Wade, "Israel Should Own Up to the Truth about the *Liberty*," *Orlando (Fla.) Sentinel*, July 1, 1997.
28. Ronald M. Wade, LVA listserver, "More on the USS *Liberty*," January 8, 2000.
29. Through a contact in Israel, information on Yohanan Levanon was obtained, as well as an introduction to Levanon. He was interviewed by this author by telephone on March 21, 2000. This author was in Miami, Florida, and Levanon was in Israel.
30. Fax received by this author from Yohanan Levanon dated March 18, 2000.

31. Copies of the e-mail are in this author's files.

32. At that interview, which took place in the Mayflower Hotel in Washington, D.C., Bamford said to this author that "Israel was a charity state of the United States," that "Israelis lie," and that "the United States should cut aid to Israel," as well as other comments that indicated Bamford's dislike of Israel.

33. Bruce Edwards, "Cover: When Friends Look Like Foe," *Rutland (Vt.) Herald Sunday Magazine*, March 11, 2001, 11.

34. James Bamford, *Body of Secrets: Anatomy of the Ultra-Secret National Security Agency through the Dawn of a New Century* (New York: Doubleday, 2001).

35. Ibid., 220.

36. On June 8, 1967, Marvin Nowicki was a chief petty officer in the U.S. Navy. Following the 1967 war he was promoted to warrant officer and returned from Navy squadron VAQ-2 at Rota, Spain, to NSA headquarters, where he was assigned to Group G and worked under Frank Raven. He became chief of G643, dealing with the Israeli military, and thereafter chief of G64, responsible for all Middle East "targets." He was promoted to chief warrant officer (CWO-2) and then commissioned lieutenant (junior grade). He retired from the Navy as a lieutenant in 1990.

37. NSA press release of April 23, 2001, quoted in Scott Shane and Tom Bowman, "New Book on NSA Sheds Light on Secrets," *Baltimore Sun*, April 24, 2001.

38. Bamford, *Body of Secrets;* Nowicki is referenced on 213, 216, 221, and 231.

39. Marvin Nowicki provided this author with a copy of his letter dated March 3, 2000, and the five enclosures mentioned therein, together with written permission to publish the same, on condition of not disclosing the names of his Navy and NSA colleagues that were set forth in the letter and enclosures.

40. Telephone interview of Clark Clifford by this author on February 9, 1989. Clifford was in Washington, D.C. He died October 11, 1998.

41. Telephone interview of George Golden by this author on March 11, 1991. Golden was in Norfolk, Virginia.

42. In an Associated Press article in the *Los Angeles Times*, November 23, 1984, 2, George Golden is quoted: "I had proof that they knew who we were. We had monitored the communications between the Israeli planes and gun boats and their headquarters in which they referred to us as an American ship. I turned my proof over to an admiral and I don't know what was done with it."

43. Telephone conversation with Roy Kirk, May 1993.

44. E-mail from Commander Bennett to this author, March 14, 2001.

Chapter 11. Did Dayan Order It?

1. "CIA Papers Cite Israelis in Attack on U.S. Navy Ship," *New York Times*, September 19, 1977, 7.

2. See Central Intelligence Agency FOIA package on the USS *Liberty* incident. This package may be obtained by written request to the CIA.

3. The program *Good Morning America* was aired to the general public on September 19, 1977.

4. Moshe Dayan, *Story of My Life* (London: Sphere Books, 1976), 372.

5. An account of the trip to Hebron, "the City of the Patriarchs," and an emotional visit to the Cave of Machpelah is set forth in Uzi Narkiss, *The Liberation of Jerusalem* (Totowa, N.J.: Vallentine, Mitchell, 1983), 271–73.

6. The site of some Israeli settlements captured and destroyed by the Jordanian Arab Legion during the 1948 war.

7. Interview of Uzi Narkiss by this author on June 19, 1990, in Tel Aviv. General Narkiss was interviewed again by this author in Miami, Florida, on July 13, 1991. He commanded the brigades that captured Jerusalem and the Western Wall; see Narkiss, *Liberation of Jerusalem*. The command post was located in the basement of a convention center at the western entrance to Jerusalem. The center was called in Hebrew Binyanei Ha'umah.

8. Eitan Haber was one of the closest aides to Yitzhak Rabin.

9. Rehav'am Ze'evi at the time of his interview was the curator of the Museum of the Land of Israel in Tel Aviv and a member of the Knesset as well as founding head of the Moledet (Homeland) Party. Rehav'am Ze'evi was assassinated on October 17, 2001, while serving as tourism minister.

10. The interview took place in Tel Aviv on June 11, 1992.

11. Interview of Yitzhak Rager by this author on December 17, 1991, in Miami, Florida. Rager became the mayor of Beersheva in 1982 and held the position until his death on June 16, 1997. In the 1967 war he commanded the battalion that captured Bethlehem and Gush Etzion.

12. Telephone interview of Sharett by this author on July 13, 1991. Sharett was in Israel, and this author was in Miami, Florida.

13. Former de facto military governor (Coordinator of Israeli Government Activities in the Territories) of the West Bank and author of *The Carrot and the Stick: Israel's Policy in Judea and Samaria, 1967–1968,* ed. Patrick R. Denker, trans. Reuvik Danielli (Washington, D.C.: B'nai B'rith, 1995). Gazit also served as Israel's chief of military intelligence.

14. Interview of Itzhak Nissyahu by this author on June 20, 1990, in Tel Aviv.

15. Aharon Bregman and Jihan El-Tahri, *The Fifty Years' War: Israel and the Arabs* (New York: TV Books, 1998, 1999), 111.

16. Fax from Rubinger to this author, February 10, 1992, stating the time on Dayan's watch.

Chapter 12. America Investigates

1. 10 USC 935 creates Art. 135 of the Uniform Code of Military Justice, enacted on August 10, 1956, which reads in part: "(a) Courts of inquiry to investigate any matter may be convened by any person authorized to convene a general court-martial or by any other person designated by the Secretary concerned for that purpose, whether or not the persons involved have requested such an inquiry."

On June 10, 1967, Commander in Chief, U.S. Naval Forces Europe, Adm. John S. McCain Jr., signed an order directed to Rear Adm. Isaac C. Kidd Jr., USN, convening a court of inquiry to inquire into the circumstances surrounding the armed attack on USS *Liberty* (AGTR 5) on June 8, 1967. The order referred to section 0402 of the JAG (Judge Advocate General) manual. The court was "directed to inquire into all the pertinent facts and circumstances leading to and connected with the armed attack; damage resulting therefrom; and deaths and injuries to naval personnel."

2. Admiral McCain's father and Admiral Kidd's father were contemporaries at the U.S. Naval Academy. McCain and Kidd were also Naval Academy graduates, but McCain graduated more than ten years ahead of Kidd.

3. Lt. Cdr. Allen Feingersch, USN, 612119/1100, was designated as assistant counsel to the court in the letter from Commander in Chief, Naval Forces Europe to Rear Adm. Isaac C. Kidd Jr., USN, 11645/1100, which created the court of inquiry. It is interesting to note that while Ward Boston was a lawyer, qualified in the sense of Article 27 of the Uniform Code of Military Justice, Allen Feingersch was not so qualified and held the designation of a line officer.

4. Although the other members of the court met the ship on June 14, 1967, the transcript of the U.S. Navy court of inquiry erroneously indicates June 13, 1967.

5. The U.S. Navy court of inquiry, list of witnesses called. Their testimony appears in the record beginning at the page indicated:

Witness	Page
Capt. R. L. Raith, USN	2
Ens. D. G. Lucas, USNR	12
Cdr. W. L. McGonagle, USN	31
Lt. (jg) L. C. Painter, USNR	55
Ens. J. D. Scott, USNR	59
Lt. G. H. Golden, USN	63
Ens. M. P. O'Malley, USN	68
Lt. (jg) M. M. Watson, USNR	72
Lt. R. F. Kiepefer, USNR (MC)	74
CTC H. J. Thompson, USN	87
CTC C. F. Lamkin, USN	91
RMC W. L. Smith, USN	94
Cdr. E. A. Flatzek, USN	99
Capt. R. L. Arthur, USN	101
CT2 J. P. Carpenter, USN	105
Lt. M. H. Bennett, USN	114
CT2 T. L. Long, USN	117
CWO J. B. Wickam, USN	122
Cdr. W. L. McGonagle, USN (Recalled)	124
Capt. R. L. Raith, USN (Recalled)	139
Cdr. C. J. Jorgensen, USN	154

6. Adm. John S. McCain Jr. was the father of U.S. senator John S. McCain of Arizona.

7. Cdr. Merwin Staring, staff judge advocate to Admiral McCain, was a perfectionist. He objected to the form of the document, but his objections were overruled by Admirals McCain and Wylie, McCain's deputy. They were much more concerned with the conclusions and with forwarding the report to the Chief of Naval Operations in Washington. Staring later became Judge Advocate General of the U.S. Navy, serving in that capacity from 1974 to 1976.

8. To be technically correct, it was to be delivered to the Chief of Naval Operations at the Pentagon, which is located just across the Potomac River in Arlington, Virginia, not in Washington, D.C. It is common to refer to the Pentagon as being in Washington, and the press and the public seldom make the distinction. Unless there is some significance in the location of the Pentagon in Virginia, the common reference to Washington is used.

9. First Endorsement to the Report of the U.S. Navy Court of Inquiry, *Liberty Incident, Record of Proceedings,* by Adm. John McCain, U.S. Commander in Chief Naval Forces Europe.

10. Interview with Adm. Isaac C. Kidd Jr. on April 18, 1991, in Washington, D.C. When this author interviewed Vice Adm. Don Engen, Engen asked if he had interviewed Admiral Kidd. When Engen was advised that Kidd had a history of not talking about this subject, Engen offered to make an introduction. As a result of that introduction, this author arranged a meeting with Admiral Kidd at the Army-Navy Club in Washington, D.C. This was the first of many meetings, visits to the Kidd home, and telephone conversations between this author and Admiral Kidd. The assistance of Admiral Kidd in the completion of this research project has been of immense value.

11. When this author interviewed Admiral McDonald on June 29, 1990, the admiral described Admiral Kidd as his "right-hand man." When Ike Kidd was told of this description he commented, "I was McDonald's trash can."

12. The court did receive communications from Israel, usually routed through the Israel Foreign Military Liaison Officer, Lt. Col. Michael Bloch, to the U.S. naval attaché, Cdr. Ernest Castle.

13. News release, Office of the Assistant Secretary of Defense (Public Affairs), Washington, D.C., No. 594–67, June 28, 1967.

14. CIA, Directorate of Intelligence, Intelligence Memorandum, "The Israeli Attack on the USS *Liberty,* 13 June 1967, SC No. 01415/67." Declassified in redacted form "per # 058375" on August 31, 1977. The June 13, 1967, memorandum consisted of seven pages plus a chronology of three pages and a map of the area.

15. The chronology and the map each show local and Washington time, with a spread of seven hours. The Washington, or EDT, times are accurate. This confirms the conclusion that the preparers of the memorandum overlooked the fact that daylight time was *not* in effect in Israel, Sinai, or the *Liberty* operating area. This discrepancy has been called to the attention of the CIA by this author, but no corrective action has been taken.

16. See the CIA *Liberty* file.

17. The Egyptian ship is named in Arabic, and when the name is transliterated to Latin script there is opportunity for great creativity. The ship has been called *El quseir*, *El Quiser*, *El Kasir*, and possibly other spellings.

18. CIA, "Israeli Attack," 4.

19. The fact-finding team was not formally approved until June 15, 1967, when Lt. Gen. B. E. Spivy, USA, director of the Joint Staff, signed a memorandum to General Russ, which he received on board the Sixth Fleet flagship in the Mediterranean. By that date he and his team had almost completed their fact-finding mission. Specifically, what the team was to study included the means used to issue and transmit operational directives of the Joint Chiefs of Staff to the USS *Liberty* and circumstances attending any conflicting directives, inordinate delays in the receipt of messages or other proper orders, or their nonreceipt.

    Further, the fact-finding team was told: "The Court of Inquiry convened by CINCUSNAVEUR to inquire into the circumstances leading to and connected with the armed attack on the USS *Liberty* will inquire into administrative, disciplinary, and internal matters within that command which are not within the scope of the examination by the fact finding team. This fact-finding team will not infringe upon the prerogatives of the Court of Inquiry."

    The members of the team were Maj. Gen. Joseph R. Russ, USA; Rear Adm. Francis J. Fitzpatrick, USN; Col. William A Garrett, USAF; Capt. William D. Owen, USN; and Maj. Harlan E. Priddle, USAF.

20. "Introduction," Report of the JCS Fact Finding Team, USS *Liberty* Incident, 8 June 1967 (Secret). This is commonly known as the Russ Report.

    5. (U[unclassified]) Inasmuch as the Fact Finding Team was not a legal investigative body, in conducting its examination the Fact Finding Team observed the following constraints:

    a. Interviews were not conducted under oath.
    b. Individuals were not warned of their rights nor designated as interested parties.
    c. Interference with the Naval Court of Inquiry was avoided.
    d. Impact on *Liberty*'s personnel was held to a minimum.
    e. Representatives of the military services were invited to accompany the team.
    (Russ Report, 3)

21. The President's Foreign Intelligence Advisory Board was created by President John F. Kennedy in 1962 following the Bay of Pigs fiasco.

22. Many of Clifford's friends in the Johnson administration were not pleased with this report, because they felt it attempted to label Israel as the aggressor when it was generally conceded that Israel had acted in preemptive self-defense as permitted by Article 51 of the UN Charter and was in fact not guilty of aggression. No charge of aggression regarding the 1967 war ever resulted in a UN resolution condemning Israel.

23. The Clifford Report is at the Lyndon Baines Johnson Library in Austin, Texas, National Security File, Memos to the President, WWR, vol. 35, box 19. The report is identified as item 82b. The report was declassified upon the appeal of this author on October 25, 1995. Sanitized ED 12356, Sec3,4; NLJ 94–389, BY CB NARA Date 10–25–95: the transmittal letter from Clifford to Rostow, item 82a, was declassified on August 30, 1995. E.O. 12356, Sec3.4; NHJ 94–389 BY CB NARA Date 8–30–95: the transmittal letter from Rostow to President Johnson, item 82, remained classified. This author appealed that decision and prevailed. The letter from Rostow to Johnson transmitting the report was declassified on June 25, 1998.

24. Clifford Report, 4–5.

25. Ibid., 5.

26. Telephone interview of Clark Clifford by this author on February 9, 1989. Clifford was in Washington, D.C. He died on October 11, 1998.

27. "Murphy's Law" was the phrase of Clark Clifford. During the interview his memory seemed quite clear and positive.

28. Possibly the Situation Room in the basement of the West Wing of the White House.

29. Telephone interview of Clark Clifford by this author on February 9, 1989.

30. Clark Clifford, *Counsel to the President* (New York: Random House, 1991), 446.

31. Bourke Blakemore Hickenlooper, a Republican, served in the Senate from 1945 to 1969.

32. Hickenlooper's dislike or distrust of the Israelis is illustrated by his remark in a closed session of the Senate Foreign Relations Committee (the transcript was declassified in 1984) when he interrupted Christian Herter, secretary of state under President Eisenhower, during a discussion of the Israeli atomic project. "I think the Israelis have just lied to us like horse thieves on this thing. They have completely distorted, misrepresented, and falsified the facts in the past. I think it is very serious, to have them perform in this manner in connection with this very definite production reactor facility which they have been secretly building, and which they have consistently, and with a completely straight face, denied to us they were building." Seymour M. Hersh, *The Samson Option: Israel's Nuclear Arsenal and American Foreign Policy* (New York: Random House, 1991).

33. U.S. Senate, Hearings before the Committee on Foreign Relations on S. 1872, A Bill to Amend the Foreign Assistance Act of 1961, as Amended, and for Other Purposes, 90th Cong., 1st sess., June 12, July 14 and 26, 1967 (Washington, D.C.: U.S. Government Printing Office, 1967).

34. Cdr. L. M. "Pete" Bucher, USN (Ret.), the commanding officer of the *Pueblo* at the time of its capture, is quoted as saying, "I never fail to relate the USS *Liberty* story and its importance to our circumstance just 6 months later and the absolute fact that if the political contrivances that put the very valuable lessons learned in a totally sealed vault, the *Pueblo* incident could not have happened." *"Liberty" News*, 4th Quarter, 1998, 1.

35. U.S. Senate, Hearings before the Committee on Armed Services, United States Senate, on S. 3293, Authorization for Military Procurement, Research and Development, Fiscal Year 1969, and Reserve Strength, 90th Cong., 2d sess. (Washington, D.C.: U.S.

Government Printing Office, 1968), 47. This hearing was held on February 1, 1968, at 2:40 p.m. in Room 212, Old Senate Office Building. Present: Senators Stennis (presiding), Symington, Jackson, Connon, McIntyre, Byrd Jr. of Virginia, Smith, Thurmond, Miller, Tower, Pearson, and Dominick.

36. Rep. Robert Lee Fulton Sikes of Florida, House of Representatives, *Report of Subcommittee on Department of Defense of the Committee on Appropriations, April 8, 1968* (Washington, D.C.: U.S. Government Printing Office, 1968), 357–58.

37. Rep. John J. Rhodes (Ariz.), *House Subcommittee Hearing Report,* 394.

38. Subcommittee on Department of Defense of the Committee on Appropriations, *House Subcommittee Hearing Report,* 398–99.

39. *Congressional Record-House,* July 12, 1968, 21055.

40. Through the assistance of Florida senator Bob Graham and his staff, this author was able to visit the restricted office of the Senate Select Committee on Intelligence. During that visit, a staff member advised that a portion of the House Appropriations Committee report remains classified as indicated.

41. U.S. House of Representatives, Report of the Armed Services Subcommittee of the Committee on Armed Services, House of Representatives, under the Authority of H. Res. 201. 92d Cong., 1st sess., May 10, 1971 (Washington, D.C.: U.S. Government Printing Office, 1971). The report was submitted for printing, with deletions for security, to the chairman of the House Armed Services Committee, Congressman F. Edward Hebert of Louisiana, on March 24, 1971. The committee studied the USS *Liberty* incident, which occurred on June 8, 1967; the USS *Pueblo* incident, which occurred on January 23, 1968; and the downing of a Navy EC-121 aircraft by North Korea on April 15, 1969. Hearings were held and a report was published.

42. U.S. House, Report of the Armed Services Subcommittee, 10.

43. Set forth in the letter of transmittal of the report, dated March 24, 1971, from the committee chair, Robert H. Mollohan, to the chair of the Armed Services Committee, F. Edward Hebert. U.S. House of Representatives, Report of the Armed Services Subcommittee, III.

44. Capt. Frank Snyder, the Sixth Fleet communications officer who was on board the USS *Little Rock* with Admiral Martin on June 8, 1967, worked with Rear Admiral Fitzpatrick in preparation of his testimony before the committee.

45. Brig. Gen. Roscoe M. Cougill (Ret.), "C3 during Desert Shield and Desert Storm," in Seminar on Command, Control, and Communications, Guest Presentations, spring 1992. Program on Information Resources Policy, Harvard University, Cambridge, Massachusetts, August 1994.

46. U.S. House, Report of the Armed Services Subcommittee, 3–4.

47. Lt. Gen. Richard P. Klocko, USAF, assumed the position of director, Defense Communications Agency (DCA), on November 15, 1967. He had begun serving in the DCA in July 1967 as deputy director of the agency and deputy director, National Military Command System Technical Support (NMCSTS).

48. U.S. House, Report of the Armed Services Subcommittee, 41–42.

49. James M. Ennes Jr., *Assault on the "Liberty"* (New York: Random House, 1979).

50. All three of the surviving pilots, who speak fluent English, have been interviewed by this author, face to face, without the intervention of a sheet. The fourth pilot was killed in an aviation accident while preparing for an air show in 1979. Under the terms of an agreement with Israel Field Security, the names of the living pilots are not to be disclosed.

51. In June 1982 the Israel Defense Forces History Department, Research and Instruction Branch, published *The Attack on the "Liberty" Incident, 8 June 1967*. Col. Uri Algom, the head of the History Department, signed the report. The report is prefaced by the following five notes:

  1. The tragic event of the attack on the American intelligence ship *Liberty* [*sic*] (8 June 1967) became, over the years, an instrument in the hands of journalists and authors, with which to contend that Israel attacked the ship maliciously.
  2. Recently, with the publication of the book, *Assault on the "Liberty,"* the American Congress appointed a committee, headed by Adlai Stevenson, for the purpose of investigating the affair and publishing the results of the investigation.
  3. Immediately upon learning of the appointment of the committee, it was decided that the History Department would research the affair and submit the official version of the State of Israel.
  4. The research is based upon all the primary and secondary evidence available.
  5. This article is the official version, written by Lt. Col. Matti Greenberg— Head of the Combat Research Branch.

  This author interviewed Matti Greenberg for the first time in Tel Aviv on August 13, 1989, and many additional times in person and by telephone.

52. In a telephone interview with this author, former Senator Adlai Stevenson stated that he had almost no recollection of the matter or the investigation. The interview took place on January 4, 1990. Stevenson was in Chicago.

53. This author visited the office of the Senate Select Committee on Intelligence in Washington, D.C., but was unable to locate any public record of the investigation. As indicated in note 52, former Senator Adlai Stevenson claimed to have no memory of the investigation. This author wrote to each of the senators who served on the committee in the 1979–81 time frame seeking information on the investigation. No senator replied.

54. This author interviewed two Israeli officers attached to the IDF spokesman who have personal recollections of the interviews. They are Col. Raanan Gissen and Maj. (later

Lt. Col.) Danny Grossman. This author also confirmed the interviews with *Kursa* Flight leader and Royal Flight leader.

55. The senators on the committee were Birch Bayh (D-Ind.); Adlai E. Stevenson (D-Ill.); Walter D. Huddleston (D-Ky.); Joseph R. Biden (D-Del.); Daniel P Moynihan (D-N.Y.); Daniel K. Inouye (D-Hawaii); Henry M. Jackson (D-Wash.); Patrick J. Leahy (D-Vt.); Barry M. Goldwater (R-Ariz.); Edwin (Jake) Gam (R-Utah); John Chafee (R-R.I.); Richard G. Lugar (R-Ind.); Malcolm Wallop (R-Wyo.); David Durenberger (R-Minn.); Charles McC. Mathias (R-Md.); and ex officio: Robert C. Byrd (D-W. Va.) and Howard H. Baker Jr. (R-Tenn.).

56. The document is entitled *Attack on the U.S.S. "Liberty."* It was originally classified top secret, because some of its contents were in that category. Other portions were categorized as secret, confidential, and unclassified. The original document, marked top secret, bore the legend "Not releasable to foreign nationals." The document was declassified per part 3, E.O. 12356 by Director, NSA/Chief, CSS COF Date 7/11/83.

This author originally obtained a copy of the document from a foreign national, not part of any intelligence community. The copy did not reflect declassification. The author spent months trying to write to the NSA. Those were the days when NSA was reputed to stand for "No such agency," and letters were either returned marked "insufficient address" or not answered. Eventually it was learned that the document had been declassified and in fact is on file in the National Archives in Washington, D.C., under document number SRH-256. The only other declassified documents relating to the *Liberty* incident in the National Archives are REP0006C, RG 218, Chairman Wheeler Files, 091 Israel-UAR Conflict, May–June 1967, Box 27, 631/8/14/4.

57. NSA, *Attack on the U.S.S. "Liberty,"* 40.

58. Allen M. Blue, from Rockville, Maryland, one of three civilian technicians employed by the NSA, also died in the attack.

59. NSA, *Attack on the U.S.S. "Liberty,"* 40.

60. Letter from Debra Rae Anderson, deputy assistant to the president and director of the Office of Intergovernmental Affairs, the White House, September 5, 1991.

61. Letter from the USS *Liberty* Veterans Association to the Honorable Nicholas Mavroules, July 1, 1991, signed by Joseph L. Meadors, chairman.

62. Meeting of this author with Roy J. Kirk and Warren Nelson at 11:00 a.m. on April 29, 1992, in Room 2120, Rayburn House Office Building. Following this meeting, all three named persons proceeded to the office of Congressman Mavroules at 2334 Rayburn House Office Building for a meeting with the congressman; that meeting lasted over an hour.

63. Presidents Lyndon B. Johnson, Richard M. Nixon, Gerald Ford, Jimmy Carter, Ronald Reagan, George H. W. Bush, and William J. Clinton.

Chapter 13. Israel Investigates

1. Section 537 states: "The Minister of Defense or the CGS may appoint a commission of inquiry for the purpose of investigating any matter relating to the Army, and such commission shall be competent to summon witnesses and to take evidence on oath or otherwise. A commission of inquiry may consist of one officer."

2. Interview of Ram Ron by this author on June 7, 1988, at Tel Aviv.

3. His report refers to exhibits up to the letter *L*.

4. Whether this is in fact an error by Ram Ron or an error in the translation from Hebrew to English is not known. This possibility should be considered regarding any of the documents originally produced in Hebrew and thereafter translated into English.

5. A preliminary inquiry under section 283 is essentially the same type of procedure as a court of inquiry under U.S. law: "283. Where the Military Advocate General has directed that a preliminary inquiry be held, he shall notify the President of the Appeal Court Martial, who shall appoint an examining judge to hold it. Sections 283 through 298 govern the conduct of a preliminary inquiry."

6. There is no record of the *Liberty* receiving the Egyptian declaration, but it appears that the judge believed that such a declaration had been made by the Egyptians well before the *Liberty*'s arrival in the area and that it had been published in *Al Ahram* and broadcast on Egyptian radio.

7. This is not exactly correct. The *Liberty* was certainly in the vicinity of the war but did not approach any closer to the coast of Israel than longitude 34-00 E, which was at least thirty-eight nautical miles from the nearest coast of Israel.

8. Examining judge's report, 16 (English translation).

9. From an outgoing telegram of the Department of State time-stamped both June 7, 1967, and June 10, 1967. The document indicates that the "text was approved in White House" and bears a number stamp 210139. Other messages from the U.S. Department of State to Israel's ambassador contain similar or identical language.

10. Clifford Report, 4–5.

11. Capt. Glenn R. Brindel had been the commanding officer of the USS *Stark* when she was hit by two Iraqi Exocet missiles on May 17, 1987. It is not unusual in the naval service to avoid a court-martial by allowing an officer to resign or retire. On April 23, 2001, Cdr. Thomas Waddle was given similar treatment in connection with the collision of the submarine *Greenville*, which he was commanding when it collided near Hawaii with a Japanese vessel; the collision killed nine people.

12. In the opinion of Captain Castle, Rehav had been an outstanding naval officer. He was talented, diplomatic, and charismatic. In the history of the Israel Navy, the second in command has almost always "fleeted up" and became the next commander. The navy of Israel was established March 17, 1948.

	Navy Commander	Second in Command
1948–49	Paul Shulman	
1950	Shlomo Sharnir	
1950–54	Mokal Limon	Shmuel Tankos
1954–60	Shmuel Tankos	Kenan
1960–66	Yochai Ben-Nun	Yitzhak Rehav
1966–68	Shlomo Erell	Yitzhak Rehav
		Avraham Botzer
1968–72	Avraham Botzer	Biny Telem
1972–75	Biny Tel	Suit Trosh
		Michael Barkaei
1975–79	Michael Barkaei	Gideon Raz
1979–85	Zeev Alrnog	Gideon Raz
		Abraham Ben-Shushan
1985–89	Abraham Ben-Shushan	Michael Ram
1989–93	Michael Ram	Ami Ayalon
1993–96	Ami Ayalon	Alexander Tal
1996–2000	Alexander Tal	Yedidya Ya'ari
2000–2004	Yedidya Ya'ari	David Ben-Bashat
2004–2007	David Ben-Bashat	Eli Marom
2007–2011	Eli Marom	Ben Yehuda
2011–	Ram Rutberg	Yaron Levi

13. Israel Defense Forces, History Department, Research and Instruction Branch, *The Attack on the "Liberty" Incident,* June 1982 [hereafter cited as IDF History], 2.

14. This author has always preferred to refer to the "attacks" (plural) rather than "the attack" (singular), as the air attack began and ended before the torpedo attack began, and there are many distinct aspects of each attack that are best considered separately.

15. IDF History, 33.

16. Ibid., 38.

17. Letter of Admiral Michael Ram, Commander in Chief, Navy of Israel, published in the *Naval Reserve Association News,* September 1992.

Chapter 14. Television's Perspective

1. Rex Bloornstein, producer and director, *Attack on the "Liberty,"* London, Thames Television, aired on BBC 2, January 27, 1987.

2. Adrian Pennink, the research editor of Thames TV, was kind enough to give the Thames research files to this author.

3. In the Thames script, 50, 51, and 52, at items 234–44.

4. Thames script, 52.

5. *Mabat shaine* translates from the Hebrew as "second view," "hindsight," or "double take." The program has a magazine format similar to that of *20/20* or *60 Minutes*. The tape was reduced from its original fifty-three minutes, seventeen seconds to about forty-nine minutes. George Golden was cut from the tape. The program was broadcast in English with Hebrew subtitles. The introductory remarks in Hebrew were translated from the original tape for this author by Oded Ben-Arie in February 1991.

6. Interview of Rex Bloomstein by this author on September 16, 1991, in London, at BBC Television headquarters. Bloomstein had become very fond of the *Liberty* crew members and very sympathetic to their situation. He was of the opinion that some of them still suffered from post-traumatic stress disorder and that they had not been treated properly by the U.S. government.

7. Rhoda Lipton, producer, "The Attack on the *Liberty*," ABC News *20/20*, show 719, aired on May 21, 1987, transcript, 2.

8. Ibid., 7.

9. *"Liberty" News*, September 1987, 3.

10. Michael Shiloh completed his tour as deputy chief of mission at the Embassy of Israel in Washington and then was appointed as Israel's ambassador to Norway.

11. Christopher Carlson, producer, and John Cosgrove, supervising director, *The Story behind the Story*, NBC, aired on January 27, 1992.

12. Justin Sturken, producer, *Now It Can Be Told*, aired on April 14, 1992, syndicated program, 1992. The program was first aired by WVUE, New Orleans, Channel 8 (an ABC affiliate). It then appeared on various channels around the country.

13. Telephone interview of producer Justin Sturken by this author on January 28, 1992, during the time that the videotape was being made. Sturken had seen the NBC program *The Story behind the Story* aired January 27, 1992, and was very unhappy with it. He felt it portrayed the *Liberty* crewmen in an unfavorable light. His exact words were, "It made them look like a bunch of jerks."

14. The crew members presented in the program are Joseph Lentini, Lloyd Painter, John Hrankowski, James Ennes, Richard Sturman, and Joseph Meadors.

15. U.S. Senate, *Hearings before the Committee on Foreign Relations on S. 1872, a Bill to Amend the Foreign Assistance Act of 1961*, 90th Cong., 1st sess., June 12, July 14 and 26, 1967, 266–67.

16. U.S. Navy Court of Inquiry, *Liberty Incident, Record of Proceedings*, testimony of Cdr. William L. McGonagle, beginning at p. 31 and again at p. 124.

17. Thames script, 18–19, items 92–94.

18. Glenn Frankel, "In Britain, Fallout from Friendly Fire: Families of Allied Dead Press Two Nations for Facts," *Washington Post*, May 18, 1992, D-1: "American officials contend they've done their best to cooperate but say the government will not compel the pilots to testify in Britain." Also William E. Schmidt, "Nine Deaths in Gulf: British Ask Why?," *New York Times*, May 11, 1992, A-3: "No Americans will be coming to England to testify about what went wrong."

19. The list of witnesses called for the U.S. Navy Court of Inquiry includes the following *Liberty* crew members. Their testimony appears in the record beginning at the page indicated:

Crew Member	Page
Ens. D. G. Lucas, USNR	12
Cdr. W. L. McGonagle, USN	31
Lt. (jg) L. C. Painter, USNR	55
Ens. J. D. Scott, USNR	59
Lt. G. H. Golden, USN	63
Ens. M. P. O'Malley, USN	68
Lt. (jg) M. M. Watson, USNR	72
Lt. R. F. Kiepefer, USNR (MC)	74
CTC H. J. Thompson, USN	87
CTC C. F. Lamkin, USN	91
RMC W. L. Smith, USN	94
CT2 J. P. Carpenter, USN	105
Lt. M. H. Bennett, USN	114
CT2 T. L. Long, USN	117
Cdr. W. L. McGonagle, USN (Recalled)	124

20. U.S. Navy Court of Inquiry, testimony of Commander McGonagle, 131.

21. Ibid., testimony of Ensign Lucas, at Malta, on June 13, 1967, 12–23; of Chief Thompson, at Malta, on June 13, 1967, 87–90.

22. Letter to this author from Susan Werbe, Vice President, Historical Programming, the History Channel, dated August 24, 2001, confirms to this author that in some cases the footage shown "is not of the actual event described." Werbe claims the practice of using footage that "is representational" or of doing reenactments has "become a quite accepted element in historical documentaries." This author would suggest that custom and practice in the documentary industry requires file film or reenactments to be orally described as such or labeled. No such oral disclosures or screen captions were included in this production.

23. Cheryl Faris, producer, and Patrick King, director, *USS Liberty Survivors* [film], Los Angeles, Sligo Productions, 1991.

24. Quoting Anthony Pearson, *Conspiracy of Silence* (London: Quartet, 1978), 319. See chapter 9, pages 112–13.

25. Telephone conversation, this author with Joe Lentini of July 23, 2002.

26. *The USS Liberty Newsletter* 3, no. 1 (January 1984), 8.

27. Reported by Robert A. Hamilton, *The Day: Connecticut,* October 29, 2002, http:/www.theday.com/mews/Is-re ASP?news UID_08D3612C-B9A2–4341–0EDEAEA.

28. Telephone conversation, this author with Joe Lentini on July 23, 2002.

29. "Attack on the *Liberty*," Thames TV.

30. Vice Adm. Connolly served as OP-05 from November 1, 1966, to August 21, 1971.

31. See *The Liberty Incident,* www.thelibertyincident.com/documents/hotline, and "The Nation: Hot Line Diplomacy," *Time Magazine,* June 16, 1967, 15–17, including a picture of the hotline teletype machine, and at Lyndon Baines Johnson, *Vantage Point:*

Perspectives of the Presidency. 1963–1969 (New York: Holt Rinehart and Winston, 1971), 297–304.

32. Bryant Jordan, "SS *Liberty* sails to Challenge Israel," Military.com, http://www.military.com/news/articles/SS_Liberty_sails_to_challenge_Israel.html? col=1186032325324, plus comments.

33. Telephone conversation, this author and John Hadden, initiated by John Hadden on February 3, 2002.

34. Ibid.

35. Cdr. David Lewis lives in Colebrook, Vermont. An interview with Lewis is included in the video production "Dead in the Water."

36. "Dead in the Water," London, Vision, 2003.

37. Review of "Dead in the Water" by Mike Weeks, posted on Amazon.com, customer reviews, August 19, 2006. See also review of Joseph (United States) on Amazon, July 25: "Absolute lies and falsified information. This film is not only severely biased, but it fails to explain why Israel would deliberately attack their only ally."

38. Associated Press report on speech of Capt. William McGonagle, June 8, 1977, carried in multiple newspapers on June 8, 1967.

39. Stephen Green, *Taking Sides* (New York: William Morrow, 1984).

40. "USAF in Sinai in the 1967 War: Fact or Fiction?," *Journal of Palestine Studies* 27, no. 1 (Autumn 1997), 67–75. Ambassador Parker served as U.S. ambassador to Lebanon, Algeria, and Morocco. After retirement he was scholar in residence at the Middle East Institute, Washington, D.C.

41. See picture in *Aviation Week & Space Technology,* July 24, 1967, 69. It was taken on June 5, 1967, the first day of the Six Day War, by Israel Air Force Squadron 119. A similar picture showing the shadow of a Mirage IIIC on the ground as it flies over three destroyed Egyptian aircraft is published in Lon Nordeen and David Nicolle, *Phoenix over the Nile* (Washington and London: Smithsonian Institution Press, 1996), the twenty-fourth picture following page 218. The caption reads: "This photograph, *taken by an IAF Mirage,* documents the severe blow inflicted upon the UARAF by Israeli jets on 5 June 1967. These three Egyptian MiG-21 fighters were destroyed on the ground by cannon fire at an air base said to be demolished before they could take off (Photo IAF)" (emphasis added).

42. *"Liberty" News,* September/October 1981, 4.

43. Ibid., August 1982, 2.

44. Ibid., 9.

45. Ibid., March 1983, 2.

46. The program titled "1967 Arab-Israeli War and USS *Liberty*" may be obtained from C-SPAN.org ID: 179892-01/12/2004-2:58.

47. This author's paper for the conference, submitted by invitation, may be viewed at www.thelibertyincident.com/docs/liberty-intelligence.pdf. It was coauthored with John Hadden, CIA chief of station in Tel Aviv in 1967, and Capt. Ernest Castle, USN, U.S. naval attaché in Tel Aviv in 1967.

48. E-mail, Brooke E. Runnette, to A Jay Cristol, November 4, 2004.

49. Reported by David Bauder, AP television writer, Thursday, March 28, 2008, New York: "Former *Nightline* reporter David Marish has quit Al-Jazeera English, saying Thursday his exit was due in part to an anti-American bias at a network that is little seen in this country."

50. James M. Ennes Jr., "The USS *Liberty* Affair," *Link* (May/June 1984), 7; James M. Ennes Jr. "The USS *Liberty*," *Link* (May/June 1992), 6.

51. USS *Liberty* Veterans Association, *Special Pre-Reunion Bulletin*, May 6, 1987.

Chapter 15. Red Herrings and Myths

1. Richard B. Parker, ed., *The Six Day War: A Retrospective* (Gainesville: University Press of Florida, 1996), 270. The entire quote is: "I'll take up the challenge of the *Liberty* with your permission. Why would Israel do such a terrible thing? We may be crazy, but we are not fools. For Israel in the middle of a war, when the Soviet fleet is on the horizon, to come out and shoot up and try to sink and bomb and kill American sailors is worse than a crime, it's damned folly. [As for] the reason being that we were going to attack the Golan Heights: that this was a reason good enough to provoke this kind of horrible thing, which would do incalculable damage to Israel is unimaginable. The Americans had many ways of finding out what our plans were. They knew what was going on, and anybody who knows Israel knows that even a truck that goes up the single road to the Golan could be spotted. We don't have to sink an American ship for that. At the risk of being laughed out of this room, I have to repeat to you that it was a terrible tragic mistake."

2. The Japanese carriers *Akagi, Kaga, Hiryu,* and *Soryu* were all lost at Midway. Mitsuo Fuchida and Masatake Okumiya, *Midway: The Battle That Doomed Japan* (New York: Ballantine, 1955), 213, 155–77. See also Samuel Eliot Morrison, *History of U.S. Naval Operations in World War II* (Boston: Little, Brown, 1964), 4: 9–93.

3. The only "rockets" were air-to-air missiles, most likely AIM-9 Sidewinders, which were heat seekers and which, if fired, would probably not have locked onto a surface ship. Shrapnel fragments were collected from *Liberty* and sent for evaluation to the Navy Scientific Intelligence Center. On June 28, 1967, the center sent a priority message to the *Liberty*, with information copies to the Chief of Naval Operations; Commander in Chief, U.S. Naval Forces Europe; Commander in Chief, U.S. European Command; Joint Chiefs of Staff (Joint Center Reconnaissance); Commander in Chief, Atlantic Command; Commander Sixth Fleet; Commander Service Force Atlantic; and the Defense Intelligence Agency. The message stated:

Confidential

Shrapnel Evaluation

a. Liberty (AGTR-5) 081715Z

1. Interim evaluation of fragments received as a result of attack Reference A indicates following types of ammunition and source:

a. 20 mm HE-T. From MTB 20K DM-11 German

b. 30 mm HC, aircraft cannon, nationality unknown

c. 40 mm tracer element from MTB. US made projectile

d. 50 caliber projectiles (several) nationality unknown.

Apparently no shrapnel fragments from rockets, missiles, or napalm canisters were collected and submitted. Though the issue of whether *Liberty* was hit by rockets remains in dispute, it is not relevant to the issue of whether the attack was intentional or a mistake.

4. Examining Judge's Preliminary Inquiry, para. 16: "It was testified to me that the area was declared by the Egyptian Authorities as one dangerous to shipping, a declaration which presumably reached all vessels to be found in the vicinity."

Chapter 16. Confirmation: National Security Agency Intercepts

1. Marvin Nowicki ultimately retired from the Navy with the rank of lieutenant commander.

2. Naval Historic Center DTG 081359Z June 1967 COMSIXTH FLEET TO FAIRECCONRON TWO [VQ-2 and others].

3. Richard Hickman is referred to in the original (i.e., first) edition of this book as the Third Hebrew Linguist (page 136 of that edition). His oral history at the National Security Agency was declassified and released on September 19, 2005, as a result of this author's Freedom of Information Act, NSA FOIA case no. 41707A.

4. Department of Defense news release 530–67 of June 6, 1967.

5. Report of House Armed Services Investigative Subcommittee of the U.S. House of Representatives Committee on Armed Services, May 10, 1971.

6. Interview of George Golden, March 11, 1991, by this author.

7. National Security Agency Report, "Attack on a SIGINT Collector, USS Liberty," National Security Agency, 1981, p. 64.

8. See U.S. District Court, Southern District of Florida, Case No. 03–20123-CIV-HUCK, *A Jay Cristol v. National Security Agency.*

9. James Bamford, *Body of Secrets* (New York: Doubleday, 2001), 185–239.

10. Scott Shane and Tom Bowman, "New Book on NSA Sheds Light on Secrets," *Baltimore Sun,* April 24, 2001.

11. "Tragic Gross Error in 1967 Attack," *Wall Street Journal,* May 16, 2001, A-23.

12. Mentioned on page 146.

13. See record of U.S. District Court, Case No. 03–20123-CIV-HUCK, *A. Jay Cristol v. National Security Agency.*

14. National Security Agency, "Attack on a SIGINT Collector, the USS *Liberty,*" 1981, 64. The audiotapes, transcripts, and 1981 report may be heard and viewed on the National Security Agency website, www.nsa.gov/liberty/.

15. See Richard W. Hickman, oral history, declassified by NSA on September 19, 2005. It may be seen at *The Liberty Incident,* www.thelibertyincident.com/hebrewlinguist3.html.

16. See Thames TV production, *Attack on the Liberty,* first aired Tuesday, June 28, 1987, at 10:39 p.m. on British television, fifty-three minutes, fifteen seconds in length.

17. See appendix 2, p. 261.

18. National Security Agency, "Attack on a SIGINT Collector, the USS *Liberty,*" 1981, vii.

19. Ibid., 64.

20. CIA intelligence memorandum, June 13, 1967, SC No.01415/67. See U.S. Department of State, *Foreign Relations of the United States, Volume XIX* (Washington, D.C., 2003), item 317.

21. CIA intelligence memorandum, June 21, 1967, SC No. 08384–67. See U.S. Department of State, *Foreign Relations of the United States, Volume XIX,* item 284.

22. Stansfield Turner, director of CIA, letter to Senator Abourzek, February 27, 1978.

23. Defense Intelligence Agency, memoranda to the chairman of the Joint Chiefs of Staff, TS-SI-0186/AP-5, 13 June 1967 (Top Secret Trine); and SS-S1–0211/AP-5, 28 June, 1967 (Secret Savin).

24. President's Foreign Intelligence Advisory Board report, July 18, 1967, p. 4. This report may be viewed, as "Clark Clifford Report," at TheLibertyIncident.com under Documents.

25. U.S. Navy Court of Inquiry, 28 June 1967, findings 1 and 6.

26. First endorsement on letter of Adm. Isaac C. Kidd, USN, 111645/1100 of 18 June 1967 from Commander in Chief, U.S. Naval Forces Europe, to Judge Advocate General, 4, para. 15.

Chapter 17. Confirmation: The Mythical Submarine

1. National Security Council Note by the executive secretary dated December 28, 1955, states "The President has this day approved the amendment of. . . . NSC 5412/1" which had created "Special Group 5412" and promulgated National Security Council directive on covert operations, NSC5412/2. See National Security File, NSA 5412/1 and NSA 5412/2, both originally classified top secret and declassified in 1977. Lyndon Baines Johnson Library, Austin, Texas.

2. Memorandum on White House stationery signed by McGeorge Bundy (at the time National Security Advisor to President John F. Kennedy). The document was declassified on December 5, 1987. Lyndon Baines Johnson Library, Austin, Texas.

3. Ennes claims to have interviewed General Steakley and to have been told "that his job with the Joint Chiefs of Staff was to win approval of such projects from the appropriate authorities. He was rarely involved in the projects themselves. He could remember nothing about FRONTLET 615." James M. Ennes Jr., "USS *Liberty*: Periscope Photography May Finally Reveal Truth," *Washington Report on Middle East Affairs* 26, no. 1 (June/July 1997), 19–20.

4. William Broe was a division chief at CIA and later inspector general of the CIA. He worked on projects related to the overthrow of Salvador Allende in Chile. It appears doubtful that Item 2, referred to in the memorandum, had anything to do with a submarine in the Mediterranean.

5. National Security File, Files of the Special Committee of the NSC, "Liberty," box 10, Lyndon Baines Johnson Library.

6. James M. Ennes Jr., *Assault on the "Liberty"* (New York: Random House, 1979).

7. Ennes, "USS *Liberty*: Periscope Photography May Finally Reveal Truth."

8. Russell Warren Howe, *Weapons* (Garden City, N.Y.: Doubleday, 1980). Howe claims the USS *Andrew Jackson* was two hundred feet below the USS *Liberty* during the attack. The deck log of the *Andrew Jackson* shows only that from April 1 through 30 June 30, 1967, she was attached to the Atlantic Fleet and operating out of Rota, Spain.

9. The deck log of USS *Trutta* shows on June 8, 1967, she was in port at Souda Bay, Crete, "moored side to starboard side USS *Tidewater* AD31."

10. The deck log of USS *Requin* shows on June 8, 1967, that she was in port at Souda Bay, Crete, "moored to buoy no. 7 in anchorage at Suda Bay, Crete."

11. Ennes Jr., "USS *Liberty*: Periscope Photography May Finally Reveal Truth."

12. An antenna at sea level could pick up sea-level transmissions at no more than two miles, line of sight. Transmissions from high-flying aircraft could be received from a greater distance. Nevertheless, some conspiracy stories claim of hearing ground controllers broadcasting from transmitters many miles away in Israel, at or near sea level, which is a physical impossibility. For example, Capt. Richard Block claims to have been on active duty with the 6931st Reconnaissance Center in Crete, more than five hundred miles away, where he heard real-time intercepts. When others who claimed they heard the intercepts in real time as far away as Viet Nam or in the United States were asked how they understood the Hebrew language of intercepts, they changed their stories to having read teletype translations of the intercepts in real time.

13. There are a possible six hundred VHF frequencies or channels (118 MHZ to 132 MHZ) and over 1,930 UHF frequencies or channels (225 MHZ to 418 MHZ) from which to select.

14. Record U.S. Navy Court of Inquiry, *Liberty Incident, Record of Proceedings*, testimony of Lt. (jg) L. Painter, 59/164/164.

15. Deck log of USS *Amberjack* for June 9, 1967, on file at the Naval History and Heritage Command (NHHC).

16. Deck log of USS *Andrew Jackson* for June 8, 1967, on file at NHHC.

17. Deck log of USS *Trutta* for June 8, 1967, on file at NHHC.

18. Deck log of USS *Requin* for June 8, 1967, on file at NHHC.

19. The original affidavit of Capt. Augustine Hubel is on file with the U.S. District Court, Southern District of Florida. It may be reviewed at *The Liberty Incident*, www.thelibertyincident.com, *Amberjack* Skipper's affidavit.

20. The original affidavit of Vice Adm. Marmaduke G. Bayne is on file with the U.S. District Court, Southern District of Florida. It may be viewed at *The Liberty Incident*, www.thelibertyincident.com, COMSUBFLOT8 Affidavit.

21. Vice Adm. Marmaduke Gresham Bayne, oral history, August 26, 1998, NHHC, 75.

22. See record of U.S. District Court, Case No. 03–20123-CIV-HUCK, *A. Jay Cristol v. National Security Agency*.

23. Ibid.

24. Nikolai Cherkashin, "On Moscow's Orders," *Russian Life,* October 1996, 13. Originally published in Russian in *Rodina.*

25. Ibid., 14.

26. Passover 1968 was celebrated from April 12 to April 20; Passover 1967 was celebrated from April 25 to April 30.

27. Cherkashin, "On Moscow's Orders," 13.

Chapter 18. Confirmation: Department of State

1. Letter

    From: "Tudda, Christopher J"

    The United States, the Middle East, and the Arab-Israeli War of 1967

    Office of the Historian, U.S. Department of State

    January 12–13, 2004

    The Office of the Historian, U.S. Department of State, will host a conference on the Arab-Israeli Crisis and War of 1967, within the broader context of U.S. relations with the Middle East during the Johnson administration. The conference will be held on January 12 and 13, 2004, in Washington, DC, and coincide with the release of the forthcoming volume in the Department of State's historical series, Foreign Relations of the United States, vol. XIX, The Arab-Israeli Crisis and War, 1967. The volume covers the period from May 1967, when Egyptian President Nasser requested the removal of the United Nations Emergency Force, to November 1967, when the United Nations passed Resolution 242. The Office of the Historian invites proposals for original papers on topics relating to the pre-war regional crises, the war itself, and the immediate post-war impact. Paper proposals should concentrate on the time period under consideration. Possible themes include:

    Origins of the 1967 war (e.g., military and strategic decisions, Arab states and leaders, Israel, the United States, and the Soviet Union)

    U.S. diplomacy leading up to and during the war

    The USS Liberty incident and the role of intelligence

    Immediate consequences of the crisis and war (e.g., for NATO, the first oil embargo, the regional balance of power)

    Regional and international economic dislocations (e.g., Suez canal closure)

    U.S. view of post-war problems (e.g., Palestinians, refugees)

    U.N. Resolution 242

    Other immediate post-war issues

    Paper proposals (abstract and c.v.) should be sent, preferably via e-mail or fax, by October 20, 2003 (NEW DATE) to:

    Laurie West Van Hook

    Conference Coordinator

Office of the Historian
U.S. Department of State
2401 E Street, NW
Room L-409
Washington, DC 20522
fax: 202–663–1289
tel: 202–663–1125

2. C-SPAN ID:179892-01/12/2004.

3. U.S. Department of State, *Foreign Relations, 1964–1968, Volume XIX, Arab-Israeli Crisis and War, 1967.* Summary released by the office of the historian, January 12, 2004, paragraphs 13–15. See www.state.gov/r/pa/ho/frus/johnsonlb/xix/28165.htm.

4. Dr. Charles Smith, *The Palestine and Arab-Israeli Conflict* (New York: St. Martin's Press, 1988).

5. The cable was passed to the White House at 6:22 p.m. Significant text of the five-page secret cable declassified on April 27, 1999, follows:

INCOMING TELEGRAM *Department of State* . . .
P 08164 0Z JUN 67
FM AMEMBASSY TEL AVIV
TO RUEHC/SECSTATE WASHDC PRIORITY . . .
S̶E̶C̶R̶E̶T̶ TEL AVIV 4020
JOINT EMBASSY/DAO . . .

1. FOLLOWING IS SUMMARY OF IDF INTELLIGENCE CHIEF'S BRIEFING OF MCPHERSON OF WHITE HOUSE JUNE 8, 11:30 A. M.

2. GENERAL YARIV SAID THAT THE PRINCIPAL TASK OF THE IDF NOW WAS TO EXPLOIT ITS SUCCESS. THERE STILL REMAINED THE SYRIAN PROBLEM AND PERHAPS IT WOULD BE NECESSARY TO GIVE SYRIA A BLOW TO GET MORE QUOTE ELBOW ROOM UNQUOTE . . .

12. . . . YARIV SAID THERE WERE NO GROUND OPERATIONS IN SYRIA YET, QUOTE UNFORTUNATELY UNQUOTE . . .

BARBOUR

6. U.S. Navy Court of Inquiry, *Liberty Incident, Record of Proceedings,* Findings of Fact, page 161 of original pagination (p. 266 of AJC and JAG pagination).

Chapter 19. Confirmation: Court of Inquiry Audiotapes

1. The testimony of Ens. John D. Scott is recorded beginning on page 59/163/163 of the U.S. Navy court of inquiry record. See below, note 2.

2. The original court of inquiry record, dated June 18, 1967 consisted of six copies. Copy number 3 is on file with the Office of the U.S. Navy Judge Advocate General. Although the entire record is posted on *The Liberty Incident,* www.thelibertyincident.com/docs/CourtOfInquiry.pdf, on June 9, 2008, this author received the following information

from the Operational Archives Branch of the Naval Historical Center: "The Court of Inquiry for the *Liberty* Incident is box 110 of CNO (00) 1969 Collection and is copy 4 of 6. Unfortunately that collection is currently closed. Records that had been reviewed for declassification under Executive Order 12958 (17 April 1995) and authorized for release have been closed pending another review. This new declassification review wsa [*sic*] mandated by Public Law 105–261, also known as Kyl-Lott. Until Kyl-Lott declassification review is completed the previously declassified records will be closed."

3. Case No. 2:07–2972-PMD-RSC, *James Scott, pro se, Plaintiff v. Naval Historical Center Operational Archives Branch, Defendant.*

4. See paragraph 10 of complaint in *Scott v. Naval Historical Center.*

5. As noted above, there were six copies of the official record of the U.S. Navy court of inquiry. The tapes were found only with the U.S. Naval Historical Center copy number 3. It is not known who made the recordings or how they got to the Naval Historical Center file.

6. The CDs may be obtained by Freedom of Information Act request to Naval History and Heritage Command, 805 Kidder Breese Street, SE, #1, Washington, DC 20374–5055.

7. See *Scott v. Naval Historical Center.*

8. Ibid.

9. Belt seven of the tapes.

10. See U.S. Navy court of inquiry record, page 174 of original pagination. The record was repaginated by the Judge Advocate General (JAG) to include additional documents and endorsements and also repaginated by this author (AJC). On the Internet, the pages contain three pagination numbers. The JAG and AJC numbers are essentially the same (p. 279 of AJC and JAG pagination).

11. Affidavit of Ward Boston dated October 22, 2003. Boston later also signed a "declaration," on January 9, 2004.

12. Telephone conversation with Capt. Bert Atkinson, May 22, 1992.

13. Handwritten letter dated 3 August 1991 on letterhead of Adm. I. C. Kidd Jr. to Judge A Jay Cristol.

14. First endorsement of CINCUSNAVEUR (Commander in Chief, Naval Forces Europe), to U.S. Navy court of inquiry dated June 18, 1967.

15. The endorsements are attached to the U.S. Navy court of inquiry. The endorsements reflect the breadth of interest in the report within the Navy.

Endorsement	Endorsing Command	Date of Endorsement
1	CINCUSNAVEUR	18 June 1967
2	CINCLANT	6 September 1967
3	JAG	3 November 1967
4	CNAVPER	13 November 1967
5	NAVSHIPSSYSTEMS	1 December 1967
6	NAVCOMMUNICATIONS	5 January 1968
7	CNO	25 March 1968

16. James Scott, *Attack on the* Liberty (New York: Simon and Schuster, 2009).

17. Phil G. Goulding, *Confirm or Deny: Informing the People on National Security* (New York: Harper & Row, 1970), 137–67.

18. See "China Rejects U.S. Explanation for Belgrade Embassy Bombing," *Washington Post,* June 29, 1999.

19. See Michael Friscolanti, *Friendly Fire: The Untold Story of the U.S. Bombing That Killed Four Canadian Soldiers in Afghanistan* (Mississauga, Ont.: John Wiley & Sons, 2005).

20. Letter from Cdr. Maurice Bennett to this author, June 3, 2003.

21. E-mail, December 23, 2003, from John Gidusko, a former *Liberty* crew member, to this author transmitting the text of an e-mail Gidusko sent to Commander Bennett in July 2003.

22. See chapter 7, pages 76 through 88.

23. On March 3, 2000, Marvin E. Nowicki sent a letter to James Bamford together with five enclosures. These materials may be viwed at *The Liberty Incident,* www.thelibertyincident.com.

24. "Tragic Gross Error in 1967 Attack," *Wall Street Journal,* May 16, 2001, A-23.

25. U.S. District Court, Southern District of Florida, Case No. 03–20123-CIV-HUCK, *Cristol v. National Security Agency.*

26. See Castle's epilogue to this book for a description of that flight.

27. *Attack on the Liberty* (London: Thames Television, 1987), aired on BBC2, January 27, 1987.

28. Telephone conversation with Hadden.

29. Hartford *Courant,* August 1, 1967, 16.

30. *National Review,* September 5, 1967, 956.

31. Lyndon Baines Johnson, *The Vantage Point: Perspectives of the Presidency 1963–1969* (New York: Holt Rinehart & Winston, 1971), 300.

32. Tom Segev, *1967: Israel, the War and the Year That Transformed the Middle East,* trans. Jessica Cohen (New York: Henry Holt , 2007). Originally published in Hebrew as *1967: Vehaaretz Shinta et Paneiha* (Jerusalem: Keter, 2005).

33. Translated for A Jay Cristol by Mitchell Dabach, University of Miami.

34. White House log, Friday, June 9, 1967, 15, Charles "Chuck" Roberts of *Newsweek* 7:55 p.m.–9:06 p.m.; pages 16–17, Mr. Hugh Sidey 9:12–10:05 p.m.

35. Telephone interview of Hugh Sidy, April 18, 1994 (A Jay Cristol in Miami, Hugh Sidy in Washington, D.C.). Sidy wrote a column titled "The Presidency" for *Life* from 1966 until 1972 and then wrote the same column for *Time.* He confirmed that the notes in the White House log sounded like Johnson, who, he said, "figured the world was against him." He said further that President Johnson liked to play being president in front of reporters and that he was a "congenital liar."

36. Johnson, *Vantage Point,* 300–301, 304.

37. See U.S. Navy court of inquiry record.

38. Johnson, *Vantage Point,* 300.

39. Ibid., 304.

40. Clark Clifford Report, July 18, 1967, 4.

41. Richard Helms and William Hood, *A Look over My Shoulder: A Life in the Central Intelligence Agency* (New York: Random House, 2003), 300–301.

42. Intelligence memorandum, Central Intelligence Agency, Washington, June 21, 1967. See U.S. Department of State, *Foreign Relations of the United States Volume XIX*, item 317, 540.

Chapter 20. Confirmation: NSA 1995 Historian's Analysis

1. Siobhan Gorman, "In a New History of NSA, Its Spies Successes Are [redacted]," *Wall Street Journal*, November 14, 2008, A1.
2. Thomas R. Johnson, *American Cryptology during the Cold War 1945–1989*, United States Cryptologic History (Fort George G. Meade, Md.: National Security Agency, Center for Cryptologic History, 1995). Originally classified Top Secret, code word Umbra.
3. Gorman, "In a New History of NSA," A1.
4. "Electronic Briefing Book No. 260," National Security Agency, *History of Cold War Intelligence Activities,* National Security Archive, George Washington University, Washington, D.C., www.gwu.edu.
5. A note from Secretary of State Edmund S. Muskie to Ephraim Evron, Ambassador of Israel, dated December 17, 1980, states, as follows:

Excellency:

I have the honor to acknowledge the receipt of your note No. AO/315 of December 15, 1980 relating to the U.S. ship "Liberty," which reads as follows: The Ambassador of Israel presents his compliments to the Secretary of State and has the honour to refer to the Embassy's note of 22 February 1978 and to consequent exchange of notes *concerning physical damage to the U.S. ship "Liberty" on 8 June 1967. Without prejudice to the legal position of the Government of Israel and to the question of liability* [emphasis added] for the tragic event the Government of Israel has the honour to propose as full and final settlement of the U.S. claim that Israel pay the United States Government the sum of $6,000,000 (six million dollars) to be paid in three annual Payments of $2,000,000 each, commencing 15 January 1981.

The Ambassador of Israel avails himself of this opportunity to renew to the Secretary of State the assurances of his highest consideration.

I have the honor to inform you that the Government of the United States agrees with your proposed settlement and that your note and my reply thereto constitute the agreement of our two Governments concerning this matter. Accept, Excellency, the renewed assurances of my highest consideration.

For the Secretary of State.

Chapter 21. Final Analysis

1. Confidential message from JCS to USCINCEUR (information copy to *Liberty*), 072230Z June 67.
2. Trevor Armbrister, *A Matter of Accountability: The True Story of the Pueblo Affair* (New York: Coward-McCann, 1970).
3. The United States continues to operate the EP-3E, which is a four-engine turboprop ELINT aircraft that replaced the Navy EC-121 in about 1971. The EP-3E community

insists that its intelligence gathering is real-time and superior to satellite collection methods. The aircraft has the ability to maintain real-time communication and carry air-search radar that can at least alert it to incoming aircraft. It is vulnerable to surface-to-air missiles. Its maximum speed is less that four hundred nautical miles per hour, which does not allow it to run away from jet fighters or even get out of their way, as evidenced by the midair collision between a U.S. Navy EP-3E Aries II and a Chinese F-8 jet fighter on April 1, 2001. Fortunately, in that incident the entire U.S. Navy crew survived. Sadly, the Chinese fighter pilot, Wang Wei, did not. The aircraft landed on Hainan island. Only the crew, NSA, and the Chinese know the extent of the compromise of highly classified sophisticated electronic equipment, some of which is believed to have been similar to classified surveillance equipment used on the *Liberty*.

4. On May 12, 1975, the U.S. merchant ship SS *Mayaguez* was seized in international waters near Cambodia by Khmer Rouge gunboats. In a failed rescue operation, forty-one U.S. Marines were killed and fifty wounded. The failure was attributed to lack of accurate intelligence and faulty communications. See John F. Guilmartin Jr., *A Very Short War: The "Mayaguez" and the Battle of Koh Tang* (College Station: Texas A&M Press, 1995).

5. It is possible that the *Liberty* had other tasks assigned in the middle-frequency/high-frequency ranges, but these tasks probably could have been accomplished from Cyprus or Turkey or even Greece. This author remains convinced that her primary task was within the VHF/UHF spectrum.

6. *UN Security Council Official Records, Twenty-Second Year, 1348th Meeting: 6 June 1967* (New York, n.d.), 2.

7. The specific official reason(s) that the NSA made the initial request is, or are, not known. However, it is known (see JCS Russ Report) that the U.S. Joint Chiefs of Staff realized that *Liberty*'s scheduled offshore operations area near the Sinai put her in direct conflict with the public announcements of U.S. government officials regarding the location of U.S. ships in relationship to the Arab-Israeli war.

8. Diplomatic note dated December 17, 1980, from U.S. Secretary of State to Ephraim Evron, Ambassador of Israel, referencing note no. AO/315 of December 15, 1980.

9. For the first eleven years following the *Liberty* incident, there was no mention of *Liberty*'s mission connected in any way with Israel's nuclear facility at Dimona. The notion was first presented by Anthony Pearson in his *Penthouse* articles and his book *Conspiracy of Silence: The Attack on the USS "Liberty"* (London: Quartet Books, 1978), 148. Wilbur Crane Eveland repeated the story in 1980 in his book *Ropes of Sand: America's Failure in the Middle East* (New York: W. W. Norton, 1980). Occasionally since 1980 various tales have been published about the *Liberty* mission as the surveillance of Dimona in order to observe and report any nuclear launch by Israel. There is no supporting evidence for these stories.

10. Dale Andrade, "The Controversy Continues," *Retired Officer,* June 1999, 59. In fact, it has been recently revealed that part of the ship's mission was to find out if the Egyptian air force's Soviet-made bombers were controlled and flown by Russian pilots.

11. Interview of Maj. Gen. Mordechai Hod on January 11, 1990, by this author, at Tel Aviv.

ACRONYMS AND ABBREVIATIONS

A-A	international maritime query, "What ship?"
A/C	aircraft
AGER	auxiliary environmental research ship
AGI	intelligence-collection ship
AGTR	auxiliary technical research ship
ARAMCO	Arabian American Oil Company
ARPA	automatic radar plotting aid
ATD	automatic tracking device
ATF	fleet tug
AWACS	Airborne Warning and Control System
CAG	carrier air group commander
CDR	commander
CHINFO	Chief of Naval Information
CIA	Central Intelligence Agency
CIC	combat information center
CINCSTRIKE	Commander in Chief, Strike Force
CINCUSAREUR	Commander in Chief, U.S. Army Europe
CINCUSNAVEUR	Commander in Chief, U.S. Naval Forces Europe
CNO	Chief of Naval Operations
CO	commanding officer
COG	course over the ground
COMDESRONTWELVE	Commander Destroyer Squadron 12
COMFAIRAIRRECONRON	Commander Fleet Air Reconnaissance Squadron
COMSERVFORSIXTHFLEET	Commander Service Force Sixth Fleet
COMSIXTHFLT	Commander Sixth Fleet
CT	communications technician
CTF	commander task force
CTG	commander task group
CVA	attack aircraft carrier
DCS	Defense Communication System
DD	destroyer
DDG	guided-missile destroyer

DIA	Defense Intelligence Agency
DIRNSA	Director, National Security Agency
DIV	division
DLG	guided-missile frigate (large destroyer-type ship)
DOD	Department of Defense
DRT	dead-reckoning tracer
EDT	eastern daylight time
ELINT	electronic intelligence
EPA	electronic plotting aid
ETA	estimated time of arrival
FBI	Federal Bureau of Investigation
FBIS	Foreign Broadcast Information Service
FOIA	Freedom of Information Act
G Group	unit within the National Security Agency
GAO	General Accounting Office
GMT	Greenwich mean time
GPS	Global Positioning System
HDQ	headquarters
HF	high frequency
HiCOM	high-command voice net
IAF	Israel Air Force
IAW	in accordance with
IDF	Israel Defense Forces
INS	Israel Navy Ship
INST	instruction
JAG	Judge Advocate General
JCS	Joint Chiefs of Staff
JRC	Joint Reconnaissance Center
KGB	Committee of State Security [Soviet foreign intelligence service]
kibbutz	a communal farming complex in Israel
LCDR, Lt. Cdr.	lieutenant commander
LVA	*Liberty* Veterans Association
MED	Mediterranean Sea
Mossad	foreign intelligence service of Israel
MSG	message
MTB	motor torpedo boat
NAVCOMUNIT	Naval Communications Unit
NAVCOMUNIT NAPLES	Naval Communications Unit Naples
NAVEUR HICOM	U.S. Navy European high command net
NCS	Naval Communication Station
NHHC	Naval History and Heritage Command
NMCC	National Military Command Center
nmph	nautical miles per hour (knot)

NSA	National Security Agency
NSA/CSS	National Security Agency/Central Security Service
OP-33	logistics unit in the office of CNO
OSD	Office of the Secretary of Defense
PARA	paragraph
PLO	Palestine Liberation Organization
PTS	patrol torpedo boat
RAF	Royal Air Force
RF-4C	reconnaissance model of F-4 Phantom aircraft
SAM	surface-to-air missile
SECNAV	Secretary of the Navy
Shin Bet	Israel's General Security Services (like FBI)
SIGINT	signal intelligence
SITREP	situation report
SOG	speed over the ground
SSB	single sideband (radio)
SSM	surface-to-surface missile
SSV	Sudno Svyazyy (Russian) communications vessel
STATE	Department of State
STBD	starboard
STEAMVALVE	U.S. Navy secure voice-telephone system
TF	task force
TG	task group
TRSSCOMM	Technical Research Ship Special Communications System
(U)	unclassified
USS	U.S. Ship
UAR	United Arab Republic (Egypt and, originally, Syria)
UHF	ultra-high frequency
UNEF	United National Emergency Force
UPI	United Press International
USAF	U.S. Air Force
USAFE	U.S. Air Force Europe
USCINCEUR	Commander in Chief, U.S. European Command
USDAO	U.S. defense attaché
USEUCOM	U.S. European Command
USG	U.S. government
USNR	U.S. Naval Reserve
USNS	U.S. Naval Ship
USUN	U.S. delegation to the United Nations
VHF	very high frequency
VQ	fleet air reconnaissance squadron
XO	executive officer
ZULU, or Z, time	U.S. military designation for Greenwich mean time

SELECTED BIBLIOGRAPHY

Books

Abu-Jaber, Faiz S. *American-Arab Relations from Wilson to Nixon.* Washington, D.C.: University Press of America, 1979.

Allison, Graham T. *Essence of Decision: Explaining the Cuban Missile Crisis.* Boston: Little, Brown, 1971.

Allyn, J. Bruce, G. James Blight, and A. David Welch. *Cuba on the Brink: Castro, the Missile Crises, and the Soviet Collapse.* New York: Pantheon Books; Toronto: Random House, 1993.

Aloni, Shlomo. *Mirage III vs MIG 21: Six Day War 1967.* Oxford, U.K.: Osprey, 2010

American Jewish Committee. *American Jewish Year Book 1968.* Philadelphia: Jewish Publication Society of America, 1968.

Armbrister, Trevor. *A Matter of Accountability: The True Story of the Pueblo Affair.* New York: Coward-McCann, 1970.

Ball, George W., and Douglas B. Ball. *The Passionate Attachment: America's Involvement with Israel, 1947 to the Present.* New York: W. W. Norton, 1992.

Bamford, James. *Body of Secrets.* New York: Doubleday, 2001.

———. *The Puzzle Palace: A Report on America's Most Secret Agency.* New York: Penguin Books, 1982/1983.

Bar-Siman-Tov, Yaacov. *Israel, the Super Powers, and the War in the Middle East.* New York: Praeger, 1987.

Bar-Zohar, Michael. *Embassies in Crisis: Diplomats and Demagogues behind the Six-Day War.* Englewood Cliffs, N.J.: Prentice Hall, 1970.

Bard, Mitchell G., and Joel Himmelfarb. *Myths and Facts.* Washington: Near East Report, 1992.

Barnes, Susan, Arsene Eglis, and Olivia Gilliam, comps. *Soviet News Media and the Middle East Crisis: A Chronological Review of Soviet Coverage (May 17–June 25, 1967).* Radio Liberty Research Paper, November 16, 1967. New York: Radio Liberty Committee, 1967.

Bassett, Ronald. *HMS Sheffield: The Life and Times of Old Shiny.* Annapolis, Md.: Naval Institute Press, 1988.

Bassiouni, M. Cherif. *The Arab-Israeli Conflict.* Vol. 2, *Readings.* Princeton, N.J.: Princeton University Press, 1974.

Belyayev, I., T. Kolesnichenko, and Ye. Primakov. *"Golub" Spushchen.* Russian. Moscow: Molodaya Gvardiya, 1968. *The "Dove" Has Been Released (Soviet Review of Israeli-Arab June 1967 Conflict),* English trans. Washington, D.C.: Joint Publications Research Service, 1968.

Ben-Adi, Herbert. *Israel's War for Peace: Private Letters of an Israeli Newspaper Correspondent.* Edited by Blanche Halpern and Abe Halpern. Edison, N.J.: Blanche Halpern and Abe Halpern, 1968.

Berkman, Ted. *Cast a Giant Shadow: The Story of Mickey Marcus, a Soldier for All Humanity.* Philadelphia: Jewish Publication Society of America, 1967.

Bigler, Philip. *In Honored Glory: Arlington National Cemetery, the Final Post.* Arlington, Va.: Bandamere, 1987.

Black, Ian, and Benny Morris. *Israel's Secret Wars: A History of Israel's Intelligence Services.* New York: Grove Weidenfeld, 1991.

Blackman, Raymond V. B., ed. *Jane's Fighting Ships, 1966–1967.* London: BPC, 1966. (Also 1955–1956, 1956–1957, 1967–1968, and 1968–1969.)

Blitzer, Wolf. *Between Washington and Jerusalem: A Reporter's Notebook.* New York: Oxford University Press, 1985.

———. *Territory of Lies: The Exclusive Story of Jonathan Jay Pollard, Who Spied on His Country for Israel, and How He Was Betrayed.* New York: Harper & Row, 1989.

Bookbinder, Hyman, and James G. Abourezk. *Through Different Eyes: Two Leading Americans— A Jew and an Arab—Debate U.S. Policy in the Middle East.* Bethesda, Md.: Adler & Adler, 1987.

Borne, John Edgar. "The USS *Liberty:* Dissenting History vs. Official History." Ph.D. diss., New York University, 1993.

———. *The USS* Liberty: *Dissenting History vs. Official History.* New York: Reconsideration, 1995.

Bornett, Vaughn Davis. *The Presidency of Lyndon B. Johnson.* Lawrence: University Press of Kansas, 1983.

Bouchard, Joseph F. *Command in Crisis: Four Case Studies.* New York: Columbia University Press, 1991.

———. "Use of Naval Force in Crises: A Theory of Stratified Crisis Interaction." Ph.D. diss., Stanford University, 1989.

Bourla, Yair. *Dictionary of Military Terms (English Index of the Hebrew Lexicon of Military Terms).* Tel Aviv: Dvir, 1988.

Brecher, Michael. *Decisions in Crisis: Israel, 1967 and 1973.* Berkeley and Los Angeles: University of California Press, 1980.

Bregman, Ahron, and Jihan El-Tahri. *The Fifty Years' War: Israel and the Arabs.* New York: TV Books, 1998/1999.

Brittin, Burdick H. *International Law for Seagoing Officers.* 245th ed. Annapolis, Md.: Naval Institute Press, 1956.

Brown, Michael, Sean M. Lynn-Jones, and Steven E. Miller. *Debating the Democratic Peace: An International Security Reader.* Cambridge, Mass.: MIT Press, 1996.

Bundy, McGeorge. *Danger and Survival: Choices about the Bomb in the First Fifty Years.* New York: Random House, 1988.

Califano, Joseph A., Jr. *The Triumph and Tragedy of Lyndon Johnson: The White House Years.* New York: Simon & Schuster, 1991.

Churchill, Randolph S., and Winston S. Churchill. *The Six Day War.* Boston: Houghton Mifflin, 1967.

Chomsky, Noam. *The Fateful Triangle.* Boston: South End, 1983.

Clifford, Clark, with Richard Holbrooke. *Counsel to the President: A Memoir.* New York: Random House, 1991.

Clingan, Thomas A., Jr., ed. *The Law of the Sea.* Honolulu: Law of the Sea Institute, University of Hawaii, 1988.

Cockburn, Andrew, and Leslie Cockburn. *Dangerous Liaison: The Inside Story of the U.S.-Israel Covert Relationship.* New York: HarperCollins, 1991.

Cohen, Avner. *Israel and the Bomb.* New York: Columbia University Press, 1998.

Cohen, Eliezer. *Israel's Best Defense.* New York: Orion Books, 1993.

Cohen, Warren I. "Balancing American Interests in the Middle East: Lyndon Baines Johnson vs. Gamal Abdul Nasser." In *Lyndon Johnson Confronts the World: American Foreign Policy 1963–1968,* edited by Warren I. Cohen and Nancy Bernkopf Tucker. Cambridge: Cambridge University Press, 1994.

Collins, Larry, and Dominique Lapierre. *O Jerusalem.* New York: Pocket Books, 1972.

Coonts, Stephen. *Final Flight.* New York: Dell, 1988.

Copeland, Miles. *The Game of Nations: The Amorality of Power Politics.* New York: Simon & Schuster, 1969.

Crenshaw, R. S. *Naval Shiphandling.* 4th ed. Annapolis, Md.: Naval Institute Press, 1975.

Curtis, Richard H. *A Changing Image: American Perceptions of the Arab-Israeli Dispute.* Washington, D.C.: American Educational Trust, 1982.

David, Ron. *Arabs and Israel for Beginners.* New York: Writers & Readers, 1993.

Dayan, Moshe. *Diary of the Sinai Campaign.* Jerusalem: Steinmatsky, Jerusalem, 1965. English ed., London: Cox & Wyman, 1966.

———. *Story of My Life.* London: Sphere Books, 1976.

Deacon, Richard. *The Israeli Secret Service.* New York: Taplinger, 1977.

Decock, Jean-Pierre. *Mirage.* London: Arms & Armour, 1985.

de Mulinen, Frederic. *Handbook on the Law of War for Armed Forces.* Geneva: International Committee of the Red Cross, 1987.

Dishon, Daniel, ed. *Middle East Record.* Vol. 3, *1967.* Jerusalem: Israel Universities Press, 1971.

Dismukes, Bradford. "Soviet Employment of Naval Power for Political Purposes, 1967–75." In *Soviet Naval Influence: Domestic and Foreign Dimensions,* edited by Michael McGwire and John McDonnell. New York: Praeger, 1977.

Donovan, Robert J. *Israel's Fight for Survival: Six Days in June.* New York: New American Library, 1967.

Draper, Theodore. *Israel and World Politics: Roots of the Third Arab-Israeli War.* New York: Viking, 1968.

Drendel, Lou. *Phantom II.* Carrollton, Texas: Squadron Signal, 1985.

Druks, Herbert. *The U.S. and Israel 1945–1973: A Diplomatic History.* New York: Robert Speller & Sons, 1979.

Dupuy, Trevor N. *Elusive Victory: The Arab-Israeli Wars, 1947–1974.* New York: Harper & Row, 1978.

Eban, Abba. *My Country.* New York: Random House, 1972.

Eisenberg, Dennis, Uri Dan, and Eli Landau. *The Mossad.* New York: Paddington, 1978.

Ennes, James M., Jr. *Assault on the "Liberty": The True Story of the Israeli Attack on an American Intelligence Ship.* New York: Random House, 1979.

———. *Assault on the "Liberty": The True Story of the Israeli Attack on an American Intelligence Ship.* New York: Ivy Books, 1987. Paperback with author's addendum, 1986.

Eveland, Wilbur Crane. *Ropes of Sand: America's Failure in the Middle East.* London: W. W. Norton, 1980.

Facts on File Yearbook 1967. New York: Facts on File, 1968.

Findley, Paul. *Deliberate Deceptions: Facing the Facts about the U.S.-Israeli Relationship.* Brooklyn, N.Y.: Lawrence Hill Books, 1993.

———. *They Dare to Speak Out: People and Institutions Confront Israel's Lobby.* Westport, Conn.: Lawrence Hill, 1985.

Fine, Morris, and Milton Himmelfarb, ed. *American Jewish Year Book 1968.* New York: American Book–Stratford, 1968.

Fisher, Eugene M., and M. Cherif Bassiouni. *Storm over the Arab World: A People in Revolution.* Chicago: Follett, 1972.

Fisher, Sydney Nettleton. *The Middle East: A History.* New York: Alfred A. Knopf, 1969.

Fraser, T. G. *The USA and the Middle East since World War 2.* New York: St. Martin's, 1989.

Gallery, Daniel V. *The Pueblo Incident.* Garden City, N.Y.: Doubleday, 1970.

Gawrych, George W. *Key to the Sinai: The Battles for Abu Ageila in the 1956 and 1967 Arab-Israeli Wars.* Fort Leavenworth, Kans.: U.S. Army Command and General Staff College, 1990.

Gazit, Shlomo. *The Carrot and the Stick.* Washington, D.C.: B'nai B'rith Books, 1995.

Gerhard, William D. *Attack on the USS "Liberty": An Edited Version of SRH-256.* Edited by Sheila A. Carlisle. Laguna Hills, Calif.: Aegean Park, 1981.

Goldschmidt, Arthur, Jr. *A Concise History of the Middle East.* Boulder, Colo.: Westview; Cairo, Egypt: American University in Cairo Press, 1983.

Goott, Amy Kaufman, and Steven J. Rosen, eds. *The Campaign to Discredit Israel.* Washington, D.C.: American Israel Public Affairs Committee, 1983.

Goulding, Phil G. *Confirm or Deny: Informing the People on National Security.* New York: Harper & Row, 1970.

Green, Stephen. *Taking Sides: America's Secret Relations with a Militant Israel.* New York: William Morrow, 1984.

Gribetz, Judah, Edward L. Greenstein, and Regina Stein. *The Timetables of Jewish History: A Chronology of the Most Important People and Events in Jewish History.* New York: Simon & Schuster, 1993.

Griess, Thomas E., et al., eds. *The Arab-Israeli Wars, the Chinese Civil War, and the Korean War.* Wayne, N.J.: Avery, 1987.

Grundman, Moshe, ed. *Israel's Security 1967–1991: An Annotated Bibliography and Research Guide.* Tel Aviv: Ministry of Defence, Israel, 1992.

Gunston, Bill. *An Illustrated Guide to the Israeli Air Force.* New York: Arco, 1982.

Halperin, Merav, and Aharon Lapidot. *G-Suit: Combat Reports from Israel's Air War.* London: Sphere Books, 1990.

Hammel, Eric. *Six Days in June: How Israel Won the 1967 Arab-Israeli War.* New York: Charles Scribner's Sons, 1992.

Heikal, Mohamed Hassanein. *The Cairo Documents: The Inside Story of Nasser and His Relationship with World Leaders, Rebels, and Statesmen.* Garden City, N.Y.: Doubleday, 1973.

Henkin, Louis, et al. *International Law,* 2d ed. St. Paul, Minn.: West, 1987.

Hersh, Seymour M. *The Samson Option: Israel's Nuclear Arsenal and American Foreign Policy.* New York: Random House, 1991.

Herzog, Chaim. *The Arab-Israeli Wars: War and Peace in the Middle East.* New York: Vintage Books, 1984.

Hinsley, Harry. *The Intelligence Revolution: A Historical Perspective.* Colorado Springs: U.S. Air Force Academy, 1988.

Hogg, Ian V. *Israeli War Machine.* London: Hamlyn, 1983.

Horwath, Stephen. *To Shining Sea: A History of the United States Navy 1775–1991.* New York: Random House, 1991.

Howard, Michael, and Robert Hunter. *Israel and the Arab World: The Crisis of 1967.* London: Institute for Strategic Studies, 1967.

Howarth, David. *Famous Sea Battles.* London: Artus, 1981.

Howe, Jonathan Trumbull. *Multicrises: Sea Power and Global Politics in the Missile Age.* Cambridge, Mass.: MIT Press, 1971.

Howe, Russel Warren. *Weapons: The International Game of Arms, Money and Diplomacy.* Garden City, N.Y.: Doubleday, 1980.

Humble, Richard, ed. *Naval Warfare.* New York: St. Martin's, 1983.

International Red Cross Handbook. 12th ed. Geneva: International Committee of the Red Cross & League of Red Cross Societies, 1983.

Ismael, Tareq Y. *International Relations of the Contemporary Middle East: A Study in World Politics.* Syracuse, N.Y.: Syracuse University Press, 1986.

Jeffers, H. Paul. *The CIA: A Close Look at the Central Intelligence Agency.* New York: Lion, 1970.

Johnson, Lyndon Baines. *The Vantage Point: Perspectives of the Presidency 1963–1969.* New York: Holt Rinehart & Winston, 1971.

Jones, Dennis. *Rubicon One.* New York: Beaufort Books, 1983.

Katz, Samuel M. *Soldier Spies: Israeli Military Intelligence.* Novato, Calif.: Presidio, 1992.

Kennedy, William V., et al. *Intelligence Warfare: Penetrating the Secret World of Today's Advanced Technology Conflict.* New York: Crescent Books, 1987.

Lenczowski, George. *American Presidents and the Middle East.* Durham, N.C.: Duke University Press, 1990.

———. *The Middle East in World Affairs.* 4th ed. Ithaca, N.Y.: Cornell University Press, 1980.

Lilienthal, Alfred. *The Zionist Connection: What Price Peace?* New York: Dodd, Mead, 1978.

Linder, Mark. *Little Boy Blue.* New York: Random House, 1992.

Loftus, John, and Mark Aarons. *The Secret War against the Jews: How Western Espionage Betrayed the Jewish People.* New York: St. Martin's, 1994.

Long, Luman H., ed. *The World Almanac and Book of Facts, 1967.* New York: Newspaper Enterprise Association, 1968.

Lynn-Jones, Sean. Preface to *Debating the Democratic Peace: An International Security Reader;* edited by Michael Brown, Sean M. Lynn-Jones, and Steven E. Miller. Cambridge, Mass.: MIT Press, 1996.

Marshall, S. L. A. *Swift Sword: The Historical Record of Israel's Victory, June, 1967.* New York: American Heritage, 1967.

McCain, John, and Mark Salter. *Faith of My Fathers.* New York: Random House, 1999.

McGarvey, Patrick J. *CIA: The Myth and the Madness.* New York: Saturday Review, 1972.

McGwire, Michael, and John McDonnell, eds. *Soviet Naval Influence.* New York: Praeger, 1977.

McNamara, Robert S., with Brian Van de Mark. *In Retrospect: The Tragedy and Lessons of Vietnam.* New York: Vintage Books, 1995.

Mercer, Derrik. *Chronicle of the Twentieth Century.* London: Longman Communications, 1988.

Merlin, Samuel, ed. *The Big Powers and the Present Crises in the Middle East: A Colloquium.* Rutherford, N.J.: Fairleigh Dickinson University Press, 1968.

Mersky, Peter B. *Israeli Fighter Aces.* North Branch, Minn: Speciality, 1997.

Moore, John Norton, ed. *The Arab-Israeli Conflict.* Vol. 2, *Readings.* Princeton, N.J.: Princeton University Press, 1974.

———. *Jane's Fighting Ships.* London: Jane's, 1987.

Moore, Molly. *A Woman at War.* New York: Charles Scribner's Sons, 1993.

Morris, James M. *History of the US Navy.* New York: Bison Books, 1984.

Morrison, Samuel Eliot. *John Paul Jones: A Sailor's Biography.* Boston: Little, Brown, 1959.

Narkis, Uzi. *The Liberation of Jerusalem.* Totowa, N.J.: Valentine, Mitchell, 1983.

Naval and Maritime Chronology. Annapolis, Md.: Naval Institute Press, 1973.

Neff, Donald. *Warriors at Suez: Eisenhower Takes America into the Middle East.* New York: Linden, 1981.

———. *Warriors for Jerusalem: The Six Days That Changed the Middle East.* New York: Linden Press/Simon & Schuster, 1984.

Noel, John V., Jr., and Frank E. Bassett, eds. *Knight's Modern Seamanship.* 16th ed. New York: Van Nostrand Reinhold, 1977.

O'Ballance, Edgar. *The Third Arab-Israeli War.* Hamden, Conn.: Archon Books, 1972.

O'Brien, Conor Cruise. *The Siege.* New York: Simon & Schuster, 1986.

O'Connell, D. P. *The Influence of Law on Sea Power.* Annapolis, Md.: Naval Institute Press, 1975.

Ofer, Yehuda. *Operation Thunder: The Entebbe Raid.* Harmondsworth, England: Penguin Books, 1976.

Patai, Raphael. *The Arab Mind.* New York: Charles Scribner's Sons, 1983.

Pearson, Anthony. *Conspiracy of Silence: The Attack on the U.S.S. Liberty.* London: Quartet Books, 1978.

Pett, Saul, ed. *Lightning Out of Israel.* New York: Associated Press, 1967.

Polmar, Norman. *Guide to the Soviet Navy.* 12th ed. Annapolis, Md.: Naval Institute Press, 1986.

———. *The Naval Institute Guide to the Ships and Aircraft of the U.S. Fleet.* 15th ed. Annapolis, Md.: Naval Institute Press, 1993.

———. *The Naval Institute Guide to the Soviet Navy.* 5th ed. Annapolis, Md.: Naval Institute Press, 1991.

Polmar, Norman, and Thomas B. Allen. *Spy Book: The Encyclopedia of Espionage.* New York: Random House, 1997.

Polmar, Norman, Warren Mark, and Eric Werthheim. *Dictionary of Military Abbreviations.* Annapolis, Md.: Naval Institute Press, 1994.

Pope, Dudley. *The Battle of the River Plate.* New York: Avon Books, 1956.

Prados, John. *Keeper of the Keys.* New York: William Morrow, 1991.

Puschel, Karen L. *US-Israeli Strategic Cooperation in the Post-Cold War Era.* Jerusalem: Jerusalem Post, 1992.

Quandt, William B. *Decade of Decisions: American Policy toward the Arab-Israeli Conflict, 1967–1976.* Berkeley and Los Angeles: University of California Press, 1977.

———. *United States Policy in the Middle East: Constraints and Choices.* Santa Monica, Calif.: Rand, 1970.

Rabin, Yitzhak. *The Rabin Memoirs.* Boston: Little, Brown, 1979.

———. *The Rabin Memoirs.* 2d ed. Bnei Brak, Israel: Steimatzky, 1994.

Rabinovich, Abraham. *The Battle for Jerusalem.* Philadelphia: Jewish Publication Society of America, 1972.

———. *The Boats of Cherbourg: The Secret Israeli Operation That Revolutionized Naval Warfare.* New York: Seaver Books/Henry Holt, 1988.

Ranelagh, John. *The Agency: The Rise and Decline of the CIA.* New York: Simon & Schuster, 1986.

Rausa, Rosario. *Skyraider: The Douglas A-1 "Flying Dump Truck."* Baltimore: Nautical & Aviation, 1987.

Raviv, Dan, and Yossi Melman. *Every Spy a Prince: The Complete History of Israel's Intelligence Community.* Boston: Houghton Mifflin, 1990.

———. *Friends in Deed: Inside the U.S.-Israel Alliance.* New York: Hyperion, 1994

Regan, Geoffrey. *Blue on Blue: A History of Friendly Fire.* New York: Avon Books, 1995.

———. *Israel and the Arabs.* Cambridge: Cambridge University Press, 1990.

Rostow, W. W. *The Diffusion of Power 1957–1972.* New York: Macmillan, 1972.

Rubenberg, Cheryl A. *Israel and the American National Interest: A Critical Examination.* Urbana: University of Illinois Press, 1986.

Rubenstein, Murray, and Richard Goldman. *Shield of David: An Illustrated History of the Israeli Air Force.* Englewood Cliffs, N.J.: Prentice Hall, 1978.

Rubinstein, Alvin Z., ed. *The Arab-Israeli Conflict: Perspectives.* Westport, Conn.: Praeger, 1984.

Rusk, Dean, as told to Richard Rusk. *As I Saw It.* New York: W. W. Norton, 1990.

Russell, John. *The Book of Seamanship.* New York: Ziff Davis, 1979.

Sachar, Howard A. *Israel and Europe: An Appraisal in History.* New York: Vintage Books, 2000.

Safran, Nadav. *From War to War: The Arab-Israeli Confrontation, 1948–1967.* New York: Pegasus, 1969.

———. *Israel: The Embattled Ally.* Cambridge, Mass.: Harvard University Press, 1982.

Sasson, Jean. *Princess: A True Story of Life behind the Veil in Saudi Arabia.* New York: William Morrow, 1992.

Saunders, Harold H. "Regulating Soviet-U.S. Competition and Cooperation in the Arab-Israeli Arena, 1967–86." In *U.S.-Soviet Security Cooperation: Achievements, Failures, Lessons,* edited by Alexander L. George, Philip J. Farley, and Alexander Dallin. New York: Oxford University Press, 1988.

Schack, Howard H., and H. Paul Jeffers. *A Spy in Canaan.* New York: Carol, 1993.

Schiff, Zeev. *A History of the Israeli Army (1870–1974).* Translated and edited by Raphael Rothstein. San Francisco: Straight Arrow Books, 1974.

———. *A History of the Israeli Army: 1874 to the Present.* New York: Macmillan, 1985.

Schindler, Dietrich, and Jiri Toman. *The Laws of Armed Conflict.* 2d ed. Alphen aanden Rijn, The Netherlands: Sijthoff & Noordhoff, 1981.

Schoenbaum, David. *The United States and the State of Israel.* New York: Oxford University Press, 1993.

Schumacher, F. Carl, Jr., and George C. Wilson. *Bridge of No Return: The Ordeal of the U.S.S. Pueblo.* New York: Harcourt Brace Jovanovich, 1971.

Scott, James. *Attack on the* Liberty. New York: Simon and Schuster, 2009.

A Seaman's Guide to the Rule of the Road. 4th ed. Bristol, England: Morgans Technical Books, 1985.

Shavit, David. *The United States in the Middle East: A Historical Dictionary.* New York: Greenwood, 1988.

Shirot, Pincus. *Yitzhak Rabin* (in Hebrew). Tel Aviv: Kol Haskanot Shmerot, 1979.

Shrader, Charles R. *Amicicide: The Problem of Friendly Fire in Modern War.* Fort Leavenworth, Kans.: U.S. Army Command and General Staff College, 1982.

Silverberg, Robert. *If I Forget Thee, O Jerusalem: American Jews and the State of Israel.* New York: William Morrow, 1970.

Simon, Reeva S., Philip Mattar, and Richard W. Bulliet. *Encyclopedia of the Modern Middle East.* New York: Macmillan Reference USA, 1996.

Slater, Leonard. *The Pledge.* New York: Simon & Schuster, 1970.

Slater, Robert. *Rabin of Israel.* New York: St. Martin's, 1993.

———. *Warrior-Statesman: The Life of Moshe Dayan.* New York: St. Martin's, 1991.

Smith, Charles D. *Palestine and the Arab-Israeli Conflict.* New York: St. Martin's, 1988.

Snyder, Frank M. *Command and Control: The Literature and Commentaries.* Washington, D.C.: National Defense University, 1993.

Sontag, Sherry, and Christopher Drew. *Blind Man's Bluff: The Untold Story of American Submarine Espionage.* New York: HarperPaperbacks, 1999.

Soustelle, Jacques. *The Long March of Israel.* New York: American Heritage, 1969.

Spanier, John. *American Foreign Policy since World War II.* 11th ed. Washington, D.C.: Congressional Quarterly, 1988.

Spick, Mike, and Barry Wheeler. *The New Illustrated Guide to Modern Aircraft Markings.* New York: Smithmark, 1992.

Spiegel, Steven L. *The Other Arab-Israeli Conflict: Making America's Middle East Policy, from Truman to Reagan.* Chicago: University of Chicago Press, 1985.

Spiro, David E. "The Insignificance of the Liberal Peace." In *Debating the Democratic Peace: An International Security Reader,* edited by Michael Brown, Sean M. Lynn-Jones, and Steven E. Miller. Cambridge, Mass.: MIT Press, 1996.

Stebbins, Richard P. *The United States in World Affairs 1967.* New York: Simon & Schuster, 1968.

Steven, Stewart. *The Spy-Masters of Israel.* New York: MacMillan, 1980.

Stevenson, William. *Israeli Victory.* London: Corgi Books, 1967.

———. *Zanek! A Chronicle of the Israeli Air Force.* New York: Viking, 1971.

Taylor, Alan. *The Superpowers and the Middle East.* Syracuse, N.Y.: Syracuse University Press, 1991.

Taylor, James. *Pearl Harbor II: The True Story of the Sneak Attack by Israel upon the U.S.S. "Liberty," June 8, 1967.* Washington, D.C.: Mideast, 1980.

Taylor, W. R., ed. *Combat Aircraft of the World from 1909 to the Present.* New York: G. P. Putnam's Sons, 1969.

Teveth, Shabtai. *Moshe Dayan: The Soldier, the Man, the Legend.* London: Quartet Books, 1974.

Tully, Andrew. *The Super Spies: More Secret, More Powerful than the CIA.* New York: William Morrow, 1969.

U.S. Congress. Office of Technology Assessment. *Who Goes There: Friend or Foe?* OTA-ISC-537. Washington, D.C.: U.S. Government Printing Office, 1993.

U.S. Department of the Navy. *Blue Jackets Manual.* 11th ed. Annapolis, Md.: U.S. Naval Institute, 1943.

———. *Commander's Handbook on the Law of Naval Operations.* NWP-9. Washington, D.C., 1987.

———. *Commander's Handbook on the Law of Naval Operations.* NWP-9 (Rev A). Washington, D.C., 1989.

———. *Law of Naval Warfare.* NWP 10–2. Washington, D.C., 1955.

Warner, Oliver. *Great Sea Battles.* New York: Exeter Books, 1981.

Watts, Allan. *Instant Wind Forecasting.* London: Adlard Coles Nautical, 1875, 1991.

Wells, Anthony R. "The June 1967 Arab-Israeli War." In "Superpower Naval Confrontation," edited by Stephen S. Roberts. In *Soviet Naval Diplomacy,* edited by Bradford Dismukes and James M. McConnell. New York: Pergamon, 1979.

Westwood, J. W. *The History of the Middle East Wars.* New York: Exeter Books, 1984.

Wheeler, Barry C. *An Illustrated Guide to Aircraft Markings.* New York: Prentice Hall, 1986.

Windchy, Eugene G. *Tonkin Gulf.* Garden City, N.Y.: Doubleday, 1971.

Wouk, Herman. *The Hope.* Boston: Little, Brown, 1993.

Wright, Quincy. "The Middle East Crisis." In *The Arab-Israeli Conflict.* Vol. 2, *Readings,* edited by John Norton Moore. Princeton, N.J.: Princeton University Press, 1974.

Wylie, J. C. "The Sixth Fleet and American Diplomacy." In *Soviet-American Rivalry in the Middle East,* edited by J. C. Hurewitz. New York: Praeger, 1969.

Yonay, Ehud. *No Margin for Error: The Making of the Israeli Air Force.* New York: Pantheon Books, 1993.

Young, Peter. *The Israeli Campaign 1967.* London: William Kimber, 1967.

Zmora, Ohad. *The Victory: The Six-Day War of 1967.* Tel Aviv: E. Lewis Epstein, 1967.

Articles

"Ahead of the News: U.S.S. *Liberty:* Caught in Political Currents?" *Newsweek.* June 26, 1967, 13.

Anderson, Jim. "New Light Shed on Israeli Attack on U.S. Spy Ship." United Press International. March 18, 1984.

Belyayev, I., and Ye. Primakov. "Kak Izrail nachal agressiyu" [How Israel began the aggression]. *Pravda,* July 27, 1967. Translated by Gregory Koldys.

Berger, Thomas J. "Parting Shot: Case Closed on USS *Liberty.*" *Soldier of Fortune* 14, no. 3 (March 1989): 96.

Berman, Sylvan M. "An Historical Note: The 1967 Israeli Attack on the American Electronic Spy Ship Revisited." *International Problems* 18 (Fall 1979): 59–63.

Bouchard, Joseph F. "Accidents and Crises: *Panay, Liberty,* and *Stark.*" *Naval War College Review* 41, no. 4 (Autumn 1988): 87–102.

Buckley, William F., Jr. "The Week." *National Review,* June 27, 1967, 673.

Caldwell, Robert J. "It's Time to Tell the Truth about Israel's Attack on the *Liberty.*" *San Diego Union,* June 14, 1987.

"C.I.A. Papers Cite Israelis in Attack on U.S. Navy Ship." *New York Times,* September 19, 1977.

(Colebrook, New Hampshire) News and Sentinel. January 27, 1988.

Crowley, Dale. "*Liberty* Survivor Fixes the Blame." *Colebrook (N.H.) News and Sentinel,* January 27, 1988.

Ennes, James M., Jr. "The Israeli Assault on the U.S.S. *Liberty.*" *Retired Officer,* June 1985, 22–24.

———. "Israeli Attack on U.S. Ship Reveals Failure of C³." *Defense Electronics* 13 (October 1991): 60–71.

———. "Spies Expect to Be Shot but the USS *Liberty* Was Humiliated." *Dossier,* no. 5 (1983): 5–9.

———. "The U.S.S. *Liberty.*" *Link* 25, no. 2 (May/June 1992): 5–6.

———. "The USS *Liberty* Affair." *Link* 17, no. 2 (May/June 1984): 1–13.

———. "The USS *Liberty:* Back in the News." *American-Arab Affairs,* no. 15 (Winter 1985–86): 19–29, 104–106.

———. "The USS *Liberty:* Israel Can't Seem to Get Its Story Straight." *American-Arab Affairs,* no. 17 (Summer 1986): 16–25, 131–40.

"An Error of War—and U.S. Seamen Die." *U.S. News & World Report,* June 19, 1967, 10.

Evans, Rowland, and Robert Novak. "Remembering the Liberty." *Washington Post,* November 6, 1991.

Le Figaro. June 8, 1967. Edition de 5 heures.

"Finis." *Newsweek,* July 3, 1967, 24.

Fishel, Reverdy S. "The Attack on the Liberty: An 'Accident'?" *Intelligence and Counterintelligence* 8, no. 3 (Fall 1995): 345–52.

Fraser, R. R. "Parting Shot: No Justice for USS *Liberty.*" *Soldier of Fortune,* 13, no. 9 (September 1988): 96.

Furmess, Adrian. "Misfortune or Murder?" *TV Times* (London), January 24–30, 1987.

Goodman, Hirsh. "The Battle over the *Liberty.*" *Jerusalem Report,* December 19, 1991, 40.

———. "Messrs. Errors and No Facts." *Jerusalem Report,* November 21, 1991, 42.

Goodman, Hirsch, and Zeev Schiff. "The Attack on the *Liberty.*" *Atlantic Monthly,* September 1984, 79–84.

Greenhouse, Linda. "The Roots and the Rudiments of Compensation to Foreigners." *New York Times,* July 13, 1988.

Herman, Edward S. "The Pro-Israel Lobby." *Z Magazine,* July/August 1994, 8–9.

"Israel Lobby: Five Former Lawmakers Form Opposition Group." *Miami Herald,* October 24, 1994.

"Israel Pays Compensation Claimed for Men Injured on U.S.S. *Liberty.*" *Department of State Bulletin,* June 2, 1969, 473.

"Israel Pays Compensation Claimed for Men Killed on U.S.S. *Liberty.*" *Department of State Bulletin,* June 17, 1968, 799.

Jacobsen, Walter L. "A Juridical Examination of the Israeli Attack on the U.S.S. *Liberty.*" *Naval Law Review* 36 (Winter 1986): 1–51.

Johnson, Lyndon B. "News Conference." *Congressional Quarterly Weekly Report,* June 16, 1967, 1039–41.

Kidd, Isaac. "View from the Bridge of the Sixth Fleet Flagship." U.S. Naval Institute *Proceedings* 98 (February 1972): 18–29.

Kilpatrick, James Jackson. "June 8, at 1400 Hours." *National Review,* September 5, 1967, 952–58.

"Lessons of the *Liberty:* Weak Spots in U.S. Defenses." *U.S. News & World Report,* July 22, 1968, 7.

"*Liberty* Signals: Misrouted, Misread." *U.S. News & World Report,* July 10, 1967, 7.

Limor, Micha. "The Attack on the USS *Liberty.*" *New York Times,* July 7, 1967.

Lynn-Jones, Sean. "A Quiet Success for Arms Control: Preventing Incidents at Sea." *International Security* 9, no. 4 (Spring 1985): 154–84.

Mallison, S. V., and W. T. Mallison. "Lawful Objects for Attack." *International Law Studies 1991: The Law of Naval Operations,* edited by Horace B. Robertson, Jr. Newport, R.I.: Naval War College Press, 1991.

Mallison, W. T. "The Zionist-Israel Juridical Claims to Constitute 'the Jewish People' Nationality Entity and to Confer Membership in It: Appraisal in Public International Law." *George Washington Law Review* (June 1964): 983–1075.

Il Messaggero di Roma, June 8, 1967.

Miami Herald, June 8, 9, and 10, 1967.

Miller, Martin J., Jr. "The Israeli Navy: Twenty-Six Years of Non-Peace." U.S. Naval Institute *Proceedings* 101 (February 1975).

"Mystery of Attack on U.S.S. 'Liberty.'" *U.S. News & World Report,* June 26, 1967, 33.

Naidy, A. G. "The United States and the Arab Israeli Conflict of 1967." *International Studies* (New Delhi) 19, no. 2 (April–June 1980): 157–96.

New York Times, June 8, 9, and 10, 1967.

Nir, Uri. "Former Israeli: Evans and Novak Distorted My Words to Defame Israel." *Haaretz,* November 7, 1991.

"The Nusses: A Tragic Mistake and a Rebuilt Life." *Newsweek,* Special Anniversary Issue, Spring 1983, 124–26.

Oberdorfer, Don, and Edward Walsh. "Iraq to Pay Damages for Attack." *Washington Post,* May 22, 1987.

Obermeyer, Eric. "Skeletons Lurk in the Closet of US-Israeli Relations." *Terminal Frost,* September 15, 1995. [Electronic].

Pearson, Anthony. "The Attack on the U.S.S. *Liberty:* Mayday! Mayday!" *Penthouse,* May 1976, 54–58, 137–47.

———. "Conspiracy of Silence." *Penthouse,* June 1976, 60–64, 147–51.

Pedahzur, Reuven. "The 'Expose' of Evans and Novak Regarding the Six-Day War Episode Is in Conflict with the Reports of Two Investigation Committees—Israeli and an American." *Haaretz,* November 5, 1991.

"The Periscope: Sinking the *Liberty*—Accident or Design?" *Newsweek,* June 19, 1967, 21.

Peterson, Iver. "Court-Martial Begins in 'Friendly Fire' Deaths in Iraq." *New York Times,* June 3, 1995.

Pipes, Daniel. "Reviews: *Encyclopedia of the Modern Middle East,* by Reeva S. Simon, Philip Mattar, and Richard W. Bulliet. "*Middle East Quarterly* 3, no. 4 (December 1996): 70–82.

Primakov, Ye. A., and I. Belyayev. "Lessons of the 1967 Middle East Crises." *International Affairs* (Moscow) 3 (March 1968): 41.

Quandt, William B. "Lyndon Johnson and the June 1967 War: What Color Was the Light?" *Middle East Journal* 46, no. 2 (Spring 1992): 198–228.

"Remember USS *Liberty,* Says VFW." *VFW Magazine,* June 1987, 28–29.

Rosenthal, A. M. "Anatomy of a Scoop." *New York Times,* November 8, 1991.

Russell, James A. "Vets Cry: 'Remember the *Liberty.*'" *Defense Week,* September 8, 1986, 2.

Scott, Richard. "Success for 'Hot Line' Diplomacy." *Guardian* (London), June 10, 1967.

"Secretary Rusk and Secretary of Defense McNamara Discuss Viet-Nam and Korea on *Meet the Press.*" *Department of State Bulletin* 58 (February 26, 1968): 261–72.

Sheehan, Neil. "Order Didn't Get to U.S.S. *Liberty.*" *New York Times,* June 29, 1967.

Sidey, Hugh. "The Presidency: Over the Hot Line—the Middle East." *Life,* June 16, 1967, 24.

"The Situation in the Near East." *Department of State Bulletin* 56 (June 26, 1967): 949–52.

Smith, Richard K. "The Violation of the *Liberty.*" U.S. Naval Institute *Proceedings* 104/6/904 (June 1978): 62–70.

Sobran, Joseph. "The Stern Gang." *New American View,* July 15, 1991, 5.

Sullivan, Antony T. Review of *They Dare to Speak Out: People and Institutions Confront Israel's Lobby,* by Paul Findley. *Middle East Insight* 4, nos. 4/5 (1986): 57–59.

The Times. Late London ed. June 8, 9, and 10, 1967.

"Tragic Error or Coverup? Case Anything but Closed on USS *Liberty.*" *Soldier of Fortune* 14, no. 6 (June 1989): 62–65.

"Unexplained Casualty: U.S.S. *Liberty.*" *Life,* June 23, 1967, 28–29.

"U.N. Security Council Demands a Cease-Fire in the Near East." *Department of State Bulletin* 56 (June 26, 1967): 934–49.

"U.S. and Iran Settle Financial Claims." *Washington Post,* February 23, 1996.

"U.S. Carrier Mistakenly Blasts Turkish Warship." *Miami Herald,* October 2, 1992.

"U.S. Electronic Espionage: A Memoir." *Ramparts,* August 1971, 35–50.

"The U.S.S. *Liberty.*" *Middle East Insight* 1, no. 1 (February/March 1982).

"The U.S.S. *Liberty* Report." *Washington Daily News,* June 30, 1967.

"A U.S. Ship Was Attacked." *Wall Street Journal,* June 9, 1967.

Velie, Lester. "The Week the Hot Line Burned." *Reader's Digest,* August 1968, 37–44.

Verhovek, Sam Howe. "Air Force Officer Is Acquitted in Downing of Army Aircraft." *New York Times,* June 21, 1995.

Wall Street Journal, Eastern ed., June 8, 1967.

Washington Post, June 8 and 9, 1967.

"When U.S. Ship Was Victim of a 'Shoot First' Policy." *U.S. News & World Report,* May 13, 1968, 12.

"Where Are They Now? The Eavesdroppers." *Newsweek,* September 29, 1969, 22.

Wilson, George C., and Anthony Astrachen. "Egypt, Syria Accept Cease Fire; Israel Hits U.S. Ship, Ten Killed." *Washington Post,* June 9, 1967.

"Wounded Liberty Crewman Ecker Tells of Attack." *American Spirit,* July 1967, 8.

Yemma, John. "Findley 'Speaks Out': Impartial Look at Arm Twisting by the Israel Lobby in US; *They Dare to Speak Out* by Paul Findley." *Christian Science Monitor,* August 2, 1985.

Zunes, Stephen. Review of *Deliberate Deceptions,* by Paul Findley. *Z Magazine,* July/August 1994, 10.

INDEX

A-A ("identify yourself") signal, 6–7, 52–53, 54–55, 72, 307–8n21

Air Force, U.S.: aircraft support for Israel, 5–6, 16, 67, 70, 109–10, 118–19, 135, 146, 207, 239, 307n15, 336n39; relationship between Israeli military and, 159

America, 3, 19, 60, 66–67, 85, 103, 210, 306nn6–7, 322n18, 325n18, 338n68

Arish, El: explosions near, 33–34, 242, 249, 317n3, 317n5; intelligence-gathering operations near, 2; Israeli control of, 33, 115; shelling of, 33, 34, 35, 38, 174, 242, 249, 317n2, 317n5; threat from burning ship off, 179; war crimes committed in, 139–40

Bamford, James, xi, 139–43, 208, 212, 226, 232, 341n32, 362n23

Bennett, Maurice, 28, 96–97, 106, 144–45, 211–12, 230–31, 352–53n19

Borne, John E., 106, 119–20, 139

Castle, Ernest: helicopter flight to *Liberty*, 61–62, 323n40; meetings and messages about attack, 60–61, 62, 66, 104, 324n42; Navy Court of Inquiry, 344n12; opinion about attack, 100–101, 232–33; panel participation and paper presentation about *Liberty*, 354n47; relationship between U.S. and Israeli military, 159; Thames TV interviews, 184; U.S. ships in combat zone, 204

Clifford, Clark: investigation of *Liberty* attack, 68–69, 93, 99, 162–63, 172, 236, 243, 345n22; Israeli responsibility for attack, feelings about, 68–69, 325n24; meeting after attack, 64–65; mistaken identity as cause of attack, 144, 146, 215; relationship between Rostow and, 68, 69; relationship between U.S. and Israel, 68, 69

communications: back-channel communications, 16, 29, 311n33, 316n24; communication link between Kirya and Stella Maris, 34, 41–42; failures in, 28–29, 31, 165–68; Mediterranean Sea, adequacy of communication system in, 29; naval communications system, 17, 207; naval liaison officers at air force command center and communication arrangements, 39, 40–42, 318n17; NSA and *Liberty*, communications between, 315n15; radio intercepts passed to enemy, 24, 125–26; between Soviet and U.S. warships, 3, 17; top-secret classification for messages, 17, 20, 27–29, 312n42; TRSSCOMM, 24, 29; U.S. practices and attack, xi, 165–68, 207

conspiracy beliefs and theories, xii, 108–29; aircraft to defend *Liberty*, 102–6, 119–20, 121–23, 186, 198, 206, 207–8, 210, 337n57; conspiracy role of NSA and State Department, x, xi; cooked telephone conversation, 110–11; cover-up claims and, 31–32, 72–73, 93, 171–72, 208–9, 252, 316n34; deliberate and premeditated act, x, xi, 94, 96, 100–101, 111–13, 116–18, 121–24, 126–29, 139–42, 144, 171–72, 211–15, 230–36, 241–42, 248–53; Egyptian

About the Author

Captain A Jay Cristol, JD, PhD, entered the U.S. Navy as an aviation cadet in November 1951. As a naval aviator, he flew day and night from the aircraft carrier *Princeton* during the Korean conflict. Upon return to civilian life, he joined the Naval Air Reserve where, during the 1960s, he flew volunteer missions to Vietnam. He wears the Meritorious Service Medal, the Navy Commendation Medal, and the Navy Achievement Medal among his more than a dozen military decorations. After eighteen years as a naval aviator, he became a Navy lawyer for another twenty years. In civilian life, he concurrently practiced civil law for twenty-five years. He is presently completing his twenty-eighth year as a federal judge. He teaches law as an adjunct professor at the University of Miami. In his spare time, he wrote his dissertation, "The *Liberty* Incident," which earned him a PhD from the Graduate School of International Studies at the University of Miami. He has written numerous articles on law, aviation, history, and other subjects. He was named a Legal Legend by the Historical Society of South Florida.